CORE AND CONTINGENT WORK IN THE EUROPEAN UNION

Labour and social security law studies have addressed the topic of the decline of the standard employment relationship mainly from the point of view of the growing number of atypical relationships. Only a limited number of studies have examined the issue from the perspective of the differentiation between core and contingent work. Such an examination is necessary as the increase in contingent work leads to complicated legal questions which vary between European states depending on the type of contingent arrangements that have become most prevalent. This book analyses, using a comparative approach, these different types of contingency from a national and EU perspective touching on the work relationship from a labour as well as a social security point of view. The aim of the book is to identify and analyse those questions adopting an innovative approach and to put forward proposals for safeguarding social cohesion within undertakings and European society.

Core and Contingent Work in the European Union

A Comparative Analysis

Edited by
Edoardo Ales, Olaf Deinert and Jeff Kenner

• HART •
OXFORD • LONDON • NEW YORK • NEW DELHI • SYDNEY

HART PUBLISHING
Bloomsbury Publishing Plc
Kemp House, Chawley Park, Cumnor Hill, Oxford, OX2 9PH, UK

HART PUBLISHING, the Hart/Stag logo, BLOOMSBURY and the Diana logo are trademarks of Bloomsbury Publishing Plc
First published in Great Britain 2017

First published in hardback, 2017
Paperback edition, 2019

A catalogue record for this book is available from the British Library.

Library of Congress Cataloging-in-Publication Data

Names: Ales, Edoardo. | Deinert, Olaf. | Kenner, Jeff.

Title: Core and contingent work in the European Union : a comparative analysis / edited by Edoardo Ales, Olaf Deinert, and Jeff Kenner.

Description: Oxford [UK] ; Portland, Oregon : Hart Publishing, 2017. | Includes bibliographical references and index.

Identifiers: LCCN 2016046231 (print) | LCCN 2016046774 (ebook) | ISBN 9781782258681 (hardback) | ISBN 9781782258698 (Epub)

Subjects: LCSH: Temporary employment—Law and legislation—European Union countries. | Employee leasing services—Law and legislation—European Union countries. | Contractors—Legal status, laws, etc.—European Union countries. | Labor laws and legislation—European Union countries.

Classification: LCC KJE2872 .C67 2017 (print) | LCC KJE2872 (ebook) | DDC 344.2401/25729—dc23

LC record available at https://lccn.loc.gov/2016046231

ISBN: HB: 978-1-78225-868-1
PB: 978-1-50993-018-0
ePDF: 978-1-78225-870-4
ePub: 978-1-78225-869-8

Typeset by Compuscript Ltd, Shannon

TABLE OF CONTENTS

LIST OF CONTRIBUTORS

Edoardo Ales is Professor of Labour and Social Security Law at the University of Cassino and Southern Lazio; he is Member of the Scientific Committee and National Expert for Italy of the European Labour Law Network (now ECE).

Olaf Deinert is Professor of Civil Law, Labour Law and Social Security Law; he is Dean of the Faculty of Law of the Georg-August-University Göttingen and Honorary Judge at the German Federal Labour Court.

Maurizio Del Conte is Professor of Labour Law at the Bocconi University.

Filip Dorssemont is Professor of Labour Law at the Université catholique de Louvain and the Université Saint-Louis de Bruxelles.

Loenzo Gaeta is Professor of Labour Law at the University of Siena, Italy.

José Manuel Gómez Muñoz is Professor of Labour and Social Security Law and Jean Monnet Chair (European Law) at the University of Seville.

Johannes Heuschmid is deputy director of Hugo Sinzheimer Institut for Labour Law and Lecturer in Law at the Goethe University, Frankfurt am Main, Germany.

Jeff Kenner is Professor of European Law, School of Law, University of Nottingham, UK; he is the University's Project Leader for FRAME (Fostering Human Rights Among European Policies), an international collaborative EU FP7 research project (2013–2017).

Thomas Klebe is director of the Hugo Sinzheimer Institut for Labour Law, Frankfurt; before he was the General Counsel of IG Metall.

Erika Kovács is Assistant Professor at the Vienna University of Economics and Business, Austria.

Antonio Lo Faro is Professor of Labour Law at the University of Catania, Italy.

Pascal Lokiec is Professor of Labour Law at the University of Paris Ouest Nanterre La Défense, France.

Franz Marhold is Professor of Labour and Social Security Law and Head of the Department of business, employment and social security law at Vienna University of Economics and Business, Austria.

Mia Rönnmar is Professor of Private Law and Dean at the Faculty of Law at Lund University, Sweden.

1

The Spirit of Pontignano

LORENZO GAETA

This book is based on a seminar held in 2014 in Gaeta, a town between Rome and Naples (it is mere coincidence that the name of the town is identical to mine!). The international seminar on Comparative Labour Law was called 'Pontignano XXXI'.

Pontignano is a small village near Siena, in Tuscany, the site of a thirteenth century Carthusian monastery, whose proud owner is the University of Siena. This peaceful place was the location of the first edition of this seminar, back in 1983. A group of labour lawyers—colleagues and friends: Gino Giugni (President of the Italian Labour Law Association, supported by the co-organiser Silvana Sciarra and Guido Balandi), Antoine Lyon-Caen, Bill Wedderburn, Wolfgang Däubler and Miguel Rodríguez Piñero—decided to organise a yearly week-long seminar, inviting young scholars from their countries. From then on, the 'trademark' stuck, and the seminars continued to be called 'Pontignano' even when they were held in places other than the monastery, and even outside of Italy. Over the first twenty years—generously funded by the Italian Association of Labour Law, and also by banks, private companies and unions—the seminar took place in Pontignano, and elsewhere in Italy (San Gaudenzio, near Pavia), as well as in France (Goutelas), Spain (Navacerrada, Sitges), Germany (Niederpöcking, Bad Orb) and England (Cambridge).

The seminar's winning formula has remained unchanged over the years: it begins with reports on the chosen topic from each participating country, followed by work sessions for the younger scholars, divided into a few working groups—with constant support from senior and junior professors, of course—and concludes with the groups' reports. But the most important aspect that has remained unchanged over the years is the special atmosphere that imbues the seminars: a few days spent in a secluded structure—an ancient convent, a small town, a research institute or a luxury resort—where intellectual reflection benefits from both the productivity isolation permits, and the unhurried yet fertile nature of informal debate between friends: old friends meeting again, and new friends who often build close relationships. In a word, I like to call it the 'spirit of Pontignano'—a spirit that has seldom waned.

At the start of the new century, this annual gathering risked cessation, due to misunderstandings between the Italian Association and some of the foreign partners: in fact, in 2002 the seminar did not take place. But a year later, as a new professor at the University of Siena, I managed to organise a new edition, with the indispensable help of my friends Thomas Blanke and Antonio Baylos. Thus began 'phase two' of the Pontignano seminars, in which Edoardo Ales plays a central role. We have rebuilt a network of relationships, renewing the foundations of the original seminar, with the help of a new group of friends and colleagues, led by Teun Jaspers; this sort of group is the key to organizing and managing such a seminar. The seminars have been extended to new countries, such as Holland, Belgium and Austria, but always following the same formula. We have struggled to overcome the difficulties arising from decreasing public and private funding, and we have organised the seminars, with the unfailing help of the Italian Labour Law Association, not only in Pontignano, but also in Montepulciano, the town of the famed Tuscan wine, thanks to the support of the local municipal administration; in the pleasant seaside town of Gaeta, with the help of the University of Cassino; and finally, in Modena, the city of fine cuisine and prestigious cars, through an agreement with the local Foundation named for Marco Biagi, the labour lawyer assassinated by the Red Brigades in 2000.

So 2014 saw the 31st edition of the seminars, which continue to bring together young scholars from all over Europe, to work and get to know one another in a very informal atmosphere: in the 'spirit of Pontignano'.

2

Methodological Introduction

EDOARDO ALES

Labour and social security law studies have addressed the topic of the decline of the standard (employment) relationship between the worker and the company mainly from the point of view of the dynamic[1] dichotomy 'typical—atypical' work. Contrary to this, the idea of this book is to address that topic adopting another dynamic dichotomy, that of 'core and contingent' work.[2]

Indeed, the 'core and contingent' dynamic dichotomy describes well the relation between the worker and the company at present. On the one hand, private and public undertakings need to react quickly, with structural and functional changes (the well-known adaptability, in the EU jargon), to competitiveness challenges deriving from the functioning of the EU Single Market and from the globalisation of world trade. On the other hand, the restriction of stable employment to workers operating at the core of the organisation seems to be the inevitable consequence of those changes. From such a perspective, fixed-term, agency work, zero hours and distance work contracts are proliferating. We can group them under the label 'contingent work'.[3]

Furthermore, the tendency of companies to (re-)organise themselves into (internal and external) network structures, in which elements of the core business are outsourced to contractors (companies or self-employed individuals) or even crowdsourced,[4] places a large part of the workforce at the margin of or even outside the 'core' company, making that workforce contingent.

All these changes are likely to have a dismantling effect on the social cohesion within the undertaking, which was once guaranteed by the equalising power of homogeneous legal and contractual arrangements.

[1] By dynamic dichotomy, we mean a dichotomy in which elements of one pole are attracted, progressively and irresistibly, to the other pole, *de facto* emptying the former and filling in the latter, so changing their nature.

[2] The idea of using this dichotomy was drawn from the German reflection on *Kern- und Randbelegschaft*, revitalised by Olaf Deinert in a recent essay: O Deinert, 'Kernbelegschaften—Randbelegschaften—Fremdbelegschaften—Herausforderungen für das Arbeitsrecht durch Reduzierung von Stammbelegschaften', in *Recht der Arbeit*, 2014, 65 ff. 'Core' as 'Kern' (an almost literal translation) and 'contingent' as 'Rand' (literally: margin) seemed to us to be the more explicative way to translate that dichotomy from German into English.

[3] See, however, Lo Faro, Ch 3 in this volume.

[4] See Heuschmid and Klebe, Ch 11 in this volume.

From the very beginning, the core/contingent dichotomy seemed to us an interesting topic of comparative legal analysis. It formed the guiding theme at the 31st Pontignano International Labour Law Seminar,[5] which took place in Gaeta (Italy) in September 2014.

In the absence of a common understanding of the very notion of contingent work, Antonio Lo Faro was asked to provide a theoretical framework for that topic. In addition to Lo Faro's authoritative opinion, the other participants to the Seminar have also provided their points of view and have been invited to develop their own reflection according to their country-of-origin perception and understanding of that notion.

As a consequence, the national reports, which characterise Pontignano's working method have, quite naturally, emphasised a number of 'country specific' legal issues, seen as national 'concretisations' of the core/contingent discourse.

Taking this into account, during the debriefing which usually concludes each Pontignano Seminar, one legal issue from each national report has been selected, putting forward the relevant country as a 'cognitive prototype' for that issue, because of the way in which the issue itself has emerged and has been regulated there. The selected issue has thus become the focus of a chapter to be defined as 'national' within the 'cognitive prototype' approach. These 'national' chapters which represent, the views of the participants to the Seminar, form the basis of this volume on 'Core and contingent work in the company' edited by Edoardo Ales, Olaf Deinert and Jeff Kenner.

As with the 29th Pontignano Seminar, held in Gaeta in 2012, from which the publication of a book on health and safety at work emerged,[6] guest authors have been invited, following the 2014 Seminar, to add further country-specific perspectives to a new book on core and contingent work in the company. Erika Kovács and Mia Rönnmar have been asked to reflect upon Hungary and Sweden respectively, and to sort out one 'country-specific' legal issue each, with reference to contingent work. Distance work for Hungary and the inter-generational collective bargaining for Sweden became the focal points of that reflection.

Thanks to the commitment and the kind hospitality of Thomas Klebe and Johannes Heuschmid, the contributors to this volume have had the opportunity to present and discuss the preliminary versions of the 'national' chapters at a workshop organised by the Hugo-Sinzheimer-Institut für Arbeitsrecht, in Frankfurt am Main on December 2014.

During that fruitful exchange, the final volume structure was agreed and successfully submitted to Hart Publishing. The final elaboration of the chapters, editorial review included has required almost two years.

[5] On the "Spirit" of Pontignano, see Gaeta in Ch 1 of this volume.

[6] E Ales (ed), *Health and Safety at Work. European and Comparative Perspective* (Alphen aan den Rijn, Kluwer Law International, 2013).

As for its structure, the volume introduces the theoretical framework propounded by Antonio Lo Faro. Lo Faro's reflection constitutes a deep and highly valuable contribution to the understanding of one of the possible meaning of the 'core/contingent' dichotomy.

Edoardo Ales, takes stock of his previous reflections on occupational health and safety law, with an eye to Italy. The author emphasises the 'risk approach' as a (positive) way to handle contingent workers, regarded as an 'especially sensitive group', to whom the entrepreneur should guarantee a qualitative and quantitative level of protection, which takes into account their contingent status within the company.

Ten 'national' chapters follow, each one focusing on one legal issue, thematised by reference to a juridical instrument, which concretise, in the view of the author, for his or her country of origin, the contingent work discourse. As already outlined above, each country is proposed as a 'cognitive prototype' of one issue, because of the way in which that issue has emerged and has been regulated there.

Olaf Deinert, proposes Germany as 'cognitive prototype' for the issue of equal treatment, thematising it by reference to agency work. Maurizio Del Conte proposes Italy as 'cognitive prototype' for the issue of the 're-structuring' of the standard employment relationship, thematising it by reference to the increasing protection contract. Filip Dorssemont, proposes Belgium as 'cognitive prototype' for the issue of conditionality in the recourse to contingent work, thematising it by reference to the fixed-term contract. Jose Manuel Gomez Muñoz, proposes Spain as 'cognitive prototype' for the issue of the 'suspicious' success of self-employment, thematising it by reference to the concept of new entrepreneurship; Jeff Kenner, proposes the United Kingdom as 'cognitive prototype' for the inversion of the flexicurity paradigm, thematising it by reference to the zero-hours contract. Erika Kovács, proposes Hungary as 'cognitive prototype' for the issue of the de-localisation of work, thematising it by reference to telework and homework. Pascal Lokiec, proposes France as 'cognitive prototype' for the issue of the externalisation of work, thematising it by reference to, among the others, co-employership. Mia Rőnnmar, proposes Sweden as 'cognitive prototype' for the issue of the intergenerational dimension of being or becoming contingent, thematising it by reference to collective bargaining. Franz Marhold, proposes Austria as 'cognitive prototype' for the issue of social protection of contingent work, thematising it by reference to the full coverage social insurance system. Thomas Klebe and Johannes Heuschmid, propose Germany as 'cognitive prototype' for the issue of the attitude of social partners towards contingent work, thematised by reference to crowdwork.

So structured, the book answers at least three crucial questions: (1) Which are the legal issues at stake when it comes to contingent work? (2) Which are the instruments that are likely (or used) to make workers contingent to the company? (3) Do national systems provide for legal measures to countervail the drift towards contingent work and/or to cope with its effects?

According to the contributors to this book, some general problematic issues are at stake when it comes to contingent work. These are: (i) equal treatment; (ii) digitalisation of work; (iii) externalisation of company's activities; (iv) increase in self-employment/new entrepreneurship. Specific to the employment relationship, on the other hand, are issues such as: (i) the weakening of job protection; (ii) working time insecurity; (iii) the breaking down of the inter-generational solidarity; iv) de-localisation of the workplace.

Closely related to those issues are the legal instruments that are likely (or used) to make the worker contingent to the company. The contributors of this book have focused on some 'usual suspects', such as: (i) agency work; (ii) fixed-term contracts; (iii) zero-hours contracts; (iv) telework and homework;[7] and on some 'new comers', like: (v) crowdwork; (vi) the increasing protection contract; (vii) co-employership; (viii) new employership.

In the final chapter, Edoardo Ales and Olaf Deinert synthesise the outcomes of the research, putting forward, in a comparative perspective, a comprehensive proposal with a view to safeguarding social cohesion within the undertaking and the society as a whole.

[7] It is debatable whether part-time work could potentially be regarded as contingent work. Since there was not enough evidence of this, we chose not to address the issue in this volume.

3

Contingent Work: A Conceptual Framework

ANTONIO LO FARO

I. Flexible, Atypical, Precarious, *Contingent*

A sort of puzzling dismay might pervade the mind of labour lawyers called to deal with the quite odd notion of contingent work.

On the one side, it cannot be denied that the issue of contingent work does unavoidably evoke the more acquainted notions of flexible, atypical or precarious work and the related contractual arrangements multifariously diverging from the traditional full-time and open-ended bilateral employment relation.

On the other side, it must, however, be stressed that most of such flexible arrangements do nevertheless presuppose the existence of an employment relation still preserving both its basic structure (in terms of a contractual relation between two counterparts plainly fitting with the traditional categories of 'employee' and 'employer'); and its basic contents (in terms of a relation essentially governed by labour law and social security protections provided by legislative and contractual sources). Within such a perspective, we could, therefore, assume that many of the flexible employment contracts fall indeed into a 'typical' notion of atypical work, insofar as they keep adhering to the traditional employment contract paradigm, though internally diversified in some of its temporal dimension.

By focusing on the idea of contingent work, on the contrary, we intend to designate a diverse kind of non-standard work, which, differently from atypical work, radically 'falls outside the employment model',[1] as some observers have noted some years ago. To say it with a formula—which for the moment could not be anything but self-assertive—while the idea of atypical work alludes to a variety of flexible arrangements within the employment contract; the idea of contingent work rather indicates a series of developments beyond the employment contract.

In the following paragraphs, an attempt will be made to fill such an assertive formula with clearer and more specific descriptive clues by asserting the

[1] S Deakin, 'A New Paradigm for Labour Law?' (2007) 31 *Melbourne University Law Review* 1161–67.

organisational context of contingent work; its interrelations with the more familiar notion of flexible work; its possible legal configuration; and its repercussions on the very same basic institutions of labour law: the contract of employment and the notion of employer.

II. Two Empirical Premises

It is part of the general assumption subtending the present book, that in order to grasp the fundamental significance of current labour market developments, the notion of contingent work might have a higher heuristic value as compared to the notion of flexible work. In justifying such statement, a double introductory premise should be declared.

First, the time has come to recognise that the category of flexible work does not really have a satisfactory explanatory capacity of the transformative dynamics affecting labour law system, in particular as far as the very same standard employment relations are concerned. Rather than concentrating on flexible employment contracts only, it should be wondered, indeed, whether the quantitative spreading of flexible/atypical arrangements has not ended up in generating a qualitative modification of standard employment contracts. Recent reforms introduced in the wake of the crisis in some European countries (Spain and Italy, for instance) reveal that it is precisely the standard employment contract—and not atypical arrangements—which has gone through the major processes of downgrading workers' rights, both in terms of reducing dismissals' protection, and in terms of limiting collective bargaining prerogatives and/or extending concession bargaining at plant level. This is why one could wonder whether nowadays the real labour protection's divide still runs along the line separating flexible from standard workers. Or whether it rather concerns the different partition between core and contingent workforce, once it is specified that 'core workforce' is not to be equated with 'standard employment contract', and 'contingent' is not to be equated with 'flexible' (see below in the concluding paragraph of this Chapter).

Second, the idea of contingent work allows to better catch the essence of a labour market reality in which the adjective 'flexible' should be referred not only to work but also to the company and to its organisational structure. In fact, it is precisely within the processes of firms' vertical disintegration[2] that the category of contingent work could be better identified, by including in it workers who—irrespective of their employment contract being a flexible or a standard one—are not part of the organisational and productive 'core' of the disintegrated firm.

[2] H Collins, 'Independent Contractors and the Challenge of Vertical Disintegration to Employment Protection Laws' (1990) 10 *Oxford Journal of Legal Studies* 353.

In the following paragraphs, each of the two premises above outlined will be separately developed, with the goal to offer a conceptual framework of the category of contingent work.

III. Deciphering Contingent Work

Contingent work is basically an American terminology. To be more precise, a 1990s US terminology, which was originally used by the US Bureau of Labor Statistics to refer to 'individuals who do not perceive themselves as having an explicit or implicit contract for continuing employment'.

In the legal academic debates, such terminology has been primarily evoked by non-European authors, either to underline the inadequacy of the binary standard/flexible divide in representing the multifarious complexity of workforce modifications at the eve of the twenty-first century;[3] or to allude specifically to workers lacking any job security; or, quite frequently, to use it as a sheer synonym for non-standard and/or substandard work relations.

However, the heterogeneous ways in which contingent work has been decoded in the past, do not automatically condemn this notion to the realm of empty catchwords deprived of any analytical significance; nor do such multiple definitions necessarily turn the category of contingent work into an 'elusive concept'[4] with limited interpretative attitude of the actual reality. In some analysis, indeed, a more precise characterisation of contingent work emerges,[5] which allows to sketch out a basic double content of contingent work: on the one side, it comprises workers whose contractual relations with their employer are so loose that it is doubtful whether they could still be qualified as employees. On the other side, it includes workers whose employment contract with a given company might also be a standard one, but whose services are managed and exploited by another company within whose organisation those workers are 'materially', albeit non-legally, incorporated.

In both cases, the common feature those two categories of contingent workers share has nothing to do with the structure of their respective employment contract; but rather with the nature of their position with respect to the core workforce employed in the production processes incorporating their work performances. As a matter of fact, both of these categories of contingent workers can be essentially characterised as being peripheral to the productive organisation which

[3] R Owens, 'Decent Work for the Contingent Workforce in the New Economy' (2002) 15 *Australian Journal of labour Law* 209.

[4] G Lester, 'Careers and Contingency' (1998) 73 *Stanford Law Review* 78.

[5] S Befort, 'Revisiting the Black Hole of Workplace Regulation: A Historical and Comparative Perspective of Contingent Work' (2003) 24 *Berkeley Journal of Employment and Labor Law* 153; K M Forster, 'Strategic Reforms of Contingent Work' (2001) 74 *Southern California law Review* 541.

their services are functional to. The notion of contingent work emerges, therefore, less as an antithesis to the standard employment contract, than rather as an alternative to the core workforce category.

This is why the notion of contingent work appears to be so challenging when analysed from a labour law perspective: because it has to be constructed as the conceptual pendant of another notion—the core workforce—that is not a legal category but rather a product of the organisational economics debates.[6] Such conceptual difficulties notwithstanding, a labour law definition of contingent work is, however, possible, on a descriptive level, and even desirable on a prescriptive level, since its 'discovery' requires policy intervention only partially identifiable with those addressed to cope with atypical or flexible work.

In order to pursue this descriptive aim, I will propose to disarticulate the notion of contingent work along the following bipartition: contingency in bilateral relations (Section IV); contingency in triangular relations (Section V).

IV. Contingency in Bilateral Relations

As has been argued by recent seminal research,[7] the progressive decline of the archetypical standard employment contract has not only thrown into crisis the correspondent model of employment legislation. It has also called into question the very same foundational issue of labour law's scope.

A. Economically Dependent Self-Employed

If we look back at the mid-1980s Atkinson's idea of core/periphery workforce divide (see below at Section V.A), we can see that the outer layer of his well-known flexible firm's model[8] was occupied, among others, by the self-employed. Thirty years later, we cannot keep assuming that the self-employed are the only category of workers excluded from the labour law protective sphere.

On the one side, it is apt to remember here how the genuine figure of self-employment has been sided over the years by a variegated galaxy of nuanced figures that are not entirely autonomous, even if they cannot be qualified as subordinate employees.[9] I am obviously referring to the category of economically

[6] J Atkinson, 'Manpower Strategies for Flexible Organizations' (1984) 16 *Personnel Management* 28.

[7] M Freedland and N Kountouris, *The Legal Construction of Personal Work Relations* (Oxford, Oxford University Press, 2011).

[8] J Atkinson, *Flexibility, Uncertainty and Manpower Management* (Brighton, Institute of Manpower Studies, 1985).

[9] Back in the sixties, the hybrid notion of 'dependent contractor' was identified by H Arthurs, 'The Dependent Contractor: A Study of the Legal Problems of Countervailing Power' (1965) 16 *Toronto Law Journal* 89.

dependent workers, which—albeit increasingly object of the sensibility of various EU institutions[10]—did not find until now an adequate legal representation at the national levels, neither as concerns its definition, nor as concerns its protective status in terms of applicable rights. Economically dependent workers, however, is not the only category of contingent workers who cannot have access to labour law protection. In addition, they do not really challenge the systematic foundation of labour law dogmatic, insofar as they belong to a category that has always been excluded, by definition, from the protective scope of labour law. The fact that they are now growing in number, poses, therefore, a quantitative challenge to labour law legislation, but not a qualitative challenge to labour law paradigms.

B. The Internal Periphery of the Workforce

On the other side of contingent bilateral relations, there is a constellation of work relationships whose complex variety could not be explained better than in the following words: 'there are many personal work relations to which different legal constructs are assigned, so that they are sometimes construed or constructed as being contracts other than employment contracts and sometimes as being only partly contractual in their nature, or as not being contractual at all'.[11]

In this regard, reference has to be made to a series of work relations where the contractual obligations of the two counterparts are so indefinite—both in terms of duties and rights—that it becomes often difficult to place such relations within labour law's scope, even if, differently from what happens with genuine and/or bogus self-employed, in these cases the existence of an employment contract could not be excluded a priori. Examples of this can be identified in zero-hours contracts,[12] job on call, mini jobs, project-workers, crowdsourcing work,[13] casual work and other arrangements which can be comprehensively labelled as the internal periphery of the workforce. Such workers are indeed 'internal' insofar as they still have a (sort of) contractual relation with the company benefitting of their services. They are, however, 'peripheral' to the extent that they do not access the firm's internal labour market in terms of personal commitment, job stability, carrier developments, training opportunities, and other company-related benefits. At times, the internal periphery workers are excluded from labour law scope due to the complete absence of an employment contract. Other times, they are excluded because even if a contract of employment exists, threshold requirements are not fulfilled in order for some or all of the legislative protection to apply. Still at other times, they fall outside the scope of labour law due to precise legislative choices.

[10] See recently the Study on *Social protection rights of economically dependent self-employed workers*, accomplished in 2013 on request of European Parliament's Committee on Employment and Social Affairs.

[11] Freedland and Kountouris, *The Legal Construction* (n 7) 6.

[12] See Kenner, Chap 10 in this volume

[13] See Heuschmid and Klebe, Chap 11 in this volume.

The declining capacity of traditional labour law paradigm in dealing with such new contingent arrangements has been discussed extensively over the past few years. Stimulating researches have been conducted investigating both the conceptual qualifications of them, and the regulatory challenges they pose.[14] The already mentioned Freedland and Kountouris research on 'personal work relations' as an inclusive alternative to the traditional employment contract, in particular, does offer a remarkable conceptual frame of analysis for contingent work, at least for descriptive ends, if not for normative goals. 'For much of the twentieth-century period of development of labour law in European legal systems'—these authors argue—'the domain of other personal work contracts existed as the largely unregulated epiphenomenon of the domain of the contract of employment'. Now, they add—together with many others[15]—the time has come to extend labour law scope towards other non-employment relations characterised in many different ways by a personal involvement of the worker, even if such involvement is legally realised through different forms than the traditional employment contract.

This is, therefore, a first conceptual challenge posed to the labour law debate by the emergence of what we have defined bilateral contingent work relations. A challenge involving the very same basic institution of labour law: the contract of employment, and its actual capacity to work as a selective tool capable of conferring protection to those who need and deserve it.

However, if the prescriptive goal of such debate is 'exploring a wide range of tools and institutions for regulating work that falls outside the traditional regulatory repertoire of labour law',[16] it must be added that legislative developments detectable at a comparative level do not always seem to follow such progressive strategy entirely. Instead of diversifying the tools capable of coping with (and protecting) the diversified arrangements emerging beyond the employment contract, the direction of legislative policies discussed and adopted in some national states in recent years is sometimes quite opposite: as a matter of fact, an effort is made to unify legislative tools to protect the heterogeneous world of workers under the heading of a renovated 'single employment contract'. This is not necessarily good news. While the declared aim of the various forms of single employment contract is to cover workers heretofore excluded from a full application of labour legislation, thus reducing the problem of labour market segmentation, its main end-effect risks to be found in a regressive transformation of the standard employment contract, which tends to be configured as a sort of common denominator of any form

[14] See K Stone and H Arthurs (eds), *Rethinking Workplace Regulation. Beyond the Standard Employment Contract* (New York, Russel Sage Foundation Press, 2013); G Davidov, 'Setting Labour Law's Coverage: Between Universalism and Selectivity' (2014) 34 *Oxford Journal of legal Studies* 543.

[15] J Fudge, S McCrystal and K Sankaran (eds), *Challenging the Legal Boundaries of Work Regulation* (Oxford, Hart Publishing, 2012).

[16] J Fudge, 'Blurring Legal Boundaries: Regulating for Decent Work' in Fudge, McCrystal and Sankaran (eds), *Challenging the Legal Boundaries* (n 15).

of 'personal work' that for this very same reason downgrades to a lower level of protection.

Hence, the question arises whether for the sake of inclusiveness, the employment contract should necessarily be emptied of its protective contents; or, on the contrary, whether the goal to also include into the protective sphere contingent workers could be pursued through different tools that, while leaving undisturbed the standard employment contract, complement it with other instruments. At the end of the day, who said that the employment contract is the one and only way to protect (contingent) workers?

C. The *Uber* Case: Can an 'App' Be An Employer?

The provocative question concluding the previous paragraph was essentially aimed at focussing the attention towards the systematic connections between the emerging reality of contingent work and the very same dogmatic construction and normative function of the contract of employment. With regard to some forms of contingent work, in other terms, the question arises whether in order to extend to contingent workers some of the labour law protection, it is necessary to qualify those workers as employees.

Some decades ago, Lord Wedderburn vividly described the judicial process of employees' qualification as an 'elephant test'. The contract of employment, he wrote, is, just as an elephant, 'an animal difficult to define but easy to recognise when you see it'. Thirty years later, we could probably say that the employment contract is still difficult to define but it has also become difficult to recognise,[17] at least when the actual reality of work relations offers 'extreme' configuration of employee-like figures—as in the case of internal contingent workers.

The recent lawsuit brought in California by an Uber driver pretending to be qualified as an employee with a view to be reimbursed of the expenses she bore to perform her driving job (tolls and parking fees),[18] offers an interesting example of what might happen when contingent workers (in this case a crowd worker) meet labour law.

[17] P Benjamin, 'Who Needs Labour Law? Defining the Scope of Labour Protection' in J Conaghan, R M Fischl and K Klare (eds), *Labour Law in an Era of Globalization. Transformative Practices & Possibilities* (Oxford, Oxford University Press, 2002), notes that '[i]t is highly unlikely that anyone writing on the state of early twenty-first century labour law would describe the test of employee in these terms' at 75.

[18] *Bervick v Uber Technologies Inc*, Case No 1146739 EK. The claim was initially brought to an administrative authority (The Labor Commissioner of the State of California) where the applicant won the case. A judicial appeal by *Uber* is currently pending before The Superior Court of California, County of San Francisco. News of the case can be read on *The New York Times*, 18 June 2015 (http://www.nytimes.com/2015/06/18/business/uber-contests-california-labor-ruling-that-says-drivers-should-be-employees.html). Text of the proceedings available at www.scribd.com/doc/268946016/Uber-v-Berwick#download.

It might be useful to recall the terms of the individual contracts subscribed by the hundreds of thousands of drivers working for Uber all over the world before dealing with the case just evoked.[19] Drivers registered within the Uber application receive requests by users via the Uber App; they do not have any obligation to accept it, but if they do, they must perform the request according to the users' demands. Their working time is not controlled by Uber, who remunerate them by electronically remitting part of the service fee paid to it by the user.

So what we have is: (a) a worker declaring from time to time through a smart phone that he is available to work, without granting however any actual job performance; (b) an actual beneficiary of the work performed by that worker who does not pay him; (c) a third party facilitating the connection between the two by offering an adequate technology and, if necessary, by providing the worker with an adequate phone. Is that enough to detect an employment relation?

According to the California Labour Commissioner, the (unexpected) answer is yes. The self-representation of Uber as just an application connecting a user with a driver, whose job is not controlled by it, was not sufficient to uphold Uber's pretention that drivers did not work for it directly. Despite its assertion that drivers had to be qualified as independent contractors of the users, rather than as employees of Uber, the labour administrative body discharged the company's allegation to be nothing more than a neutral technological platform, designed simply to enable drivers and passengers to transact the business of transportation. The reality is—the Commissioner objected—that 'Defendants are involved in any aspect of the operation [...] Plaintiff's work was integral to Defendants' business. Defendants are in business to provide transportation services to passengers. Plaintiff did the actual transporting of those passengers. Without drivers such as Plaintiff, Defendants' business would not exist'.

The California Labour Commissioner's decision, together with other preceding and subsequent decisions affirming the opposite, is now being extensively discussed in the US, even if primarily in the bar associations[20] and in the non-specialised media rather than in academic journals. Its relevance to the issue of contingent work is, however, crucial, since it demonstrates that the challenges posed by contingent work are to be found more in the dogmatic reconstruction of labour relations than in the actual regulation of their substantive content. Aside from the profitable results it has granted to Mrs Bervick, the questionable systematic argumentation adopted by the Commissioner in the *Uber* case testifies indeed how the substantive goal to assure a certain degree of protection to contingent workers can hardly be pursued by perpetuating the 'existing strongly

[19] Just to give an idea of the dimension of the issue, the CEO of Uber recently declared that he expects to have 42.000 drivers in London by early 2016.

[20] See the report prepared in 2015 by the American Bar Association—Section for Labor and Employment Law on *Independent Contractors and the Sharing Economy: Uber, Lyft, and Other 'Tech' Business Models*.

felt but intellectually cramping constraints, the most significant [of which] is the dominant paradigm of the contract of employment'.[21]

Within such a perspective, the cautious wording used by another US Court dealing with identical issues to those examined by the California Labor Commissioner is perhaps more adequate and more 'useful' if intended as an intellectual stimulus for the current labour law debate. Talking about the choice to classify a crowd worker as an independent contractor or as an employee, the judge concluded that:

> 'the jury in this case will be handed a square peg and asked to choose between two round holes. The test the California courts have developed over the 20th Century for classifying workers isn't very helpful in addressing this 21st Century problem [...] perhaps Lyft drivers should be considered a new category of worker altogether, requiring a different set of protections'.[22]

Identifying the concrete content of such 'different' sets of protections; and verifying whether those protections might reach also workers who are not employees, is one of the main task of a future labour law finally emancipated from the conceptual chains of the contract of employment.

V. Contingency in Triangular Relations

In the introductory pages of this chapter, a suggestion has been made to define the notion of contingent work by opposing it to that of core workforce, rather than comparing it to the standard employment contract. By the same token, it has also been anticipated that the idea of a divergence from a 'standard' model—which characterises the very same concept of contingency—could be better appreciated insofar as it is referred not only to work but also to the firm.

While in the preceding paragraph we have dealt with contingent workforce as an expression of non-standard work, in the present paragraph we will deal with contingent work as an expression of a 'non-standard firm', if I may say so. And in order to refine the argument, a further premise should be put forward. Investigating the firm's organisational strategies under the specific perspective of their impact on the issues at stake in the present chapter, implies that attention should be focused not so much on the firm itself, as on its 'labour law image': ie the employer, and the way 'the received unitary concept of a single-entity employer'[23] has been changed over the last decades.

[21] Freedland and Kountouris, *The Legal Construction* (n 7) 316.

[22] *Cotter and al v Lyft, Inc*, Case No 13-cv-04065-VC United States District Court—Northern District of California. The case was brought against Lyft Inc, a company organising driving services according to the same modalities as Uber. Text of the decision is available at www.cand.uscourts.gov/filelibrary/1575/Order%20Denying%20Motions%20for%20Summary%20Judgment%203.11.2015.pdf.

[23] So defined by J Prassl, *The Concept of the Employer* (Oxford, Oxford University Press, 2015).

A. Splitting the Economic and the Legal Boundaries of the Firm

Theoretical explanation of the reasons subtending the changing organisation of the flexible firm have been developed in a well-known economic debate which—started in the 1940s—was fully developed as the 'three bigs' of the post-war industrial model began to decline: big government, big unions and, precisely, the big firm. Since that moment, approximately identifiable with the 1980s, firms began to turn to a model of organisational flexibility essentially consisting in internalizing core competencies and in outsourcing non-strategic activities to external suppliers. Many firms began to follow a model of lean production, downsizing their internal organisation and, thus, segmenting the workforce they needed to manage the production process into core and periphery workers—the former being hired directly by the 'main' company, the latter being employed by others.

It is worth clarifying from the outset that such entrepreneurial practices of organisational flexibility cannot in any way be equated with employment flexibility, since those practices primarily affect the very structure of the production process, rather than the contracts concluded with the workers employed within the new organisation. In principle, nothing excludes both the outsourcing and the supplier firms from hiring all of their workers with standard employment contracts.

Downsizing core organisation, furthermore, cannot be equated with a reduction of the economic business. Right on the contrary, the flexible firm deciding 'to buy rather than to make', aims at increasing its business through a different organisation made of subcontracting, networking, partnership agreement, long-term relations with other economically dependent smaller firms or even with individual independent contractors. In short, a lean production process implying a diminution of direct employment relations is often sided by an increase of commercial relations concluded with other functionally specialised supplier firms. It is precisely in such a trade-off between employment and commercial transactions that the divide between core and contingent workers emerges.

Before dealing with the impact of such strategies on labour law (and industrial relations too),[24] it is opportune to briefly mention some of the theoretical insights that have been forged in the past within the intellectual itinerary which from economics, to organisational studies, to general contract theory has finally linked the issues of outsourcing to their labour law dimension.

Starting with the economic analysis, it is clear that the Ronald Coase transaction costs theory must be placed at the origin of any subsequent modelling of the make/buy alternative that firms are called to take into account when deciding to shift from hierarchy to the market. Coase's early assumptions have been

[24] J Drahokoupil (ed), The Outsourcing Challenge. Organizing Workers Across Fragmented Production Networks (Bruxelles, European Trade Union Institute, 2015).

subsequently refined by neo-institutional economics in the late 1970s and 1980s, particularly by Oliver Williamson,[25] whose work has detailed the nature of the costs inducing employers to outsource. The Williamson notion of 'asset specificity' is particularly relevant for labour law, since it explains why workers (or activities) outsourced are the less skilled; and why, correspondingly, the vertical disintegration of the outsourcing firm is usually not such a big problem for skilled, asset-specific, and contractually strong workers.

In the field of organisational studies, the partition between a core and a periphery of the workforce, already implied in the mentioned economic theories, has been openly and fully asserted in the mid-1980s by John Atkinson,[26] whose model of the flexible firm—although sometimes criticised[27]—is still a landmark reference point for all those who deal with organisational flexibility. In his model, core workers are the only employees who benefit from job security and high earnings to compensate them for being functionally flexible across different traditional skills boundaries. The firm invests in these workers in terms of training, and they develop new skills, which make them increasingly separate from the contingent workers relegated to the external labour market. High commitment, high involvement, high performance for the core workforce; exactly the contrary for the rest.

When finally referred more specifically to labour law, such transferal of activities and workers from the internal hierarchy to the external market, determines a final end-product which can be read in terms of what has been called the 'commercialisation of employment'.[28] As long as part of the activities—and/or of the workers performing them—are outsourced to other organisations, a change is produced in the traditional view of labour market as a place where the work demanded by firms is supplied by individual workers. Labour market becomes on the contrary a place where both labour demand and labour supply might be the object of an exchange accomplished by firms. The actual development of such inter-firm exchanges, however, does not entirely fit with the assumptions prompted by transaction costs theories. The neo-institutional economic analysis describing outsourcing processes in terms of a sheer substitution of the internal hierarchy in favour of an external market made of 'spot' or 'on-off' transactions, is misleading and in any case contrasting with what actually happens. Firm-to-firm contractual relations replacing employer/employees contractual relations, indeed, far from being managed through market spot transactions, tend to be rather structured as a sort of hybrid between market and hierarchy. Such hybrid is a network where the contractual integration between the 'main' outsourcing firm and the other supplier firms might become so intense that the notion of the 'quasi-firm' has been

[25] See generally O Williamson, The Economic Institutions of Capitalism: Firms, Markets, Relational Contracting (London, Free Press, 1985).

[26] See above Atkinson (n 6 and n 8).

[27] A L Kalleberg, 'Organizing Flexibility: The Flexible Firm in a New Century' (2001) 39 *British Journal of Industrial Relations* 479.

[28] Fudge, 'Blurring Legal Boundaries' (n 15).

proposed in the literature in order to describe a scenario where 'the latticework of collaborations with "outsiders" blurs the boundaries of the firm, making it difficult to know where the firm ends and where the market or another firm begins'.[29]

Such reality of blurring boundaries between different firms economically integrated within a single network contractual organisation could be read in legal terms through the category of the long-term relational contracts developed by one of the world-leading scholars in the field of contract law, Ian McNeil.[30]

The sociological observation of the development of inter-firms' co-operative networks,[31] as rationalised by the legal analysis through the idea of a 'contractual integration'[32] heavily relying on relational contract theories, have all been evoked in the above, to the extent that all of those visions might help to find out now why and how the vertical disintegration of the firm[33] affects the issue of contingent work, particularly as far as the external periphery of workforce is concerned.

B. The External Periphery of the Workforce

While the developments affecting bilateral employment relations give rise to an internal periphery of the workforce already dealt with above, the development of triangular relations between the outsourcing firm, the supplier and the workers sees an external periphery of the workforce clearly emerge.

By contrast to what happens in the first case, in the case of external peripheral workforce we are confronted with contingent workers having no contractual relation whatsoever with the firm which often directs, controls and finally benefits from their performances.

It is clear that one of the legal forms that such external contingency might assume is constituted by temporary agency work[34] where the already mentioned modification of the employer's figure is more clearly detectable. And it is precisely this 'visibility' which has favoured a prompt—albeit partly inadequate—reaction on the part of legislators willing to provide, at a national as well at a supranational level, a body of protection aimed at mitigating the negative effects of contingency in agency work cases.

Still, when projecting the vertical disintegration of the firm upon the issues of contingent workforce, a second kind of external peripheral workers comes into play, raising completely different questions to existing labour law categories.

[29] W Powell, 'The Capitalist Firm in the Twenty-First Century: Emerging Patterns in Western Europe', in P Di Maggio (ed), *The Twenty-First-Century Firm: Changing Economic Organization in International Perspective* (Princeton, Princeton University Press, 2001) 58.

[30] I Macneil, 'The Many Futures of Contract' (1974) 47 *Southern California Law Review* 691.

[31] S Macaulay, 'An Empirical View of Contract' (1985) *Wisconsin Law Review* 465.

[32] L Corazza, Contractual Integration e rapporti di lavoro (Padova, Cedam, 2004).

[33] Introduced in the labour law debate following the publication of the influential essay by Hugh Collins cited at n 2.

[34] See Deinert at Chapter 4 in this volume.

An outsourcing strategy could be implemented by a flexible firm through two different options: (a) either the firm might decide to outsource just the workforce, and in this case, agency work is the issue, both in the temporary and in the indefinite form of staff leasing arrangements; or (b) it might decide to outsource segments of production by contracting out a service, and in this case subcontracting is the issue.

Whereas, in an economic sense, the two kinds of externalisation are considered homogeneous, since they are equally conceived as an expression of the employer's option to 'buy' (it does not matter whether what is bought is a service, a product, or a worker), from a labour law perspective, these two kinds of outsourcing are usually kept clearly separate.

On the one hand, agency work is considered as a form of contingent work where a certain connection between the worker and the final beneficiary of his work might be detected; and, therefore, some form of responsibility for the legal obligations deriving from the employment relation could be assigned also to the user firm, despite the fact that it is not the formal employer. This is, more or less, the European model, as it is to some extent recognised and regulated by EU Directive 2008/104/EC.

On the other hand, when talking of subcontracting and of other forms of outsourcing, it is usually argued that since the outsourcing firm limits itself to buying services or goods, it has no responsibility whatsoever towards the workers producing it.

Such double standard is hardly justified, if one looks at the concrete modalities through which an outsourcing process is generally accomplished, and to the actual contractual relationships generally connecting the two (or more) firms. Outsourcing is hardly a way to dismiss, or not commence, an activity by completely entrusting it to another firm. More often, outsourcing enables an activity to be carried on by developing functionally specialised contractual partnerships with other firms linked by long-term collaborations, involving (also) different forms of joint-utilisation of the workers concerned, regardless of whether they are employed by the outsourcing or by the supplier firm.

Within such a perspective—which as research shows is far from being marginal or speculative—the regulatory separation between service contracts and labour-only supply contracts is or could be arbitrary and irrational, since in many cases the two situations are in point of fact very close as far as the concrete situation of the workers involved in the two cases is concerned. As a report of the International Labour Organization (ILO) notes, 'triangular employment relations [...] may present a technical difficulty as the employees concerned may find themselves interacting with two (or more) interlocutors, each of whom assumes certain functions of a traditional employer'.[35] If it is true that this happens in agency work cases, it is

[35] International Labour Conference 95th Session 2006 Report, The Employment Relation (Geneva, ILO Publications).

also true that it happens too in many cases of inter-firm organisational agreements originated by an outsourcing strategy.

All of the various co-operative models developed in such a 'relational outsourcing'[36] have resulted in a great deal of heterogeneity in organisational arrangements, whose common denominator could be indicated in a series of key assumptions to be expressed in the following terms: the economic and the labour-law boundaries of the firm do not overlap anymore; the traditional bi-univocal connexion between productive organisation and employment contracts is broken. The changes affecting the 'work of organisations' have finally modified the 'organisation of work'.[37]

C. Who is my Employer?

A recent article on outsourcing in French manufacturing firms is entitled: 'Avoiding the employment relationship'.[38] Such a provocative title could be of great help in introducing additional considerations aimed at clarifying further what sub-contracting, quasi-firm, networks, partnership agreements, supply chains and other forms of relational outsourcing have to do with contingent work.

As has been specified on a number of occasions above, it would be erroneous to associate outsourcing with employment flexibility. Workers concerned with any of the various form of relational outsourcing, in truth, are not necessary flexible workers. And yet, it is not by mere chance if the great part of the labour law doctrine dealing with these issues has resolutely and repeatedly warned about the potential risks that the firms' vertical disintegration strategies might procure to labour law's effectiveness and to its scope.

Crucial to the comprehension of such risks is the awareness of how, in blurring boundaries such as those characterizing relational outsourcing models, it might become problematical to ascertain 'which entity bears the responsibility for legal obligations owed to employees in different legal contexts'.[39] The traditional answer assuming that the outsourcing firm has no responsibilities at all toward supplier's employees, cannot survive a reality in which 'just as workers have become a very heterogeneous group, so have the firms employing them: as a result of the [...] wide availability of a labour force which can be sourced from external providers,

[36] R Gibbons, 'Firms (and Other Relationships)', in P Di Maggio (ed), *The Twenty-first-century Firm: Changing Economic Organization in International Perspective* (Princeton, Princeton University Press, 2003).

[37] I owe this sort of pun to W Powell, in 'The Capitalist Firm', who actually framed it in the reverse form ('the changes remark not only the organization of work but also the work of organizations' (n 29) 59).

[38] C Perraudin, N Thèvenot and J Valentina, 'Avoiding the employment relationship: Outsourcing and labour substitution among French manufacturing firms, 1984–2003' (2013) *International Labour Review* 152, 525.

[39] Fudge, 'Blurring Legal Boundaries' (n 15) 11.

modern work arrangements frequently involve more than one entity with control over where, when and how work is done'.[40]

The spreading of sub-contracted services and supply chains organised on a permanent basis, thus gives rise to masses of workers who do not know who their 'real' employer is. As the above mentioned ILO Report noted, in a triangular employment relation where the normal functions of an employer (assigning tasks, providing the means to perform them, giving instructions and supervising their performance, paying wages, assuming risks, making profits and terminating the employment relationship) 'are assumed separately or jointly by more than one person and anyone or a number of them may be perceived as the employer, in which case the employee may reasonably wonder: who is in fact my employer?[41] That in the context of such an existential dilemma, an open-ended, full-time employee employed by a supplier firm might perceive himself as being a contingent worker, is something that does not need to be further discussed.

What on the contrary deserves to be investigated is the possible response that labour law might provide to cope with the problems under consideration.

In the abovementioned challenging inquiry into the notion of the employer, Jeremias Prassl has observed that, in case law reports, a clear disproportion exists between the abundance of judgments on the definition of employee, and the few cases decided regarding the legal identification of the employer. Such statement, based on English case law, may well be extended to the generality of labour law discourse at a comparative level, even if signals of a revived attention are visible in the most recent debates on the re-configuration of the notion of employer in groups of enterprises[42] and on temporary agency work.[43]

It is exactly in the absence of a structured legal entity, such as in the context of triangular work relations, that the precise identification of the employer is most problematic and where a revived interest in the notion of employer is most needed. In such cases, the time has certainly arrived to find out who bears the responsibility towards workers fluttering in firms' networks characterised by the blurring of the traditional organisational boundaries. Is there any normative or conceptual tool capable of inducing us to say that a contingent worker might have more than one single employer? Should the consolidation of stable partnership arrangements within relational outsourcing processes suggest, or even require, that the recognition of some form of joint-employership be identified on the plane of labour law dogmatic? The 'multi-functional' conception of the employer proposed by Prassl, identifying the responsible subject on a case-by-case basis, according to each of

[40] Prassl, The Concept of the Employer (n 23) 4.

[41] ILO, *The Employment Relation* (n 35) 10–11.

[42] O Razzolini, 'Contitolarità del rapporto di lavoro nel gruppo caratterizzato da unicità di impresa' (2009) 31 *Giornale di diritto del lavoro e di relazioni industriali* 263.

[43] M Wynn and P Leighton, 'Will the Real Employer Please Stand Up? Agencies, Clients Companies and the Employment Status of the Temporary Agency Worker' (2006) 35 *Industrial Law Journal* 301.

the different employer's functions that each time come into question, is certainly a promising scheme to reduce contingency of the external periphery workforce.

VI. Conclusions

The fundamental aim of the present Chapter has been to dissipate the conceptual fog often obfuscating the notion of contingent work. Having started from an apparent equivalence between contingent workforce and flexible employment, we came to the conclusion that contingency and flexibility are not at all synonymous. And this is so on the basis of a double assessment. First, the flexible firm is not a firm that makes use of flexible employment contracts; the flexible firm is the one that separates core from periphery (or contingent) workforce. Second, core workers do not inevitably have a standard employment contract; and periphery workers do not automatically have a flexible employment contract.

Turning away from the notion of employment flexibility, then, contingent workers might be better identified by reference to a notion of 'periphery' as opposed to one of core workforce. Just as a periphery is best defined as an area not included in the city centre, so the most suitable definition of peripheral, or contingent workers is a 'negative' one, essentially aimed at revealing what they are not.

In the view expressed in the previous paragraphs, a contingent worker can be identified as such to the extent that he is not bound by an employment contract with the firm actually benefitting from his work. Such 'negative' requisite might occur in two different cases, which have been investigated separately in the above: (a) either contingent workers do have direct contractual relations with the firm which profit from their work, but such contracts are not employment contracts (Section IV); or (b) they do have an employment contract, but such contract is concluded with an entity that is not the one to the benefit of which their work is ultimately performed (Section V). According to such double requisite, contingent workers could be either located in what we have called the internal periphery of the workforce, as is the case for economically dependent workers, zero-hours contracts, project-workers, on-call workers, casual workers and crowd workers. Or they could be placed in the external periphery of the workforce, as occurs in the case of agency workers and other workers involved in the variegated triangular relations springing out from an original decision to outsource.

In terms of labour protection's coverage, both categories of contingent workers share similar problems, consisting in an exclusion from the scope of labour law, which is not justified in view of the underlying economic ratio subtending their relationship with the ultimate beneficiary of their performances. The debated issue of quantitative thresholds limiting labour law application, for instance, is certainly one of the topics in most need of reform once it is assumed that the legal boundaries of the firm cannot but follow the economic boundaries of it, thus including in the threshold both core and contingent workers. Outside the field of individual labour protection, the spreading of contingent work negatively affects the effectiveness of a collective bargaining system still essentially designed to cover core workers only. Collective agreements aimed at covering also employees of other employers involved in a supply chain or in a multi-firm network, are still extremely rare. And the same can be said of many social security benefits which do not apply to the majority of workers falling outside the core workforce.

It is precisely the common problems the variegated contingent population shares that justifies or better necessitates the use of a unifying concept and a unifying terminology—contingent workforce,—aimed at keeping together something which in the labour law analysis and in labour law policies is usually kept separate. If considered under the same conceptual umbrella of contingent work, other apparently disparate issues—zero-hours contracts and subcontracting, just to mention but two—may also find a common ground of analysis and of regulatory intervention. Contingent work, in this perspective, is not an analytical concept. It is a rather a synthetical or holistic concept, emphasising, as such, the importance and the usefulness of comprehensive hermeneutical tools able to catch and govern the great transformations affecting the organisation of work in a post-industrial era.

It is furthermore apt to note, by way of conclusion, that contingent work is not a contingent phenomenon. It is rather a structural effect due to the spreading of flexible organisational models implemented by large and small enterprises since decades. Far from being a vague or obscure concept, contingent work challenges traditional labour law categories much more than flexible employment has done heretofore. Depicted as one of the most inclusive concept aggregating many of the labour law effects of the new organisational models, contingent work obliges labour lawyers to face a number of demanding tasks: not only a redefinition of the worker, but above all a re-conceptualisation of the employer going beyond the formal imputation of the employment contract, and a re-foundation of the employment contract itself.[44]

[44] See B Caruso, 'The Employment Contract is Dead! Hurrah for the Work Contract!' in K Stone and H Arthurs (eds) *Rethinking Workplace Regulation Beyond the Standard Employment Contract* (New York, Russel Sage Foundation Press, 2013).

4

Equal Treatment as a Problem: Germany and Agency Work

OLAF DEINERT

I. Introduction

German experiences with the equal treatment principle are somewhat ambivalent. On the one hand, the German legislator introduced the principle in order to secure employment protection for agency workers after deregulating agency work in other fields; and on the other, the system was open to abuse. This led to a weakening of the agency workers' position. In 2011, the Parliament took the opportunity to react with some changes besides regulation of equal treatment principle when it transformed the temporary agency work Directive.[1] However, companies used to benefit from a foreign (cheaper) workforce, soughtout new alternatives. The practice of subcontracting with self-employed individuals and foreign companies supplying their own workforce began to emerge. This appeared as real subcontracting in some cases but also as hidden employment contracts respectively agency work in other cases.

II. The Ancient Agency Work Regime

Shortly after the Second World War, agency work became subject to controlled recruitment. Agency work recruitment was, due to a legal monopoly, the exclusive business of the Federal Job Agency. In this way, agency work was prohibited for private enterprises. The Federal Job Agency's monopoly was considered compatible with the German Constitution ('Grundgesetz').[2] However, the European

[1] Directive 2008/104/EC of the European Parliament and of the Council of 19 November 2008 on temporary agency work, OJ L 327/9.

[2] Bundesverfassungsgericht4 April 1967—1 BVR 126/67—21 *BVerfGE* 245 (Federal Constitutional Court).

Court of Justice subsequently decided that the monopoly was incompatible with European Community Law as far as management workforce was concerned.[3] As a result, the monopoly was eliminated in 1993[4] and, in 2002, the need to hold a licence in order to run an agency was removed.[5] Although the Federal Constitutional Court considered the monopoly to be compatible with the Constitution, it did not adopt the same position with regard to the prohibition of private agency work. The Court felt that such monopoly was incompatible with the freedom of profession (article 12 of the Constitution).[6] Two premises in the decision are of considerable importance. The Court focused on the legal circumstance that it was not lawful to link the duration of the labour contract with the duration of the operation in the user enterprise. Further, the Court was convinced that long term operation in the user's enterprise would not occur in practice. Both premises are not valid yet: The interdiction of synchronisation of labour contract and duration of the operation has been abolished later by the legislator and in reality, after the beginning of the millennium long term operations became customary. However, in the end of the 1960s, the judges were not able to read the future—and nowadays anyone pleads for a new general prohibition of agency work (which would be incompatible with European Union laws as well).

In 1972, the legislator reacted by adopting the Federal Temporary Employment Act ('Arbeitnehmerüberlassungsgesetz') in which the necessity of a licence and the conditions of the work of agency workers are regulated.[7] The German law follows the idea of a labour relation between the agency and the user. In practice, the number of temporary work agencies and the number of agency workers grew after that. Nevertheless, the enterprises worked with their own workforce as ordinary way of operation. Agency work was an option for firms in transitional need of workers. This changed drastically after the labour market reforms were introduced by the government under Chancellor Gerhard Schröder in the early 2000s.

III. Labour Market Reforms since 2002 ('Agenda 2010')

The coalition of Social Democrats and The Green Party introduced a new social security and labour market policy under the label 'Agenda 2010'. Among others, the agenda was supposed to reduce the unemployment rate drastically. The

[3] Case C-41/90 *Höfner and Elser v Macrotron* GmbH, 1991 ECR I-1979.

[4] Erstes Gesetz zur Umsetzung des Spar-Konsolidierungs- und Wachstumsprogramms (1. SKWPG), 21 December 1993, 1993 *Bundesgesetzblatt I* 2353 (Federal Law Gazette).

[5] Gesetz zur Vereinfachung der Wahl der Arbeitnehmervertreter in den Aufsichtsrat, 23 March 2002, 2002 *Bundesgesetzblatt I* 1130 (Federal Law Gazette).

[6] Bundesverfassungsgericht 4 April 1967—1 BvR 84/65—21 *BVerfGE* 261 (Federal Constitutional Court).

[7] Gesetz zur Regelung der gewerbsmäßigen Arbeitnehmerüberlassung (Arbeitnehmerüberlassungsgesetz—AÜG) und zur Änderung anderer Gesetze, 7 August 1972, 1972 *Bundesgesetzblatt I* 1393 (Federal Law Gazette).

government set up a commission, chaired by Peter Hartz, the former labour manager of the Volkswagen Company, in order to find solutions for the unemployment problem. The proposal of the commission[8] was—among others—to promote agency work as an instrument to reduce the unemployment rate or shorten periods of unemployment.[9] In this way, agency work was viewed as a bridge helping unemployed people find regular employment, namely through labour service agencies ('Personalserviceagenturen').[10] The commission, therefore, recommended the deregulation of agency work. In response to the commission recommendations, the legislator adopted four statutes dealing with 'modern services in the labour market' ('Moderne Dienstleistungen am Arbeitsmarkt'). The reform and deregulation of agency work has been put into the first statute dealing with modern services in the labour market.[11] It was one of four statutes implementing the recommendations of the Hartz Commission which have colloquially been called 'Hartz-Gesetze'.

In the first stage, this new legislation led to a deregulation of agency work:[12]

— A special prohibition on fixed-term contracts with agency workers was abolished.
— A prohibition on the re-engagement of former agency workers was eliminated.
— The prohibition of synchronisation disappeared.
— A maximum period of performance in the user enterprise was abolished.

According to the explanatory statement, the rationale for these deregulations was an equal footing protection for agency workers through a new equal treatment principle. Up to that point, Germany was one of the biggest opponents to the equal treatment principle during the European discussions about the agency work Directive. From then on, German policy changed due to the fact that the equal treatment principle became the 'one and only' instrument for social labour protection in the field of agency work.

In fact, the equal treatment principle was introduced to agency work law one year earlier via the Job-AQTIV-Gesetz (statute on activation, qualification, training, investment and recruitment service).[13] However, in the older version of the law the principle was only applicable after 12 months in an operation unit. This obstacle disappeared from 2003. According to articles 9, 10 of the agency work statute, the employee is usually entitled to the same working conditions which the normal workforce in the operation plant enjoy from the very beginning of

[8] *Moderne Dienstleistungen am Arbeitsmarkt*, Bericht der Kommission, 2002, accessible at http://www.bmas.de/DE/Service/Medien/Publikationen/moderne-dienstleistungen-am-arbeitsmarkt.html

[9] *Moderne Dienstleistungen am Arbeitsmarkt* 157.

[10] *Moderne Dienstleistungen am Arbeitsmarkt* 147 ff.

[11] Erstes Gesetz für moderne Dienstleistungen am Arbeitsmarkt, 23 December 2002, 2002 *Bundesgesetzblatt I* 4607 (Federal Law Gazette).

[12] See Krause, 'Arbeitnehmerüberlassung als Instrument zur Flexibilisierung von Arbeitsmärkten' in *Zeitschrift für internationales und ausländisches Arbeits- und Sozialrecht* (2014) 123–24.

[13] 10 December 2001, 2001 *Bundesgesetzblatt I* 3443 (Federal Law Gazette).

the operation. As the Federal Constitutional Court pointed out, this rule does not interfere with the Constitution.[14]

IV. The Equal Treatment Principle

A. The Equal Treatment Principle in General and its Exceptions

The new equal treatment principle is applicable starting from the moment an agency worker starts performing work in the user enterprise. However, there were two exceptions:

— if the employee entered into the labour contract immediately after a period of unemployment, the remuneration could, for a maximum period of six weeks, justifiably be lower than the wages an employee in a similar job in the user enterprise earned, provided that it was not lower than the level of unemployment benefits the employee would have been entitled to,

— if a collective agreement existed which was applicable to the parties of the labour contract, the employee could only lay claim to the working conditions set out in that agreement, regardless of whether these conditions were more or less advantageous than the working conditions applicable to a similar employee in the user's enterprise. This rule was not only applicable where the parties to the labour contract were bound to the collective agreement by membership or by generally binding declaration, but also where there was a reference to the collective agreement in the labour contract even though the parties were not bound to the agreement by membership or generally binding declaration.

B. The Practice of 'Equal Treatment'

The first mentioned option was rarely applied because of the second option offered to temporary work agencies. This latter option led to a race to the bottom that the legislator perhaps had not envisaged. According to the explanatory report, the authors of the new law sought to promote flexible solutions for agency workers. They explicitly mentioned the possibility of flat rate solutions and stabilising wages, which could be an advantage in comparison to constant changes in the amount of the wages where an employee performs his or her work for several short periods in different enterprises, perhaps with breaks by periods of any operation.[15]

[14] Bundesverfassungsgericht 29 December 2004—1 BvR 2283/03, 1 BvR 2504/03, 1 BvR 2582/03—2005 *Der Betrieb* 110 (Federal Constitutional Court).

[15] *Bundestags-Drucksache* 15/25, 38 (Parliament Document).

This idea was accompanied by the hope that collective bargaining structures in relation to work agencies, which had not existed before, could be established. If the agencies were interested in advantages that they could only obtain by collective agreements, they could become interested in bargaining collectively although the unions were not strong enough to put pressure on them via collective action.

The impact of this new rule was rather disappointing. Normally, one would have expected the unions to have enough bargaining power to claim better conditions for the agency workers because they had the possibility to fall back on the conditions set out by the law, ie the principle of equal treatment. If they declared an index of lowest level —not to go beyond the benefits that the agency workers could claim on average under the equal treatment principle—they could refuse to bargain on lower conditions. Due to a predicament which the legislator has tried to solve, this did not work out: If the exception from the equal treatment principle had been applicable only to those who were bound to the agreement by membership and not to those who were bound by reference to it in the labour contract, this could have led to the result that union members could fall under a disadvantageous regulation while outsiders could work under better conditions. This might apply pressure on the unions indirectly. Therefore, the law tried to eliminate this dilemma by allowing deviations from the equal treatment principle by reference in the labour contract. Usually, this is at the employer's discretion since he sets out the terms of employment.

This had an unfortunate impact: The employers became quite interested in the option of concluding collective agreements which were—from their point of view—more advantageous than being subject to the equal treatment principle. Moreover, they found some organisations that were willing to take advantage of the exceptions available to the equal treatment principle.[16] A number of so-called Christian unions founded an umbrella network, the Christian Unions for Temporary Agency Work and Labour Service Agencies ('Christliche Gewerkschaften Zeitarbeit und Personalserviceagenturen', also known as 'CGZP'). Under this network, they concluded low-level collective agreements offering wages of 7.21 € per hour. Since every labour contract in the field of agency work has reference clauses, these agreements allowed employers to evade the equal treatment principle and remunerate employees at a different rate. On the other hand the unions organised in the German Trade Union Confederation ('Deutscher Gewerkschaftsbund', also known as 'DGB') lost their bargaining power because employers no longer had a need to bargain with them. They were no longer in the position only to refuse to bargain collectively.[17] Therefore, the DGB-unions were under pressure to bargain

[16] cf Schüren, P, 41 *Jahrbuch des Arbeitsrechts* 49, 51 ff; Krause, R, 'Arbeit in der Holzklasse—Gesetzliche und kollektivvertragliche Rahmung der Leiharbeit' in *Kritische Justiz* (2013) 124–25; Waltermann, R, 'Fehlentwicklung in der Leiharbeit' in *Neue Zeitschrift für Arbeitsrecht* (2010) 482, 483, 485.

[17] According to Nielebock, H, 'Regelung europarechtskonformer Ausnahmen vom Gleichbehandlungsgrundsatz durch die Änderung des AÜG 2011?' in *Festschrift für Klaus Bepler* (München, C.H. Beck-Verlag, 2012) 455, 456, the DGB-unions had found a compromise with the employers on roundabout 11 € per hour, which was not laid down in a collective agreement after the agreement of the so-called Christian unions became public.

collectively 'besides the shadow of the law'. Due to the lack of organisation in the field of agency work and, consequently, due to their specific lack of bargaining power, the DGB-unions were only able to conclude an agreement at a level not much higher than that of the CGZP-agreements. It is possible to discuss at length the motives which led those so-called Christian unions to conclude such low-level agreements. It is rumoured that those unions were yellow dog unions. However, this has never been proved. Employers usually argue that those unions did not have less potential than the DGB-unions, including the metal workers union and the chemical industry, mining and energy union, because the latter were not able to conclude higher-level agreements. This is only half the story because the DGB-unions, aware of their lack of bargaining power in that sector, refused at the beginning to conclude agreements with good reasons.

The result of this practice was disastrous. Collective bargaining became an instrument to deregulate the legal entitlements of employees.[18] One should bear in mind that the equal treatment principle was the only essential entitlement left to agency workers for their protection since the other labour law protections have been eliminated by the first statute on modern services in the labour market.[19]

This is not only a problem of lack of labour protection in the field of agency work, but also a problem regarding the European agency work Directive. The Directive allows Member States in Article 5(3) to accept collective agreements that differ from the working conditions under the equal treatment principle, but only 'while respecting the overall protection of temporary agency workers'. It is obvious that this condition cannot be fulfilled by a rule that allows deviating without any restrictions and without securing labour protection in any other way.

The result was impressive. Temporary agency work grew. By the middle of 2006, Germany had 300,000 agency workers. The number increased to 742,000 in 2010. In this respect, one could argue that the main challenges under the 'Agenda 2010' have partly been settled by the liberalisation of agency work. This is, once again, only half the story. The scientific institute of the Federal Labour Agency (the 'Institut für Arbeitsmarkt- und Berufsforschung'—Institute for Employment Research) discovered that roughly 50% of the number of jobs that appeared in the temporary agency branch after agencies adopted the first statute on modern services in the labour market have disappeared in other branches.[20] The bridge function of agency work became questionable.[21] Although 30% of agency workers are later hired in operation plants,[22] it is uncertain if they are hired under fixed-term contracts, and, whether those contracts extended after the first period.

[18] Thüsing, G, 'Equal Pay bei Leiharbeit—Zur Reichweite der Gleichbehandlungspflicht nach dem AÜG' in *Der Betrieb* (2003) 446, 448, in this context speaks about wrongful use of collective agreements.

[19] See III *supra*.

[20] IAB-Kurzbericht 2/2013.

[21] Hohendanner, C and Walwei, U, 'Arbeitsmarkteffekte atypischer Beschäftigung' in WSI-Mitteilungen (2013) 239, 241.

[22] Böckler impuls 8/2008, p 1.

The German legislator, in the early 2000s, saw temporary agency work as a flexible instrument, to be used by the user enterprises in the event of temporary need for additional workforce. Promoting a sector that could fulfil those wishes was supposed to create new jobs in that sector. In order to facilitate this, Parliament deregulated the agency work law but also recognised that agency workers are members of the workforce in the user enterprises, though not the core workforce. The Federal Labour Court has upheld this on several occasions,[23] eg:

— agency workers are included in the calculation of the threshold for social protection against dismissals (Article 23 of the unfair dismissals Act, *Kündigungsschutzgesetz*);[24]
— agency workers who can take part in works council elections after three months of operation in the plant shall be considered as part of the workforce in order to calculate the number of workers. This is of importance eg for the size of the works council according to Article 9 of the Works Constitution Act ('Betriebsverfassungsgesetz'),[25] or for determining the threshold at which the employer has an obligation to bargain with the works council about the social plan in the event of modifications in the plant (Articles 111, 112 of the Works Constitution Act);[26] or
— the right to be elected on a works council depends on how long an employee has been part of the workforce (article 8 of the Works Constitution Act). When calculating the length of time, periods spent in a foreign enterprise can also be taken into account.[27]

From that point of view, it is only natural that agency workers should enjoy the same working conditions as the core workforce. According to the law, they are contingent workers, not second-class workers. The second aspect is reflected in the equal treatment principle, the first one in the construction that the work agency is the debtor and takes also the risk of lack of operation possibilities.[28] The reality looks different: agency workers became second-class workers because they did not enjoy equal treatment in reality and remained a foreign workforce.

[23] See Deinert, O, 'Kernbelegschaften—Randbelegschaften—Fremdbelegschaften: Herausforderungen für das Arbeitsrecht durch Reduzierung von Stammbelegschaften' in *Recht der Arbeit* (2014) 65, 69.

[24] Bundesarbeitsgericht 24 January 2013—2 AZR 140/12—2013 *Neue Zeitschrift für Arbeitsrecht* 726 (Federal Labour Court).

[25] Bundesarbeitsgericht 13 March 2013—7 ABR 69/11—2013 *Neue Zeitschrift für Arbeitsrecht* 789 (Federal Labour Court); with regard to the role of agency workers in the works constitution see: Linsenmaier, W and Kiel, H, 'Der Leiharbeitnehmer in der Betriebsverfassung—"Zwei-Komponenten-Lehre" und normzweckorientierte Gesetzesauslegung' in *Recht der Arbeit* (2014) 135 ff.

[26] Bundesarbeitsgericht 18 October 2011—7 ABR 69/11—2012 *Neue Zeitschrift für Arbeitsrecht* 221 (Federal Labour Court).

[27] Bundesarbeitsgericht 10 October 2012—7 ABR 53/11—*Arbeitsrechtliche Praxis* § 8 BetrVG 1972 n° 15 (Federal Labour Court).

[28] This has been stated explicitly by the Federal Labour Court (16 April 2014—5 AZR 483/12—2014 *Neue Zeitschrift für Arbeitsrecht* 1262) when deciding that the adoption of a flexitime wage record aiming at evading of the law was incompatible with the Temporary Employment Act.

A vivid illustration of such deviation from the equal treatment principle and the division of the workforce into core workforce and contingent workers is provided by the drugstore chain Schlecker:[29] They transferred workers to a legally autonomous enterprise which was member of the group and posted them to workplaces in chain stores similar to their old jobs. This led to the emergence of two classes of workers. De facto agency work was used as an instrument to reduce labour costs by lowering the working conditions.

C. The Reactions of Courts, Trade Unions and Parliament

For a certain period, agency work was seen as a 'good remedy' by human resource managers. As it evolved over time, the active ingredient of this 'remedy' began to decline, due to the evolution described below.[30]

i. Jurisprudence

As already intimated, the motives behind an organisation concluding collective agreements against the interests of the organised workforce were questioned. Furthermore, the competing unions within the German Trade Union Confederation denied the trade union status of the Christian Unions for Agency Work and Labour Service Agencies. In the last instance, the Federal Labour Court had to decide on the capacity of the Christian Unions to conclude collective agreements for agency workers.[31] The CGZP was an umbrella organisation, composed of some organisations, which alleged to be trade unions in a legal sense, but doubts arose about whether all of them really were trade unions. It should be noted that according to German collective agreements law only trade unions in a legal sense have the capacity to conclude collective agreements. The Federal Labour Court did not go into detail on this question. It decided that an umbrella organisation like the CGZP could only have the capacity to conclude collective agreements on its own once it gets the capacity from all its member organisations in full range. That means that the capacity to conclude collective agreements cannot go beyond the capacity of all the members. It is the same for the competence according to the statutes of the member organisations: a trade union is only able to conclude collective agreements once given the competence to do so according to its statute. Therefore, the competences of a federation cannot go beyond that of all the

[29] See 'Fall Schlecker beunruhigt Zeitarbeitsbranche', *Frankfurter Allgemeine Zeitung*, 12 January 2010.

[30] See Deinert, *Recht der Arbeit* (n 23) 65, 69–72; M, Lembke and J, Rothmann, *Zeitschrift für Europäisches Sozial- und Arbeitsrecht* (2014) 372; Krause, R, 'Flexibler Personaleinsatz—Arbeitnehmerüberlassung und Werkverträge zwischen Markt und Regulierung' in *Zeitschrift für Arbeitsrecht* (2014) 349, 368–84.

[31] Bundesarbeitsgericht 14 December 2010—1 ABR 19/10—2011 *Neue Zeitschrift für Arbeitsrecht* 289 (Federal Labour Court).

member organisations taken together. However, the agreements concluded by the CGZP went beyond the capacities and competences of its member organisations. Therefore, the CGZP was not able to conclude valid collective agreements in order to lower the working conditions in comparison to the conditions of the equal treatment principle.

The decisions of the Federal Labour Court seemed to be at first glance to focus only on an *ex nunc* situation. However, later the Court also decided that the legal situation according to the judgment had effects *ex tunc*.[32]

Due to this jurisdiction, deviations from the equal treatment principle became impossible. This was not only true for collective agreements which were enforceable on their own by reason of membership of the contract parties in the trade organisations, but also in the case of reference in the individual employment contract to the collective agreement because this reference referred to something which did not exist.[33] During the legal proceedings before the labour courts, which led to the mentioned decision of the Federal Labour Court, the employer's organisations and the members of the CGZP changed their tactics and started to conclude collective agreements whose parties on the labour side were the member organisations of the CGZP. Legally, this was a composition of several collective agreements in one document. This tactic was unsuccessful. The Federal Labour Court decided that a reference to such collective agreements could not result in deviation from the equal treatment principle because the reference in the labour contract was not transparent enough in the sense of Section 307 para 1 of the German Civil Code ('Bürgerliches Gesetzbuch'): no one knew which of the numerous agreements was the one to be incorporated with the labour contract. The last mentioned point was legally important because the different agreements incorporated in the labour contract were identical at the beginning but could have different developments, eg in the case of termination only by some of the unions.

As a result, it was discovered that many agency workers had undercharged wages. The legal services team of the German Trade Union Federation reported about 1,500 claims for higher wages amounted to €5 million. However, those claims were only possible for the past three years because wages from earlier periods fell under the statute of limitations. The limitation was not interrupted during the period of uncertainty about the status of CGZP according to the Federal Labour Court.[34] Much more drastic consequences arose from the law of social security contributions: if the agency workers were entitled to higher wages according to the equal treatment principle in the past, the employers were obliged to

[32] Bundesarbeitsgericht, 23 May 2012—1 AZB 58/11—2013 *Neue Zeitschrift für Arbeitsrecht* 623; Bundesarbeitsgericht, 23 May 2012—1 AZB 867/11—2012 *Neue Zeitschrift für Arbeitsrecht* 625; Bundesarbeitsgericht, 24 July 2012—1 AZB 47/11—2012 *Neue Zeitschrift für Arbeitsrecht* 623 (Federal Labour Court).

[33] Bundesarbeitsgericht, 13 March 2013—5 AZR 954/11—2013 *Neue Zeitschrift für Arbeitsrecht* 680, n° 26 ff (Federal Labour Court).

[34] Bundesarbeitsgericht, 24 January 2013—2 AZR 140/12—2013 *Neue Zeitschrift für Arbeitsrecht* 726 (Federal Labour Court).

pay the social security contributions on the higher level which depended on the real entitlement of the agency workers.[35] The pension's insurance carrier therefore claimed for higher contributions. With regard to limitation periods, the rules on social security contributions are covered by a special regime: the period is four years—but in the case of intention, it is 30 years according to Section 25 Para 1 (1) of Book 4 of the Social Code. The Federal Social Court had decided in an earlier decision that intention is given in any case in which the employer may think it could be possible that he is obliged to pay higher contributions.[36] Such a case of intention has been given for all the work agencies at the latest from the moment in which the proceedings on the question of capacity to conclude collective agreements of the CGZP became public.[37] Additionally, the user enterprises are liable like guarantors for the social security contributions of the work agencies according to Section 28g Para 2 (1) of Book 4 of the Social Code. Until the end of May 2013, the pension's insurance carrier claimed contributions totalling €200 million. Although the employees usually have to pay towards half of the social security contributions, the agencies were not able to seek redress for the full amount. Besides the fact that many of the agency workers still were not employees of the firm and it is not always possible to find out the address of a former employee, it is legally not possible to get redress from the former employees. According to Section 28g of Book 4 of the Social Code the employer can only get redress by reducing the wages during the following three payment periods.

ii. Collective Bargaining

Further measures for combating the misuse of agency work to undermine working conditions in the user enterprises were established via collective agreements.[38]

One measure was the establishment of a minimum wage level for agency workers. Such a measure was introduced by a law of 28 April 2011 (see below). It allows for bargaining on minimum wages between trade unions and employers organisations which shall be made applicable *erga omnes* by ministerial regulation. Such a minimum wage level cannot be avoided by individual labour contracts or by collective agreements of other organisations. Under this new regime, a group of trade unions under the German Trade Union Confederation reached a first agreement on minimum wages for agency workers, which became applicable *erga omnes* by regulation from December 2011.[39] Following a second regulation[40] founded on

[35] See eg Berchtold, J, 'Nachforderung von Sozialversicherungsbeiträgen bei Nichtigkeit von Tarifverträgen der CGZP' in *Soziale Sicherheit* (2012) 70; Deinert, 2012 *Arbeitsrecht im Betrieb* 255, 257 ff.

[36] Bundessozialgericht, 25 October 1990—12 RK 10/90—1992 *Der Betrieb* 2090.

[37] Deinert, O, 'Zahlung der Sozialversicherungsbeiträge' in *Arbeitsrecht im Betrieb* (2012) 255, 258 (Federal Social Court).

[38] See in detail Krause, *Zeitschrift für Arbeitsrecht* (n 30) 349, 372–74, 381–84.

[39] *Bundesanzeiger* n° 195, 28 December 2011, 4608.

[40] Second regulation on minimum wage level in the field of agency work, 21 March 2014, *Bundesanzeiger* AT 26.3.2014 V1 (Federal Bulletin).

collective bargaining, the minimum wage for agency workers as of April 2014 was €8.50 in Western Germany and €7.86 in Eastern Germany; this increased in April 2015 to €8.80 in Western Germany and €8.20 in Eastern Germany; as of April 2016 the minimum wage is €9.00 (West) and €8.50 (East) respectively.

It is clearly recognisable that the minimum wage in the field of agency work can only affect drastic low price policies of so-called unions, which only conclude agreements in order to facilitate deviation from the equal treatment principle. However, this cannot prevent employers from deviation of the equal treatment principle by individual labour contract as such. Therefore, the trade unions under the German Trade Union Confederation tried to bargain on the employment and working conditions of agency workers directly in the plant. Two routes were chosen: one route was to bargain with the user enterprises about possible ways to give the equal treatment principle effect. A first success in this field was reported in 2010 from the steel industry.[41] Afterwards, a breakthrough was settled in the metal industry in 2012:[42] The user enterprises became obliged to only conclude contracts with agencies, which pay wages according to collective agreements. Further, a co-determination right of the works council was installed. The second route was addressed to the agencies: the metalworkers union succeeded in different industry sectors to conclude on a wage uplift for agency workers ('branch supplements'). Similar agreements were later concluded by the service union Ver.di and the union for mining, chemistry and energy. Especially the branch supplements were supposed to have direct effects on the—decreasing—number of agency workers.[43]

iii. Legislation

A third actor in this field was the legislator. Soon after the Schlecker practice became public, the former Minister of Labour, Ursula von der Leyen, declared such practice to be unacceptable and sought to promote legislation against the misuse of agency work. On the occasion of the implementation of the agency work Directive, the ministry adopted a proposal for a first amendment of the agency work statute. The following new law from 28 April 2011[44] was made up of several instruments of implementation of the Directive on the one hand and careful new developments in the national law on the other hand in order to prevent enterprises from using agency work as an instrument to get cheap workforce from outside:

[41] 'Erstmals gleicher Lohn für Leiharbeiter', *Süddeutsche Zeitung*, 2 October 2010, 2.

[42] See *IGM direkt* 2012 n° 7, 3; Krause, R, 'Neue tarifvertragliche Regeln für die Leiharbeit in der Metallindustrie' in *Neue Zeitschrift für Arbeitsrecht* (2012) 830; Krause, R, 'Tarifverträge zur Wiederherstellung von Equal Pay' in *Arbeit und Recht* (2012) 55; Krause *Kritische Justiz* (n 16) 119, 127 ff; Schumann, D, 'Tarifverträge zur Leiharbeit in der Metall- und Elektroindustrie—Verbesserte Arbeitsbedingungen für Leiharbeitnehmer' in *Arbeitsrecht im Betrieb* (2012) 423.

[43] 'Leiharbeit kostet mehr', *Süddeutsche Zeitung*, 23 May 2013, 20.

[44] Erstes Gesetz zur Änderung des Arbeitnehmerüberlassungsgesetzes—Verhinderung von Missbrauch der Arbeitnehmerüberlassung, 28 April 2001, 2011 *Bundesgesetzblatt* I 642 (Federal Law Gazette).

- The legal framework for agency work is no longer restricted to agencies that run under a trade business; instead the Temporary Employment Act is applicable to any agency work which is performed within an economic activity. This also covers work agencies that lease workforce within a group for only original costs.[45]
- Agency workers' rights regarding information and participation in facilities in the user enterprise have been established.
- Agency work has to be performed occasionally.
- The equal treatment principle became subject of reform to a small degree (see (ii) below).
- A measure of high publicity was the introduction of the minimum wage level for agency workers in Section 3a of the Agency Workers Statute. It should be noted that, in Germany, statutory minimum wages have no legal tradition. Instead, Parliament trusted in collective bargaining for a long time and for several years in sectoral minimum wage agreements which are to be declared generally binding by ministerial decree or regulation under the Posting of Workers Act ('Arbeitnehmerentsendegesetz'), which became an instrument of minimum working conditions after the amendment from 2009[46] not only for posted workers but for every worker who performs their labour on the German territory.[47] It was not before the elections of 2013 that a general statutory minimum wage (€8.50 per hour) could be implemented by law from 2014[48] under the new 'great coalition' of Social Democrats and Conservatives which is still in power.

Previously, the question as to which industry sector could bargain on the issue of minimum wage was subject to political debate. Under the former 'great coalition' of Social Democrats and Conservatives (2005–2009), a minimum wage for agency workers supported by trade unions was rejected.[49] The liberal-conservative government of Chancellor Merkel from 2009–2013 initially stood against minimum wages. The breakthrough came following a political deal with the opposition during the debates about the amount of the minimum social benefits for unemployed people in 2011.

The minimum wage level not only sets a minimum wage for agency workers. It also excludes the deviation from the equal treatment principle via or by reference to collective agreements that undercut the minimum wage level. Therefore, the

[45] Hamann, W, 'Die Reform des AÜG im Jahr 2011' in *Recht der Arbeit* (2011) 321, 323 f.

[46] Gesetz über zwingende Arbeitsbedingungen für grenzüberschreitend entsandte und für regelmäßig im Inland beschäftigte Arbeitnehmer und Arbeitnehmerinnen (Arbeitnehmer-Entsendegesetz—AEntG), 27 April 2009, 2009 *Bundesgesetzblatt I* 799 (Federal Law Gazette).

[47] See with further Deinert, O, *Internationales Arbeitsrecht* (Tübingen, Mohr Siebeck Verlag, 2013) § 10 n° 93.

[48] Gesetz zur Stärkung der Tarifautonomie (Tarifautonomiestärkungsgesetz) from 11 August.2014, 2014 *Bundesgesetzblatt I* 1348 (Federal Law Gazette).

[49] See Deinert, O and Kittner, M, 'Die arbeitsrechtliche Bilanz der Großen Koalition 2005–2009' in *Recht der Arbeit* (2009) 265, 276.

minimum wage level needs to be seen as a pillar for the equal treatment principle. Although a statutory minimum wage of €8.50 exists in Germany, the minimum wage for agency workers is still of importance because any sectoral minimum wage which is higher than the statutory minimum wage has priority (with an exception for an interim period until the end of 2017).[50]

(a) The EU Directive

The Concept

The EU Directive on temporary agency work focuses on the 'flexicurity' approach which means that temporary agency work shall not only promote the employers' interests in flexible workforce but also the employment interests of the agency workers which is expressly stated in preamble (11). Article 2 of the Directive points out that temporary work agencies should be recognised as employers and Article 4 aims at abolishing restrictions and prohibitions except for some fundamental interests of society which includes the protection of the agency workers. There is more to it: Article 2 of the Directive mentions the protection of the agency workers as an aim of the Directive in cooperation with the 'flexicurity' approach which is referred to in preamble (9).

This indicates that a complete deregulation of labour rights of agency workers is in contradiction with the agency work concept of the Directive. The former German model could not comply with that policy. Taking a closer look at the equal treatment principle of the Directive as set out in Article 5, it becomes very clear.

Article 5(1) of the Directive stipulates that any agency worker should benefit from the basic working and employment conditions during the time of operation as if they had been hired directly by the user enterprise. Although this dictates an equal treatment principle, the approach is a different compared to the one adopted under German law: under German law, the criterion is not how the employee would have been treated if he was an employee of the user;[51] the question is how a comparable employee of the user is treated or would have been treated.[52,53] An exception to the equal treatment principle with regard to pay (equal wages) can be envisaged by the Member States in the event that the agency worker has a

[50] Section 1 Para 3 and Section 24 Para 1 of the Minimum Wage Act.

[51] This is the approach of the Directive, see Engels, C, 'Regulating Temporary Work in the European Union: The Agency Directive', in: Blanpain, R and Hendrickx, F (eds), *Temporary Agency Work in the European Union and the United States* (Wolters Kluwer, 2013) 1, 14.

[52] This is the test according to the German Agency Work Statute, although scholars often focus on the conditions that would have been applicable in the case of being a regular employee of the user enterprise, see Sansone, P, 'Leiharbeit' in U Preis and A Sagan (eds), *Europäisches Arbeitsrecht* (Köln, Otto Schmidt, 2015) § 8 n° 56.

[53] Boemke, B, 'Die EG-Leiharbeitsrichtlinie und ihre Einflüsse auf das deutsche Recht' in *Recht der internationalen Wirtschaft* (2009) 177, 182; Waas, B, 'Der Gleichbehandlungsgrundsatz im neuen Arbeitnehmerüberlassungsgesetz' in *Zeitschrift für Europäisches Sozial- und Arbeitsrecht* (2012) 7.

permanent contract and gets a continued pay during times of operation and times of non-operation (Article 5(2)).[54]

At first glance, this seems to justify the practice of collective agreements for agency workers: if a collective agreement sets out wages for agency workers who are usually under a permanent labour contract because—according to the law—an agency worker's labour contract is not limited to the time of operation, the agreement may allow deviation from the equal treatment principle irrespective of the level of wages. But this interpretation would ignore the rules set out in Article 5(3) of the Directive.[55] According to this section collective agreements on working and employment conditions of temporary agency workers may differ from the equal treatment principle, but only 'while respecting the overall protection of temporary agency workers'. This means that a mere undercutting of the equal treatment principle by collective agreements is not possible under the Directive because the overall protection of temporary agency workers would not have been respected in that case. It should be clear that, although respecting the autonomy of social partners according to article 28 of the EU Charter of Fundamental Rights, collective agreements, which do not respect a minimum of protection for agency workers, are incompatible with European Labour Law.[56] The same applies with respect to the individual employee's right to healthy, secure und fair working conditions according to Article 31 of the Charter[57] and with respect to the fundamental right of equal treatment according to article 20 of the Charter.[58] Moreover, Article 5(5) of the Directive stipulates the obligation of the member states to take appropriate measures with a view to preventing misuse. This also shows that collective agreements which deviate from the equal treatment principle without providing any

[54] See for the potential for misuse, Schlachter, M, 'Transnational Temporary Agency Work: How Much Equality Does the Equal Treatment Principle Provide?' in *International Journal of Comparative Labour Law and Industrial Relations* (2012) 177, 193.

[55] See for this provision, Schlachter, *The International Journal of Comparative Labour Law and Industrial Relations* (n 54) 177, 193–196.

[56] See Sansone, in Preis and Sagan (eds), *Europäisches Arbeitsrecht* (n 52) § 8 n° 76; also Waas, *Zeitschrift für Europäisches Sozial- und Arbeitsrecht* (n 53) 7, 9; Blanke, T, 'Der Gleichbehandlungsgrundsatz in der Arbeitnehmerüberlassung' in *Der Betrieb* (2010) 1528, 1531 ff. Focusing on the national minimum wage or the minimum wage for agency workers is no respect on the overall protection of agency worker (Zimmer, R, 'Der Grundsatz der Gleichbehandlung in der Leiharbeitsrichtlinie 2008/104/EG und seine Umsetzung ins deutsche Recht' in *Neue Zeitschrift für Arbeitsrecht* (2013) 289, 291; Waas, *Zeitschrift für Europäisches Sozial- und Arbeitsrecht* (n 53) 7, 9 ff; see also Heuschmid, J and Klauk, M, 'Zur Primärrechtswidrigkeit der Leiharbeits-Richtlinie' in *Soziales Recht* (2012) 84, 93; against see Sansone, in Preis and Sagan (eds), *Europäisches Arbeitsrecht* (n 52) § 8 n° 77; Sansone, P, *Gleichstellung von Leiharbeitnehmern nach deutschem und Unionsrecht* (München, C.H. Beck-Verlag, 2011) 546, because this is only the lowest level of protection which fits for any worker in Germany and nota bene a national statutory minimum wage cannot be treated as a measure of protection which is provided by the social partners.

[57] Zimmer, *Neue Zeitschrift für Arbeitsrecht* (n 56) 289, 290.

[58] In this way the equal treatment principle in the Directive could be understood as a specification of the fundamental right in article 20 of the Charter. Moreover, Heuschmid and Klauk, *Soziales Recht* (n 56) 84 ff, argue that the Directive is incompatible with this fundamental right because it allows—irrespective of the overall protection of the agency worker—to deviate from the equal treatment principle for a long-standing period which is not justified.

substantive protection to agency workers are not compatible with the Directive. Instead, the Directive follows some kind of dual channel protection system. Temporary agency workers shall be protected:

— either by equal treatment with the core workforce of the user enterprise; or
— by a special regime of labour protection which is tailored exactly for agency workers by collective agreement. (A similar possibility to set out an agency worker's protection regime is foreseen in Article 5 Section 4 of the Directive for Member States, which have no possibility to declare such collective agreements generally binding.) This special regime must achieve an equivalent quality of protection of agency workers compared to the equal treatment principle.

One could assume that the first route is designed for Member States which have a legal system in which temporary agency work contracts are commonly synchronised with the operation period, while the second route focuses on Member States with a temporary agency work regime in which the labour contract is independent from the operation period in the first place. However, the Directive creates no direct links between the two routes and the two possible systems. Moreover, the Directive indicates a preference to the equal treatment principle. This principle is the general rule and the special regime for temporary agency work is an exception in a technical sense.

Details

Article 5(2) allows for deviation from the general equal treatment principle only under two preconditions:[59] The exception only concerns the payment and is merely applicable to permanent employment contracts. The reason for this exemption is that temporary agency workers who have a permanent contract of employment with a temporary work agency continue to be paid in the period between assignments and the work agency should have the option of paying the employee a lower rate. Departing from this rule, German law allows further deviation from the equal treatment principle in cases of fixed term contracts and not only with respect to payments. The German exemption is not covered by Article 5(2) of the Directive.[60]

[59] Engels, 'Regulating Temporary Work' (n 51) 1, 16; Ulber, J, 'Die Richtlinie der Leiharbeit' in *Arbeit und Recht* (2010) 10, 13; Riesenhuber, K, *Europäisches Arbeitsrecht* (Heidelberg, C.F. Müller Verlag, 2009) § 18 no 15.

[60] See Blanke, *Der Betrieb* (n 56) 1528, 1530 ff; Zimmer, *Neue Zeitschrift für Arbeitsrecht* (n 56) 289, 293; Düwell, FJ, in *Bundestag, Ausschussdrucksache* 17 (11) 431, 56, 57 (Committee of Parliament Document); Ulber, *Arbeit und Recht* (n 59) 10, 13; Rieble, V and Klebeck, U, 'Lohngleichheit für Leiharbeit' in *Neue Zeitschrift für Arbeitsrecht* (2003) 23, 25; Riederer von Paar, in Schüren, P and Hamann, W (eds), *Arbeitnehmerüberlassungsgesetz*, 4th edn (München, CH Beck-Verlag, 2010) Einleitung no 611; Schüren, in Schüren and Hamann (eds), *Arbeitnehmerüberlassungsgesetz*, § 9 no 170; Thüsing, in Thüsing, G (ed), *Arbeitnehmerüberlassungsgesetz*, 3rd edn (München, CH Beck-Verlag, 2012) Einführung no 29c; Lembke, in Boemke, B and Lembke, M, *Arbeitnehmerüberlassungsgesetz*, 3rd edn (Heidelberg, Deutscher Fachverlag Fachmedien Verlag Recht und Wirtschaft, 2013) § 9 no 17.

Article 5(3) allows for deviation from the general equal treatment principle by collective agreement while respecting the overall protection of temporary agency workers. This rule applies not only to pay questions but to any working conditions covered by this exception.[61]

In the German literature, a discussion arose about whether this exemption also covers the possibility of deviating from the equal treatment principle by reference to a collective agreement.[62] Such deviation is surely not mentioned in the wording of Article 5(3). However, on the one hand, it should be stressed that in other Member States collective agreements are—different to German collective agreements law—applicable to outsiders on the employee's side by law.[63] And the technique of reference in the labour contract for outsiders in German law has the same function. On the other hand, scholars point out that the way of covering outsiders, according to the Directive, is the generally binding declaration and not a reference in the labour contract since Article 5(4) of the Directive sets out a further exemption to the equal treatment principle for Member States that do not have an instrument of generally binding declaration.[64] Nevertheless, the legislator surely did not think of the technical way of making collective agreements applicable and it cannot depend on the national system of collective agreements law if an exception should be applicable only for union members or also for outsiders. This is also indicated in Preamble (17) of the Directive in which it is stated that Member States should be able to derogate 'on the basis of an agreement' which does not only cover the case of being bound to the agreement under a statutory rule. It should furthermore be noted that the way the German legislator chose has the following function: If it were not be possible to deviate from the law by reference in the labour contract, only union members would get worse labour conditions in comparison to outsiders.[65] The possibility to refer to an agreement therefore seeks to avoid that result. If scholars refuse this interpretation and refer to bad experience in the German practice,[66] it should be noted that those are not really laid

[61] Sansone in Preis and Sagan (eds) (n 52) §8 no 75; Engels, 'Regulating Temporary Work' (n 51) 1, 16 ff.

[62] Claiming for incompatibility: Blanke, *Der Betrieb* (n 56) 1528, 1529; Rödl, F and Ulber, D, 'Unvereinbarkeit von § 9 Nr. 2 Halbs. 4 AÜG mit der Leiharbeitsrichtlinie' in *Neue Zeitschrift für Arbeitsrecht* (2012) 841 ff; Zimmer, *Neue Zeitschrift für Arbeitsrecht* (n 56) 289, 292 ff; Nielebock, in *Festschrift für Klaus Bepler* (n 17), 455, 463; also doubting Weiss, 'Regulating Temporary Work in Germany', in Blanpain and Hendrickx (eds), *Temporary Agency Work in the European Union and the United States*, 113, 121; Waas, *Zeitschrift für Europäisches Sozial- und Arbeitsrecht* (n 56) 7, 11 ff; holding the rule as compatible with the Directive: Sansone, *Gleichstellung von Leiharbeitnehmern* (n 56) 547 ff; Sansone in Preis and Sagan (eds), (n 52) § 8 no 79; Nießen, T and Fabritius, B, 'Gleichbehandlungsgebot in der Arbeitnehmerüberlassung durch Bezugnahmeklauseln und bei Befristungen' in *Fachanwalt Arbeitsrecht* (2013) 294 ff; Boemke, *Recht der internationalen Wirtschaft* (2009) 177, 183.

[63] Nießen and Fabritius, *Fachanwalt Arbeitsrecht* (n 62) 294, 295.

[64] Blanke, *Der Betrieb* (n 56) 1528, 1529; Rödl, F and Ulber, D, 'Unvereinbarkeit von § 9 Nr 2 Halbs. 4 AÜG mit der Leiharbeitsrichtlinie' in *Neue Zeitschrift für Arbeitsrecht* (2012) 841, 842.

[65] See Nießen and Fabritius, *Fachanwalt Arbeitsrecht* (n 62) 294, 296.

[66] Zimmer, *Neue Zeitschrift für Arbeitsrecht* (n 56) 289, 293; Nielebock, in *Festschrift für Klaus Bepler* (n 17) 455, 464.

down in the possibility of reference to a collective agreement as such. The German practice of undermining the equal treatment principle is just founded on the basis of a race to the bottom by competition of organisations.

To summarise, Article 5(3) allows for deviation from the equal treatment principle by collective agreement as a result of a binding declaration or by reference in the contract of employment to a collective agreement. However, it should also be stressed that such a reference is only possible for labour contracts between employees and employers in cases where the employer is bound to the agreement because it is only in this situation that the idea of non-discrimination of union members is justified. For this reason, it seems that the German legislator would have done better to allow deviation from the equal treatment principle only by way of reference in labour contracts with employers who are bound to a collective agreement by membership or by being party to the agreement.[67]

Another question which arose was whether the exception in Article 5(3) only covers permanent employment contracts of agency workers.[68] This is surely not laid down in the wording of the article but could follow from the scope of Article 5(2). However, nothing indicates that the additional and wider exception rule (which refers to any working conditions) shall have the same small scope as the one before.

Finally, Article 5(4) allows exemptions from the equal treatment principle where the legal system of a Member State does not allow for the provisions to be extended to outsiders. This stipulation is not applicable to Member States that do have a generally binding declaration possibility such as Article 5 of the German Collective Agreements Statute.[69] On the other hand, this does not exclude the possibility of deviating from the equal treatment principle by reference to a collective agreement in the labour contract (see above).

(b) The Prevention of Misuse Legislation

As pointed out at an earlier stage of this report the German legislator wanted to follow this concept in principle: the Agency Work Statute was amended by implementing the equal treatment principle. However, this principle could be deviated from via collective agreements. Moreover, the legislator had the idea of finding tailored solutions for agency workers such as regulating wages on a stable level during times of operation and times of non-operation. The practice, however, was far from that: collective agreements became instruments for deviating from the equal treatment principle without establishing an alternative protection regime as specified in the Directive and the national law. Once the practice became public,

67 See with regard to agency work Rödl and Ulber, *Neue Zeitschrift für Arbeitsrecht* (n 64) 841, 843, 845.

68 Against, see Nießen and Fabritius, *Fachanwalt Arbeitsrecht* (n 62) 294, 296.

69 Sansone in Preis and Sagan (eds) (n 52) § 8 no 67; Nielebock in *Festschrift für Klaus Bepler* (n 17) 455, 459; Ulber in Ulber (ed), *Arbeitnehmerüberlassungsgesetz*, Einleitung no 61; Lembke in Boemke and Lembke (eds) (n 60) § 9 no 21.

the legislation should have been amended to restrict deviation via collective agreements or by securing an equivalent protection of temporary agency workers. However, the new statute—although under the label of preventing misuse—did not manage this in a satisfactory way.

The exception to the equal treatment principle in the case of a labour contract concluded directly after a period of unemployment was incompatible with the Agency Work Directive. Therefore, this rule was eliminated. The effect in reality was rather small because that exception had no real significance due to the fact that it was very easy to deviate from the equal treatment principle by application of or by reference to a collective agreement.

The exception from the equal treatment principle by collective agreements remained. So far, evidence indicates that collective agreements are assumed by law to create proper rules.[70] This assumption goes back to the idea that contracts are assumed to create proper rules for the parties because they would only conclude agreements under the precondition that they feel that their interests are protected by the contract: the rules of a contract are 'good' if both parties agreed to them. This assumption may not be true for an individual labour contract but for a collective agreement because in theory the social partners bargain on an equal footing due to the industrial action system.[71] In the field of agency work this consideration seems to be questionable.[72] As pointed out before, the Directive does not allow deviating from the equal treatment principle regardless of the protection's quality.[73] Perhaps one could argue that providing overall protection of temporary agency workers is only possible in a real representation of interests of the employees and such a representation would be inconceivable if an organisation did not aim at bargaining for better rights for the employees.[74] In addition, the compatibility of the German regime with the Directive has been brought into question due to the fact that the Directive allows deviation only 'while respecting the overall protection of temporary agency workers'.[75] The idea that the overall protection of temporary agency workers could be secured by the institution of collective bargaining as such has been discovered as an error in practice. The assumption of proper rules by collective bargaining is founded on a balance of power. Therefore, a balance of power needed another basis. This basis could have been the situation of bargaining in the shadow of the law as long as the unions were able to refuse bargaining at a lower level without compensations. From the moment the Chris-

[70] *Bundestags-Drucksache* 17/4808, 9 (Parliament Document).

[71] See eg Deinert in Kittner, M, Zwanziger, B and Deinert, O (eds), *Arbeitsrecht Handbuch für die Praxis*, 8th edn (Frankfurt am Main, Bund-Verlag, 2015) § 1 no 22.

[72] Schüren, P and Wank, R, 'Die neue Leiharbeitsrichtlinie und ihre Umsetzung in deutsches Recht' in *Recht der Arbeit* (2011) 1, 5.

[73] Waltermann, *Neue Zeitschrift für Arbeitsrecht* (n 16) 482, 485 f.

[74] Schüren, in Schüren, P and Hamann, W (eds), *Arbeitnehmerüberlassungsgesetz*, 4th edn (München, CH Beck-Verlag, 2010) § 9 no 171.

[75] Waltermann, *Neue Zeitschrift für Arbeitsrecht* (n 16) 482; Zimmer, *Neue Zeitschrift für Arbeitsrecht* (n 56) 289.

tian unions decided to conclude an agreement at a lower level, this power was lost. On the other hand, one could argue that the Christian unions concluded on the basis of a stable bargaining power. This was not the reality. The membership basis is quite unclear and from a legal point of view, there is a lack of bargaining power for the simple reason that the CGZP had no capacity to conclude collective agreements. To conclude, the whole experiment shows a history of misusing the instrument of collective agreements.[76]

To summarise, the 2011 instruments implementing the EU Directive on temporary agency work and to prevent misusing were not satisfactory with regard to the equal treatment principle: the minimum wage level does not prevent deviation from the equal treatment principle and allows a protection only at the lowest level and the rules allowing exemptions from the equal treatment principle by collective agreement do not contain any requirements to ensure the appropriate protection of agency workers. Although it seems to be possible to interpret this rule compatibly with the Directive on agency work,[77] it is at least disadvantageous that management and labour cannot read this in the letter of the law and agency workers will continue to be left in the dark about their rights.[78]

In practice, the legal situation is not as harmful as it would seem from the wording of the law. Since the decision of the Federal Labour Court about the incapacity of the CGZP to conclude collective agreements, this way of professional undermining of the equal treatment principle seems to have disappeared. Nevertheless, this result does not follow from the legal rules concerning the equal treatment principle.

V. What Happened After This?

A. Increase of Service Contracts

Agency work in Germany was reformed as a result of the Federal Labour Court's case law, the collective agreement policy between trade unions and employers and recent legislation. Agency work was no longer seen as an instrument introducing a second class workforce in the enterprise; it came to be viewed as an instrument for flexible solutions in the case of temporary need for further workforce.

In August 2011, the total amount of temporary agency workers reached its peak level with 927,000 agency workers.[79] Although the total number declined to

[76] Schüren, P, 'Tarifunfähigkeit der CGZP wegen Missbrauchs der tariflichen Normsetzungsbefugnis in der Leiharbeit' in *Arbeit und Recht* (2008) 239.

[77] Ulber, *Arbeit und Recht* (n 59) 10, 14; Fuchs, M, 'Das Gleichbehandlungsgebot in der Leiharbeit nach der neuen Leiharbeitsrichtlinie' in *Neue Zeitschrift für Arbeitsrecht* (2009) 57, 62 ff.

[78] cf Zimmer, *Neue Zeitschrift für Arbeitsrecht* (n 56) 289, 291.

[79] Bundesagentur für Arbeit (BA) *Der Arbeitsmarkt in Deutschland, Arbeitsmarktberichterstattung—Juli 2013*, 8.

720,000 by April 2013,[80] the number had increased again by December 2013 to 815,000.[81]

This shows an orientation of the industry sector 'temporary agency work' to its core function.[82] This trend is indicative of how user enterprises seek ways of lowering working conditions and human resources managers have searched for new ways of dividing the workforce in core workforce and low price workforce. The solution seemed to reside in service contracts.[83] These started being used around the time the 2010 Agenda was launched. One of the labour market reform instruments according to the second statute on modern services in the labour market[84] ('Hartz II') was the 'Ich-AG' (Me Inc), an instrument to promote self-employment under a label with reference to a stock company ('AG—Aktiengesellschaft'). After this measure, the number of solo self-employed persons increased from 1.85 million in 1998 to 2.35 million in 2011.[85]

After the re-orientation to the core function of agency work, the number of service contracts with foreign enterprises increased.[86] However, the phenomenon is not only an indication of misuse. It seems to be normal if e.g. an enterprise that runs a factory concludes a service contract with an installation enterprise for servicing the heating system or a logistic enterprise concludes a service contract with a garage for servicing the lorries. But the more the service contractors work in the field of core competences of the user[87] and the more they work in the operation plant of the user (on-site contracts), the more the question arises as to whether this is a real service contract with an independent self-employed person or whether this is a service contract with an enterprise which performs its obligation by using its own workforce.[88] The answer depends on the existence of instruction power of the user.[89] If the undertaking that runs the operation plant

[80] See *Deutschlands Zukunft gestalten*, Koalitionsvertrag zwischen CDU, CSU und SPD, 18. Legislaturperiode, 169.

[81] *Bundestags-Drucksache* 18/2363, 2 (Parliament Document).

[82] Deinert, *Recht der Arbeit* (n 23) 65, 72.

[83] Siebenhüter, S, 'Der Betrieb als Projekthaus—Wie Werkverträge die Arbeitswelt verändern' in *WSI-Mitteilungen* (2014) 306 ff.

[84] Zweites Gesetz für moderne Dienstleistungen am Arbeitsmarkt, 23 December 2002, 2002 *Bundesgesetzblatt I* 4621 (Federal Law Gazette).

[85] Nebe, K, 'Spaltung des Arbeitsmarktes durch Krisengesetzgebung—eine kritische Analyse des deutschen Arbeits- und Sozialrechts vor und nach der Krise' in *Soziales Recht* (2013) 1, 7.

[86] Deinert, *Recht der Arbeit* (n 23) 65, 72.

[87] See for the constant practice: Helfen, M and Nicklich, M, 'Gewerkschaften zwischen Konkurrenz und Kooperation? Inter-organisationale Beziehungen in der Facility Services-Branche' in 20 *Industrielle Beziehungen* (2013) 181; also Helfen, M, 'Netzwerkförmige Tertialisierung und triangularistische Beschäftigung: Braucht es eine interorganisationale Personalpolitik?' in *Managementforschung* (2014) 171.

[88] Hamann, W, 'Fremdpersonal in Unternehmen—Industriedienstleistung statt Leiharbeit?' in *Neue Zeitschrift für Arbeitsrecht* (2014) 1st Suppl 3 ff; Greiner, S, '"Personalhoheit" als Schlüsselbegriff der Abgrenzung von echtem Fremdpersonaleinsatz und verdeckter Arbeitnehmerüberlassung' in *Recht der Arbeit* (2014) 213.

[89] Hamann, *Neue Zeitschrift für Arbeitsrecht* (n 88) 3, 5 ff.

has instruction power over the workforce of a foreign enterprise, the contract is an agency-work contract and not a service contract as declared. And if the undertaking that runs the operation plant has instruction power over a so-called self-employed person, this person is legally not self-employed but an employee. This is not always easy to prove because any work can be performed as a free and independent service contract or in the form of a labour contract. According to the case law of the Federal Labour Court, the qualification does not depend on the declaration by the parties but on the content of the contract as performed in reality.[90] Therefore, a claimant has to prove that the user enterprise enjoys instruction power. To a certain degree, the courts facilitate this. The Federal Labour Court has decided that evidence of the existence of a labour contract comes from the fact that the workforce in question is integrated in the operation in such a way that the demand of the user enterprise for the service will implicitly include a decision on content, time, duration and place of performance of the foreign workforce.[91] And the Regional Labour Court of Baden-Württemberg has decided to apply a lower burden of proof if the decision depends on facts that the employee cannot know but the employer knows.[92]

The problems that arise from the use of service contracts for the workforce are numerous:[93]

— Solo self-employed persons are not employees. Therefore, the labour laws are not applicable. Only some statutes apply to self-employed persons with employee-like status.[94]
— Solo self-employed individuals normally do not fall within the scope of collective agreements. Although Article 12a of the Collective Agreements Act allows for collective agreements for solo self-employed individuals with employee-like status,[95] those collective agreements are rare and not every solo self-employed individual has an employee-like status.
— The Minimum Wage Act ('Mindestlohngesetz') is not applicable to solo self-employed individuals.[96]

[90] Bundesarbeitsgericht, 14 March 2007—5 AZR 499/06—2007 *Neue Zeitschrift für Arbeitsrecht—Rechtsprechungsreport* 424, 425; Bundesarbeitsgericht, 23 August 2008—7 AZR 269/07—*Entscheidungen zum Arbeitnehmerüberlassungsgesetz* § 10 Fiktion n° 121 (Federal Labour Court).

[91] Bundesarbeitsgericht, 25 September 2013—10 AZR 292/12—2013 *Neue Zeitschrift für Arbeitsrecht* 1348 (Federal Labour Court).

[92] Landesarbeitsgericht Baden-Württemberg, 1 August 2013—2 Sa 6/13—2013 *Neue Zeitschrift für Arbeitsrecht* 1017, 1020 (Regional Labour Court of Baden-Wuerttemberg).

[93] Deinert, *Recht der Arbeit* (n 23) 65, 73 ff, 76; see also Krause, *Zeitschrift für Arbeitsrecht* (n 30) 349, 389–393.

[94] See Däubler, W, 'Der Arbeitgeber—ein Fixpunkt des Arbeitsrechts?' in *Kritische Justiz* (2013) 137 ff.

[95] See concerning the compatibility with the TFEU, Case C-413/13 *FNV Kunsten Informatie en Media v Staat der Nederlanden*, 4 December 2014, ECLI:EU:C:2014:2411.

[96] Däubler, W, 'Der gesetzliche Mindestlohn—doch eine unendliche Geschichte?' in *Neue Juristische Wochenschrift* (2014) 1924, 1926.

- Since the Temporary Employment Act is not applicable, the minimum wage level is not applicable either.
- The same applies to the equal treatment principle: a self-employed person is not entitled to equal treatment with the core workforce of the operation unit.
- Solo self-employed people do not enjoy the unfair dismissal protection.
- Due to the fact that solo self-employed individuals are not members of the workforce, they are mostly not covered by immunities from civil law liability towards their colleagues and the user/employer.

Similar problems arise from the performance of foreign workforce under service contracts with foreign enterprises:[97]

- The foreign enterprise may fall within the scope of another collective agreement, eg the foreign workforce may perform their work under the agreements of the cleaning branch while the same work would fall within the scope of the metal industry agreements if the work was performed under a direct labour contract with the user enterprise.
- The Temporary Employment Act is not applicable; in particular, the equal treatment principle and the minimum wage level do not apply.
- The works council has no co-determination rights with regard to the integration of the service contractor's workforce, while such a co-determination right would exist if there was a direct labour contract with the user enterprise.
- Organising an industrial action is much more complicated if only a part of the workforce has a labour contract with the user enterprise and is covered by the intended collective agreement.
- Although the foreign workforce is entitled to unfair dismissal protection vis-a-vis its employer, it runs the risk of dismissal for economic reasons when the service contract with the operation enterprise is terminated; a selection between the employees with respect to social criteria as foreseen in the Unfair Dismissals Act only refers to the labour under a contract with the service contractor and does not include the core workforce of the operation plant.

B. Political Arena

As pointed out before (see Section V.A above), it is rather difficult to differentiate between 'normal service contracts' and service contracts which actually are hidden labour contracts or hidden contracts of agency work. And it is even more complicated to differentiate between 'normal service contracts' and service contracts which are by function an instrument to substitute agency work and core labour.

[97] See Krebber, S, *Unternehmensübergreifende Arbeitsabläufe im Arbeitsrecht* (München, CH Beck-Verlag, 2005) 165 ff; for the health and safety matters see Wiebauer, B, 'Arbeitsschutz im Fremdbetrieb' in *Zeitschrift für Arbeitsrecht* (2014) 29.

The first problem is a mere legal question; challenges only arise in respect of proof. The second question is a political question. Both problems have been subject to legal proposals.

In 2013, the Green Party adopted a proposal for a reform act concerning agency work.[98] It aimed at forcing temporary work agencies to declare a service contract as agency work in advance; otherwise it should be impossible to rely on a licence for agency work if a 'service contract' is discovered as agency work. This would have the result that the labour contract with the agency would be null and void by law and the worker would have a fictitious labour contract with the user.

Nearly simultaneously, the Social Democrats—who were in opposition at that time—proposed an amendment of the co-determination rights of the works council.[99] The works council was supposed to be involved in all cases of integration of foreign workforce under the business concept of the user's enterprise. Currently, the Works Constitution Act envisages a co-determination right only where the user wants to conclude an agreement whereby it has managerial powers over the foreign workforce.[100] The new statutory proposal sought to broaden its scope and not only focus on illegal service contracts in the sense of hidden labour contracts or hidden agency work, with the aim of making it easier to discover an unfair practice.

A combination of both proposals has been pushed by some federal states ('Bundesländer') which were governed—among others—by Social Democrats.[101]

The Social Democrats also proposed to adopt a list of legal criteria in the law to discover hidden labour contracts and hidden agency work under the label of 'service contracts',[102] as the left-wing party had done—in combination with an amendment of co-determination rights.[103]

All this happened shortly before the elections in autumn 2013 and may be understood as part of the election campaign. Therefore, it is quite interesting to assess what happened after the elections and the building of a 'great coalition'. The coalition treaty between the Christian parties and the Social Democrats deals with this topic as follows. The political goal is combating misuse of service contracts and agency work.[104] The measures considered seem, however, to be very vague.[105] In only two paragraphs, the coalition promises:

— more effective control by public authorities;

[98] *Bundestags-Drucksache* 17/13106 (Parliament Document).

[99] *Bundestags-Drucksache* 17/13476 (Parliament Document).

[100] Bundesarbeitsgericht, 13 May 2014—1 ABR 50/12, 2014 *Neue Zeitschrift für Arbeitsrecht* 1149 (Federal Labour Court).

[101] *Bundesrats-Drucksache* 687/13; see Franken, JP, 'Erforderliche Nachbesserungen im Arbeitnehmerüberlassungsgesetz' in *Neue Zeitschrift für Arbeitsrecht* (2013) 1192.

[102] *Bundestags-Drucksache* 17/12378 (Parliament Document).

[103] *Bundestags-Drucksache* 17/12373 (Parliament Document).

[104] 'Deutschlands Zukunft gestalten', Koalitionsvertrag zwischen CDU, CSU und SPD, 18. Legislaturperiode, 8.

[105] For the following see 'Deutschlands Zukunft gestalten', Koalitionsvertrag zwischen CDU, CSU und SPD, 18. Legislaturperiode, pp 49 ff.

- securing and clearly defining of information rights of the works council;
- sanctions in the event of hidden agency work, such as in the case of agency work without a licence;
- securing health and safety for foreign labour in the case of service contracts;
- regulation of the jurisprudence criteria for differentiation between 'normal service contracts' and 'misuse'.

With regard to agency work, the coalition plans to:

- define exactly the overall maximum length of 18 months for operation which can be rearranged by collective agreements or plant agreements;
- re-orientate agency work to its core function which means:
  - equal payment without any exceptions after nine months of operation,
  - prohibition of strikebreaking by agency workers, and
  - agency workers considered as core workforce with regards to thresholds.

These are only some noted items and will surely be subject to political debate once the draft regulation goes before Parliament.[106]

VI. The Lessons to be Learned

Following the amendment of the Agency Workers Statute, the new collective bargaining policy and the recent case law of the Federal Labour Court is that agency work can no longer have the effect of creating a second-class workforce in the plant. Agency work cannot be used as an instrument for reducing labour costs by lowering the working conditions. Agency work is some kind of contingent interim work which provides user enterprises with the flexibility they need whilst upholding the protection of agency workers as employees by treating them like any other employees. This enables work agencies to be considered as 'normal' employers. Taken altogether, this seems to be a coherent concept: the Directive tries to recognise temporary work agencies as normal enterprises and employers who conduct a business in which they offer services to other enterprises by providing workforce flexibility. This allows defining temporary agency work as providing workers who are assigned to user undertakings to work 'temporarily' (Articles 1(1), 3(1)(b) of the Directive). And what allows work agencies to be considered as 'normal employers' is the overall appropriate protection of agency workers which is realised in the first place by the equal treatment principle and which can be altered—not avoided—by another appropriate protection tailored especially to agency workers. The equal treatment principle which underpins the labour protection afforded to agency workers achieves its justification from the subject of the ser-

[106] For some first ideas see Schüren, P and Brors, C, 'Neue gesetzliche Rahmenbedingungen für den Fremdpersonaleinsatz' in *Neue Zeitschrift für Arbeitsrecht* (2014) 569.

vice which a work agency provides: providing the user undertaking with human resource flexibility—the employees who carry out their work in the agency could (if it was not a situation of temporary need) also have concluded a contract with the user enterprise under the same conditions as all the other employees of the user enterprise. The German Federal Labour Court seems to be aware of this when holding that equal treatment means that the agency worker should be treated as if he was an employee of the user enterprise.[107]

The German experience is a good example which helps shed light on this topic and provide a better understanding of the interaction between work agencies, fulfilling the needs of user enterprises for a flexible workforce and the need to protect agency workers. Nevertheless, good example does not mean good experience. It was a high price to pay for those workers who were exploited during the period when the equal treatment principle was systematically undermined.

Another lesson that can be learned from the German experience is that the circumvention practices of using service contracts could undermine the 'flexicurity' concept of the Agency Work Directive. If the European Union has decided to balance the interests of the parties in this way, it should realise the political need to fill the gaps that allow such circumvention. It seems that the Court of Justice of the European Union has realised this in its decision on the possible exception from the competition rules for collective agreements dealing with solo self-employed persons.[108] The European legislator should follow.

[107] Bundesarbeitsgericht 19 February 2014—5 AZR 700/12—2014 *Neue Zeitschrift für Arbeitsrecht* 1097 (Federal Labour Court).

[108] See CJEU Case C-412/13 (n 95).

5

'Making' Contingent Work Conditional: Fixed-Term and Temporary Agency Contracts in Belgian Law

FILIP DORSSEMONT

I. Introduction

Belgian Labour Law is suspicious about the recourse to fixed-term or temporary agency contracts. By submitting recourse to fixed-term or temporary contracts to conditionality, it confirms that the contract for an indefinite term or the contract with a permanent or core worker is 'the standard' contract.[1] In this contribution, the issue of conditionality under EU secondary law as well as under Belgian Labour Law will be analysed. The relationship between conditionality and combatting abuse will be highlighted. These conditions put a restriction on the recourse to contingent work, thus securing the interests of (actual and future) workers with a standard contract.

Since this paper deals with workers with a fixed-term contract as well as with temporary agency workers, the word 'contingent' is used in a double meaning. In a seminal contribution, Summers referred to contingent as designating two different concepts, ie as employment which was atypical or peripheral.[2] In his contribution to this book, Lo Faro restricts the use of contingent to employment which 'radically 'falls outside the employment model', or 'as a series of developments beyond the employment contract. In his approach, atypical work alludes to a variety of flexible arrangements within the employment contract.[3] In his contribution on the occupational risks, Ales argues that the distinction is to some extent irrelevant, insofar as EU law vests a liability on an employer managing an enterprise towards

[1] J Buelens, K Reyniers, 'Standard and non-standard work in Belgium', in J Buelens and J Pearson (eds), *Standard work: an anachronism?* (Antwerpen, Intersentia, 2013) 17–40.

[2] C Summers, 'Contingent employment in the United States', *Comparative Labor Law Journal* (1996–97) 503–22.

[3] See Ch 3 by A Lo Faro in this volume.

both core and contingent workers.[4] Ales' and Lo Faro's analyses are not deprived of some thought-provoking Hegelian inversions. Lo Faro rightly points out 'that many of the flexible employment contracts fall indeed into a "typical" notion of atypical work' whereas Ales by qualifying contingent workers as a particularly sensitive risk group, demonstrates that the protection of contingent workers is at the core of health and safety regulations.

In the case of workers with a fixed-term contract, contingent is being opposed to the workers who have concluded a less precarious contract with the same employer. These workers are not contingent to the undertaking managed by their employer. Their employment relation can be called contingent, in the meaning of precarious. In the case of temporary agency workers, the latter are opposed to the 'core' workers of a different employer, ie the employer who is managing the user undertaking. Whether the so-called permanent workers of the user undertaking have a standard contract or not is not relevant. In this scenario, the user undertaking has recourse to 'contingent' workers in an indirect way, by concluding a commercial contract instead of an employment contract.

II. Conditionality In EU Directives on Atypical Work

Conditionality has been construed as a means to prevent abuses in the Framework Agreement on Fixed-Term Work (1999) implemented by means of Council Directive 1999/70/EC of 28 June 1999.[5] In the so-called general considerations of the Framework Agreement, the social partners state that: 'the use of fixed-term employment contracts based *on objective reasons* is a way to prevent abuse' (emphasis added).[6]

The CJEU has highlighted the scope of the notion of objective reasons in *Adeneler and others*.[7] The definition of the CJEU fills a gap insofar as the notion of objectivity has not been defined in the Framework Agreement. The Court has clarified that 'objective reasons' refer to 'precise and concrete circumstances characterising a given activity, which are therefore capable in that particular context of justifying the use of successive fixed-term employment contracts'.[8]

The Court elucidates that these 'circumstances may result, in particular, from the specific *nature* of the tasks for the performance of which such contracts have been concluded and from the *inherent characteristics* of those tasks, or, as the case

[4] See Ch 14 by E Ales in this volume.

[5] OJ L175/43, 10 July 1999. See M Schlachter, '1999/70/EC: Fixed-Term Contracts' in M Schlachter (ed), *EU Labour Law. A Commentary* (Alphen aan den Rijn, Wolters Kluwer, 2015) 221–48.

[6] Framework Agreement on Fixed-Term Work 1999, general considerations (7).

[7] Case C-212/04 *Adeneler and others v ELOG*, CJEU, 4 July 2006.

[8] ibid § 69.

may be, from the pursuit of a legitimate social policy objective of a Member State' (emphasis added by author of this chapter).[9,10]

If given a closer look, it is clear why these reasons can be called 'objective'. They are not related to the parties in the employment relations, but *in se et per se* to the tasks which need to be performed. The distinction in this context between the nature and the inherent characteristics of these tasks is puzzling. Both are intertwined, since indicating inherent characteristics seems to be a logical way to describe the nature of the task. The last example given by the Court is puzzling as well. It boils down to the assessment that objective reasons relate to circumstances resulting from 'objectives'.

Hence, the word 'objective' is being used in two different meanings. In fact, the Court implicitly states that reasons do not just need to be 'objective', but justified as well. These justifications for the recourse to fixed-term contracts can flow from the very nature of the tasks or from a more extrinsic social policy objective. To some extent, the reference to a social policy objective is redundant, since the measures to prevent successive contracts are already said to be preventing abuse. It is hard to see why the prevention of abuse could not be qualified as a social policy objective.

The Court of Justice has indicated in this case that a proper implementation of the Framework Agreement cannot be reduced to a copy or paste operation. The objective reasons concerned need to be substantiated.[11] Thus, the Court in *Kücük* acknowledged that making recourse to fixed-term contracts conditional upon the requirement that it serves a temporary need for replacement staff could constitute such an objective reason.[12] However, the assessment of the justified character will be dependent upon the circumstances at hand. Insofar as a renewal is made dependent in order to meet temporary needs, which are in fact fixed and permanent, the CJEU has ruled that Article 5 of the Fixed-Term Work Directive has not been properly implemented.

The analysis of the fifth clause of the Framework Agreement on fixed-term work tends to mitigate the requirement of objective conditionality in a threefold way.

Firstly, the clause restricts the risk of abuse to the use of successive fixed-term contracts. Hence, there is no need to put forward objective conditions right from the start; neither is there an obstacle against successive fixed-term contracts for the same job concluded with successive workers.

Secondly, conditionality based upon objective reason is only one way among others to prevent abuse. The social partners have been reluctant to oblige Member States to introduce unprecedented measures. They are not obliged to introduce the measures mentioned in the Agreement, provided that equivalent measures exist.

[9] Framework Agreement on Fixed-Term Work 1999, general considerations (7).

[10] ibid § 70.

[11] ibid § 71.

[12] Case C-586/10, *Bianca Kücük v Land Nordrhein-Westfalen*, CJEU, 26 January 2012.

Thirdly, the social partners have indicated two other measures in order to prevent abuses. The first consists of setting a maximum to the total duration of successive fixed-term employment contracts or relationships, the second deals with restricting the number of renewals of such contracts or relationships.

The CJEU has stated that these three measures are alternatives offered to the Member States. There is no duty for the Member States to implement *all* the measures indicated, in the absence of equivalent measures.[13]

In the sixth general consideration Framework Agreement on fixed-term work, the Court stated that the 'employment contracts of an indefinite duration are the general form of employment relationships and contribute to the quality of life of the workers concerned and improve performance'.

The idea that an employment contract is atypical and the necessity to prevent abuses do not go hand in hand. Part-time work deviates from the traditional 'full-time' standard contract concluded with an employee. However, the Framework Agreement on Part-Time work, implemented by Council Directive 97/81/EC of 15 December 1997,[14] does not provide any obligation to combat abuse arising out of the conclusion of part-time employment contracts. The mere fact that the Framework Agreement is mute on this issue might be seen as the sign of the emancipation of the part-time contract. It is not made subject to any suspicion. To some extent, the Framework Agreement on Part-Time Work heralds the idea that part-time work needs to be promoted. Member States as well as social partners are obliged to 'identify and review obstacles of a legal or administrative nature which may limit the opportunities for part-time work and, where appropriate, eliminate them'.[15] Furthermore, the Framework agreement tends to treat and promote transitions from part-time work to full-time work as well as vice versa on equal footing.[16]

The issue of the prevention of abuse in Directive 2008/104/EC on Temporary Agency Work[17] is much more ambiguous. As in the Framework Agreement on Fixed-Term Work, there is a statement corroborating the idea that employment contracts of an indefinite duration constitute the standard contract. The fifteenth recital states, in an identical way as in the Framework Agreement on Fixed-Term Work that '[e]mployment contracts of an indefinite duration are the general form of employment relationship'.

[13] Case C-378/07 to 380/07 *Kiriaki Angelikaki and others*, CJEU, 23 April 2009.

[14] OJ L14/9, 20 January 1998. See G Kiss, '97/81/EC: Part-Time Work', in M Schlachter (ed), *EU Labour Law. A Commentary* (Alphen aan den Rijn, Wolters Kluwer 2015) 195–220.

[15] See Clause 5(1) Framework Agreement on Part-Time Work.

[16] See Clause 5(3) Framework Agreement on Part-Time Work; see, however, Case C-221/13 *Mascellani v Ministero della Giustizia*, CJEU, 15 October 2014. In this judgment, the CJEU ruled that this clause does not preclude 'national legislation pursuant to which the employer may order the conversion of a part-time employment relationship into a full-time employment relationship without the consent of the worker concerned'.

[17] OJ L327/9, 5 December 2008. See further B Nyström, '2008/104/EC: Temporary Agency Work', in M Schlachter (ed), *EU Labour Law. A Commentary* (Alphen aan den Rijn, Wolters Kluwer 2015) 249–79.

However, the recital is not being used as a prelude to a discourse on the prevention of abuse, but as a justification for allowing Member States to lower the standard of protection provided for by the Directive. In the body of the Directive, the idea of the prevention of misuse, in particular to prevent 'successive assignments designed to circumvent the provisions of this Directive' pops up in Article 5. This article is not dedicated to the prevention of abuse as such, but to one of the most important tools offering some 'security' to agency workers, ie the principle of equal treatment.

It is very difficult to understand how any misuse could be generated by the application of such a provision.[18] Furthermore, the best way to allow for the circumvention of the provisions of the Directive is paradoxically the recourse to temporary agency workers who have a permanent contract of employment with a temporary work agency. 'Provided, that they are paid in the time between assignments, Member States can derogate from the principle of equal treatment'.[19]

In sum, successive employment contracts with a temporary agency worker might provide much more protection. However, such a succession continues to be problematic, insofar as it does not offer any genuine employment security at all. The Temporary Agency Work (TAW) Directive does not provide any protection against such an abusive use of a succession of TAW contracts. The safeguards of Article 6 of the TAW Directive are not construed as anti-abuse measures, but seek to facilitate the access of temporary agency workers to find employment in the undertaking of the user undertaking based upon a contract of employment concluded between that worker and the user undertaking. These measures are fairly soft.

They relate to a right to be informed of any vacant post, to a prohibition of clauses impeding the conclusion of a contract of employment or impeding an employment relation and to a prohibition for temporary work agencies to charge temporary agency workers any fees in exchange for arranging for them to be recruited by a user undertaking, or for concluding a contract of employment or an employment relationship with a user undertaking after carrying out an assignment in that undertaking, as well as to an obligation to adopt measures to improve the access to vocational training.

These provisions, which pretend to facilitate transitions, are inferior to those in the Framework Agreement on Fixed-Term Work and Part-Time Work. Thus, the TAW Directive does not indicate that the user undertaking should give consideration 'as far as possible' to a request of a temporary agency worker to work for him.

This 'loophole' cannot be circumvented by integrating temporary agency workers within the ambit of the Framework Agreement on Fixed-Term Work, despite the fact that a lot of temporary workers are bound by a fixed-term work contract with the temporary work agency. In *Della Rocca*, the Court shielded temporary

[18] See in the same vein, K Riesenhuber, *European Employment Law* (Antwerp, Intersentia, 2012) 475.
[19] Article 5 § 2 TAW Directive.

agency workers from the protection afforded by this Agreement. Though the exclusion of temporary agency workers in the general considerations of the Agreement was not decisive, this was taken into account in the interpretation of the scope of application of the Agreement, which refers in Clause 3 (1) to: 'a person having an employment contract or relationship entered into *directly* between an employer and a worker' (emphasis added by the author of this chapter).[20,21]

In my view, the best way to prevent abuse of recourse to temporary work is to insist on the temporary character of the work concerned. Though this condition for the recourse to temporary agency workers is self-evident, the TAW Directive does not indicate any criterion at all to clarify the temporary nature of temporary agency work, despite the fact that the definition of a TAW clearly indicates that these workers are assigned to a user undertaking to work temporarily under their supervision and direction.

Conditionality of temporary agency work is dealt with in a rather negative way. In Article 4, Member States are being required to reconsider existing prohibitions or restrictions regarding the recourse to temporary agency work. Provisions introducing conditionality will fall within the ambit of Article 4 of the TAW Directive. Such an approach to conditionality is at odds with the more deferential attitude to conditionality provisions mirrored in Article 3(1)(d) of Directive 96/71/EC on the posting of workers[22] which integrates 'the conditions of hiring-out of workers, in particular the supply of workers by temporary employment undertakings' into the famous hard core of applicable host country labour law. This reference is consistent with the explicit inclusion of posted temporary agency workers into the ambit of Directive 96/71.[23]

III. Conditionality of Fixed-Term and Temporary Contracts in Belgian Law

A. Five Avenues

The Belgian law is being studied as a classical example of making the conclusion or the renewal of fixed-term and temporary contracts conditional upon the fulfilment of objective conditions.

[20] Framework Agreement on Fixed-Term Work 1999, general considerations (7).

[21] Case C-290/12 *Oreste Della Rocca v Poste Italiane SpA*, CJEU, 11 April 2013, ECLI: EU: C: 2013:235.

[22] Directive 96/71/EC of the European Parliament and the Council of 16 December 1996 concerning the posting of workers in the framework of the provision of services, OJ L18/1. See further F Schierle, '96/71/EC: Posting of Workers', in M Schlachter (ed), *EU Labour Law. A Commentary* (Alphen aan den Rijn, Wolters Kluwer, 2015) 163–94.

[23] In *Della Rocca* (n 19) § 41, the CJEU refers to Directives 96/71/EC and 91/383/EEC (OJ L206/19, 29 July 1991) by means of a contrast, insofar as the legislator explicitly mentions temporary agency workers as being included within the scope of these directives.

For a proper insight into the matter, it is essential to distinguish five avenues to fixed-term or temporary employment relations in the private sector.

The most classical avenue is the contrat à durée déterminée (fixed-term contract). Article 10 of the Law on Individual Employment Contracts[24] is not a textbook example of the legislative precision or detail that the CJEU seems to require from Member States implementing Article 6 of the Framework Agreement. It states:

> 'Lorsque les parties ont conclu plusieurs contrats de travail successifs pour une durée déterminée sans qu'il y ait entre eux une interruption attribuable au travailleur, elles sont censées avoir conclu un contrat pour une durée indéterminée, sauf si l'employeur prouve que ces contrats étaient justifiés par la nature du travail ou par d'autres raisons légitimes.'[25]

In case of a succession of fixed-term contracts, provided that the interruption is not due to the employee, the fixed-term contract will be converted to a contract for indefinite duration, unless the recourse to a subsequent fixed-term contract is due to 'the nature' of the work or to other 'legitimate reasons'.

Despite the lack of precision of this provision and despite the absence of any catalogue, the Belgian judiciary has taken great care to elucidate these reasons.[26]

Thus, recruitment for 'research purposes', which is dependent on subventions, is usually seen as justifying recourse to successive fixed-term contracts.[27] This cannot be extrapolated to any kind of recruitment that is dependent upon subventions. The economic and financial situation of the enterprise cannot as such constitute a legitimate reason to have recourse to subsequent fixed-term contracts.[28] An exceptional increase in the demand of work does constitute such a reason.[29] The judicature is lenient as well, when it considers the recourse to subsequent fixed-term contracts to be in the interest of the worker.[30]

A second avenue stems from the same statutory instrument on individual employment contracts. Thus, Article 11-*ter* provides for the so-called contract of replacement. It allows an employer to have recourse to a fixed-term contract sui generis. This contract derogates from applicable rules with regard to the duration of the contract and the notice period. Hence, it can only be concluded in

[24] Loi relative aux contrats de travail, 3 July 1978, *Moniteur belge*, 22 August 1978.

[25] Translation: 'When the parties have concluded several consecutive employment contracts for a fixed term without interruption between them due to the worker, they are deemed to have concluded a contract for an indefinite period, unless the employer proves that these contracts were justified by the nature of work or other legitimate reasons.'

[26] See H Deckers and A Mortier, 'Durée du contrat de travail et durée du travail', in S Plasschaert and O Ryckaert, *Le droit social en chantier(s)* (Bruxelles, Larcier, 201) 261–66.

[27] Cour du Travail, Bruxelles, 25 February 1981, *Revue de droit social* (1981) 305; Cour du Travail, Bruxelles, 21 December 1983, *Revue de droit social* (1984) 85; and, Cour du Travail, Gand, 23 December 1998, *TijdschriftvoorGentserechtspraak* (1999) 120.

[28] Tribunal du Travail de Bruxelles, 3 July 1984, *Jurisprudence de travail de Bruxelles* (1985) 380.

[29] Cour du Travail, Liège, 26 November 1983, *Jurisprudence de Liège* (1984) 259.

[30] Cour du Travail, Anvers, 18 June 1993, *RechtskundigWeekblad* (1993–94) 929.

order to replace a worker whose contract of employment has been suspended. The rule that a legitimate suspension of a worker warrants the recruitment of a replacement worker on the basis of such a contract, is subject to some exceptions which have been enumerated explicitly. They relate to a suspension for economic reasons, bad weather, strike and lock out.

Three other avenues to fixed-term work have not been enshrined in the Law on Individual Employment Contracts. They are provided for in a complementary statutory instrument that constitutes the statutory basis for recourse to 'agency workers' by user undertakings. This statutory instrument of 24 July 1987 consecrates a fundamental principle that has not been enshrined in the Agency Work Directive. Article 31 states that it is prohibited for employers to post their workers to another undertaking, while delegating a part of their authority to the latter.

Article 31 of this statutory instrument delimitates what constitutes the delegation of a part of the authority of the employer. This provision does not constitute an exception to the principle, but an attempt to define or delimitate the principle.

Recourse to Agency work constitutes the most important exception to that principle.

Two other exceptions are fleshed out in Articles 32 and 32-*bis* of the statutory Instrument. The latter deal with the posting of workers by an employer who does not post workers within the framework of his normal activities and with the recruitment employees under a scheme for the integration of employees in the labour market ('un trajet de mise au travail'). The recourse to posted workers in the first hypothesis is subject to a previous authorisation by the Social Inspectorate, unless the posting of a permanent workers has an exceptional character, which is based upon a collaboration between undertakings which constitute an economic and financial unit and provided that the posting is done in view of the ad hoc performance of specialised tasks requiring particular skills.

The recourse to agency works too is conditional under Belgian law. It can only be done insofar as the work undertaken by the agency worker has a 'temporary' character. Article 3(1)(c) of the TAW Directive also stresses that agency workers are assigned to user undertakings to work there 'temporarily' under their 'supervision and direction'. However, it does not indicate in any explicit way that the temporary character of their assignment is due to the nature or the characteristics of the work. Neither is the notion 'temporarily' defined in anyway at all.

The Belgian legislator has filled that gap. It defines what kind of work can be considered to be temporary. The definition is based upon a limitative enumeration of scenarios justifying recourse to agency work. According to an Act of 24 July 1987, agency work is justified in case of:

(i) (temporary) replacement of a 'permanent worker';
(ii) temporary increase of work;
(iii) exceptional work.

Two of these main scenarios have been fleshed out in minute detail. Thus, the Statutory Instrument of 1987 identifies what needs to be considered as the (temporary) replacement of a worker. Furthermore, a national and inter-sectoral collective agreement extended erga omnes defines what constitutes an exceptional work.[31] The scope of the notion of a temporary increase of work has not been defined.

Last but not least, the Statutory Instrument also seeks to promote recourse to agency work as the stepping stone towards the conclusion of a permanent contract of employment with the user undertaking or as a means to integrate unemployed workers into the regular labour market. Both avenues are regulated in two distinct instruments. The avenue to a permanent contract is regulated by a collective agreement,[32] whereas the avenue of integration is regulated in a royal decree.[33] Both instruments provide some added value in respect of the TAW Directive. Despite the flexibility discourse in the TAW Directive, it does not contain many provisions that effectively facilitate access to 'permanent' employment.

B. Three Main Scenarios of Recourse to Agency Work

The conditionality which is inherent in the three main avenues listed above (i, ii; iii) for recourse to agency work will now be studied.

i. Replacement of A Permanent Worker of the User Undertaking

This scenario is available in case of a suspension of a permanent worker in the user undertaking or in case of a termination of the employment relation of a permanent worker.[34] For obvious reasons, recourse to agency work in order to replace a permanent worker suspended due to absence of work for economic reasons or due to the climate ('intempéries') is not allowed. The legislator has also recognised the competence of the social partners to regulate the recourse to agency workers in a very specific case of suspension of the employment contract, ie the strike and the lock out.[35] The social partners have prohibited the recourse to agency workers and the use of posted agency workers at the user undertaking in case of strike or lock-out.

ii. Temporary Increase of Work

The notion of a temporary increase is not defined, neither in the statutory instrument nor in the complementary collective agreement. According to the Travaux

[31] Convention Collective de Travail (CCT) No 108, 16 July 2013, declared generally binding by Royal Decree 26 January 2014.

[32] CCT No 108, Articles 24 to 32.

[33] See Royal Decree of 15 June 2006 (concernant la procédure à suivre pour le travail intérimaire dans le cadre d'un trajet de mise au travail reconnu).

[34] See Loi du 24 July 1987 sur le travail temporaire, le travail intérimaire et la mise de travailleurs à disposition d'utilisateurs, Article 1 § 2.

[35] Loi du 24 July 1987 sur le travail temporaire, le travail intérimaire et la mise de travailleurs à disposition d'utilisateurs, Article 1 § 5. See also CCT No 108, Article 19.

préparatoires, this is work that constitutes an extraordinary character in relation to the normal workload of the user undertaking

iii. Exceptional Work

The Convention Collective du Travail (CCT) No 108, Article 6 § 1 defines in an exhaustive way which kind of activities can constitute exceptional work at the user undertaking. For these activities to be recognised as exceptional, they cannot be 'habitual'.

These 'objective' conditions, which need to be fulfilled in order to have recourse to agency workers, go hand in hand with some procedural prescriptions. In some scenarios, an authorisation is needed, in other scenarios a notification is sufficient. The actors concerned are state officials and/or actors who represent workers in the Belgian dual channel system of industrial relations.[36]

Thus, an authorisation from the trade union delegation is required for the replacement of a permanent worker after the termination of his or her employment contract (CCT No 108, Article 4 § 2):

— in case of a temporary increase of work (CCT No 108, Article 10 § 1).
— in case of exceptional work (CCT No 108, Article 6 §1).

Such a far-reaching impact of the trade union delegation is unprecedented. In essence, in Belgium, the prerogatives of trade union and elected representatives tend to be limited to information and consultation rights. The power given to trade union delegates to veto entrepreneurial decisions in the field of the working organisation is unprecedented. It raises two major issues. First, the question arises, as to how the trade union delegation should adopt such a decision (unanimity or majority). Secondly, the question arises as to whether the employer can attack such a decision in court. Neither of these issues has been solved. There is neither a statutory instrument nor a collective agreement providing any indication whatsoever. There is only one unpublished case that is related to a refusal of the trade union delegation to authorise recourse to agency work in a case of a temporary increase of work. The employer, a producer of candles, was confronted as usual with an increase of work in view of the end of the year. Confronted with the refusal, he initiated a summary proceeding upon a unilateral request of the employer asking the President of the Tribunal du Travail of Hasselt to grant an authorisation in lieu of the trade union delegation. The President without ever hearing the trade union delegation, let alone asking for their motives considered that the refusal of the delegation was abusive, insofar as it had apparently not been motivated. In the aftermath, the dispute was settled between the trade union

[36] On this dual system, see F Dorssemont, 'Trade union representation in Belgium', in C La Macchia (ed), *Representing employee interests: trade union systems within the EU* (Albecete, Editorial Bomarzo, 2012) 53–74.

delegates and the employer, thus allowing the Court of Appeal to conclude that the appeal was inadmissible.[37]

Furthermore, a notification to the Social Inspectorate is required in case of replacement of a worker whose contract has been terminated with notice or for a 'motif grave' in case of increase of work and in case of exceptional work. Since this obligation is introduced by a collective agreement and is incumbent[38] upon employers, it cannot entail further obligations for the Social Inspectorate. The missions of the Social Inspectorate obviously fall beyond the scope of the social partners.

IV. Assessment

The question arises as to how these objective conditions need to be assessed from the point of view of European labour law. In my view the question needs to be examined differently, depending on whether the contingent worker is an agency worker or a fixed-term worker. As highlighted above, the Fixed-Term Work Agreement urges Member States to prevent abuses. Making the conclusion of successive fixed-term contract subject to conditionality is one among the avenues suggested by the Agreement. Insofar as Belgium seems to opt for the avenue of conditionality, the question might arise whether the implementation of this alternative is in conformity with the EU Directive.

The issue of conditionality under the TAW Directive is different. This EU Directive seeks to promote recourse to agency work, where Article 4(1) states unambiguously, that prohibitions or restrictions on the use of temporary agency work shall be justified only on grounds of general interest relating in particular to the protection of temporary agency workers, the requirements of health and safety at work or the need to ensure that the labour market functions properly and abuses are prevented'. In view of this substantive rule, the TAW Directive has obliged Member States after consulting the social partners in accordance with national legislation, collective agreements and practices, to review any restrictions and prohibitions on the use of temporary agency work in order to verify whether they are justified on these grounds.

In my view, this rule could never be based upon a provision under the Social Policy Title (Title X) of the Treaty on Functioning of the European Union, essentially dealing with the relations between employers and undertakings. Such a rule,

[37] See President Tribunal du Travail of Hasselt, 2 October 2009 (no 5684) and Court of Appeal, Labour Court of Antwerp, 10 February 2010 (no 2009/AC/3). For a critical analysis by a Belgian Labour Law Professor (Patrick Humblet) for a non-legal audience, see www.vonk.org/Syndicaal/arbeidsrechtbank-hasselt-zorgt-voor-primeur.html.

[38] See CCT No 108, Article 4 § 2.

which deals with the freedom of user undertaking to have access to services of agencies concerns a commercial relationship outside the scope of the Social Policy Title.

The Belgian State did not take such a stance, in its Report to the European Commission on the existing prohibitions and restrictions. It defended the conditionality as an expression of the temporality that is inherent in the concept of temporary agency work. The Commission was not dissatisfied with such an argument and did not consider these provisions on conditionality to be at odds with Article 6 of the TAW Directive.

As far as the Fixed-Term Work Agreement is concerned, there is a major lesson to be drawn. The CJEU has insisted that Member States opting for the objective avenue, should refrain from general and abstract formula defining these objective conditions. It is very difficult not to interpret the Belgian statutory provisions as an example of such a bad practice, despite the fact that the Belgian Courts have tried to fill the legislative gap or rather the legal insecurity created by the law.

Some might consider the Belgian legal system's obsession with conditionality as a disproportionate obstacle to the freedom to conduct a business, a principle that was erroneously promoted to the status of a fundamental right in the Charter of Fundamental Rights of the European Union. In my view, the Belgian model honours the very first meaning the Oxford English Dictionary attributes to the notion 'contingent'. Indeed, 'contingent' is being defined as 'conditional'. These conditions need to be made explicit by the legislator. Insofar as they do take into account 'objective' or technical needs, which are inherent and restricted to a system of production, they will not be an obstacle to economic development. The abolition of these conditions will increase the recourse to contingent workers in a way that is not consistent with objective needs of a given system of production. It only serves to loosen the bounds, hence the social responsibility of an employer in respect of employees which will be replaced by employees of another employer or which will be recruited under precarious patterns of employment. It is a paradox of our time, that whereas employers progressively tend to loosen these ties with the workforce in the name of flexibility, they more loudly start to boost their attachment to corporate social responsibility.

6

Externalising the Workforce: Lessons from France

PASCAL LOKIEC

I. Introduction

In a context of globalisation and severe competition, firms tend to optimise their efficiency and to cut costs, among which labour costs. One of the answers to the problem of social costs consists in externalising part of the work by transferring some of the functions of the organisation to an external partner.

Externalisation is one of the main challenges for the future of labour law, all the more so as it is likely to extend considerably. We have moved from the Fordist firm, based on a model of integration, where all functions (design, production, distribution) were handled by a single company, to a model of vertical disintegration where the firm is organised as a network. Externalising is not, for these companies, an accessory policy that can be used for very specific purposes (cleaning, accounting …) or in case of saturation of production, but an essential part of their business model. From the 1980s, companies started to focus on their core business and to develop networks of subcontractors for their remaining activities. IKEA, Dell or Nike could not function without their hundreds or thousands of subcontractors.

Often linked with the issue of relocation, this phenomenon develops at such a point that it calls today into question both the company's structure and the forms of organisation of labour that have developed in the past hundred years. The classical approach, based on an integrated firm that functions with employment relationships, that is to say contracts of employment, now competes with new business models. The twentieth century consisted, in France, as in most developed countries, in the rise of employment relationships. The twenty first century could well be, if nothing changes, that of the decline of labour law, at least in developed countries, with the transfer of the workforce to subcontractors located in low cost countries.

It appears easier, in order to resist the pressure of competition and to adapt permanently to the needs of the market, to breach a commercial contract with a temporary agency or with a subcontractor, than to dismiss employees under a collective redundancy plan. Companies are also keen on not having to deal with hiring, firing, payroll, unemployment insurance and workers' compensation payments. The challenge is considerable for labour law and workers' rights, since the protections (wages, working time, employment protection) are usually substantially lower where work is externalised, even more where externalisation takes place abroad.

II. The Strategies of Externalisation

The same work can be carried out under different statutes; for instance, computer maintenance can be accomplished by an employee of the firm, by a temporary worker or by outsourcing to a subcontractor. Why should a firm have recourse to externalisation rather than hiring its own employees? This is a strategic choice with major legal consequences.

A. Fraud versus Economic Efficiency

Externalisation is not, by itself, contrary to the law. Yet, the firm that decides to externalise has to respect a certain number of rules, particularly in the field of labour law.

i. Fraud

Organising a company's structure to escape most of employee protection rules or the payment of social security contributions is possible. The fragmentation of the firm sometimes responds to a strategy to escape from the protection afforded by social security and labour law. For instance, the company may be divided into different entities to avoid the thresholds that necessitate the creation of a works council or the nomination of union delegates.

Numerous mechanisms exist to fight against this type of fraud, starting with the criminal law. In France, as in most European countries, the supply of temporary staff for financial gain, can only be developed through temporary work agencies,[1] and is subject to a number of rules (only specific reasons are admissible, the same as those which enable recourse to fixed-term contracts; equality of treatment with employees of the user, etc).

On the other hand, outsourcing does not aim, directly, at providing staff, but at delivering a service. If the requested service does not match a clearly defined task within a specific competence of the contractor, one can suspect that the provision

[1] Labour Code, Art L1251-1; 'Temporary agency work in the European Union and the United States' (2013) in *Bulletin of comparative labour relations*, Kluwer, June 2013.

of staff is the only object of the contract. From a labour law perspective, the risk is a requalification of the employment relationship, in case of confusion as to the exercise of executive power and the existence of a relationship of subordination with the user.[2]

These risks are particularly acute in certain fields, such as that of computing, since employees are permanently in the user undertaking and follow, most of the time, the client's direct instructions. Such workers could take an action to be requalified as employees if a relationship of subordination with the user can be established. In the worst cases, the breakup of the company will even aim to escape the establishment of employee representation, playing on the workforce size thresholds. For example, a company composed of 80 employees will split into two companies of 40 employees to escape the 50 employees' threshold beyond which the creation of a works council or a committee on health and safety (CHSCT) becomes mandatory. If the judges find that many businesses, though legally distinct, form between them an 'economic and social unit', they will add up their numbers and require them to set up these bodies.[3]

Fraud can also consist in the illegal use of outsourcing, or in the creation of subsidiaries, with the aim of organising the bankruptcy of a corporate entity. The activity previously carried out by the parent company is transferred to one or more subsidiaries, sometimes created for that purpose. In a typical case, the subsidiaries, and their employees, are sacrificed if their business is not profitable. The strategy is, more precisely, as follows. The parent company intends to reduce the group's workforce, eliminating an unprofitable activity without having to set up a redundancy plan. It transfers this activity, with its staff, to a subsidiary. Employees are now those of the subsidiary, which will be declared, by chance, bankrupt and will dismiss them. The main company has managed to separate itself from its employees, without bearing any social costs![4] It is one of the main challenges for the law to fight against such devices (the main answer is the concept of joint-employers: see below).

The fight is all the more difficult when the legal devices applied are more and more sophisticated such as suppressing jobs, not by the liquidation of the assignee, but by the implementation of a voluntary departure plan of the latter. The SFR (one of the main mobile phone companies in France) case is a typical outsourcing case. In order to focus on its core activity, the operator decided to transfer its customer relations centres (based in Toulouse, Lyon and Poitiers) to a subsidiary of the Teleperformance Group, one of the world leaders in customer service, technical support and call centres.

[2] Cour de Cassation, 2nd Chambre civile, 9 March 2006, no 04-30.220; ML Morin, 'Les frontières de l'entreprise et la responsabilité de l'emploi' (2001) *Droit social* 478; ML Morin, 'La sous-traitance' (2003) *Semaine sociale Lamy*, 1140.

[3] Cour de Cassation, Chambre Sociale, 23 April 1970, no. 68-91333; *D*, 1970, 444; G Blanc-Jouvan, 'L'unité économique et sociale et la notion d'entreprise' (2005) *Droit social*, 68.

[4] P Lokiec, *Il faut sauver le droit du travail* (Paris, Odile Jacob, 2015).

For this, it proceeded in two stages. First, according to the law on transfers of undertakings, the employees of SFR were transferred to Teleperformance. Once integrated into Teleperformance, they were asked to enter into a 'voluntary departure plan' ('plan de départs volontaires'). The fraud lies in the fact that this plan was devised in co-ordination with SFR before the transfer and was meant to avoid the application of the rule on transfers of undertaking. The plan was successful among employees both because the indemnities offered to them were attractive and because the collective status at Teleperformance was less advantageous than that of SFR. Nevertheless, SFR and Teleperformance were condemned before the courts on the ground that they established fraudulent collusion, detrimental to employees.[5]

ii. Economic Strategy

Externalisation is, in most cases, a business strategy, not meant to play with the rules of labour law. Subcontracting is mostly motivated by the choice to externalise the least profitable and the most costly (notably in terms of labour costs) operations. Economically speaking, it enables the company to improve its productivity (the least productive activities are relocated, which is a strong trend in the USA and partly explains the high rate of productivity of labour over there)[6] and to absorb the variations of activity, without problems as to labour, whose management is transferred to subcontractors.

In the most elaborate cases, we can talk of business networks. Following activities such as catering, cleaning and security, it is now strategic functions, IT accounting through logistics and, in some cases, the manufacture of products that are affected. IKEA and Decathlon have become companies without factories, based on subcontractor networks scattered around the world. IKEA turned in 1961 to communist Poland for mass production. Today, the strategic functions of the multinational are still in Sweden, where it employs designers who plan collections and technicians who test products. The design of its communication tools, such as the famous catalogue and the assembly instructions, comes from Icom, a subsidiary of the IKEA group.

Although IKEA presents itself as a Swedish company, it is a company with 1,220 suppliers in 55 countries, a third of which are in Asia.[7] Nike is also a company that has massively used outsourcing; today, it mainly focuses on design and marketing. Toyota has built a pyramid of subcontracting, called 'kereitsu' which consists of more than ten thousand companies, fully connected together.[8] It is easy to understand how this type of strategy is a threat for employment in European

[5] Cour de Cassation, Chambre Sociale, 18 June 2014, no 12-18.589; Lokiec (n 4).

[6] *Etudes économiques* (OCDE: Royaume-Uni, 2007) 42.

[7] N Nahapétian, 'Ikea: un modèle low cost, alternatives économiques', 17 February 2010, www.alternatives-economiques.fr/ikea---un-modele-low-cost_fr_art_633_48117.html.

[8] K Aoki and Th Taro Lennerfors, 'The new, improved Keiretsu', *Harvard business review*, September 2013.

countries in the coming decades, especially for low qualified employees whose jobs are delocalised in Asia.

Employment or self-employment; the new business models—The development of outsourcing is part of a broader movement towards the development of 'business models' that are no longer based on contracts of employment. In the case of outsourcing, the firm prefers commercial contracts to labour contracts.

Avoiding the application of labour law is a phenomenon that is growing, taking its model from firms like Uber. Given the cost of labour, companies are looking to get out of labour law. In the US, companies in the new economy (personal services, carpooling, etc) face a growing number of requests for requalification into employment contracts with employees lodging claims (including class actions) to obtain the requalification of their contract as a contract of employment. US jurisdictions are starting to admit actions for requalifying. The classical criterion is that of control. Does the firm have control on the worker? For instance, in the case of Uber, drivers argue that they have to register their car, that the clients grade them with the possibility for Uber to prohibit them from connecting to the application if the grade is below a certain level. In the case of Handy, a company that lets consumers book maid or handyman services through its website or smartphone app, workers argue that the firm dictates what its cleaners wear, how they should operate, and what they should say to the client after the end of work: 'Thanks for using Handy!'[9]

Another criterion was adopted by the Superior Court of California in June 2015, in a case concerning Uber. According to the Court, 'Plaintiff's work was integral to Defendants' business. Defendants are in business to provide transportation services to passengers. Plaintiff did the actual transporting of those passengers. Without drivers such as Plaintiff, Defendants' business would not exist'.[10]

The Court asks a fundamental question for the future of these business models that function with a very limited number of employees (millions of drivers for Uber and only thousands of employees): Are our societies, which are built on employment contracts, ready to admit that the organisations operate on the model of self-employment? For instance, Uber has built its 'business model' on the use of self-employed workers, with savings in terms of social security and insurance costs or vehicle maintenance. The company describes itself as an intermediation platform between service providers and clients, and invokes the autonomy enjoyed by its drivers in terms of timetables and hours worked. The drivers put forward the obligations imposed upon them by the platform and the situation of economic dependence in which they find themselves.

If these disputes deserve attention, it is not only because this type of business operates in Europe but also because with the planned development of a new

[9] A Griswold, 'Are uber drivers employees? The trial that could devastate the "sharing economy"', www.slate.fr.

[10] Superior Court of California, *Uber Technologies, Inc v B Berwick*, 16 June 2015.

economy, including personal services,[11] in the coming decades, there is a real risk of seeing an increasing proportion of the working population excluded from the protection of labour law. It is likely that more and more companies in the service sector will have recourse to this business model, in order to reduce costs. Again, if the activity of the company collapses, it is easier to terminate the contract of independent contractors than that of employees.

It must be noted that recourse to externalisation is not necessarily economically efficient compared to employment. Although these business models have gained in importance, using its own employees is not necessarily less efficient. These firms have difficulties in training, managing and motivating workers whose link with the firm is distant. Some companies resist this movement, in the name notably of consumers' satisfaction, such as a firm called 'MyClean', based in New York City, which discovered that the ratings of customers were higher if it used permanent workers, rather than contract workers.[12] The preceding remarks do not apply less developed countries where the issue is radically different and the rate of independent workers much more important.

Telework—Telework is a form of so-called organisational externalisation. The workers remain employed by their company but their work is 'externalised' outside the site of the firm. Teleworking has many advantages both for businesses and for employees. For the former, it saves costs. For the latter, it means more flexibility in schedules and autonomy in carrying out the work. These advantages can nevertheless turn into problems. The fact of having workers in different places, including private places, makes it very difficult to develop collective actions. How can unions put workers together to develop collective actions if workers are located in different places, and even more at home? Another problem is the risk of unlimited working hours, especially when the use of telework is accompanied by a work by project or objectives. E-employment is another issue for labour law but it does not necessarily imply organisational externalisation. E-employment may indeed be exercised at home, within the premises of the firm or in a tele-centre.

Umbrella work (*Portage salarial*)—Since 2015, French firms have been using a new tool for hiring workers without being their employer: 'umbrella work'. This term encompasses a form of employment that concerns workers that have a mission in a company in the form of service delivery but do not want to lose the benefits of labour law. The umbrella company that behaves like a temporary work agency, hires an employee, pays him a salary and bills its customers. However, contrary to temporary work, it is the worker who approaches the user company and then goes to see the umbrella company to ask it to become his employer.

According to the French labour administration, approximately 15,000 workers work on this model. For a while, this model did not have a proper legal basis.

[11] Trades 2022, Dares, France-Strategy, 2015 (http://www.strategie.gouv.fr/sites/strategie.gouv.fr/files/atoms/files/fs_rapport_metiers_en_2022_27042015_final.pdf).

[12] www.economist.com/news/briefing/21637355-freelance-workers-available-moments-notice-will reshape-nature-companies-and.

Historically, 'umbrella work' has long been tolerated but not legalised. In 2008, it was introduced into the labour code,[13] but essentially through collective agreements; statute law contented itself with a definition and delegated to collective bargaining the construction of the legal regime. The Constitutional Court argued that this was contrary to Article 34 of the French Constitution which requires that statute law should define the 'fundamental principles of labour law'.[14]

Consequently, a new statute law was adopted in April 2015, with a more detailed regime. The new law[15] provides that 'umbrella work' is not opened to all types of work: the work must require a certain level of expertise, diploma and experience which guaranties, in theory at least, that the worker will have a certain degree of bargaining power. Accordingly, the worker benefits from a contract of employment but has autonomy in his work. The new law also requires that the worker should be paid a minimum of 2,380 euros monthly (in the year 2015, including taxes) for full-time work; it also requires a maximum of 36 months service in the same company and the exclusion of services to the person.[16]

B. Externalisation Outside the Firm versus within the Firm

To tackle the phenomenon of outsourcing, in its connections with labour law, a distinction is necessary between internal and external outsourcing. Outsourcing does not always mean that work will be carried out by subcontractors at the other corner of the planet. It can also take place in the same site in a joint operation. Outsourcing on site is extremely diverse, from general services (security, catering, etc) to project work that brings together engineers, designers coming from different firms. We can speak of co-activity[17] (the term is used by the circular letter of 18 March 1993).[18]

Here we face two main difficulties. The first one relates to respect for the principle of equality. How to justify that, for the same job within the same site, two workers are paid, one 2,000 euros per month, the other 3,000 euros per month, because that they have contracted with a different legal entity? The justification, here, lies both in the theory of contract and in that of legal personality. Since employer A and employer B are, legally speaking, different entities, there is no reason why their employees should be paid the same wages. Contracts are concluded with different employers and, accordingly, may contain different rules. The second difficulty relates to health and safety. Here, the issue is not contractual and there is every reason for the rules to be determined, not according to contractual theory,

[13] Labour Code, Art L1251-64; L Casaux-Labrunée, 'Le portage salarial: travail salarié ou travail indépendant?' (2007) *Droit social* 69.

[14] Conseil Constitutionnel, Déc no 2014-388, QPC, 11 April 2014.

[15] Ordonnance No 2015-380 du 2 April 2015 relative au portage salarial.

[16] Labour Code, Art L1254- 2.

[17] www.inrs.fr/media.html?refINRS=ED%206180.

[18] Circulare letter DRT No 93/14, 18 March 1993.

but according to the place of work. As far as health and safety at work is concerned, the employee is not treated by law as a party to a contract but as a human being that deserves protection whatever the contract.

Under French law, a Decree of 20 February 1992 and a Law of 31 December 1991[19] on the prevention of industrial accidents, transposing Directive 89/391/EEC on health and safety of workers, recognise the risks associated with the interference of activities, where several companies are working together on the same site. Integrating employees in the same economic process justifies the application of the same rules, at least in certain areas of law such as health and safety. Again, the works rule (called 'règlement intérieur' in French), in its provisions relative to health and safety, applies to all individuals who perform work within the firm, should they have a contract of employment with the firm or not.[20]

Where it is external, outsourcing may lead to relocation in a foreign country (with additional legal difficulties, such as social dumping; see below). Here, we have problems of autonomy with technical requirement specifications (quality requirements, deadlines), pressure on prices and, more generally, a situation of economic dependence that may have consequences, not only on the subcontractor but also on its employees who bear the risk of breaching the subcontracting contract. The essential issue, here, is that of social dumping.

III. The Legal Organisation of Outsourcing

In principle, outsourcing is legal, provided the rules of competition law are respected and the employees' representatives are informed and consulted. The outsourcer as well as the recipient must inform, in due time, their workers' representatives of the reasons for, measures and consequences of the prospective operation, notably in relation to employment.

Some countries have introduced specific limitations. There is a famous case in Finland concerning the collective agreement made for paper and pulp mills. The collective agreement used to contain a prohibition concerning all but temporary use of outside labour in the normal production and maintenance tasks inside a paper mill. In 1995, the Supreme Administrative Court decided that the prohibition was in conflict with national competition law considering it prevented traders in cleaning, security and similar businesses from offering subcontractor services to companies in the paper industry. This prohibition was later replaced by a bargaining procedure, which must be followed if a paper company intends to outsource such activities. Outsourcing is then subject to the consent of the Paper Workers' Trade Union.[21]

[19] Loi No 91-1414 of 31 Dec 1991; Décret No 92-158 of 20 Feb 1992.

[20] Labour Code, Art L1321-1.

[21] www.ilo.org/wcmsp5/groups/public/---ed_dialogue/---dialogue/documents/meetingdocument/wcms_159885.pdf.

In most countries, recourse to temporary work is under control (control of temporary work agencies notably). In Finland, there is also control for subcontracting through the 'Act on the Contractor's Obligations and Liability when Work is Contracted Out'.[22] It concerns situations where temporary agency workers or subcontracting are used. According to the Act the ordering party has the duty to check a contracting partner's ability to discharge their statutory obligations. At the same time, it has to ensure that the subcontractors and agencies hiring out workers discharge their obligations as employers. The obligations laid down are also intended to ensure that the minimum terms of the employment relationship are fulfilled, also in the case of subcontracting and temporary agency workers. The Act entered into force on 1 January 2007.[23]

One of the main legal constraints regarding outsourcing concerns transfer of undertakings. In a globalised economy, businesses are winning and losing contracts, with potential consequences as to the legislation on transfer of undertakings.

In particular, a company that decides to separate from one activity to transfer it to a subcontractor may fall within the law on transfer of undertakings and, thus, has to transfer the contracts of the employees of the entity to the subcontractor. The transfer occurs if there is an organised grouping of resources pursuing an economic activity, which is transferred and its identity is substantially retained in the hands of the transferee.[24] Originally directed at the sale of a business, Directive 2001/23/EC now applies,[25] under some circumstances to outsourcing. If recourse to outsourcing results in a transfer of undertaking, the employees are transferred automatically to the transferee with the same rights and duties; notably, remuneration of the employee remains and all modifications (except those that fall within the unilateral power of the employer)[26] require the consent of the employee. In France, rights or advantages created by custom or unilateral commitment of the former employer (outsourcer) are also transferred.[27]

The *Albron Catering* case gives a wide interpretation of Directive 2001/23/EC in the context of outsourcing. According to the Court, the Directive does not prevent the non-contractual employer, to which employees are seconded on a permanent basis, from being regarded as a 'transferor', within the meaning of the Directive. More precisely, an employee hired by a company of a group but working for another permanently follows the activity of the latter when transferred outside the group. This means that the existence of a contractual relationship between an employee and a company is not in itself an obstacle to the transfer of the employment contract with the activity of another.[28]

[22] Loi 1233/2006, Contractor's Liability Act.
[23] www.tem.fi/files/34074/TEM_ESITE_Tilaajavastuuta_EN_22032013.pdf.
[24] Famous French case, *Vittel Perrier*, Cour de Cassation, Chambre Sociale, 12 July 2000, (2000) *Droit social* 845, comment by G Couturier.
[25] OJ L82/16, 22.03.2001.
[26] The transferee is also allowed to change the work conditions if they are not contractual.
[27] Cour de Cassation, Chambre Sociale, 27 May 2009, no 08-42555.
[28] Case C-242/09, *Albron Catering BV v FNV Bondgenoten & John Roest*, CJEU, 21 October 2010.

In general, the legislation on transfers of undertakings may apply in three circumstances, as far as outsourcing is concerned: on an initial outsourcing to a service provider; on a change from one service provider to another; on taking a service back in-house.[29] The typical case is the following: company A has a commercial contract with company B for computer maintenance and decides to contract with company C instead of B. This may result in a transfer of undertaking from company B to company C with the transfer of the contract of employees working on computer maintenance.[30]

Reflections have developed in France concerning the legal regulation of outsourcing. A draft advisory opinion was adopted by the Conseil Economique et Social (Economic and Social Council) in 2005 which adopted several propositions for a National Charter of Outsourcing, among which: the adoption of the 'site', ie the place where the employees carries out their work, as a level of social dialogue and the creation of joint boards for site social dialogue; the creation of unions and employer organisations at this site level; the conclusion of site agreements; granting a right to the transferred employee to refuse the transfer of his contract of employment.[31]

IV. The Temptation for Social Dumping

In a globalised world, the rules, notably those applicable to labour, have become, for companies, an essential factor to decide in which country to invest. A reform of labour law in a country may lead companiesthat do not wish to increase prices of goods and services to terminate or not renew outsourcing contracts with local businesses and to move part of their operation to a country with lower social costs. This strategy is highly debatable (a lower cost of labour can lead to having employees that are less efficient, less productive) and it generates one of the biggest challenges for employees protection nowadays: social dumping which has become a central aspect of outsourcing.

A. The Fight against Social Dumping

We mean here social dumping outside the country of the concerned firm. The abuses of outsourcing become headlines, with employees hired in deplorable conditions by a subcontractor thousands of kilometers away. Mattel, distributor of

[29] www.acc.com/legalresources/publications/topten/tupe-its-effect.cfm; 'Sous-traitance et relations salariales' (1994) 60 *Travail et Emploi* 23.

[30] www.personneltoday.com/hr/tupe-and-outsourcing-advice-on-two-common-scenarios/.

[31] www.ilo.org/wcmsp5/groups/public/---ed_dialogue/---dialogue/documents/meetingdocument/wcms_159885.pdf.

the famous Barbie doll, Samsung or Apple have been questioned by the NGO, China Labor Watch, for having recourse in China to suppliers guilty of multiple violations of labour law: working time up to 13 hours a day, low pay, housing in overcrowded dormitories, lack of protective equipment, discrimination against people over 40 years etc. In the absence of a sufficiently binding international legal corpus, and despite the rise of corporate social responsibility (CSR), legal means currently mobilised are too weak.

The European Union has not reached a sufficient degree of integration to avoid the phenomenon of social dumping within its borders, favoured by strong disparities in wage costs between Member States. The absence of a European minimum wage, and the fact that some countries of the European Union (Denmark, Finland, and Sweden in particular) have no legal minimum wage, does not help. To reduce fraud and prevent social dumping, the Directive on the posting of workers provides for the automatic application of the core rules of the host country, including health and safety and minimum wage.[32] It should be noted that, in Finland, legislation provides for the application of the collective agreement of the user if the subcontractor has no collective agreement.[33]

Despite this Directive, the abuses are numerous, especially in sectors such as food or construction such as undeclared workers, non-compliance with provisions on health and safety and working time, employees partly paid in compensation costs, fraud in social security contributions, and sophisticated legal arrangements, as illustrated by the *Flamanville* case which attracted much attention in 2011 in France. Employees were Polish; they were recruited in Cyprus through a temporary employment agency based in Ireland, to work on behalf of the French company Bouygues on the site of Flamanville.[34]

How can such practices be stopped? The Enforcement Directive[35] contains provisions on subcontracting liability. It obliges Member States to introduce subcontracting liability, or other appropriate enforcement measures, in the construction sector as part of a comprehensive approach to better enforcement. The liability is limited to the direct subcontractor.[36] This Directive follows the finding that numerous posted workers are exploited and left without full payment (or with no payment at all) of the wages they are entitled to. The reason sometimes is that their employer has disappeared or never existed legally. An indication of how serious

[32] Directive 96/71/EC, 16 December 1996. See C Barnard, *The Substantive Law of The EU* (Oxford, OUP, 2013).

[33] www.ilo.org/wcmsp5/groups/public/---ed_dialogue/---dialogue/documents/meetingdocument/wcms_159885.pdf.

[34] www.metiseurope.eu/flamanville-ou-les-contradictions-du-droit-social-europeen_fr_70_art_29177.html.

[35] Directive 2014/67/EU of the European Parliament and of the Council of 15 May 2014 on the enforcement of Directive 96/71/EC concerning the posting of workers in the framework of the provision of services and amending Regulation (EU) No 1024/2012 on administrative cooperation through the Internal Market Information System ('the IMI Regulation').

[36] http://europa.eu/rapid/press-release_MEMO-14-344_en.htm.

France is in combatting social dumping is demonstrated by its early adoption of the Directive.

The French Act of 10 July 2014 on 'social dumping'[37] provides, in addition to joint liability (France joins countries such as Austria, Germany, Spain, Finland, Italy, The Netherlands and Belgium which already had a system of subcontracting liability),[38] the establishment of a blacklist on the web of businesses convicted of illegal work, for a period of two years, by decision of a judge.

The fight against social dumping is not only a concern for labour law. It is also a concern for social security law. It is essential to limit abuse by reducing distortions of competition in terms of levels of social security contributions. The charges applicable to wages are currently 13% in Romania, 17% in Slovenia and 21% in Poland, against about 45% in France.[39] However, under European regulations, payroll taxes remain payable in the country of origin, which, in fact, allows an employer to hire lower-cost workers and send them to work in countries with higher social contributions.

B. New Tools

New instruments have emerged against social dumping, particularly under the impact of corporate social responsibility.[40]

Codes of conduct—The companies that have created networks of subcontractors tend, more and more, to lay down codes of conduct. The objective is to ensure that the subcontractors respect human and social rights.[41] For instance, IKEA, attacked in the middle of the 1990s for child labour among its subcontractors, especially carpet manufacturers in India, has implemented measures to fight against these abuses. Not only did the Swedish company react by encouraging schooling for adolescents, especially in Asia, but it also had to adopt a code of conduct to maintain its reputation (as most codes of conduct, it is mainly influenced by the norms of the ILO, as far as social rights are concerned). Similarly, Apple requires from its subcontractors that they do not hire children below the legal age and that weekly hours should not exceed 60 hours. The Apple code of conduct starts as follows:

> 'Apple is committed to the highest standards of social and environmental responsibility and ethical conduct. Apple's suppliers are required to provide safe working conditions,

[37] Statute law 2014-790, 10 July 2014; M Segonds, 'Les limites imposées à l'optimisation sociale par la loi n. 2014-790 du 10 juillet 2014 visant à lutter contre la concurrence sociale déloyale' Revue sciences criminelles 2014, 828.

[38] http://europa.eu/rapid/press-release_MEMO-14-344_fr.htm.

[39] http://europe-liberte-securite-justice.org/2013/12/10/travailleurs-detaches-leurope-sociale-sera-t-elle-rattachee-a-la-libre-prestation-de-services/.

[40] Commission Green Paper 2001, 'Promoting a European Framework for Corporate Social Responsibility', COM(2001) 366; Ch Walker-Said and J D Kelly (eds), *Corporate social responsibilty? Human rights in the new global economy* (University of Chicago Press, 2015).

[41] R Jenkins, R Pearson, G Seyfang (eds), *Corporate responsibility and labour rights: Codes of conduct in the global economy* (London, Routledge, 2013).

> treat workers with dignity and respect, act fairly and ethically, and use environmentally responsible practices wherever they make products or perform services for Apple.'[42]

The big issue about codes of conduct concerns control. Internal control, that is to say control by organs within the firm, is not sufficient. External control is absolutely necessary, even though it often turns out to be complex: record keeping is often rudimentary, employees may be reluctant to answer questions concerning their working conditions for fear of sanctions.[43]

The 'duty of diligence'[44]—In reaction notably to the drama of the 2013 Rana Plaza collapse,[45] several countries are thinking of creating new duties in the context of subcontracting. Too often, tragic accidents occur in subsidiaries or with subcontractors without any possibility for victims to have recourse to true compensation. It is now clear that the prime contractor and the subcontractor cannot be considered anymore as completely separate entities (although they have autonomous legal personalities); the former cannot delegate activities to the latter with 'eyes closed' and must integrate more stringent legal constraints when considering outsourcing. A few countries have already adopted provisions like Canada, the USA, Italy, Belgium and the UK.[46]

The debate in France has been intense since 2013.[47] A bill to create a presumption of liability of parent companies for damage caused by their subsidiaries and subcontractors was filed in November 2013.[48] Here again, we come across the problem of autonomy of legal personality. The project is not limited to fighting corruption (like in the UK) but also to preventing:

> 'violations of rights and fundamental freedoms, serious physical or environmental damage and health risks resulting from the company's operations and those of the companies it controls […] directly or indirectly, as well as activities of their subcontractors or suppliers with which it has an established business relationship'.

More precisely, the text aims to make companies with 5,000 or more employees directly responsible for violations of human rights and environmental law committed by their subsidiaries or subcontractors abroad. This change, it is hoped, will help prevent the occurrence of such tragedies. The text has a long history.

[42] www.apple.com/jp/supplier-responsibility/pdf/Apple_Supplier_Code_of_Conduct.pdf.

[43] www.oecd.org/daf/inv/investment-policy/WP-2001_3.pdf.

[44] Devoir de vigilance in French.

[45] D Berliner and AR Greenleaf, *Labor standards in international supply chains: aligning rights and incentives* (Cheltenham, Edward Elgar Publishing Ltd, 2015); Committee on Foreign Relations United States Senate, Worker Safety and Labor Rights in Bangladesh's Garment Sector, Create Space Independent Publishing Platform, 2015.

[46] www.carefrance.org/partenaires/entreprise-fondation/actualites-entreprises/refus-proposition-loi-RSE.htm#.

[47] I Vacarie, 'Le travail dans un marché sans frontières' (2015) *Revue de droit du travail* 634. PL Périn, 'Devoir de vigilance et responsabilité illimitée des entreprises: qui trop embrasse mal étreint' (2015) *Revue Trimestrielle de droit commercial* 215.

[48] Proposition de loi relative au devoir de vigilance des sociétés mères et des entreprises donneuses d'ordre, Assemblée nationale, 30 March 2015.

The initial version of the bill was about sanctioning companies—criminal and civil—which would not have been able to demonstrate that they had put in place all the measures and taken all the necessary guarantees to prevent accidents. It was liability without causal link between the damage and the fault, which was considered too broad by some parliamentarians.[49] Due to criticism, criminal liability has disappeared, replaced by civil penalty of up to €10 million and an advertising sanction. Companies will have to protect themselves, through a vigilance plan whose quality will determine whether the firm should be deemed responsible for human rights abuses or not.

The text, both in its contents and philosophy, is under severe criticism. It is argued that the control of direct and indirect subcontractors is difficult, let alone for subcontractors established abroad. For employers' organisations, the standards which they are expected to abide by are too wide (human rights, environmental, corruption, freedom etc) and not sufficiently explicit.[50] Added to this, is the fact that such duties would make France less attractive if the other countries do not have the same rules. A national and isolated action is certainly not sufficient. A commitment at European level or, ideally, worldwide level, would be much more appropriate.

C. Social Dumping and Low-Cost

The problem of social dumping is not limited to relationships between firms located in different countries. Social dumping takes other forms when it occurs not between states but between companies in the same country. This is the growing phenomenon of 'low cost'. The firm compresses social costs (salary level, the organisation of working time, complementary social protection) to gain a competitive advantage. This can be obtained by reorganising the firm so as to have a subsidiary or a subcontractor with lower costs (lower wages; more flexibility of working time etc).

This phenomenon requires a specific legal context, that is to say the possibility for the firm to subcontract with a company which has different rules. This is favoured by the decline of statute law to the benefit of collective bargaining, especially to the benefit of company or factory agreements. Most countries have encountered this issue. Air France was criticised for developing its low cost subsidiary Transavia, and offer the Transavia pilots lower wages, more working hours (the pilots of traditional companies like Air France, Lufthansa or British Airways work between 700 and 750 hours per year; those of low-cost companies like Ryan Air or EasyJet around 900 hours), less advantages as to complementary social

[49] S Schiller and C Hannoun, 'Quel devoir de vigilance des sociétés-mères et des sociétés donneuses d'ordre?' (2014) *RDT* 441.

[50] PL Périn, 'Devoir de vigilance et responsabilité illimitée des entreprises: qui trop embrasse mal étreint' (n 46).

protection. For instance, pilots under contract with Air France benefit from more generous social benefits, such as supplementary pensions, mutual health or advantages linked with the works council, than those of Transavia France.[51]

The problem is more complex than seems at first glance because the disadvantages for employees are, in some cases, benefits for low-income consumers. It is with this type of argument that the retail giant Wal-Mart, the world's largest company by turnover as ranked by Fortune magazine in 2014, denies charges of treating its employees worse than its competitors. While negative for employees that have to tolerate lower wages and an absence of unionisation, the social dumping effect caused by the opening of a Wal-Mart supermarket is good for consumers with modest incomes who benefit from lower prices both at Wal-Mart and among competitors who have no choice but to line up.[52]

V. Joint Employers

For a long time, identifying the employer was an easy task. It was enough to read the payroll or the employment contract. One of the collateral effects of externalisation is to make it complex, in some cases, to identify the real employer. The identification of the employer is not a new problem for labour law. It is, indeed, an enduring question concerning temporary work, with a debate as to the identification of the true employer between the legal employer (the temporary agency) and the real employer (the user who, often, has in fact power over the employee). The issue is the same with regard to subcontracting, for instance in the case of call centres, which today hire approximately 300,000 workers in France under social conditions more precarious than those of the employees of the user company. In law, the employer is the call centre company; it signs employment contracts, is responsible for non-compliance with social rules and is the contact for employees in case of claims. However, orders and directives mostly emanate from the users.

Under classical labour law, there is a single employer; the objective of the law should be to identify the employer who has power over the employees. The concept of joint employer or co-employment has been invented to deal with this situation.[53]

The recognition of a co-employment situation makes it possible for employees to ask, for example, the payment of their salary or their redundancy payments to a company other than the one with which they are bound by a contract of employment, which is very useful when their employer becomes insolvent. The other company is called 'co-employer'.

51 'Air France ou Transavia, où fait-il être meilleur pilote', www.lefigaro.fr, 29 Sept 2014.

52 See CC.

53 JF Cesaro, 'Le co-emploi' (2013) 1 *Revue de jurisprudence sociale* 3.

In France, to be recognised as co-employer, the employees must establish either the existence of a relationship of subordination, or a confusion of activity, direction and interest between both companies.[54] With this second criterion, by far the most controversial, it is now possible for employees to require from a company the payment of wages, of redundancy indemnities without having to prove subordination. In a famous case,[55] the mother company called 'Metaleurop' was liable for the redundancy payment that its subsidiary, insolvent, was supposed to pay to its employee. To consider the existence of co-employment, the judges found that the decision to restructure the subsidiary had been taken by the board of the parent company, that directors were common and that the main company was interfering in the management of the staff of its subsidiary.

Co-employment has become one of the main targets of those who see labour law as an obstacle to the implementation of foreign groups in France. The British or the German firm might well apprehend being qualified, by French courts, as the co-employer of the employees of their subsidiary or their subcontractor in France. To reassure groups about the fear of requalification as co-employer, French courts have stated that the necessary co-ordination of economic actions inside groups of companies and supervision of decisions are not enough to characterise co-employment.[56] We must now distinguish between the management of the group by the parent company (definition of group policy, commitment to provide the funds needed to cover social measures of the subsidiary) and abnormal intrusion in the management of the subsidiary or subcontractor.

Co-employment is not a French specificity. It exists in Italy where it is used for dismissals, especially economic dismissals; it is also used to push the limits of the obligation of reclassification to individual redundancies, and to extend 'to more than one company the financial liability for unpaid wage claims demanded by the workers.

In 2013, the Italian legislature introduced two standards in the Legislative Decree no 276 of 2003: the first concerns the posting of workers and admits co-employment of employees of different companies belonging to the same network;[57] the second allows the joint hiring from several companies, provided they are agricultural or belong to a network contract in which at least half of the firms are agricultural enterprises.[58]

The concept of 'associated employers' in the United Kingdom, only allows to take into account, as part of continuity of service (qualifying period notably for the application of unfair dismissal legislation),[59] the previous working relationships with different companies of the same group. English law also allows the

[54] Cour de Cassation, Chambre Sociale, 25 Sept 2013, no 12-14.353, P Bailly, 'Le co-emploi: une situation exceptionnelle' (2013) *Semaine juridique (JCP), édition sociale* 1441.

[55] Cour de Cassation, Chambre Sociale, 28 Sept 2011, no 10-12278.

[56] Cour de Cassation, Chambre Sociale, 2 July 2014, no 13-15208.

[57] Article 30 par 4-*ter*.

[58] Article 31 par 3-*bis*, 3-*ter*, 3-*quater*, 3-*quinquies*.

[59] Employment Rights Act (ERA) 1996 s 231.

court to order the reinstatement, following an unfair dismissal, with the employer who decided the dismissal but also in another company (associated) group.[60]

One of the most famous cases concerning associated employers concerns the conflict between McDonald's and the National Labor Relations Board (NLRB)[61] in the US. This concept is, as in Europe, used to treat different entities, that are in appearance independent but in reality constitute one integrated enterprise, as a single entity; there will be joint employers where separate entities 'share or co-determine those matters governing the essential terms and conditions of employment'.[62] In April 2015, the NLRB decided that McDonald's is a joint-employer of its franchisees. The reasoning seems as follows:

> 'If a franchisor's involvement prevents employees from meaningful bargaining with their employer, such as using corporate check ins to determine employee policies, the general counsel believes the franchisor should be held responsible as a joint employer. In the Freshii's case, the franchisor does not fit this conception of joint employer. In McDonald's case, the board argues that it does.'[63]

The NLRB press release reads as follows, concerning Mc Donald's:

> 'Our investigation found that McDonald's, USA, LLC, through its franchise relationship and its use of tools, resources and technology, engages in sufficient control over its franchisees' operations, beyond protection of the brand, to make it a putative joint employer with its franchisees, sharing liability for violations of our Act.'

In the case of the healthy fast-casual chain, Freshii's, the NLRB concluded in April 2015 that Freshii's was not a joint employer.[64] The board considered that the chain did not have a significant role in employee issues, such as hiring, firing or discipline. 'At most, Freshii's control over Nutritionality's operations are limited to ensuring a standardised product and customer experience, factors that clearly do not evince sharing or codetermining matters governing essential terms and conditions of employment', the board wrote.

If the co-employment is undoubtedly the toughest response to the problem of fragmented business, other routes are open, starting with the commitment of the civil liability of the parent company that, through its own fault,[65] contributed

[60] ERA 1996, s 115(1).

[61] The NLRB is an independent federal agency vested with the power to safeguard employees' rights to organise and to determine whether to have unions as their bargaining representative. The agency also acts to prevent and remedy unfair labour practices committed by private sector employers and unions, www.nlrb.gov/what-we-do.

[62] *NLRB v Browning-Ferris Industries*, 691 F.2d 1117, 1123 (3rd Cir 1982).

[63] K Taylor, 'Why the NLRB Says This Franchise Isn't a Joint Employer, But McDonald's Is', May 2015, www.entrepreneur.com/article/246364.

[64] Advice Memorandum regarding Nutritionality, Inc, d/b/a Freshii from Barry J Kearney, Associate General Counsel, NLRB Office of the General Counsel, to Peter Sung Ohn, Regional Director, NLRB Region 13 (28 April 2015), available at www.nlrb.gov/case/13-CA-134294.

[65] This would require the making of a decision deliberately prejudicial to the interest of the subsidiary (Cour de Cassation, Chambre Criminelle, 4 February 1985, no 84-91581, (1986) 2 *Semaine juridique* (JCP) édition générale, 20585, note W Jeandidier, *Rev. sociétés* 1985, p 648, note B Bouloc) or the subcontractor.

to the collapse of its subsidiary or subcontractor and the loss of jobs within it. Outsourcing poses significant problems collectively. For example, the right to conclude collective agreements is a difficult one to assert when faced with such networks of companies. A recent report ordered by the French Government encourages the development of collective bargaining in supply chains, with the idea that the centralised firm cannot be the only model for collective bargaining anymore.[66]

Indeed, companies rarely perform the same activity, which means that they do not fall within the same sector. Company A, which is a mobile phone operator, is subject to the sector agreement on telecommunication, whereas its subcontractor, Company B, in charge of call centres, will be subject to the collective agreement on service providers. Another difficulty concerns collective representation of the employees of the subcontractor. For instance, French law provides that employees of the subcontractor may be voters in the elections in the user undertaking if they are present for 12 continuous months.[67]

VI. The Issue of Risks

An essential aspect of labour law is the link between risks and power. The risk of bankruptcy and consequently of losing the job is higher if one is an employee of the subcontractor than of the main company. In the case of subcontracting, labour law is a problem for the subcontractor, not for the main company.

What role for labour law in this scheme? A residual one. For instance, rather than hiring an employee to perform accounting of the company, the company will enter into commercial contracts, and transfer the risk on the subcontractor. In this example, the company will be able, in case of lower activity, to terminate the commercial contract—usually through a simple notice—which is considerably easier than terminating hundreds of labour contracts individually. It will be the subcontractor, as in the case envisaged above, to manage the consequences for its own employees of the termination of the commercial contract. Indeed, from the standpoint of commercial law, the subcontractor is an independent contractor who works on an equal basis with the main company. When Dell or Ikea project the closure of a site, there are hundreds of subcontractors concerned. A former secretary general of the CGT warned that, throughout France, 'as long as Peugeot announces the suppression of 8,000 to 10,000 jobs, multiply by three or even four, to measure the impact in terms of jobs for the entire country.'[68]

[66] JD Combrexelle, *La négociation collective, le travail et l'emploi, Rapport au Premier ministre*, France Stratégie, 2015.

[67] Labour Code, Art L2314-18-1.

[68] B Thibault, in T Thuillier, 'PSA: quel avenir pour les sous-traitants?', www.L'Express.fr, 12 juillet 2012.

Should labour law evolve to deal with the issue of subcontracting? In other words, should we adapt the wage figures to better meet the demand for flexibility? This is the challenge around the project contracts. The idea is to set up a contract that would automatically end once the project, for which the contract has been concluded, is completed. This contract would replace the indeterminate contract, and it is meant to be particularly attractive for employers. Here we take on the Italian model project contract, removed by Legislative decree no 82 of 2015. This is a challenge for labour law; with such contracts, the link between the worker and the employer is close to that of a commercial partner, that is to say a commercial link. It is a form of 'controlled autonomy'.[69]

VII. Externalisation of Management

Until now, we have dealt with outsourcing the activity of the company. Another aspect of outsourcing is growing: outsourcing of firm management. A company in trouble or about to enter a process of merger, invites external consultants to manage the firm. From a legal perspective, transition management is not an easy issue. First, abuses have been identified[70] when a firm has recourse to this type of management to get rid of a trade union in the firm. Second, a third party to the firm cannot exercise the powers and responsibilities of the employer (dismissal, collective bargaining etc). What status should these atypical managers have within the firm? Is it appropriate to give them a managing director's mandate or to sign with them a work contract of limited duration?[71]

In conclusion, labour law has to face the challenge of the transforming of the firm and the development of outsourcing inside and outside Europe. Is this transformation necessarily correlated with the development of contingent work? Efficient tools already exist but have to be developed, both in the individual and collective spheres of labour law, so that the employees of subcontractors do not become a permanently contingent and precarious workforce. This is one of the main challenges for the future of labour law.

[69] Th Coutrot, *Critique de l'organisation du travail* (Paris, La Découverte, 1999) 20.

[70] Cour de Cassation, Chambre Criminelle, 2 Sept 2008, no 07-81.661.

[71] P. Lokiec, Il faut sauver le droit du travail, Odile Jacob, 2015, p. 140.

7

Do We Really Wish You Were Here? Hungary and Distance Work

ERIKA KOVÁCS

I. Development of Distance Work—From Homework to Crowdwork & Co

A. Introduction

The umbrella term 'distance work' covers a wide range of work forms starting with the ancient homework through the telework up to the most recent types of work performance, which are still emerging and dynamically evolving, like crowdwork. The mentioned various forms of work share one common feature, namely the work is usually—not necessarily all the time—performed in a place different from the employer's premises or the places determined by the employer or clients.

Homework can be labelled as the pioneer of distance work, since it appeared over one hundred years ago. It is the oldest form of work performance different from the traditional form in the sense of the Fordist model, but cannot be regarded as the archetype of atypical work, as before the emergence of factory work, homework was the 'typical' work. With the emergence and establishment of the typical employment relationship, homework has taken its place at the periphery of the labour market with relatively little practical significance.

The onset of the digital era has fundamentally changed the earlier dull phenomenon of distance work. The emergence of ICT (Information and Communication Technology) in work life brought about not only new working equipment, but put the performance and organisation of work into a new dimension and challenged the legitimacy of the traditional sense of basic terms like workplace, working time and personal dependency.

The next, recent change in the world of work is the emergence of 'crowdwork',[1] where even the last, major bastion of employment relationship falls, namely the durable connection of the worker to a particular employer. Having the picture in mind, when crowdworkers manage the tasks outsourced in a crowdsourcing platform one by one, one can't help thinking that crowdwork reproduces the brave new world by the digital, electronic version of Ford's assembly line.

B. The Most Common Forms of Distance Work

i. The Oldest One—Homework

Homework cannot be qualified as an atypical work, as it is one of the oldest forms of work performance, but it could be regarded as contingent work when taking a broad definition of the latter. The technological development brought about the renaissance of the work performed from home, but the use of ICTs created a new quality of employment, which simply cannot be subsumed under the classical term of homework. On the one hand, the regulation of homework occurred in an area of social policy, when most (Western) European states established a network of social legislation to guarantee a (basic) level of welfare protection to all those engaged in a kind of employment. An important pillar of this tendency was to extend the personal scope of legislation to cover new categories of wage earners and, at the end, all professional categories of workers. The regulation of homework fitted into this trend (in Germany, France and Austria in the 1950s).[2] On the other hand, the emergence and regulatory need of telework occurred in an area characterised—at least partly—by the opposite trend, namely by the fragmentation of employment relationship and the following fragmentation of the regulation.

In Hungary, homework was first regulated in 1967[3] and again in 1981 and 2004 by Ministerial Orders.[4] Finally the new Labour Code (LC) of 2012 integrated

[1] See the articles of Comparative Labour Law & Policy Journal, Vol. 37/3, 2016; C Benner (ed), *Crowdwork—zurück in die Zukunft?, Perspektiven digitaler Arbeit*, (Frankfurt/Main, Bund-Verlag, 2015); MA Cherry, 'A Taxonomy of Virtual Work', (2011) *Georgia Law Review* 951–1013; W Däubler/T Klebe, 'Crowdwork: Die neue Form der Arbeit—Arbeitgeber auf der Flucht?', (2015) *Neue Zeitschrift für Arbeitsrecht* 1032–42.; A Felstiner, 'Working the Crowd: Employment and Labor Law in the Crowdsourcing Industry', (2011) *Berkeley Journal of Employment and Labor Law* 143–204; available at SSRN: http://ssrn.com/abstract=1593853; M Risak, 'Crowdwork—Erste rechtliche Annäherungen an eine "neue" Arbeitsform', (2015) *Zeitschrift für Arbeits- und Sozialrecht* 11–19.

[2] B Veneziani, 'The Employment Relationship', in B Hepple and B Veneziani (eds), *The Transformation of Labour Law in Europe—A Comparative Study of 15 Countries 1945–2004*, (Oxford, Hart Publishing, 2009) 105–6.

[3] 16/1967. (XII.27.) MüM rendelet a bedolgozók foglalkoztatásáról [No 16/1967. on 27.12. Order of the Ministry for Labour on Homework].

[4] 10/1981. (IX.29.) MüM. Rendelet a bedolgozók foglalkoztatásáról [No 10/1981. on 29.11. Order of the Ministry for Labour on Homework].

homework into the LC bringing about its recognition as an atypical employment.[5] Ironically, the spread and legal recognition of numerous kinds of atypical forms of employment were needed to recognise homework—the oldest form of employment—as an atypical form of employment.

The legal qualification of homework has been controversial in the Hungarian literature for a very long time. The prevailing opinion was that it is rather a sui generis relationship than an employment relationship due to the missing element of personal dependency.[6] This view was also expressed in the separate legislation for several decades. The 1994 Order turned round this rule and clarified that homeworkers operate within the framework of an employment relationship according to the rules of the LC, but the specific rules of the Order apply to them. Remarkably, the Order strongly relativised the personal dependency of the homeworker by expressly stating that he can make use of the services of other persons, provided they live in the same household and are entitled to create an employment relationship.

The broad definition of homework in the Order required the fulfilment of only two conditions: firstly, the relationship is established for work which can be performed independently and, secondly, the performance can be defined by quantitative or qualitative indicators.[7] This definition did not exclude the application of the regulation on teleworkers.

Despite the recognition of homework as employment, the Order provided significantly less protection to homeworkers than to typical workers. So for example, it provided a short notice period of 15 days for both parties and, in case of unlawful termination, the party liable for the termination was only obliged to pay the minimum wage for the set 15 days.[8] Furthermore, it was precarious, for although the worker was entitled to four weeks annual holiday, the payment of this leave was subject of their agreement and the Order only stated the upper limit, which was 30 per cent of the minimum wage.

ii. The Recent Regulation of Homework

Homework is now regulated in the new LC[9] as a form of atypical employment, so in addition to the special rules, the general rules of the LC apply to this employment relationship. Even if the LC assumes that this kind of work is performed within the framework of an employment relationship, this does not change the

[5] G Berke and G Kiss (eds), *Kommentár a Munka Törvénykönyvéhez* (Budapest, Complex Kiadó Kft. 2012) 498 and T Gyulavári, 'A gazdaságilag függő munkavégzés szabályozása: kényszer vagy lehetőség?', (2014) 1 *Magyar Munkajog, E-Folyóirat. 1-2*;.available at www.hllj.hu/A-gazdasagilag-fuggo-munkavegzes-szabalyozasa-Kenyszer-vagy-Lehetoseg--pdf-38.html.

[6] G Kiss, *Munkajog* (Budapest, Osiris Kiadó, 2005) 120.

[7] § 3 of the Order of the Government of 24/1994. (II.25.) on the employment of homeworkers.

[8] § 10 and 22 of the Order of the Government of 24/1994. (II.25.) on the employment of homeworkers.

[9] § 198-200. of the new Labour Code.

fact that homework in Hungary falls within a grey area between employment and self-employment.[10] The sparse regulation—the majority of which is optional anyhow—allows the parties to form a relationship with minor personal though strong economic dependency. Consequently, this relationship can, in theory, be seen as belonging to a third category of workers.[11] Nonetheless, homework is regarded, under current Hungarian labour law, by definition as a form of employment relationship. The recognition of homeworkers as employees means that basically the provisions of the LC apply to homeworkers which significantly improves their protection. To the contrary, if a person performs his work from home by means of ICT tools mainly independently from his client(s), he will be regarded as being self-employed. In this case, the rules of the LC do not apply to him, so he will not have any labour rights. However, if the relationship and the performance of work show the prevailing features of employment, the relationship is regarded as fake self-employment and the person is considered to be a teleworker (and as such an employee).

The law gives a broad definition of homework. The possibility of the independent performance of work and the exclusive performance-related determination of the remuneration are the two differentia specifica of homework. It is difficult to understand why the remuneration has to be specified as solely performance-related, instead of allowing the combination of time- and performance-related payment. The statutory definition of homework does not theoretically exclude the application of these rules to telework. The two main statutory conditions of homework can be noticed in several forms of telework and thus makes the distinction between homework and telework more difficult. Traditional characteristics of homework, like the performance of simple, manual work is not required.

Furthermore, the parties are free to specify the working place. However, there is an obligation to agree on it, so the worker is basically not free to determine or change his working place unilaterally.

Under Hungarian labour law, it is a long-lasting opinion that it is necessary to require a written employment contract, in any case, in order to protect the interests of the worker. In line with this general idea, there is an obligation to conclude a written employment contract with homeworkers and to specify the activity of the worker, the working place and the amount of wages agreed and the method of payment.

The new LC sets out compulsory rules regarding the payment of the worker. According to the basic rule, the worker is entitled to the reimbursement of his

[10] Under the Hungarian legal order there is no third, middle category of persons performing work between workers and self-employed persons. See in detail, G Kiss, 'The problem of persons having a similar legal status as employees and the absence of regulating this legal status in the Hungarian labour code: The "third estate" of the labour market', in G Kiss (ed) *Recent Developments in Labour Law* (Akadémiai Kiadó, Budapest, 2013) 259 –279; available online in English: http://real.mtak.hu/25658/1/Kiss_259to_279.pdf.

[11] Gyulavári, 'A gazdaságilag függő munkavégzés szabályozása: kényszer vagy lehetőség ?' (n 5) 14.

costs rooted in the employment relationship or, if the actual costs cannot be specified, to a lump sum. More controversial is the rule on the elimination of the right to wage and also the reimbursement of the costs, if the result of the performance does not satisfy the requirements due to a reason for which the worker is accountable.[12]

The regulation contains several optional rules on instructions, control, working equipment and working time, which shall only be applied in the absence of differing agreement between the parties. The new LC basically authorises the employer to define the method of control and if the control takes place in the working place, then the shortest period between the notification and the beginning of the control. Even if it is an optional rule and the parties can deviate from it, this rule puts the workers in an adverse situation. To counterbalance it, the LC declares that the control cannot become an inappropriate burden for the worker and for other persons using the same place.

The working time is—in the absence of deviating regulation—unbound, meaning that the worker has the right to allot his time for work independently. According to this, the new LC leaves open the possibility for the employer to determine certain rules regarding working time (eg the worker has to be available for certain hours of the day etc).

iii. Crowdwork & Co

Crowdwork and similar kinds of work have recently become the focus of attention of labour lawyers.[13] The legal qualification of such work is certainly controversial but not only because of the broad variety of the different forms of work performance. Crowdwork may show certain features of employment, but the qualification of the relationship as employment is made particularly difficult by the presence of several 'atypical features' of an employment relationship, such as the short, casual assignments, distant working place, self-determined working time, little power of direction, etc. Crowdworkers show usually little personal dependency on the client/employer, but are often economically dependent either on the crowdsourcing-platform or directly on the crowdsourcer, as they earn their living from these activities.[14] One has to be cautious, as any general finding regarding crowdwork is a strong simplification, as the qualification varies on a case-by-case basis. It is also conceivable, that in specific cases, the work relationship is established

[12] § 200 par 2 of the new LC.

[13] See eg the 7th Annual Legal Seminar of the European Labour Law Network on 'The New Forms of Employment and EU Law', on 27–28 November 2014 in the Hague and the 4th Conference on Regulating for Decent Work on 'Developing and Implementing Policies for a Better Future at Work' organised by the ILO on 8–10 July 2015.

[14] M Risak, 'Crowdwork—Erste rechtliche Annäherungen an eine "neue" Arbeitsform', (2015) *Zeitschrift für Arbeits- und Sozialrecht* 11, 13.

as one of personal dependency with the result that the relationship is qualified as one of employment.[15]

Crowdwork should be regarded as the next step of an organic development of work performance by ICT. In my opinion, one of the major differences between telework and crowdwork lies in the short duration of work and consequently the presence of many clients/employers. These features can make a qualitative difference when compared with telework. Crowdwork poses the problem of the identification of the actual employer. Regulation of crowdwork is a huge challenge, which certainly cannot be appropriately managed at national level, but calls for supranational solutions.

iv. Telework—A Uniform Category?

Telework is recently the prevailing form of distance work, but even telework cannot be regarded as a uniform category, since there are several expressions highlighting different aspects of the situation, when the employee performs his work outside of the employer's premises by electronic devices. The commonly used expressions 'teleworking', 'telecommuting' or 'e-work' show that the major characteristic of this kind of work is obviously the performance in a place different from the employer's place. Whereas the notion 'telecommuting' is preferably used by US researchers, the 'e-work' refers to the way of performing work.[16] There are no commonly used and accepted definitions of these expressions, but the meaning of them depends mainly on the country or the discipline in which they are used. In the following, the term telework will be used to cover also the other terms mentioned above, as this expression has been long established in the terminology of the ILO[17] and in the European legal language following the adoption of the European Framework Agreement on Telework.[18]

It is useful to categorise telework according to the workplace and the working time or regularity. Firstly, based on the place of work, we can differentiate between home, mobile and satellite telework. Telework can be performed in another country, where the employer has its premises, which is called 'transborder teleworking'. Secondly, according to the working time and regularity, one can differentiate between casual, alternating and permanent telework. Casual telework shows similarities to crowdwork.

[15] ibid 16.

[16] The Irish social partners named their agreement Code of Practice on 'e-working' and the Code equates teleworkers with e-workers. See *Implementation of the European Framework Agreement on Telework*, Report by the European Social Partners, adopted by the Social Dialogue Committee on 28 June 2006 at 15.

[17] See ILO, *Conditions of Work Digest: Telework*, (Geneva, 1990), Vol 9 no 1 and V Di Martino and L Wirth, 'Telework: A new way of working and living', (1990) *International Labour Review* 529.

[18] The same expression is used in the US legislation, see Telework Enhancement Act of 2010; available at www.gpo.gov/fdsys/pkg/PLAW-111publ292/pdf/PLAW-111publ292.pdf.

In this chapter, addressing mainly telework, I will not deal in detail with certain issues, where I do not see—from a Hungarian point of view—great shortcomings, like the maintenance of the employee's status when changing to telework, equal treatment, the voluntary nature of assignment to telework or training and career development. When teleworkers are regarded as employees, the general labour law applies to them regarding these issues, and provides more or less appropriate protection to this group. I selected certain issues, which are more controversial in my view.

II. The Great Image of Telework—False Expectations?

Telework has an exceptionally great image, particularly compared with other atypical forms of employment. Both employers and workers have a positive perception of it—although among workers the positive connotation is definitely stronger—and public policy regards telework as a development worth subsidising. Workers appreciate the great freedom and autonomy and the improved reconciliation of work and private life by flexible working time. For employers, telework can bring about the reduction of costs and a new results-based management. The need of the companies for flexible production motivates employers to decentralise and even outsource many functions. Distance work suits this tendency as it allows for important functions to be exercised out of the employer's premises.

The EU and Member States consider telework as the manifestation of the knowledge-based economy and information society in the world of work and as an excellent instrument to reconcile flexibility and security.[19] Already the White Paper of 1993 emphasised the significance of telework in the creation of new service markets, which should be promoted.[20] Telework was assumed to be the phenomenon in the world of work which represented the changeover towards an information society. The follow-up Bangemann report in 1994 confirmed the importance of the promotion of telework and pointed out that all stakeholders will benefit from it, ie companies will profit from productivity gains and increased flexibility, the general public enjoys advantages in terms of reduction in pollution, traffic and energy consumption. For the employees it can also be beneficial, particularly for those who are homebound or living in remote locations.[21] Telework was expected to be an appropriate instrument to support the employment of certain

[19] Commission Staff Working Paper, *Report on the implementation of the European social partners' Framework Agreement on Telework*, Brussels, 2.7.2008 SEC (2008) 2178 [COM (2008) 412 final]. 4.

[20] *Growth, competitiveness, employment—The challenges and ways forward into the 21st century*, White Paper, Commission of the EU, COM(93) 700, 5 December 1993. Bulletin of the European Communities Supplement 6/93. 96–97.

[21] *Europe and the global information society*, Recommendations of the high-level group on the information society to the Corfu European Council (Bangemann report), 1994. Bulletin of the European Union, Supplement 2/94. 29.

disadvantaged groups, like disabled workers. It was often regarded as an instrument to overcome mobility 'laziness' and contribute to the increase of employment in certain regions with high unemployment rates.[22] Altogether, in the 1990s, telework seemed to be the ultimate wonder drug for many problems.

These were, to a great extent, false hopes, as studies proved first that employers do not perceive telework as an appealing way of employing new workforce, but rather as an opportunity to change the organisational form of work of those tried and trusted. This opinion reflects the deep distrust of employers for telework, particularly noticeable among those in small and medium companies.[23] Another major obstacle to using telework as a successful employment policy instrument for the support of certain groups disadvantaged in the labour market is that in practice most teleworkers are highly qualified experts, which is clearly not the target group of employment policy. Furthermore, statistics show that telework is most commonly used in cities; however, this statement only refers to the location where the employer's premises are and says nothing about the actual place of work of the teleworker.[24] Consequently, telework is hardly a suitable instrument of the employment policy, but is still a good opportunity for certain professionals.

Telework has an extremely positive image among workers, but it has been acknowledged for early on that telework entails certain serious risks, eg it can lead to the social isolation of the worker with the result of following psychosocial diseases, can cause difficulties with internal motivation, can jeopardise the worker's privacy and although it can contribute to the better reconciliation of work and family life, it also can blur the line between them.

The Framework Agreement (FA) on Telework in 2002 was certainly an important step in awareness raising and promoting telework in the Member States, but also by providing a practical guidance on the issues most important when regulating telework. The importance of the FA from a labour law point of view is the fact that it identifies the main fields requiring particular attention when people perform telework, such as data protection, privacy, health and safety, etc.

III. Spread of Telework in Hungary

A. Search for Reasons of Low Use

The spread of telework varies enormously between the countries of the EU. Telework is more popular in the Western European countries, while usually less

[22] *Implementation of the European Framework Agreement on Telework*, Report by the European Social Partners, 6.

[23] S Asztalos and I Czibere et al, *Az atipikus formában szervezhető munkalehetőségek feltárása és elterjesztésének lehetőségei, Kutatási zárójelentés*, (Budapest, Konszenzus Alapítvány, 2011) 109.

[24] Á Hárs, 'Atipikus foglalkoztatási formák Magyarországon a kilencvenes és a kétezres években', (2013) *Közgazdasági Szemle* 247.

widespread in the Eastern European countries. It is nearly impossible to find reliable comparable national statistics on telework, mainly due to the facts, that national definitions are different, they are often broad, the measurement of alternating telework is extremely difficult, and the separation of telework from homework often causes troubles for statistics.

In Hungary, telework is definitely less widespread than in most parts of Europe and lags far behind the great expectations. It is difficult to present reliable numbers on the teleworkers for two reasons. First, the difference between homework and telework is not always clear[25] and surveys can deliver false results, when treating homework and telework as one group, as persons performing these activities can be very different in terms of qualification, age, labour market expectations, etc.[26] Second, the LC contains a narrow definition on telework requiring the regularity of employment away from the place of the employer making it difficult to define whether a worker can be regarded as a teleworker, if he performs alternating telework. This narrow definition prevents employers from the extended use of this kind of employment. If the criterion of the narrow definition is not fulfilled, but the worker performs his job in personal dependency, he should be regarded as a typical, 'normal' worker (with flexible working time and working place).

In 2010, about 2.6 per cent of the employees were teleworkers and altogether 8.6 per cent of the employees worked in unbound working time.[27] Another survey confirmed that about 3 per cent of the workers were teleworkers and about 8 to 9 per cent of the workers performed work at home in 2010.[28] It is impossible to estimate the number of workers performing telework outside an employment relationship.[29]

It is instructive to analyse the composition of teleworkers. Telework is most widely spread among the persons with tertiary education; 8 per cent of the men and 5 per cent of women with tertiary education worked as teleworkers, while those with primary education do not even reach 1 per cent of the workforce.[30] Telework seems to be the form of employment for the best qualified young men, who are over proportionally represented among teleworkers.[31]

[25] ibid 245–46.

[26] Hárs argues to the contrary, that the conditions influencing the probability of homework and telework are nearly similar. Hárs, 'Atipikus foglalkoztatási formák Magyarországon a kilencvenes és a kétezres években', (n 24) 2013, 246.

[27] M Lakatos and R Váradi, 'Az atipikus munkát végzők demográfiai és munkaerő-piaci jellemzői, az atipikus munka szerepe a foglalkoztatottság alakulásában', in Fordam Kft *Az atipikus foglalkoztatás helye és szerepe*, (Budapest, 2013) 134. Available at www.kjmalapitvany.hu/category/kutatoi-palyazatok/kutatoi-palyazatok.

[28] Hárs, 'Atipikus foglalkoztatási formák Magyarországon a kilencvenes és a kétezres években', *Budapesti Munkagazdaságtani Füzetek*, (Magyar Tudományos Akadémia Közgazdaságtudományi Intézete, 2012) 145. Available at www.econ.core.hu/file/download/bwp/bwp1207.pdf.

[29] Z Bankó, '*Atypical Employment Relationships in the Hungarian Labour Law*', 74.

[30] Hárs, Atipikus foglalkoztatási formák Magyarországon a kilencvenes és a kétezres években', (n 24) 2012, 147, 148.

[31] Lakatos and Váradi, 'Az atipikus munkát végzők demográfiai és munkaerő-piaci jellemzői, az atipikus munka szerepe a foglalkoztatottság alakulásában', 134–137.

In Hungary, one reason for the low level of the spread of telework is certainly the negative approach of the employers to this kind of employment. Among employers, telework has a negative association assuming the lower level of efficiency and less result in a quantitative and qualitative sense. Companies tend to favour a conservative approach and insist on the possibility of regular physical control of the worker.[32] The best target audience for possible telework is certainly not the less educated person coping with finding employment, as employers are very unlikely to employ them in telework. Employers are usually only willing to employ well-educated, experienced workers as teleworkers.[33]

B. Promotion and Subsidy of Telework

When considering telework as an attractive model of employment, it is necessary to think about possible measures to support its proliferation. In particular, employment policy, labour law and tax law measures should be taken into account.

The Hungarian State tried to make use of certain employment policy measures. In 1998, the so-called 'telework-programme' started and the 'Telework Coordination Public Benefit Organisation' ('Távmunka Koordinációs Közhasznú Társaság') was established, which operated as a service centre to bring together offer and demand. The first tenders addressed the partly disabled persons and those women, who are on maternity leave or are single parents. A great number of potential workers registered, but employers were not interested in these opportunities. In 1998, 15,000 workers registered for a job in the form of telework, but only 60 employers participated in the tender and, in the end, 27 were supported, who created altogether 197 new jobs as telework.[34] This public organisation ceased to exist in 2002 and the financial support of the State—basically with the co-finance of the EU—is irregular.[35] The target group of the few existing tenders in the last couple of years were women, particularly those returning from maternity leave and persons living in disadvantaged regions.

Employment law provisions can support the spread of telework by providing the worker the right to change to telework. The employer should have the obligation to consider (seriously) this request. The Commission too suggested the involvement of a rule on the access to telework into the FA.[36] According to its proposal, objective criteria should be elaborated based on which the decision on the access to telework can be delivered. Such regulation already exists in Hungary, Poland

[32] Á Hárs, '*Az atipikus foglalkoztatás: mítoszok, lehetőségek és korlátok az atipikus foglakoztatási formák lehetőségeinek kihasználásában*', (Kopint Konjunktúra Kutatási Alapítvány, Budapest, 2013) 13–15.

[33] ibid 15.

[34] Z Bankó, *Az atipikus munkajogviszonyok* (Pécs, Dialóg Campus Kiadó 2010) 170.

[35] § 19/C. 1991. évi IV. törvény a foglalkoztatás elősegítéséről és a munkanélküliek ellátásáról [IV. Statute of 1991 on the support of employment and the maintanance of unemployed persons].

[36] Commission Staff Working Paper, *Report on the implementation of the European social partners' Framework Agreement on Telework* 47–48.

and the UK. Recently, the Netherlands adopted a new law which gives workers the right to require the change of the working time (increase or decrease of the length and distribution) or the workplace.[37] The employer is not obliged to approve the request if there are serious business grounds to refuse it and such grounds are broadly defined. However, the employer is obliged to consult with the employee and, in case of refusal, communicate the reasons of refusal in written form.[38] The increased individualisation of the right to change the form of work organisation and shift into telework could certainly bring additional flexibility and can give impetus to the spread of telework.

The old Labour Code (old LC) of 1992 contained the right of workers to initiate the modification of the employment terms to facilitate the transition from typical work to telework and vice versa. The employer had great margin to refuse the offer and take the reasonable interests of the company into account. The old LC expressly mentioned the circumstances of the work organisation, the criteria of efficient operation and the requirements of the specific job, which were allowed to be considered in the decision-making process.[39] In practice, this rule did not really work. According to the new LC, in case the worker initiates the modification of the employment, the employer has to provide an answer within 15 days of the request in written form, but the LC does not specify the reasons of refusal anymore, which provides a great margin to the employer.[40]

Tax law measures can contribute to make telework an attractive form of employment. The Hungarian legislator adopted the Statute on Personal Income Tax which specifies that workers can pay-off the purchase of ICT tools, the fee for the use of internet, a lump sum amount for overhead costs in case of homeworking, or, if the teleworker works from a place different from home, the rental costs and, in this way, the reimbursement of these costs will be tax free for the employer.[41]

IV. Regulatory Considerations

A. Which Principles for Best Regulation?

Telework contains a priori the dilemma of the best regulation. The inquiry for the best form of regulation is preoccupied by the special situation of the adoption of

[37] The right is limited to those who have at least 26 weeks length of service and are employed by a company with at least 10 employees.

[38] See Article 2 of the Act of June 9, 2015 which aims to promote flexible work: 'Wet van 9 juni 2015 tot wijziging van de Wet aanpassing arbeidsduur ten einde flexibel werken te bevorderen' to find under https://zoek.officielebekendmakingen.nl/.

[39] § 84/A and § 192/E (3) of the old LC.

[40] § 61 of the new LC.

[41] 3. számú melléklet, 24. pont, 1995. évi CXVII. törvény a személyi jövedelemadóról, [3. appendix, Nr. 24 of the Act Nr CXVII of 1995 on Personal Income Tax].

the first framework agreement at European level and its implementation in the Member States through a wide variety of legal instruments including trade union guidelines, collective agreements and legislation.[42]

Before adopting a regulation on telework, the legislator should have regard to at least two major questions. Firstly, whether there is a need at all to provide special regulation for telework or whether the existing general rules can regulate this kind of work appropriately and secondly, which legal relationship should be promoted as a form of telework.

Regarding the first question, the great advantage of a special regulation on telework certainly is that it can take into account the special features of this kind employment. If the State intends to provide tax and social security provisions for this kind of work performance, it is necessary to define telework.[43] However, the type of regulation which is adopted can determine the future of this kind of employment. The adoption of the FA certainly created a beneficial environment for regulation by either soft or hard law methods.[44] The instruments chosen are multifaceted. This diversity does not weaken the effect of the regulation, but allows different solutions to be tested and lessons to be drawn from the diverse experiences of the countries.[45] One of the major achievement of the FA was its contribution to raising awareness of this kind of employment, particularly because before the FA only a few regulatory instruments existed. The adoption of the FA has resulted in bringing telework into the mainstream and generating a discussion on how best to regulate this form of work.

The regulation of telework counters to a certain extent the recent trend of deregulation of labour law, which removes or reduces employment rights in the interests of the assumed positive effects on productivity and employment rates,[46] even if the chosen soft regulatory methods in many States significantly leaven the sharpness of the regulation.

What form should the regulation take and how detailed should it be? The legislator should be measured and only regulate what is absolutely necessary to protect the parties and enable this kind of employment to work. I do not plead for a floor of rights for all teleworkers, but would restrict the scope of legislative measures to the specific, sensitive features, like privacy and data protection, health and safety issues or the reimbursement of costs. There is a serious risk that over regulation would hinder the adoption of this form of employment.[47]

[42] *Implementation of the European Framework Agreement on Telework*, Report by the European Social Partners 7.

[43] Bankó *Az atipikus munkajogviszonyok* (n 34) 171.

[44] See on the instruments chosen to implement the FA in the Member States: Commission Staff Working Paper, *Report on the implementation of the European social partners' Framework Agreement on Telework* 49.

[45] Commission Staff Working Paper, *Report on the implementation of the European social partners' Framework Agreement on Telework* 49.

[46] See on this Veneziani, 'The Employment Relationship' (n 2) 114.

[47] Bankó *Az atipikus munkajogviszonyok* (n 34) 171.

Should the law regard telework either as an atypical form of employment or self-employment or possibly as an intermediary form? The regulation can provide beneficial legal environment for a certain legal form, as the FA does by acknowledging telework as an atypical form of employment. This however does not change the fact that if the work is performed without a certain level of personal dependency, it cannot be qualified as an employment relationship.

B. Regulation in Hungary

The evolution of the diverse forms of distance work and their regulation in Hungary is similar to that in many other European states in the sense that homework was regulated early on (in 1967), while telework became subject to statutory regulation in the course of implementation of the FA in 2004. These two forms of distance work are now regulated in the new LC.

After many years of debate as to whether it was necessary to regulate telework in Hungary, the FA provided the final incentive for a regulation.[48] The FA was implemented by the integration of a regulation into the old LC[49] and into the Occupational Safety Act.[50] The reason for implementation through legislation was the general weakness of the social partners and their low representativeness. The social partners were, however, consulted on the proposal of the act in the tripartite 'National Interest Reconciliation Council' (Országos Érdekegyeztető Tanács).

Since teleworkers are regarded as employees, the general rules of the LC applied to them. The FA was basically implemented word for word. Regulating telework was seen as an employment policy measure that would drive employment.[51] The legislation has been based on the same idea as the FA, namely that telework is performed in the context of dependent employment. The qualification of the relationship of a teleworker was based on the actual circumstances of the work performed dependent on which the teleworker could be qualified as either an employee or a self-employed.[52]

The regulation of telework in the new LC is significantly shorter than that in the old LC. The legislator's goal in the adoption of the rules on atypical employment was to provide the greates possible freedom to the parties by restricting the regulations on the necessary rules in order to protect the employees' rights and public interests.[53] The reduction in length is also the consequence of an intended simplification of the rules and the involvement of certain general rules in the new LC regarding, for example, the privacy protection of workers.

[48] Kiss, *Munkajog* (n 6) 118 and Bankó, 'Az atipikus munkajogviszonyok' (n 34) 80, 171.
[49] Chapter X/A. on telework of the old Labour Code.
[50] Act No XCIII of 1993 on Occupational Safety.
[51] Bankó, *Az atipikus munkajogviszonyok* (n 34) 80.
[52] ibid 172–173.
[53] The minister's explanatory statement for the Labour Code, General Explanation, 7.14.

V. Telework as Employment Relationship—Protection or Segmentation?

Teleworkers have by definition less personal dependency than normal workers and this makes it possible for this kind of job to be performed in the context of different relationships. The qualification of telework as employment, self-employment or an intermediary category entails the same risks as other blurring forms, in particular as regards the complexity of the identification of appropriate criteria to characterise the employment relationship. The criteria commonly used in labour law to distinguish self-employed individuals from employees should be applied to teleworkers as well. As these criteria are controversial and hotly debated in most legal systems, the labelling of telework is extremely difficult. The great diversity in the specific forms of telework makes it even more difficult to set down general statements regarding the qualification of the relationships in which telework is performed. Telework can take on many different forms depending on whether the employee can define independently his workplace and working time. The level and intensity of control and instructions given are also factors which help define the relationship. At the one end of the spectrum are those workers, whose working place and—at least to a certain extent—also working time is co-determined by their employer. At the other end are crowdworkers, who usually have the least personal dependency.

It is crucial to notice the special nature of subordination and personal dependency regarding telework. As telework is often the domain of highly skilled employees, the scope of the managerial prerogatives is necessarily limited to the assignment of work and determining deadlines for delivery. The supervisors usually do not possess the skills and expertise necessary to instruct the way of work should be performed, as teleworkers outclass their managers as regards technical and professional know-how.[54] This fact has led in the case of telework to the 'depersonalisation of subordination' limiting the employer's power of command.[55]

The FA expressly covers only those teleworkers who carry out their work in the framework of an employment contract/relationship. The exclusivity of the FA in terms of personal scope entails the usual risk, namely the danger that it will produce a dual labour market, enhance the segmentation of teleworkers, and thus exclude a great proportion of individuals from the protection afforded by the beneficial regulation. The FA and the national measures exclude self-employed persons from the scope of labour law rules. This does not change the fact—and probably even intensifies the problem—that a high proportion of teleworkers perform their job as self-employed persons. The Commission emphasised the need

[54] See Veneziani, 'The Employment Relationship' (n 2) 120–121.
[55] ibid 126.

to take appropriate measures to prevent any abuse of self-employment in relation to telework.[56]

The Hungarian legislation continues to adopt the classical binary typology of work performance, which allows for work to be performed in a relationship of dependency or autonomously, without accepting the profound transformation of the way work has been performed in the labour market in the last couple of decades and introducing an intermediary category.[57] The binary system regarding the scope of labour law does not recognise the intermediary category of persons performing work similar to the employees. The first draft of the new LC contained a definition and specific rules on this third category, but it was quickly removed from the later drafts mainly due to the allied opposition of the social partners to this proposal. The employers feared the increased burdens and unions assumed that this new category would weaken the existing protection by drawing employees into this category.[58]

Consequently, telework in Hungary can be performed either within the framework of employment or that of self-employment. However, the provisions of the Labour Code on telework only apply to those who perform their tasks in the context of an employment relationship. The situation regarding qualification of an employment relationship is worsened by the lack of definition of self-employment.[59] In Hungary, the employment relationship is the focus of attention and the qualification of a particular type of work is determined by the content of the relationship and the degree of personal dependency on the employer.[60] The nature and content of work, but also the way the work is performed should play a significant role in the determination of the legal status of the person performing the work.

VI. The Definition of Telework

A. Broad Definition—Blurring Borders

The definition of telework is the key point in the regulation, as it determines the kind of employment covered by or excluded from the scope of the regulation.

[56] Commission Staff Working Paper, *Report on the implementation of the European social partners' Framework Agreement on Telework*, 37.

[57] See to this Veneziani, 'The Employment Relationship' (n 2) 108–113.

[58] G Kiss, 'A munkavállalóhoz hasonló jogállású személy problematikája az Európai Unióban és e jogállás szabályozásának hiánya a Munka Törvénykönyvében', (2013) Jogtudományi Közlöny 13. and T Gyulavári, 'A bridge too far? The Hungarian regulation of economically dependent work', (2014) *Hungarian Labour Law E-journal* 82, 95–98.

[59] Gyulavári, 'A bridge too far? The Hungarian regulation of economically dependent work' (n 58) 82, 91–92.

[60] T Prugberger and G Kenderes, 'Az atipikus munkaviszonyok a munkaerő-kölcsönzés és a távmunkavégzés tükrében', (2009) II *Miskolci Jogi Szemle* 49.

Taking a broad definition of telework has the clear advantage that certain new forms of employment can fall within the definition of telework.

The evolution of telework was shaped by the uncertainties surrounding its definition. This connects with the diverse forms of employment which fall within this term. The birthplace of telework, the USA, specifies only one differentia specifica of telework, namely that the employee performs the duties and responsibilities 'from an approved worksite other than the location from which the employee would otherwise work.'[61]

In my opinion, two key factors can help define employment as telework, namely the distant workplace and the use of ICT tools. The latter is only necessary if one wishes to separate telework from homework. The Commission also recognised these two factors as crucial in the qualification of telework.[62] Defining these two factors makes it possible, firstly, to cover all forms of employment, where work is performed at a distance (from home, mobile and in telework centres) and, secondly, to include some of the new, upcoming forms of distance work.[63] One should be cautious about including other criteria into the definition of telework, because any further condition will necessarily restrict the range of employment that can fall within this term.

Regarding the place where teleworkers perform their activities, the old LC specified that the worker was usually freely to choose it, whereas the new LC only specifies that the place needs to be distant from the employer's premise.[64] Consequently, the parties can agree that the worker performs the activity in his home, or a place chosen by him or even in a place determined by the employer (eg in a telecottage). The parties are obliged—as in case of all employment—to specify the working place in the written employment contract. This rule should provide a guarantee for the worker that the employer cannot change the place of work unilaterally.

Both the first and the recent Hungarian definitions of telework require that the completed work is delivered electronically.[65] The reason for this criterion in the definition was to make the distinction between homework and telework easier.[66] It is namely conceivable to perform certain activities that can be described as performance-related within the frame of homework. However, with telework, the completed work needs to be transmitted by means of an electronic device. In my opinion, the adoption of this condition unnecessarily restricts the scope of telework, as it is quite possible for the completed work not to be delivered directly to

[61] Telework Enhancement Act of 2010, § 6501. Definition available at www.gpo.gov/fdsys/pkg/PLAW-111publ292/pdf/PLAW-111publ292.pdf.

[62] Commission Staff Working Paper, *Report on the implementation of the European social partners' Framework Agreement on Telework* 33.

[63] See also ibid 34.

[64] Berke and Kiss, *Kommentár a Munka Törvénykönyvéhez* (n 5) 494.

[65] § 196 (1) of the new LC.

[66] Berke and Kiss, *Kommentár a Munka Törvénykönyvéhez* (n 5) 495.

the employer but to be uploaded into a cloud.[67] However, a broad interpretation of the wording can resolve this issue if electronic transmission can involve uploading to the net or storing data in a pen drive.

Further significant challenge to the definition of telework resides in its relation to homework. Homework shows certain distinctive features, as it covers usually simple manual work carried out by low-skilled people and paid by piece. However, the similarities between the two kinds of employment are also obvious, mainly distance working, self-determined working time and reduced personal dependency from the employer. The common features can give rise to a common regulation. There are also certain overlapping activities as for example offline work with a computer can be qualified as homework.[68]

Both the old and the new LC require that the parties agree in the written employment contract on the fact that the work is telework. This rule should guarantee that telework is performed voluntarily and any change to the relevant conditions of work needs the agreement of the parties.

B. Alternating Telework—The Future of (Tele)Work

I am firmly convinced that alternating telework is the future common form of work performance. The situation where the worker performs his work on some days away from the employer's premises and, on other days, is expected to work from the employer's premises is quite common.[69] Alternating telework combines many advantages of telework and typical work and can reduce certain shortcomings of telework, such as the isolation of the worker, the possible lack of feedback and motivation, and can contribute to the greater involvement in the collective representation organisations etc. Surveys have clearly shown that an appropriate level of physical, face-to-face contact is also necessary to maximise the outcome of telework.[70]

There are three ways in which this situation can be regulated. Recently in Hungary, the spread of such working method has just been ignored and is regarded as typical work. It is, however, conceivable for such work to be regulated within the framework of flexible working time and place. The third option is to integrate this kind of employment under the definition of telework.

[67] Same opinion: 'A távmunka növelésének lehetőségei a munkavédelmi szabályozás átalakításával', A Munkáltatók Esélyegyenlőségi Fóruma előterjesztése a Nemzetgazdasági Minisztérium részére, (The possibilities to increase telework by the change of the law on health and safety protection, Proposal of the Employers' Association for Equal Treatment to the Ministry of National Economy) 2015, 3, 4.

[68] Z Bankó and J Ferencz, *Atipikus munkajogviszonyok* (Budapest, Wolters Kluwer Kft, 2015) 87.

[69] F Hohmeister/A Küper, 'Individualvertragliche Arbeitszeitgestaltung bei der alternierenden Telearbeit', *Neue Zeitschrift für Arbeitsrecht*, 1998, 1206.

[70] M Coenen and R A W Kok, 'Workplace flexibility and new product development performance: The role of telework and flexible work schedules', (2014) *European Management Journal* 564, 573. Available at SSRN http://ssrn.com/abstract=2369211.

Particularly controversial is the question, whether distance work requires a certain regularity or continuity. This issue determines, whether the definition of telework covers alternating telework. I perceive this question as crucial for the success of the regulation and the spread of telework. The Commission required that 'at least a considerable proportion of working time' shall be performed at a distance by ICT.[71] This definition would have made it possible to involve not only permanent but also alternating telework into the definition. The wording of the FA, however, is slightly different from this suggestion, as it requires that work is carried out under the mentioned circumstances 'on a regular basis'. This phrasing opened the door for failed interpretation and implementation under national laws. This also happened in Hungary, where it is questionable, whether a worker can be qualified as a teleworker, if he spends only certain working days away from his workplace.[72] The new LC—similar to the old one—requires that the activity is regularly performed in a place distinct from the employer's location.[73] According to certain authors, the regularity of the performance of work is only important in establishing that the worker's activity is recurring and continuous and is, in this respect, similar to typical workers and proves the existence of an employment relationship.[74]

Recently, a Hungarian employer's association suggested including alternating telework in the definition of telework, as in practice this kind of work performance occurs very often and the exclusion of alternating telework from the definition seriously hinders its development. The association suggested that in case of alternating telework the specific rules on telework should only be applied on the days when the worker performs his work in a different place from the employers' location, so alternating telework should bring about the partial application of the special rules.

In my opinion, a major challenge for the future labour law will be to find an appropriate regulation for alternating telework either within the framework of the regulation on telework or on flexible working time.

VII. Rights and Obligations

A. Information or Agreement Obligations?

It is important to determine certain issues on which the employer is obliged to inform the teleworker, which go beyond the general information duty of the

[71] Commission Staff Working Paper, *Report on the implementation of the European social partners' Framework Agreement on Telework* 34.

[72] Bankó, *Az atipikus munkajogviszonyok* (n 34) 162.

[73] § 196 (1) of the new LC.

[74] Berke and Kiss, *Kommentár a Munka Törvénykönyvéhez* (n 5) 494.

employer included in Council Directive 91/533/EEC. The main question in this context is on which issues the parties shall agree and on which questions can the employer unilaterally make a decision and simply inform the worker of the decision.

The FA specifies two main additional information obligations. First, the teleworker should be informed of the organisation unit to which he is attached in order to be able to make contacts with colleagues, enjoy their collective rights, etc. Teleworkers must be informed also of is "his/her immediate superior or other persons to whom she or he can address questions of professional or personal nature, reporting arrangements, etc."[75] The old LC followed narrowly these rules.[76] The new LC states that the employer has to guarantee that the worker can enter the location of the employer to make and keep contact with other workers.[77] It is important to guarantee that the workers receive all information relevant to the performance of their work and also to enable them to make contact with their colleagues, as usually they work isolated, as this can impair their ability to exercise their rights and obligations.[78]

In order to protect privacy and personal data, the new LC obliges the employer to provide information to the teleworker on the forms of the employer's control and on the use of ICTs.

Other issues regarding working time or place and working equipment are subject to the agreement of the parties. The LC does not stipulate any other circumstances on which the parties can or must agree, but it is useful to agree on how the parties keep contact, the person, who will provide the working equipment and on the method of reimbursement of the reasonable and necessary costs of telework. The old LC required the agreement on these issues and in particular the last one which provides a guarantee to the worker. The Commission also suggested that the employer should entirely cover the costs of equipment, installation, maintenance, insurance and telecommunication.[79] The FA requires—at least for alternating telework—that the employer compensates or covers the costs directly caused by the work.[80] Such rule is missing from the regulation.

B. Limited Managerial Prerogative

Teleworkers perform their work with great independence and thus the right of the employers to give instructions to the workers is significantly restricted. The

[75] Clauses 3 and 11 of the FA.
[76] Clause 3 of the FA
[77] § 196 (5) of the new LC.
[78] Berke and Kiss, *Kommentár a Munka Törvénykönyvéhez* (n 5) 496.
[79] Commission Staff Working Paper, *Report on the implementation of the European social partners' Framework Agreement on Telework* 40.
[80] Clause 7 of the FA.

limited managerial prerogative of the employer does not only emerge from the fact that the worker is physically absent from the employer's premise, but is linked to the circumstance that most teleworkers—as highly qualified workers—perform their activity with great autonomy; and they would do it in the same way, even from the employer's location. Therefore, the limitation in the power of employers to give instructions is more the result of the kind of profession, than the distant performance of work.

Regarding the control facilities, the picture is more differentiated, as ICT provides the opportunity for the employer to have thorough control over the activity of the teleworker. Both the old and new LC provide the employer with a greater margin of control. In the absence of agreement between the parties, the employer can unilaterally determine the method of control, but he has to observe the proportionality rule; ie the level of control cannot give rise to unjustified and unreasonable burden on the worker and on other persons using the same place.[81] As the control of teleworkers is a very sensitive issue and can be the source of disputes, it is highly advisable to agree in advance the level and way in which the control is exercised.[82]

The old LC maintained the general rule of the broad managerial prerogative of the employer over teleworkers, but allowed the parties to agree on its limitation. The new LC rightly turned round this principle and, as general rule, provides that the employer's power of discretion is limited to the determination of the work of the workers, although the parties can agree on different rules, ie can, for example, extend the scope of issues on which the employer can give instructions.[83] However, taking into account the special feature of telework and the loose dependency of the workers from their employers, the scope of such differing agreements should be kept narrow.[84]

C. Flexible Working Time—Inflexible Workload

Telework is regarded as a tool which facilitates flexible working arrangements, particularly working time. However, flexibility should be granted to teleworkers only regarding the organisation of work, but not concerning the basic minimum and maximum rules (maximum working time, rest breaks, annual paid holiday, night work, etc).[85] Flexibility should be limited to working time management with parallel observance of the standards.

[81] § 192/G (4) of the old LC and § 197 (4) of the new LC.

[82] Berke and Kiss, *Kommentár a Munka Törvénykönyvéhez* (n 5) 495.

[83] E Kajtár, 'A munkáltatói utasítás helye a 21. század munkajogában', (2014) II *JURA* 214, 221.

[84] Berke and Kiss, *Kommentár a Munka Törvénykönyvéhez* (n 5) 495.

[85] The same opinion represented the Commission, see Commission Staff Working Paper, *Report on the implementation of the European social partners' Framework Agreement on Telework*, 43–44.

The new LC only stipulates that the working time of the teleworker is—in the absence of any differing agreement—unbound. This basically means that workers have the right to decide when they want to perform work and can independently organise their working time. The parties can, however, also specify certain working time. Pursuant to the general rules, the working time is considered as unbound, even if the worker can perform certain part of the work—due to its specific feature—only at a specific time or period.[86] One of the major questions regarding working time is—especially from a health and safety point of view—how to guarantee the observance of the general rules on working time—not only by the employer, but also by the teleworker himself. The new LC provides that in case of unbound working time the statutory provisions on maximum working time, daily break, daily and weekly rest period, overtime, as well as on-call and stand-by duty do not apply.[87] The exclusion of the application of these rules certainly contradicts the FA.

Under the FA, the teleworker has control over his working time. However, this provision cannot exclude the possibility for certain working hours to be determined by the employer, for example to keep contact. The narrow interpretation of the self-determination of working time would exclude alternating telework from the scope of regulation. Complete unbound working time is the less common form anyway, as it is useful to determine when the worker can be contacted by the employer and when he can ask for technical support.[88]

It is a huge challenge for the employer, but also for a possible regulation, to define the quantity of the work which can be performed in the working time and which limitations can be set in order to protect the workers from excessive workload.[89] The old LC required—in line with Clause 9 of the FA—the equal treatment of teleworkers with workers performing the same or similar activities for the employer at the employer's premise or in the absence of such workers with workers in the same branch.[90] The employer had to consider, in the determination of the tasks, the working time of the teleworker, and the nature and the quantity of the work as well as the necessary physical and mental effort required of the workers.

The background idea of this regulation is that instead of sticking to the working time—which is in practice not measurable—the workload of the teleworker should be determined and limited. The comparator test, however, entails the risk of missing comparable employees in typical employment, which is very likely in the case of teleworkers.

[86] § 96 (2) of the new LC.

[87] § 96 (3) of the new LC.

[88] See also the national solutions in *Implementation of the European Framework Agreement on Telework*, Report by the European Social Partners, 17.

[89] Bankó, *Az atipikus munkajogviszonyok* (n 34) 174.

[90] § 192/G (2) of the old LC.

Currently, there is no statutory limit regarding the workload of the teleworker. Coupled with this is the fact that the minimum and maximum standards of working time do not apply to teleworkers, who are, as a result, in a vulnerable situation in terms of overload and long working time.

D. Liability for Damages

The new LC does not contain special rules on the liability of teleworkers and their employer, but the general rules on liability apply to them. The employer is liable to provide compensation to the worker for damages caused in connection with an employment relationship.[91] However, the employer shall be relieved of liability if he is able to prove either that the damage occurred in consequence of unforeseen circumstances beyond his control and it was not reasonable to expect action to be taken to prevent or mitigate the damage; or that the damage was caused solely by the unavoidable conduct of the teleworker. Some authors express concerns since the performance of telework usually falls outside the scope of control of the employer and, therefore, he will be only exceptionally liable for damages incurred by the teleworker.[92] The Hungarian regulation gives employers relief from liability under the mentioned circumstances, which could deprive workers from significant protection. However, the new LC also stipulates that the employer can only be exempted from liability if he has previously fulfilled the health and safety requirements and established the safety of the working place.

Furthermore, breach of privacy and data protection can also give rise to possible damage and the employer has to take appropriate measures to protect the teleworker from risk of damage in this field. If the employer fails to comply with his obligation in this area, he cannot be relieved.

E. Health and Safety

The health and safety protection of teleworkers is a difficult area to regulate. The conflict lies in the desire to protect teleworkers against risks while limiting the degree of control.

Teleworkers are certainly increasingly exposed to psycho-social risks due to their social isolation and also partly due to the high level of self-determination of the work organisation that can lead to heavy workload on certain days. The risk of musculo-skeletal disorders is also higher in the case of teleworkers due to the

[91] § 166 of the new Labour Code.

[92] I Horváth and T Szabó, *Munkajogi Navigátor—Az új Munka Törvénykönyve a gyakorlatban*, (Kaposvár, Adónet Zrt. 2012) 386.

typical sitting work performance, even if it is usually difficult to prove the direct causality between work and disease.[93]

The FA adopted the European Commission's proposal and puts the employer clearly in a position of responsibility for the health and safety of the teleworker. However, employers can discharge their obligation if they inform the worker of the company's policy on health and safety and on the requirements relating to the use of visual display units and verify that the worker applies these provisions correctly.[94] On the other hand, the worker is obliged to observe the rules and follow the instructions regarding health and safety as well as provide access to safety officers and maintenance personnel.[95]

In Hungary, the respective Act on Occupational Safety[96] provides detailed regulation on occupational health and safety issues. The regulation is even stricter than the FA requirements. Workers performing distance work enjoy full protection, as the Act has a broad personal scope covering all persons who perform work within the framework of an 'organised employment', which means every form of dependent work. Further, the statute gives a very broad definition of working place, which covers all open or closed places, where workers stay for the purpose of or in the context of work performance, even if it is a coffee shop or a metro train. Consequently, most provisions of the statute shall be applied to teleworkers.

The Act on Occupational Safety includes some special provision for teleworkers.[97] It requires that the employer control the working tools provided by the employee in advance. The place of work has to be qualified by the employer in advance as appropriate for work and the employee may change the working conditions, which are relevant for health and safety only with the prior permission of the employer.[98] This obligation significantly restricts the freedom of the teleworker to choose or change his actual place of work.[99] In case the worker changes the place of work unilaterally, the employer can probably be relieved from the liability in case of injury.

The statute specifies that the employer may regularly control the employee to make sure that the working conditions meet the requirements and that workers know and observe the rules. The employer has the right to enter the property, which is serving as a place of work to perform the health and safety checks, ie

93 See in detail on the Hungarian situation E Kovács, 'Chapter 6—Occupational Health and Safety in Hungary: Changes in the Name of Competitiveness?', in E Ales (ed) *Health and Safety at Work, European and Comparative Perspective* (The Netherlands, Kluwer Law International, 2013) 151, 160.

94 Clause 8 of the Framework Agreement.

95 Commission Staff Working Paper, *Report on the implementation of the European social partners' Framework Agreement on Telework* 42.

96 Act Nr. XCIII of 1993 on Occupational Safety.

97 Chapter VII/A. Differing occupational safety rules for telework, section 86/A. Act XCIII of 1993 on Occupational Safety.

98 § 86/A (3) of the Act on Occupational Safety.

99 Berke and Kiss, *Kommentár a Munka Törvénykönyvéhez* (n 5) 497.

install the tools, assess the risks, control or examine the circumstances of an accident. These rules put the employers in a difficult position, as they obviously cannot freely change, re-organise or re-built the workplace, particularly, if it is the home of the worker.

Recently, a Hungarian employer's association provided a proposal to loosen the mentioned rules.[100] According to the proposal, the mentioned rules prevent the employers from using this kind of employment. They argued that the employers usually do not have appropriate access to the workplace and, thus, it is against common sense to oblige them to guarantee the health and safety of the teleworker, particularly to assess the risks and take preventive steps to avoid danger and accidents. It is certainly the case that the working place of the teleworker is not under the control of the employer, as it is in the case of normal employees. However, for this reason, the liability of the employer for risks emerging from the work of the teleworker is limited and the worker has increased responsibility for his own health and safety.

F. Privacy and Data Protection

The FA clearly delegates the responsibility for data protection to the employer. However, it also provides ways in which this responsibility can be loosened up especially by setting internal rules and limits to the use of ICT by the worker coupled with appropriate sanctions in case of non-compliance.[101]

Teleworkers are in an extremely vulnerable position if they are monitored in the working place which happens to be their home. The new LC contains general rules on privacy protection of all employees, which also apply to teleworkers.[102] It states that the personality rights of the worker can only be limited, if the restriction is absolutely necessary for a reason directly connected to the goal of the employment relationship, provided that the limitation is proportionate to the achievement of the goal. It is worth noting that until now there has been little case law on the proportionality test, which makes it difficult to interpret it in practice. The employer is obliged to inform the employee of the method, criteria and expected duration of such limitation.[103]

The control of the teleworkers via ICT tools is one of the most sensitive issues of telework, as the employer can get access to the worker's private data of; therefore, the crucial question is how to control teleworkers without violating their privacy. The other major concern is that teleworkers, in most cases, perform the work

[100] 'A távmunka növelésének lehetőségei a munkavédelmi szabályozás átalakításával', A Munkáltatók Esélyegyenlőségi Fóruma előterjesztése a Nemzetgazdasági Minisztérium részére, (The possibilities to increase telework by the change of the law on health and safety protection, Proposal of the Employers' Association for Equal Treatment to the Ministry of National Economy) 9.7.2015.

[101] Clause 5 of the Framework Agreement.

[102] §§ 9–11 of the new LC.

[103] § 9 (2) of the new LC.

in their home and so the physical control necessarily takes place in their home. The new LC states in general, that the employer may only control the behaviour of the worker related to his employment relationship. The control of the worker and the tools and methods used cannot bring about the violation of human dignity, but have to be necessary and proportionate.[104] The private life of the worker must not be controlled.[105] Furthermore, it is important that, in line with Directive 90/270/EEC on visual display units, the employer is obliged to inform the worker in advance on the use of the technical devices controlling him.[106] The general framework of data protection is also guaranteed by a separate statute.[107]

In line with the FA, the employer may limit the activities that the workers are allowed to perform by ICT tools and the employer is entitled to exercise control, whether or not the worker observes this limitation or prohibition.[108] To protect the privacy of teleworkers both the old and new LC lay down that the employer is not allowed to access and get an insight into data not related to the work stored in the computer of the teleworkers.[109]

The new LC also states in general that the employer may only communicate facts, data or opinion relating to the worker to third parties based on a statutory regulation or the approval of the worker.[110]

The regulation of privacy and data protection in Hungary complies with the required standards. In the absence of sufficient case law on the topic, there are concerns as to the correct application of the rules. Particularly alarming, however, is the elimination of the position of the Ombudsman for Data Protection in 2011 (after 16 years of existence) and its replacement by a public authority, which reflects the attitude of the State to privacy and data protection.

G. Collective Representation

It is remarkable and proves the weakness of the social partners and of the collective labour law system as a whole that in certain Eastern European states (Czech Republic, Hungary, Poland), the social partners wished to implement the FA by way of regulation into the Labour Code.[111]

The difficulty regarding the collective representation of teleworkers lies not in the legal guarantee of their rights, but in the practical realisation of them, ie how

[104] Berke and Kiss, *Kommentár a munka törvénykönyvéhez* (n 5) 51.

[105] § 11 (1) of the new LC.

[106] § 11 (2) of the new LC.

[107] Act CXII of 2011 on the right to information self-determination and the freedom of information, [2011. évi CXII. törvény az információs önrendelkezési jogról és az információszabadságról].

[108] § 192/G (3) and (6) of the old LC and § 197 (2) of the new LC.

[109] § 197 (3) of the new LC.

[110] § 10 (2) of the new LC.

[111] *Implementation of the European Framework Agreement on Telework*, Report by the European Social Partners 12–13.

trade unions and other collective organisations can reach and engage teleworkers. Teleworkers have the same status as other workers in terms of collective representation, trade unions, right to conclude a collective agreement or create a works council, so teleworkers have to be counted regarding these institutions as typical employees.[112]

In Hungary, the real problem is that collective organisations and collective agreements in general do not play an important role in the regulation of employment relationship.[113] Unions are weak, the unionisation rate is low (approx 10 per cent)[114] and the dominant level of bargaining is the enterprise level. Only a few branch or industry-wide collective agreements have been concluded.[115] There is no union specialised for teleworkers and there is no data available to indicate whether the established unions would expressly represent the interests of these workers. Teleworkers as employees are generally covered by collective agreements, but the author has found neither special collective agreements directed to teleworkers, nor agreements which expressly mention this group.[116]

Hungarian works councils have limited consultation rights regarding the introduction of telework for a 'bigger group of employees',[117] as the Labour Code states.[118] The employer has to inform the works council of the planned measure 15 days prior to the introduction of telework and consult with it. In some other Member States, like Germany or Austria, works councils play a more significant role in the introduction and implementation of telework.[119]

H. Full Coverage in the Social Security System

Teleworkers—and homeworkers as well—are completely covered by the general social security protection, if they perform the activity in an employment relationship or as self-employed.

[112] Berke and Kiss, *Kommentár a Munka Törvénykönyvéhez* (n 5) 496 and Clause 11 of the Framework Agreement.

[113] See in more detail E Kovács, 'Hungarian Unions: How Representative? How Effective?', *Comparative Labor Law and Policy Journal*, 2011 891–914; see http://papers.ssrn.com/sol3/papers.cfm?abstract_id=1908427.

[114] ibid 903.

[115] ibid 891–914.

[116] On the first collective agreement on teleworkers in Austria see N Melzer-Azodanloo, 'Erster Kollektivvertrag für Tele-Arbeit', *Arbeits- und SozialrechtsKartei*, 1997 349; in Germany, 'Tarifvertrag über Telearbeit bei der Deutschen Telekom AG/T-Mobil', *Neue Zeitschrift für Arbeitsrecht*, 1998 1214 and Hohmeister/Küper, 'Individualvertragliche Arbeitszeitgestaltung bei der alternierenden Telearbeit' (n 69) 1206 ff.

[117] The term 'bigger group of employees' cannot be uniformly defined; it depends inter alia on the size and organisation of the employer; see Berke and Kiss, *Kommentár a Munka Törvénykönyvéhez* (n 5) 597.

[118] § 264 (2) f) of the new LC.

[119] On the German situation see T Schmechel, 'Die Rolle des Betriebsrats bei der Einführung und Durchführung von Telearbeit', *Neue Zeitschrift für Arbeitsrecht*, 2004 237; on the Austrian situation in detail, see N Melzer-Azodanloo, *Tele-Arbeitsrecht*, (Linde Verlag, Wien, 2001) 124 ff.

The Hungarian social security system has maintained certain features from the socialist system where social insurance was based on citizenship. Article 5 of the respective statute[120] specifies a long list of assured persons including nearly everybody performing work in whatever legal form. People in all kinds of typical and atypical employment are insured without any limit of a minimum income, so even part-time or homeworkers with a very small working time and low income are fully insured and enjoy protection. Even those falling under protection, who do not work as registered self-employed persons, but based on a contract of service or a contract for services, if their income reach 30 per cent of the minimum wage.[121]

Self-employed persons are fully insured, but have to pay social security and pension contributions themselves from their income. The bottom line for the calculation of pension contribution is the statutory monthly minimum wage and regarding the social security contributions one and the half of that.[122] Self-employed persons have to pay regularly these contributions, even if their income do not reach the minimum wage.

VIII. Closing Remarks

Distance work is the work of the future. I regard in particular alternating telework as an essential form of future work, which should be acknowledged and increasingly promoted.

Telework is a flowing term covering several different forms of work performance. This fact challenges the legislators to provide an appropriate protection and maintain the freedom of the contracting parties at the same time. A modern regulatory framework should provide a broad definition with basic rules focusing on the crucial points. Key issues are the determination of the status of teleworkers and the regulation of working time, privacy and data protection, as well as health and safety. In practice, numerous issues remain unsolved, due, in particular, to the sparse regulation and the missing case law.

The regulation of telework in Hungary has been aligned to the detailed rules of the European Framework Agreement on Telework. Although the comprehensive rules may provide (overall) protection to the teleworkers, they can also increase the segmentation of the labour market[123] and create an obstacle to employers who wish to opt for this kind of employment.

[120] Act LXXX of 1997 on the assured persons of the social security and private pension, as well as on the coverage of these services [1997. évi LXXX. törvény a társadalombiztosítás ellátásaira és a magánnyugdíjra jogosultakról, valamint e szolgáltatások fedezetéről].

[121] § 5 (1) g) of the Act LXXX of 1997.

[122] § 10 (1) a) and § 29 of the Act LXXX of 1997.

[123] On the pros and cons of equal treatment of atypical workers see A Davies, 'Regulating atypical work: beyond quality', in N Countouris and M Freedland (eds), *Resocialising Europe in a Time of Crisis*, (Cambridge University Press, 2013) 230–49.

By placing the Hungarian law on teleworkers within the concept of core and contingent work, we notice a certain duality between the legal framework and the practice. The law certainly considers teleworkers as part of the core workforce, as they are employees and the general rules of LC apply to them. However, this legal classification cannot hide the fact that teleworkers—in some respect—are at the periphery of the workforce and share certain features with contingent workers. The little personal dependency of the teleworkers and their absent place of work enhance the externality of these persons. The geographical distance from the employer's premises brings about negative side effects, such as remoteness from colleagues and the collective organisations of workers, which can lead to isolation and the inappropriate representation of their interests. This kind of work performance entails higher risks regarding privacy protection and health and safety. Nevertheless, based on the overall estimation of the current Hungarian situation, I come to the conclusion that teleworkers belong to the core workforce, mainly because they are recognised as employees and fall under the scope of the LC. Taken as a whole, the inclusion of teleworkers into the LC outweighs the special features of their relationship.

8

Re-structuring the Standard Employment Relationship: Italy and the Increasing Protection Contract

MAURIZIO DEL CONTE

I. Premise

There has been much discussion among academics and in the media about the transformation of the work model, which passed in a few decades from a Fordist-style to 'lean production', and more recently has been put to the test by the Internet,[1] which thanks to its mobile applications, is said to have subverted the paradigm of the separation of production means between capital and labour.[2] In this perspective, the archetype of permanent subordinate jobs, by now evidently obsolescent, is drawing close to its definitive demise. However, in the last few years a parallel debate has arisen on the evils of dualism in the job market, the fact that the latter brings with it an unjust and inefficient contrast between 'insiders' and 'outsiders', ie between 'typical' stable and protected workers on one side and 'atypical' unprotected workers on the other.[3] The term precariousness has come to describe the ugly situation of the rising numbers of workers with no fixed jobs, normally on low incomes and without any concrete prospects of accessing the good part of the market, where permanent subordinate employment is on

[1] See E Brynjolfsson and A Mcafee, *The Second Machine Age* (New York, WW Norton & Company, 2014); CB Frey and MA Osborne, *The Future of Employment: How susceptible are jobs to computerisation?* (Oxford Martin School, 2013). See also the report of the Boston Consulting Group, *The Mobile Revolution. How Mobile Technologies Drive a Trillion Dollar Impact*, 2015. Lately, the mediatic debate has been revamped by The Economist, 'Workers on tap, The rise of the on-demand economy poses difficult questions for workers, companies and politicians', 3 January 2015.

[2] F Seghezzi, *Le grandi trasformazioni del lavoro, un tentativo di periodizzazione. Appunti per una ricerca*, Working Paper ADAPT, 2015, no 169.

[3] For a 'dual' job market we sum it up here briefly as one offering unequal terms of work and income to workers, together with different possibilities of accessing social security and job security. For a review of the international literature on the subject of job market segmentation, see J Davidsson and M Naczyk, *The Ins and Outs of Dualization: a Literature Review* (Oxford, Department of Social Policy and Social Work, 2009).

offer, with an accompanying treasure chest of rules, regulations and guarantees. How can such opposite visions of employment make for coherence, held up both as a virtuous model to emulate and as a malaise to be phased out? And caught between this contrast in interpretations, what direction has the Italian legislation taken, which over the last twenty years in particular has repeatedly put hand to the Labour Law with reforms carried out by alternately centre-right and centre-left governments, which both declared a common intent to increase employment levels, reduce dualism and improve job quality?

To try to understand the present scenario, this paper will begin its investigations back with the foundations of Italian Labour Law, highlighting the way it developed on the social model of employment. It will be seen how one of the basic suppositions of the entire protective legislation was protection against illegal firing, backed by the general ruling—for bigger companies—of reinstatement in the case of unfair dismissal. The most meaningful passages of the criticism against the real stability of labour relations will be identified, and an attempt will be made to put the light on the role of the new directions taken by European social policies over the last fifteen years. The last part will put forward an interpretation of the new course of Labour Law set in motion by the Jobs Act, the reform desired by the centre-left backed Renzi Government. The result is that it has given a strong stimulus to companies to adopt open-end contracts for subordinate work, by means of three levers: a) reducing social security costs; b) introducing a subordinate work contract subject to increasing protection, together with sure costs for unfair dismissal and limiting reinstatement protection to last resort; c) extending the legislation of subordinate work to irregular forms of collaboration offered by the employer. An explanation will be given as to why this focus back on subordinate work is not born of nostalgia, but on the contrary promotes the evolution of more efficient organisational models to answer the transformation of productivity caused by technological evolution. Not that it must lead to a marginalisation of self-employment but on the contrary, enhance it, partly by means of a specific support intervention, announced several times but as yet not realised. Finally, the paper will conclude with an attempt to reconstruct a new balance between core and contingent work and offer an explanation of how this equilibrium can contribute to giving equity and efficiency to the Italian job market in the prospect of worldwide economic competition.

II. The Central Position of Subordinate Permanent Jobs at the Origins of Italian Labour Law

As mentioned above, with its complex interweaving of different levels of normative sources and collective bargaining, Italian Labour Law was historically constructed around the archetype of the permanent subordinate work contract.

The condition of subordination to the directive power of the employer/entrepreneur is the theoretical basis of Labour Law legislation, which is distanced in some parts from the general principles of private law in matters of contracts on the presupposition of an asymmetry of powers between the parties 'in which power or autonomy is attributed to only one of the parties' and is 'characterized by a disvalue which permanently weighs on the other party'.[4] The central importance of the subordinate work contract was consecrated in the 1942 Civil Code which in Article 2094 defines subordinate workers those who constrict themselves via compensation to collaborate in a company, by means of their intellectual or manual work, in the employ or under the direction of the entrepreneur.

From this definition onwards, the work of the legislators and the collective parties was for decades dedicated to strengthening the contractual position of weak, subordinate workers in their relations with their entrepreneurial counterparties. A relation which was desired to be solely bilateral per force, as emerges from Law 1369 (1960), which decreed that any form of work with a third party contemplated in the contract between entrepreneur and worker was forbidden and liable to the most serious of sanctions, ie the application of the Penal Code. As for the effects on contracts, ownership of the contract was transferred *ope iudicis* from the intervening third party to the company using *de facto* the worker's services.

But the most important step towards affirming the stability of the job as a condition for, and for the effectiveness of, the whole legislation protecting the worker was the combination of regulations limiting dismissal—firstly partially realised by the collective autonomy by means of sectorial interconfederal agreements and then universally recognised by Law No 604 (1966) and Article 18 of the 1970 Law No 300, more familiarly known as the 'Statute of Workers' Rights', which added the regulation decreeing in companies staffed by more than fifteen, the reinstatement of workers held to have been unfairly fired, without either just cause or justified motive. The control over reinstatement, allowing the entrepreneur no word in the destiny of the contract, has been lived over time as the necessary premise

[4] See M Pedrazzoli, *Democrazia industriale e subordinazione* (Giuffrè, Milano, 1985) 103. On the origins of Italian Labour Law see L Barassi, *Il contratto di lavoro nel diritto positivo italiano*, (Milano, Società editrice libraria, 1901) which identifies the nucleus of subordination in the concept of hetero (other) direction, or the employer's power to modify unilaterally the contract's content (directive power). The need to give the right weight to the 'personal implication' of the worker in the productive organisation by the employer is highlighted by F Santoro Passarelli, *Nozioni di diritto del lavoro* (Napoli, 1944). Particular emphasis on corporate organisation as employer specification of the duties inherent in employment is given by GF Mancini, *La responsabilità contrattuale del prestatore di lavoro* (Giuffrè, Milano, 1957) who holds that the results of organisation depend on the employer and he/she is therefore extraneous to the duty, which is up to the worker. For L Mengoni, 'Il contratto di lavoro nel diritto italiano', in AaVv, *Il contratto di lavoro nel diritto dei paesi membri della C.E.C.A.* (Milano, Giuffrè, 1965) 436, the directive power is to be found in the 'global organisation of the service' given the 'functional link of the service of each employee with his/her colleagues' while for M Persiani, *Contratto di lavoro e organizzazione* (Padova, Cedam,1966), the basic function of a subordinate work contract is organisation. The employer uses the collaboration of the worker to satisfy the interests of labour organisation and, therefore, production.

for additional controls over other subordinate work contracts.[5] Therefore, the stability of employment relations guaranteed by effective tutelage against unjust firings has contributed towards strengthening, in Italian legislation, the tendency to construct the whole protective branch of Labour Law around the figure of the subordinate worker on a permanent contract. It is no coincidence that the legislation against unfair firing started off what in the literature has been called the 'expansive tendency of Labour Law', which has been more widely applied by virtue of a more inclusive interpretation of the subordinate work contract as defined by Article 2094 of the Civil Code.

Certainly favoured by the prevailing model of productive organisation, permanent subordinate work seemed destined to dominate over all other forms of work, with the consequent marginalisation of self-employment. It was above all a political phenomenon, in that while being widespread in the Italian productive fabric, self-employment had actually been forgotten by both legislators and trade unions. In this moment of history and cultural perspective, all forms of contract distancing from the archetype of the bilateral company-worker relationship based on a permanent subordinate work contract was seen not only as residual but even pathological, surrounded by suspicions of it eluding the regulatory body of Labour Law and, therefore, treated with disapproval by the legal system.

III. The Transformation of the Productive Systems and the Spread of Consultancy Work

Already in the 1970s, however, the progressive transformation of productive systems had caused a gradual appearance of ways of collaborating with companies, which, in spite of being very different from the standard prototype of subordinate work, contributed to meeting the interests of the modern company. The gradual appearance of forms of self-employment leading to an integration between services given and corporate organisation so as to weaken subjection to the employer's power, had brought about a crisis in the traditional distinction between self-employment and subordinate work and the steady affirmation of a

[5] For a reconstruction of the system offering protection against unfair dismissal see M Napoli, *La stabilità reale del rapporto di lavoro* (Milano, F Angeli, 1980). The same author confirmed the importance of reinstatement protection in cases of unfair dismissal in his article 'Elogio della stabilità', in *Quaderni di diritto del lavoro e delle relazioni industriali* (2002) 26 (1) 9. A different stand is taken by P Ichino, 'La riforma dei licenziamenti e i diritti fondamentali dei lavoratori', in L Nogler and L Corazza (eds) *Risistemare il diritto del lavoro. Liber amicorum Marcello Pedrazzoli* (Milano, F Angeli, 2012) 792, who notes the disastrous effects of protected reinstatement on the job market, recalling also the theory of property vs liability rules introduced by G Calabresi and AD Melamed, 'Property Rules, Liability Rules, and Inalienability: One View of the Cathedral' in *Harvard Law Review* (1972), 85(6), 1089–1128.

new category of consultancies, which take on board those who collaborate with companies in a 'prevalently personal' activity (Civil Code, Article 2222), but do not enjoy the same tutelage as subordinate workers.

Though in a legislative ruling about procedural profiles, an indirect normative recognition of these models of collaboration came with Law No 533 (1973), which extended the application of court hearings also to controversies about 'relations with agencies, sales representatives and other relations of collaboration which result in a continuous and coordinated service given, even though not subordinate'. Only towards the mid-1990s, partly because of the increasing resort to forms of consultancies, the Law provided a specific social security tutelage by setting up a specific and separate branch of the social security administration (Article 2, par 26–31, Law No 223/1995).

The flight from the standard work model in Italy became a flight from subordinate work to self-employment in a wide variety of forms. Differently from in other European countries, the quota of non-standard subordinate work, particularly fixed-term, via agencies or part-time, was relatively low, while the number of consultancy contracts rose. As has been recently noted, Italy is the country of self-employment. Indeed, there are today around 6.3 million self-employed, 23 per cent of the total workforce, almost 10 per cent more than in France and Germany (15 per cent). Some are entrepreneurs, but most of them are self-employed without dependent workers. Many of them would most likely be employees in any other European State. Most of the consultants have project contracts (502,000) or are company administrators or auditors (506,000). The two figures are very different for average age and earning power: young and on a low income, the consultant-workers; old and well-paid, the administrators.[6]

Overall, the dualism of the Italian market can be said to be perceived above all in the dichotomy between subordinate work and self-employed consultancies. Therefore, from the D Lgs (Legislative Decree) No 276/2003 (the 'Biagi Law'), Italian legislators have sought above all to stem the spread of consultancies, establish more precise limits and above all force companies using consultancy collaborations to declare their real contents, with the aim of bringing to light—and repress—slippery cases in the field of subordinate work.

The most significant point in this legislative strategy was the introduction, via Article 61 ff of the Biagi Law, of 'project work' ('lavoro a progetto'). Deliberately recalling the co-ordinated and continuous collaboration in Article 409 of the Code of Civil Procedure, the Biagi Law built up the 'lavoro a progetto' as a real standard contract for a typical job, equipping it with a specific legislation. The norm provides for project workers to enjoy a minimum tutelage, and in particular, remuneration must be in proportion to the quantity and quality of the work carried out. Given the particular nature of the service and the contract

[6] M Leonardi, 'Cosa succede con la fine di collaboratori e finte partite Iva', in *Lavoce.info*, 24 febbraio 2015, www.lavoce.info/archives/33308/succede-collaboratori-finte-partite-iva.

regulating it, it cannot be under the minimum payment established for each sector by the collective contracts jointly signed by the most representative trade unions and employers' organisations. The project worker has the right to be acknowledged as the author of what he has invented at work; pregnancy, illness and injury do not end the contract; it is suspended, without remuneration, with the understanding that in the case of illness or injury, the suspension of the contract does not mean it being extended. It ends on the due date, while in the case of pregnancy, the contract is extended for another 180 days; the norms of safety and hygiene of the workplace are applicable, as well as the protection standards against work injuries and occupational illnesses.

Nevertheless, it is easy to note how the contractual protection set up by the Biagi Law for project workers was fragile, and certainly not able to discourage entrepreneurs from misusing it in their search for ways of evading subordinate work costs. The real—if not the only—anti-evasion instrument contained in the 'lavoro a progetto' legislation lay, as we have mentioned above, in the fact that employers were obliged to put down in the contract an analytic description of the forms of co-ordination and times of the employment, thus allowing judges to verify concretely the presence of elements of autonomy, and in their absence reclassify the contract as subordinate employment.

IV. The Monti Government and the Role of the European Institutions in the Job Market Reform

Between late 2011 and spring 2012, during a very serious sovereign debt crisis, the government headed by Mario Monti pushed through a series of structural reforms in an attempt to relaunch a competitive Italian productive system, and above all to regain the confidence of Europe's political and financial powers. In this scenario, one of the pressing structural reforms was that of the job market, going well beyond protection for unfair dismissal, particularly in cases where it was due to economic reasons. At the same time, workers had to have the guarantee of a universal instrument supporting pay for involuntary unemployment, until then inexistent in Italy, though present in most European countries. In other terms, it was the case of starting off in Italy a path leading towards the model of flexicurity, which had been taken as the reference point for reforms in the job market in EU member countries.

It needs to be recalled that at the beginning of the twenty-first century, the EU's social policy took a fairly radical turn in comparison to the previous phases in which it had concentrated on trying to bring about a generalised increase in worker protection. From the year of the Lisbon strategy (2000), the main objective of the EU has been to make Europe's labour market more flexible, in order to bolster both employment levels and productivity and aim at 'good employment', ie a type of employment that generates higher added-value to offer greater competition on the global market.[7]

At the close of 2006, before the post-2008 financial crisis economic downturn and slump, the European Commission launched its new political manifesto on social policy in a Green Paper entitled 'Modernising labour law to meet the challenges of the 21st century'.

The declared objective of the Paper was to promote a public debate in the EU to reflect on the way to modify Labour Law so as to uphold the objectives of the Lisbon strategy, namely, to generate sustainable growth with more and better jobs. From that perspective, the Green Paper maintained that Europe's labour markets would have to meet the challenge by combining greater flexibility with maximising security for all.

Denouncing the risk of a two-track labour market with, on one hand, workers on permanent contracts and on the other the 'excluded', in particular the jobless, those outside the labour market and those with precarious or informal jobs, the Commission immediately asked Member States to evaluate and possibly review the level of flexibility in standard contracts, for terms of notice, costs and procedures for individual or collective dismissals or the definition of unfair dismissal.

Such measures were to be part of a broader flexicurity-inspired social policy which includes life-long learning, allowing workers to keep abreast of the new pressing competences; active policies designed to help the jobless and inactive get back into the labour market; more flexible rules in the social security sector to answer the needs of those changing jobs or temporarily exiting the market.

But Italy's official stand, at least up to the arrival of Monti, had been very cool, if not foot-dragging, as shown by its answer to the Green Paper, 'Modernising labour law to meet the challenges of the 21st century' launched by the European Commission at the close of 2006. Thus, in answer to the Commission's guidelines, the 2007 Italian document points out that:

> 'Any reflection on the Green Paper cannot preclude an explicit reference—which is instead absent from the text—to the Fundamental Charter of Rights of Nice insofar as the latter already represents today, and before its desired insertion in the constitution, a safeguard and political and legal constriction for social rights, too, as proven by the Commission's 2001 decision to take the Charter as the foundation for its action, and in various decisions in cases in Italian and European Law. Any future modification of labour law, whose intents are to uphold the original reasons and functions as they are still valid, could only take place within the bounds of the principles and the rights sanctioned in the Charter.'[8]

[7] On the new balance between 'social rights' and 'economic issues' in the European multi-level legal framework, see E Ales, 'Diritti sociali e 'discrezionalità' del legislatore nell'ordinamento multilivello', in *Giornale di Diritto del Lavoro e di Relazioni Industriali*, 2015, no 3 455.

[8] http://eur-lex.europa.eu/legal-content/EN/TXT/?uri=URISERV%3Ac10312

And again:

> 'The central question that the Green Paper raises regards the ways and means to ensure the flexibility needed by companies in the new international context, guaranteeing at the same time security for the workers. After having established that this objective has been pursued over the last few years by means of "flexibility on the margins", which has expanded work contracts and has segmented the labour market, the Green Paper suggests that a more adequate solution could be to ease the regulations on standard employment relationships, including severance payment, alongside bolstering protection measures to encourage mobility and employability and increase employment. Starting from the fact that no empirical evidence exists to prove beyond all doubt the existence of a positive correspondence between regulations on severance terms and trends for companies to take on personnel, this hypothesis implies an exchange between protecting employment and the market when, instead, both are necessary to ensure stable labour conditions and create good employment.'[9]

Indeed, the significant passage of the Italian answer contends that:

> 'To prevent flexibility from transmuting into precariousness, it is necessary for non-standard employment contracts to be made sustainable both by sufficient legal and contractual norms, by developing protection for the labour market and incentives aimed at bringing about permanent contracts. Recent Italian legislation is moving in this direction and wants to make it "convenient" for companies to offer permanent employment contracts.'[10]

But the Monti government was born with the precise aim to push through the reforms which Europe for some time had been calling for, and differently from his predecessors, the new Prime Minister was very much in line with the political and financial institutions of Europe. There were, indeed, the political premises for a reform of the job market which translated into positive norms the general lines of the European stand on flexicurity.

V. The 2012 'Monti-Fornero' Reform. The Squeeze on Freelance Collaborations

The declared objectives of comma one of article 1 of the 2101 Law No 92—the 'Monti-Fornero Reform', named after the Prime Minister and the Minister of Labour who presented it—were quite ambitious.

The reform proposed to introduce:

> 'measures and interventions designed to realise an inclusive and dynamic job marker, able to contribute to creating employment, both in quality and quantity, social and

[9] ibid.
[10] ibid.

> economic growth and cut definitively the rate of unemployment, in particular by: a) promoting more stable labour relations and confirming the priority of subordinate permanent employment, the so-called "dominant" contract, as the most common form of labour relationship; b) enhancing apprenticeships as the main mode for the young to enter the world of work; c) redistributing in a more equal way job protection, on one hand contrasting the improper and instrumental use of the elements of flexibility introduced with the legalization of various contract types. On the other hand, gradually adapting the norms for dismissal to meet the new context, with the provision of a specific judicial procedure to speed up the judgements on controversies; d) making more efficient and fair the structure of the social safety nets and active policies in order to universalise and strengthen employment possibilities; e) opposing tax and contribution evasion; f) promoting a greater inclusion of women in the economic life; g) favouring new opportunities for jobs, or protecting the income of over 55s in the case of job loss; h) promoting participative modes of industrial relations according to the directions taken at a European level, in order to improve the competitive spirit of companies.'

Already clear from the premise is the influence of the European model of flexicurity and the aim of reducing the precariousness resulting from the dualism of the job market, with a special emphasis on subordinate, permanent employment, understood as the 'dominant contract'.

Law 92/2012 faced the excess of self-employed collaborations following a double track. On one hand providing for co-ordinated and continuative employment, 'lavoro a progetto', too, (except for highly professional services) to be considered subordinate in the case in which the collaborator's services were carried out in a similar mode to those of dependent workers. On the other hand, having the services carried out by a party with a VAT taxable status eligible unless proved otherwise, continuous and co-ordinated employment, with at least two of the following conditions: that the collaboration lasts more than eight months less than a year for two consecutive years; b) that the payment for the collaboration, even if invoiced to more parties and the same centre of interest, makes more than 80 per cent of the annual sum received by the collaborator in the span of two consecutive solar years; c) that the collaborator has a fixed workstation in one of the seats of the employer. Nevertheless, these criteria were not operative when the services were of a high level of theoretical competences or technical skills or when carried out by a party with an autonomous income above a certain level, established by the law itself. Again it could be with reference to services carried out in the exercise of professional activity, for which the law required enrolment in a professional order or due register.

So with Law 92 of 2012 there entered for the first time in the law quantitative indexes (referring to income and the quota coming from one client) as determinants for distinguishing between autonomy and subordination. As is obvious, the legal presumption based on quantitative requisites is a rough and sometimes distorting instrument, but it was efficient in reducing the number of self-employed collaborations. It must be noted, however, that the effect was partly due to the progressive increase in the contribution rates, which made the system economically less advantageous for companies.

It can, however, be said that the 2012 reform contributed to reducing the phenomenon of false self-employed collaborations by penalising them both in terms of risking requalification in the case of litigation and in terms of gross overall costs for the collaborator. The negative aspect of such an approach was that it created a general hostility in the Law for autonomous work and, therefore, companies distanced from these forms of collaborations without replacing them with the dominating typology of permanent subordinate employment contract. In other terms, while it is true that the 2012 Law contributed to reducing the number of self-employed collaborations, it did not help redirect the demand for work towards the typology of subordinate work in that it created no incentive in absolute terms, but only made self-employment more costly. Consequently, the dualism of the market was reduced, thanks to the loss of a good quota of precarious work, for which as yet there has been no corresponding increase in the demand for subordinate work.

A. The next step: Flexicurity

On the level of real effects, the two new lines of reform in Law 92/2012 intended to create the overall structure of flexicurity, turned out to be less impactful than announced. The aim had been the passage from protective reinstatement to indemnity for unfair dismissal (flexibility) and the creation of social safety nets for a national coverage of involuntary unemployment (security). For what concerns the realisation of a system of indemnity protection, in the case of unfair dismissal, the 2012 reform was conditioned by the need to reach a series of compromises with the different groups in the coalition backing the Government, to such a point as to produce a somewhat complex regulatory table which did not really meet the legal need for certainty. The Law faced the modification of Article 18 of the Workers' Statute—which, as we have noted above, provided for companies with over 15 on the payroll a protective reinstatement in all cases of unfair or incorrect dismissal, imposing a different sanction according to the diverse illegitimate reasons for dismissal. Put briefly, the table that emerged is the following: 1) discriminatory dismissal remains as in Article 18, so an invalid dismissal and reinstatement plus compensation for lost wages, with the understanding that the worker has the right to 15 months wages/salary as an alternative to reinstatement; 2) for disciplinary dismissal, ie, for justified subjective reasons (evident non-performance) and dismissal for right causes (very serious reasons interrupting employment), it is foreseen that where the extremes for justified reasons or right causes for the absence of the facts contested, or because 'the fact is part of conduct punishable with a conservative sanction on the basis of the previsions of collective contracts or applicable disciplinary codes', the sentence contains the order for reinstatement as well as compensation for damage, with a ceiling of twelve monthly pay cheques. This case is referred to as attenuated integration protection. In the other cases of illegitimate dismissal for the absence of a justified reason or just cause, the judge declares the contract terminated and condemns the employer to pay an all-inclusive compensation between 12 to 24 months' instalments of the most recent pay level; 3) a compensatory sanction between 6 and 12 months' pay is foreseen for cases of non-essential formal misdeeds (excluded therefore any oral forms, which remains with the nullity of the dismissal and right to full reinstatement); 4) for dismissal for 'a justified objective motive' linked to physical suitability, attenuated reinstatement protection is foreseen, as a principle (with a maximum of 12 months' pay as compensation); 5) in the case of a 'justified objective motive' (the so-called economic dismissal) attenuated protective reinstatement is foreseen in the case of 'manifest absence' of the fact at dismissal, although the judge can opt—at his discretion—for a merely compensatory protection between 12 and 24 months' pay; 6) in other cases of absence (non-manifest) justification, a compensatory protection between 12 and 24 months is foreseen.

Finally, there is a specific obligatory procedure of conciliation for cases of dismissal and lawsuits, as was foreseeable, a great juridical uncertainty over interpretations, with the formation of opposing directions, so that dismissals have become more difficult than before the reform.

For financial support in the case of involuntary unemployment, Law 92/2012 took an appreciable step forward in establishing ASPI (Social Insurance for Employment), a far more generous and inclusive form of unemployment benefits than before. But the reform of the social safety nets was not completed, both for lack of sufficient funds to guarantee truly nationwide benefits and a structural reform of redundancy funds system, which in Italy is still the major expense item in the whole system of the social safety net.

So in spite of what it announced, the 2012 reform was no turning point in the direction of a flexicurity system, but it left many critical aspects of the Italian job market unsolved.

VI. The Renzi Government's Jobs Act

All the most important indicators in Italy's macro-economic data for the period 2012 to 2014 were negative. The GDP went on contracting, marking the longest period of recession in the post-WWII period, while unemployment went on rising, until in late 2014 it reached a rate of 13 per cent, with 40 per cent for the under 29s. Matteo Renzi's government had called for a vote of confidence and presented Parliament with a programme of reforms, among which, once again, the rewriting of the job market rules. But since the Italian job market had been the object of an almost interrupted flow of legislative interventions from the late 1990s, a new reform could only have meaning if it produced strong signals of breaking with the past, both in content and dimension.

Therefore, the reform project presented by the Renzi government—significantly baptised 'the Jobs Act', with a direct recall of Obama's Jobs Act of

September 2011—had right from the beginning, the declared ambition to make radical changes: from the introduction of subordinate contracts with increasing protection to the abolition of the contribution cost for new staff; to the establishment of a generalised protection system or incomes against involuntary unemployment, to the creation of a nation network of services for the active policies of employment. Also proposed was the downsizing of income assistance; from the introduction of new conciliatory instruments between life time and work time to a more efficient protection of working mothers; from the streamlining of the regulations and existing contract types to the strengthening of ways of contrasting irregular work.

The reform programme started with Proxy Law No 183, approved on 16 December 2014, and was completed with the passing of eight legislative decrees, the latter coming into force in September 2015. Although, looking at it well, the most important act on the level of public financial commitment was the estimate in the 2015 budget law, for tax reductions for all new open-end appointments taking place in the solar year of 2015, valid for the three following years.

Among the above-mentioned provisions, this paper will limit itself to recalling those that have specific impact on the dualism of insiders and outsiders in the job market. There is no doubt that the abolition—up to a ceiling of 8,060 euros a year—of the contribution charges for new employees with a permanent subordinate work contract is the greatest economic incentive towards the stabilisation of precarious workers ever experimented in Italy.

A. The 'Contratto a Tutele Crescenti' (Contract with Increasing Protection)

The main innovation at the level of regulations is the new structure of norms for the permanent contracts, known as 'contratto a tutele crescenti' (contract with increasing protection), in combination with the expansion of all the protection foreseen for subordinate work, to cover also differently organised collaborations.

The contract with increasing protection, which becomes the standard form for new permanent employees, lies at the heart of the reform because legislators pictured they could use it as the barycentre of the job market.[11] In reality, contracts with increasing protection are nothing other than normal permanent subordinate contracts, with all the same terms, but with a new ruling about dismissals.

[11] On the 'contratto a tutele crescenti' see Carinci, F and Tiraboschi, M (eds), *I decreti attuativi del Jobs Act: prima lettura e interpretazioni* (Bergamo, ADAPT University Press, 2015)?; MT Carinci, A Tursi (eds), *Jobs Act, Il contratto a tutele crescenti*, (Torino, Giappichelli, 2015); L Fiorillo, A Perulli (eds), *Il contratto a tutele crescenti e la Naspi, Decreti legislativi 4 marzo 2015, n. 22 e n. 23* (Torino, Giappichelli, 2015); R Pessi, C Pisani, G. Proia, A Vallebona (eds), *Jobs Act e licenziamento* (Torino, Giappichelli, 2015); M Rusciano, L Zoppoli (eds), *Jobs Act e contratti di lavoro dopo la legge delega 10 dicembre 2014 n. 183*, WP C.S.D.L.E. 'Massimo D'Antona', Collective Volumes—3/2014.

In particular, the principle of needing justification for dismissal is the same, and therefore the ruling in Law No 604 (1966), according to which dismissal must be backed by a just cause or justified subjective motive (dismissal for wrong done by the worker, or disciplinary) or by a justified objective motive (including dismissal for economic reasons). On the other hand, the sanction for unfair dismissal changes radically. The general rule is that in cases where no room is found for justified dismissal, justified subjective motive or just cause, the judge declares null and void the contract from the date of the dismissal and condemns the employer to pay a compensation without deductions for social security contributions, equal to two months' pay at the present salary for every year of service—however not less than four and not more than 24 months' pay. So, the sanction for unjustified dismissal is economic, whether the employer's motive be disciplinary or economic, and the calculations for the compensation have been subtracted from the judge's duties. They are tied to the objective factors of number of years in that employment. Reinstatement is confirmed for discriminatory dismissal in those cases where the employer's accusations prove unfounded.

An innovation of great impact in the reform is the procedure for facilitated conciliation. It provides for an offer made by the employer to the worker, within 60 days after dismissal, of a cheque for half the sum he would pay if the judgment went against him. To encourage the worker to accept the cheque, the law provides for the sum offered in conciliation to be tax and contribution free. In practice, that means that the conciliatory cheque corresponds to a net sum slightly lower that the gross he/she would have in the case of a victory in court. In this way, the parties are most likely to choose the rapid solution without litigation.

From this new framework, there emerges a clear outline of the costs of dismissal, also for bigger companies, which should play down apprehensions about taking on permanent personnel even when the prospects of development are uncertain. Here again, we see the aim to incentivise companies to opt for standard permanent contracts rather than go for precarious forms, unless of course they have a specific requirement for temporary workers.

B. The Demise of Some Marginal Contracts and Extending Protection for Subordinate Work

The other piece completing the reform strategy, easing out precarious employment not sustained by any real need, is the process of elimination for some forms of non-standard contracts, too often used as a way out, like project work and joint ventures with specified job performance or job sharing, which is of little practical use.

The repeal of project work, so important in the plan for reducing precariousness, could have created the paradoxical effect of further weakening the protection given to self-employed co-ordinated and continuous collaborators. But, as mentioned above, the law provided for the extension of the protection of subordinate work to 'collaboration which is configured inexclusively personal continuative work, executed according to the manner, time and place organised by the employer'.

This means that the collaborators—the category most used by employers for circumvention—who do not have the freedom to organise their work, will enjoy all the protective coverage of subordinate workers.

Naturally, it will be up to jurisprudence to clarify the concept of hetero-organisation,[12] reworking past interpretations, which are not always in order on a theoretical-dogmatic plane, condensed in the pronunciations already attributing a qualifying note of the subordination to the fact that the work was inserted in the company's organisation. And passing thus a vast production of jurisprudence which had created the figure of 'attenuated subordination' in an attempt to respond to the 'juridical transformation'[13] of the steering power which, in the context of work characterised by a particularly high level of intellectual content or in contrast to a low, elementary and repetitive content, presents a selective 'attenuated' efficiency, since carrying out such work does not require precise, specific and constant directions, but general and planned.[14]

Extending the situation of subordinate work to hetero-organised collaborations is, therefore, the 2015 answer of Italian legislators to the problem of collaborators lacking any real organisational autonomy in their activity.

Other opinions had also been aired and had entered academic debate, often inspired by experiences matured over the last few years in various European countries. In particular, in the debate that had preceded the reform, one of the scientifically accredited proposals had been to create a special contract for economically dependent collaborators, furnishing them with some protection to

[12] The problem of distinguishing between the hetero-organisation of the new norms and the co-ordination of collaborators had been already signalled (Art 409 of cod proc Civ) in the literature. According to T Treu, 'In tema di Jobs Act. Il riordino dei tipi contrattuali', (2015) *Giornale di Diritto del Lavoro e delle Relazioni Industriali* 155 ff, 'Co-ordination would concern those cases in which the relations between the parties and the ties of place and time for the collaborator are only those necessary for reaching the result of the collaboration; while vice versa in services organised by the employer, the modes of execution and the relative ties of time and place asked of the collaborator are more general and in a certain way indeterminate, like those of someone taking part in an organisation and inserted in it'. See also M Magnani, 'La riforma dei contratti e del mercato del lavoro nel c.d. Jobs Act. Il Codice dei contratti', (2015) *Dir Rel Ind* 961; L Nogler, 'La subordinazione nel d.lgs. n. 81 del 2015: alla ricerca dell'"autorità del punto di vista giuridico"', in WP CSDLE 'Massimo D'Antona', IT—267/2015; A Perulli, 'Prestazioni organizzate dal committente e collaborazioni coordinate e continuative. Il nuovo quadro normativo', in L Fiorillo, A Perulli (eds), *Tipologie contrattuali e disciplina delle mansioni, Decreto legislativo 15 giugno 2015, n. 81*, (Torino, Giappichelli, 2015); G Santoro Passarelli, 'I rapporti di collaborazione organizzati dal committente e le collaborazioni continuative e coordinate ex art. 409, n. 3, c.p.c.', in WP CSDLE 'Massimo D'Antona'—278/2015, 6 ff; M Tiraboschi, 'Il lavoro etero-organizzato', in M Tiraboschi (ed), *Le nuove regole del lavoro dopo il Jobs Act* (Milano, Giuffré, 2016) 261; P Tosi, 'L'art. 1, comma 1, d.lgs. n. 81/2015: una norma apparente?', (2015) 6, *Arg Dir Lav*.

[13] V A Supiot, 'Les nouveaux visages de la subordination', in *Droit Social* (2000) 131 ff, which speaks of 'the juridical metamorphoses of power'.

[14] The question is efficiently summed up in the following terms: O Razzolini, 'La nuova disciplina delle collaborazioni organizzate dal committente', in *WP CSDLE 'Massimo D'Antona', IT*—266/2015.

make up for their weakness in the market. The idea was basically to follow the path already taken by the Monti-Fornero Reform and identify the selective criteria in economic weakness, which were to have been deduced from the fact that the collaborator's income depended on one employer.[15] A proposal of this kind means that legislators indicate a threshold. For example, as happened in the Spanish experience, the threshold could have been established to at least 75 per cent of income from work, economic and or professional activity.[16] Nevertheless, certain criticisms were levelled against such a solution. First of all, the introduction of a threshold very quickly makes companies resilient and they modify their behaviour to get round the negative aspects of the threshold. Furthermore, as has been observed in the literature:

> 'the single employer, measured via quantitative requisites of remuneration, arouses perplexity for the protection of the contractual will of the employer faced by an imputation based on circumstances which are neither denotative nor of a particular way of working, or a certain balance of powers and interests between the parties.'[17]

Put aside, therefore, the idea of creating a 'tertium genus' of economically dependent workers, half way between subordinate work and self-employment, the outline of the reform must be completed by entirely new norms for autonomous work, which can lead to an equilibrium between the protection foreseen in the Law for all forms of work and can also find a solution to the problems in all the different forms of collaboration.

VII. Conclusions

In conclusion, we return to the questions raised in the premise. First of all, how can we make coherent two contrasting visions of subordinate work, perceived both as a model of virtue and as an outdated mechanism?

The contradiction is in reality only apparent, simply because however disrupted work is in some sectors, putting aside a work model inserted functionally and

[15] For a recent, ample treatment of the subject see M Pallini, *Il lavoro economicamente dipendente*, (Padova, Cedam, 2013). With specific reference to the debate immediately before the 2015 Reform see A Perulli, 'Un Jobs Act per il lavoro autonomo: verso una nuova disciplina della dipendenza economica?' in WP 'Massimo D'Antona', no 235/2015.

[16] See J Cruz Villalon, 'Il lavoro autonomo economicamente dipendente in Spagna', in *Diritto lavoro mercati* (2013) 287 ff.

[17] O Razzolini, 'La nuova disciplina delle collaborazioni organizzate dal committente'. On the subject, see also S Liebman, 'Prestazione di attività produttiva e protezione del contraente debole fra sistema giuridico e suggestioni dell'economia', (2010) *Giorn dir lav rel ind* 589 with reference to the d.d.l. no 1873 promoted by Senator Pietro Ichino; M Roccella, 'Lavoro subordinato e lavoro autonomo, oggi', *WP 'Massimo D'Antona'*, no 65/2008, 41; also F Carinci, 'Provaci ancora, Sam: ripartendo dall'art. 18 dello Statuto', (2012) WP CSDLE 'Massimo D'Antona'no 128, 39 now in (2012) I *Riv It Dir Lav*, 36 and ff, for whom restraining the will of the two parties makes for greater rigidity in the dynamics of the economy.

stably in corporate organisations belongs more to the fantasy than the real world. Even looking beyond our borders, we cannot find any country, especially among the more economically developed ones, in which structural reforms have been realised to do away with the central importance of dependent work. Some interesting attempts can, however, be mentioned, like the experiments in Spain and France, to reduce the differential between subordinate work and self-employment. On the other hand, European social legislation, including its most advanced point summarised in the 'Europe 2020' strategy, rotates around the importance of permanent, subordinate work, intended to improve employability by means of training and life-long learning.

It is with this scenario in mind that the Jobs Act faced the issue of precariousness, breaking away from the sterile ideological dispute between 'bad precariousness' and 'good flexibility', and moving adroitly and unexpectedly: returning to the importance of subordinate work though reducing indirect economic costs and the unsustainable complexity and uncertainty of the norms. It must be said that few explanations are needed for the measures and extraordinary reasons contained in the 2015 stability law[18] which almost abolished the tax wedge, the choice to place in the centre of the system open-end contracts was not so obvious. On the contrary, it risked appearing backward-looking in a more and more fluid job market with production in continuous evolution. This choice measures the distance between the Jobs Act and the methodological structure of the Biagi Law, which had followed the evolution of the market by introducing into the juridical system new types of contracts, worked out in great detail, with the aim of answering the new needs of the companies, always more troubled by the monolithic rigidity of Labour Law. Of course, for its period it was a courageous operation, which certainly contributed to questioning a system that was instinctively fearful of innovation. However, with the passing of the years, this approach to the modernising of Labour Law has revealed the limits of its axiological premises. To trace the evolution of the complex real world via the legal micro-typologies would produce precocious normative obsolescence, because companies go faster that the legislative engine and when they find themselves up against the hypertrophic complexity of the law, they tend to go round it. The Jobs Act's approach to the challenge of innovation went down a different road. Its fundamental paradigm was the reduction of the complexity of the rules and the contract models imposed by the law. The first step in this direction was to make the costs of dismissal certain and foreseeable, without touching the premises for legitimacy, which continue to be just cause or a worker's obvious non-performance, and the objective reasons of company downsizing. The introduction of the mechanism of increasing protection with years of company service makes the dismissal of new employees relatively cheap, which obviously encourages

[18] Act n.190, Dec. 23, 2014.

open-end contracts. If then is added tax exemption for three years, we see a decided move towards the open-end subordinate contract, which should thus return to its natural function of prevalent form, given the re-found economic and normative advantages, and not because of the heavier costs of alternative flexible contracts. Because flexible contracts, where they are functionally necessary, are not discouraged, they must not be transformed into an escape route for companies desperately trying to avoid the high costs of standard work. Nevertheless, the promotion of the open-end employment would have been unbalanced if at the same time it had not faced the age-old problem of the vast 'grey' zone of contracts which pass as self-employment, but really hide jobs lacking any organisational autonomy: a parallel world made of fake self-employment, mostly populated by young people available for any kind of work, paid a fraction of the minimum foreseen in collective contracts and incorrectly used by the companies. With this group of atypical and ontologically precious workers, two different directions could have been taken: recognise for them a special stature, in some way carrying on from 'project work', perhaps introducing some new form of protection, but confirming their segregation or—more simply—extending the protection area of the norms of subordinate work to cover them, too. The choice made by the 2015 reform goes in the latter direction. By extending the norms of subordinate work to collaborators de facto inserted structurally in the productive organisation of a company, our norms do away with the hypocrisy of a para-subordination composed of self-employed workers on paper but substantially subordinate workers in substance. Here, too, can be recognised a sign of conceptual and normative streamlining, which marks the difference between the Jobs Act and the repeated reforms of the job market following on from one another over the last fifteen years. While for a long time attempts were being made to put a roof of norms over the homeless, the Jobs Act tried to lead them towards the rules governing employment.

Now there are two more steps to take: on one hand, once the cloudy area between self-employment and subordination has been cleared up, determined action must be taken to protect, enhance and incentivise genuine self-employment, which our economic and productive fabric so sorely needs. A relevant quota of professionalism of the highest added value is concentrated in self-employment, which also guarantees small and medium-sized companies the specialised competences needed to continue the process of technological and organisational innovations. It is necessary, therefore, to back all those—particularly the young—who want to put themselves on the line with only their professional training and experience on their side. It is necessary to work to overcome a Byzantine fiscal system, assure a balanced system of contributions and social security, guarantee the certainty and punctuality of payment and offer adequate instruments for familiarising with and accessing the market.

On the other hand, the market of subordinate permanent work must be evolved beyond the Fordist model of organisation, allowing 'core' employees to work also outside the worksite and the predefined schemes of timetables, so evaluating their performance by the result and not the time made available to the employer.

A revolution in organisation called 'smart work', which is not only needed to exploit the distance work opportunities made possible by ICT and portable computers, but would be of great need in Italy, where space is a scarce resource and commuting is made difficult by mostly inefficient transport and infrastructures, and where women give up working more than in other European countries, in order to stay at home and look after their families, purely because of the lack of public welfare services.

These steps have just been taken by the Government with the draft of the so-called 'Statute of Self-Employment' and an unprecedented regulation of the 'smart work'.

9

Re-addressing Self-employment: Spain and the New Entrepreneurship

JOSÉ MANUEL GÓMEZ MUÑOZ

I. Difficulty of Classifying Self-Employed Workers in a Legal Category

One of the most singular features of Spanish Labour Law is the classification of subjects included in and excluded from the scope of application of labour regulations. This may complicate an identification of the workers that may be classified as 'core and contingent workers' for the purposes of the conclusions of this collective work, since there is no direct correlation between these terms and the legal categories established in our system. In the case of self-employed workers, this becomes especially significant and difficult. We must keep in mind that in our 'Estatuto de los Trabajadores' (Workers' Statute—ET), no labour regulations apply to self-employed work to the extent that it is not even mentioned in the employment relationship exclusion clauses or Article 1 ET. Its paragraph three establishes that the terms of this regulation do not apply to: (1) service relationships of civil servants; (2) compulsory personal services; (3) activities of company directors or members of corporate governing bodies; (4) work performed on grounds of friendship, good will or good neighbourliness; (5) work performed in family-owned business by relatives to the second degree of kinship by blood or by marriage; (6) work of traders undertaking operational risks; (7) licenced transport services operators driving vehicles controlled by them; and (8) finally, all other work relationships lacking the features identifying the employment relationship established in Article 1.1 ET, ie voluntary nature, employment by another party, dependence and compensation.[1]

[1] See, M R Alarcón Caracuel, 'La ajenidad en el mercado como criterio definitorio del contrato de trabajo' (1986) *Revista Española de Derecho del Trabajo* no 36; A Martín Valverde, 'Fronteras y zonas grises del Derecho del Trabajo en la jurisprudencia actual' (2002) *Revista del Ministerio de Trabajo y Asuntos Sociales* no 38; M Rodríguez-Piñero, 'Contrato de trabajo y relación de trabajo' (1967) *Anales de la Universidad de Huelva*; T Sala Franco and F López Mora, 'Contrato de trabajo' in *Comentarios a las*

At the same time, the legal regulation of Article 2 ET places within the boundaries of the labour law system, employment relationships of a special nature, similar to what in Italy is known as 'parasubordinato', 'parasubordonné' in France, or 'arbeitnehmerähnliche' in Germany, which includes: (1) senior management staff; (2) domestic servants; (3) convicts serving prison sentences; (4) professional athletes; (5) public entertainment artists; (6) traders not undertaking any operational risks; (7) disabled workers in special work sites; (8) stevedores; (9) junior doctors in training; (10) solicitors working in law firms; and (11) religion teachers. Therefore, we can state that all professional activities taking place in these categories, which are excluded from labour regulations, or regulated as special employment relationships would fall within the category of self-employed work. However, the Final Clause 1 of the ET determines that work on one's own account, which is how it is also known in our legal terminology, will not be subject to labour regulations, unless where otherwise specifically established by law.[2]

Some labour regulations apply in this way to self-employed workers, among them Article 3.1 of the Freedom of Association and Right to Organise Act, which allows self-employed workers that are not employers to join class trade unions. Likewise, Article 24.5 of the Occupational Risk Prevention Law sets forth that self-employed workers have co-operation, information and training duties in occupational risk prevention whenever they are working on worksites in which two or more companies are operating, either directly or as subcontractors; therefore, they must comply with any co-ordination measures established in such sites for prevention purposes. In this case, it can be considered that these self-employed workers enjoy the same protection granted to core workers employed by companies; it additionally establishes occupational safety obligations typically required from employers.

At a less specific level, we will see that self-employed workers enjoy typical labour rights such as equal treatment and non-discrimination, dignity and privacy, professional training and retraining, associations and collective actions, or those aiming at ensuring the protection of minors and reconciliation of working and family life. However, such rights are granted to them by Law 20/2007 of 11 July on the Statute of Self-Employed Workers (LETA), which cannot be considered as labour legislation, raising the issue of sources of governing law, which will be discussed below.

leyes laborales. El Estatuto de los Trabajadores (Madrid, Edersa, 1990); S González Ortega, *La presunción de existencia del contrato de trabajo* (Madrid, Ministerio de Trabajo y Seguridad Social, 1990); J López Gandía, *Contrato de trabajo y figuras afines* (Valencia, Tirant lo Blanch, 1999).

[2] See M Areta Martínez and AV Sempere Navarro, *La contratación laboral (especial) entre abogados* (Pamplona, Thomson/Aranzadi, 2006); P Rodríguez Ramos, *La relación laboral especial de los estibadores portuarios* (Madrid, Trotta, 1997); A Val de Tena, *Los trabajadores directivos de las empresas* (Pamplona, Thomson/Aranzadi, 2010); R Quesada Segura, *El contrato de servicio doméstico* (Madrid, La Ley, 1991); T Huertas Bartolomé, *Mediación mercantil en el ordenamiento laboral* (Madrid, Tecnos, 1991); C Molero Manglano, *El contrato de alta dirección* (Pamplona, Thomson/Civita, 2011).

As opposed to wage earners, the relationship of self-employed workers in Spain with their client or user company, takes place by means of civil or commercial contracts (order, work under contract, leasing of services, agency or transport contracts) as well as by a whole range of new emerging agreements related to the new technologies. This is the case for example of workers operating in the Uber or Blablacar environments; these companies are networked technological businesses providing taxi services among users. The rolling out of these companies has generated a debate in some European Union countries, and they have been legally banned in the case of Spain, France and Germany. Community managers and other social media operators have the same legal consideration in Spain. This is not the case of teleworkers, who clearly enjoy the legal status of employee under Spanish Law.[3]

The problems of delimiting the figure of the self-employed worker arise when they work in a continued and regular manner for the same company or client, something frequent in activities related to the transportation and courier industries, construction sector or commercial activities in large shopping centres. In these cases, self-employed workers are 'collaborators' of the company-client which is directly involved in the performance of their activity and they work as if they were core workers. Here we are faced with the difficulty of separating this self-employed worker from the figure of the economically dependent self-employed worker (TAED) established in 2007, which would be some kind of tertium genus between the core worker and the self-employed worker, which in turn raises a series of new questions that will be addressed below.

From the point of view of the evolution of regulations, it is not possible to establish a fixed date for the enactment of the concept of self-employed worker, beyond the approval of the LETA in 2007; however, some activities have been gradually incorporated into areas related to Labour Law, such as home-based work in 1931, presently regulated in Article 13 ET at the same level of provisions as telework,[4] the work of travelling salespeople in 1962, or senior management work in 1985. Other activities, such as those performed based on an agency contract in 1992,[5] or brokerage in the field of private insurance in 2006,[6] have become part of a hybrid regulation of labour and commercial legislation. The members of worker co-operatives since 1999,[7] who would later be governed by the Social Economy Law[8] and

[3] See, F Ortiz Chaparro, *El Teletrabajo* (Madrid, McGraw-Hill, 1996); E Rojo Torrecilla, 'Cambios en el mundo del trabajo: nuevos empleos y nuevos trabajadores' (2002) *Revista de fomento social* vol 57 no 226, 241.

[4] According to the regulation of Law 3/2012, [2012] BOE 7 July, on urgent measures for the reform of the labour market.

[5] Law 12/1992 of 27 May 1992, [1992] BOE 22 May.

[6] Law 26/2010 of 17 July 2010, [2010] BOE 21 August.

[7] Law 27/1999 of 16 July 1999 on Co-operatives, [1999] BOE 17 July.

[8] Law 5/2011 of 29 March 2011, [2011] BOE 30 March.

the partners of professional partnerships,[9] also fall within this same blurry environment. Certain labour regulations in the field of occupational risk prevention, labour jurisdiction and working and family life balance apply to partners-workers who produce goods or services for third parties. However, they are not wage earners or employees, but rather self-employed workers that may have employees themselves, although it is clear that the irradiation of labour standards in the regulation of their activity is greater than in the case of self-employed workers stricto sensu.

In 1966, a Special Scheme for Self-Employed Workers (RETA) was established within the Social Security system.[10] It determined that it should include all workers working for someone else or self-employed that performed in a regular, direct and personal manner an economic activity for profit not subject to an employment contract, including those using paid work of other people. The law assumed that self-employed workers ran a business establishment open to the public as owners, lessors, users or some other similar concept.[11] This assumption does not apply anymore; therefore, a worker can be considered self-employed without having any business establishment open to the public.

Neither does the Spanish Tax legislation allow for identifying self-employed workers, since the subjects obliged to pay the Economic Activity Tax (IAE)[12] are all those obtaining income from economic activities arising from personal work or capital without distinction, in which the taxpayer manages on his own account production means and human resources or either of them, with the purpose of taking part in the production or distribution of goods or services. This legal provision applies to individuals, legal persons and professionals, and does not make any distinction among them. For tax legislation, there is an economic activity when a taxpayer manages on his own account production means and human resources or either of them, with the purpose of taking part in the production or distribution of goods or services. The obligation to declare and pay Value Added Tax (VAT) does not allow for the establishment of differences between self-employed workers and all other taxpayers.

Finally, it is necessary to point out that self-employed workers who hire employees have in our legal system (Article 1.2 ET), the status of employer (*datore di lavoro, Arbeitgeber*) for labour law purposes. Such effects are different from the consideration of company-employers, since in this case an individual receives and uses the work of the persons defined in Article 1.1 ET as employees.[13] In this

[9] Law 2/2007 of 15 March 2007, [2007] BOE 16 March. Other less relevant categories can be identified, such as share farming, which is governed by Article 1579 of the Civil Code and involves the farming of land, livestock and agricultural establishment with owner and tenant sharing profits, which is regulated by the Farm Lease Law, Law 49/2003 of 26 November 2003, [2003] BOE 27 November.

[10] Law 22 April 1966, [1966] BOE 23 April, on Social Security.

[11] Article 2, Decree 2530/1970, of 20 August 1970, [1970] BOE 15 September, regulating the Special Social Security Scheme for Self-Employed Workers.

[12] Article 35.4 of the General Tax Law 58/2003 of 17 December 2003, [2003] BOE 18 December.

[13] Supreme Court Judgments of December 22, 1989 and July 17, 1993.

respect, the self-employed worker becomes the holder of employment rights and obligations, inasmuch as he exercises management powers over his employees (Article 20 ET) and holds all the labour law powers and responsibilities resulting from the enforcement of labour regulations.

II. Impact of the Economic and Social Crisis on Self-Employed Work

In order to understand the quantitative bases of the self-employment readdressing process in Spain, it is necessary to undertake a brief analysis of employment before and during the deep economic, financial and labour market crisis. In the second quarter of 2015, Spain had the same number of occupied workers as twelve years ago, slightly over 17.4 million including employees and self-employed workers. There were 3,151,605 self-employed workers registered in the RETA in April 2015, a 0.8 per cent increase over 2014 and a 2.5 per cent increase over 2010, which implies that one out of every five occupied workers in Spain is self-employed. Out of this total, 2.2 million are self-employed workers without employees. And the figure keeps growing.

These figures mean that only 38 per cent of the total population is working, as compared to 46.1 per cent in 2000. The level of people at work implies that, whereas in 2007 90 per cent of the people at work had a full-time job, in 2015 the percentage has decreased to just 79 per cent. This has happened in spite of the fact that there are an additional 340,000 active people over 2007, reaching a present total figure of 22.8 million people. The worst figures are unquestionably those of unemployment, which has grown from 1.8 million unemployed at the end of 2007 to 4.1 million in the second quarter of 2015 according to the Active Population Survey.[14] In addition to these figures, it is necessary to consider emigration for work reasons, affecting especially highly qualified young workers. This is a process that has reappeared in Spain for the first time since massive immigration of workers started in 1987, leading to an inversion of the migration balance existing prior to the crisis, with a total of 450,000 workers having left Spain since 2009.

As far as self-employed workers are concerned, the largest numbers can be found in retail trade (25.9 per cent), construction (11.3 per cent), hospitality industry (11.3 per cent), agriculture (8.5 per cent), professional, scientific and technical activities (7.8 per cent), industry (7.3 per cent), transportation and warehousing

[14] In Spain, the unemployment registered by the Public National Employment Service (SEPE) includes all the unemployed registered at Employment Offices, which results in 5.4 million job seekers in the second quarter of 2015. However, the Active Population Survey (EPA), based on 60,000 interviews, is more reliable; it excludes from the total figure the unemployed that are not actively seeking a job, such as for example students aged 16 to 23.

(6.1 per cent), administrative activities (3.8 per cent), healthcare activities (3.1 per cent), education (2.4 per cent), finance and insurance (1.8 per cent), arts and entertainment (1.7 per cent), and information and communication (1.5 per cent).[15] Considering all the above economic sectors, the most relevant increases in the last year since the beginning of the economic recovery are 3.3 per cent in education, 2.2 per cent in real estate, 2.0 per cent in artistic activities, 1.6 per cent in information and communication and 1.5 per cent in the hospitality industry. These increases indicate the growing phenomenon of the 'false self-employed workers' i.e. employees that are moved to the condition of self-employed workers through production outsourcing processes and spill over to related companies, mostly in the information and communication, healthcare, finance and insurance, transportation and warehousing, and education sectors.[16] These figures provide us with a quite reliable image of the evolution of the economic and production sectors where there is self-employed work in Spain.

III. Stages in the Readdressing of Self-Employment Work in Spain

The redirecting of self-employed work has been a direct consequence of the financial, economic and unemployment crisis that has affected the Spanish productive system since 2008. While the favourable economic conditions experienced by Spain between 1998 and 2007 allowed for an initial confluence of the legal, economic and social protection schemes of self-employed workers and employees, leading to the Self-Employed Work Statute of 2007, the severity of the crisis has led the Government to focus away from this confluence and opt in a resolute manner for facilitating the transitions paths from work under employment to self-employed work. Indeed, it is a mere acceptation of the fact that the speed of job losses in Spain has not been reduced by the numerous legal reforms implemented since the approval of Law 35/2010, of 17 September, on urgent measures to reform the labour market. This regulation was encouraged by the serious warning given by the troika to the Spanish Government in May 2010 urging it to undertake substantial reforms in our labour relationships system.[17] Since the enactment of this regulation, a whole series of reforms have been approved along the same direction.

[15] Federación Nacional de Asociaciones de Trabajadores Autónomos (ATA).

[16] *Boletín del Instituto Nacional de Estadística*, (2015) no 1.

[17] Previously the Government approved Law 17/2009, of 23 November 2009, [2009] BOE 24 November, on free access to and exercise of service activities, which has partially incorporated into Spanish Law, Directive 2006/123/EC [2006] OJ L376/36 of the European Parliament and of the Council, of 12 December 2006, on services in the internal market, hereafter the Directive. The

All political and economic sectors in Spain have become aware of the fact that labour market reforms aimed at encouraging employment based on social security contribution discounts and direct subsidies for the recruitment of specific groups of unemployed workers have not yielded the expected results. This process has led to the fifty types of contracts currently existing, with all kinds of tax and social security benefits, which have turned our employment contract panorama into an unco-ordinated labyrinth of overlapping measures that are fully inefficient to stop job destruction, especially in economic crisis conditions. Although Spain's GDP is expected to grow by almost 3 per cent in the second quarter of 2015, the reality is that the number of indefinite full-time employment contracts signed in 2010–2015 accounts for barely 10 per cent of all employment contracts. Active employment policies connected to a commitment to employability and training require a thorough reform of the Public Employment Service (SEPE), which is capable of matching barely 1 per cent of the job offers and demands in Spain. Therefore, it is not surprising that redirecting work to self-employment has now become a top priority in governmental action. This action has been implemented in several stages as detailed below.

The first stage started with the enactment of Royal Decree 3/2012, of 10 February,[18] which focuses on the creation of jobs by small and micro-enterprises—less than 50 employees—using the instrument of the employment promotion contract for entrepreneurs in order to encourage indefinite full-time employment. It includes a one-year probationary period, in which the contract can be terminated without any compensation, and a direct payment together with a reduction of the employer's social security contribution of up to 100 per cent. The impact of this controversial employment contract intending to encourage job creation by self-employed workers and micro-enterprises has been negligible in terms of reduction of unemployment figures, with just 23,400 contracts made since its approval.[19] Measures aimed at encouraging the recruitment of young workers by self-employed workers have been maintained afterwards with mixed success in the regulations discussed below, indicating that despite the relatively low impact of these measures in the first stage, the Spanish Government has maintained its focus on the creation of jobs by micro-enterprises.

In the following period, we find Law 11/2013, of 26 July, on support measures for entrepreneurs and incentives for growth and job creation. Its Article 1 establishes a series of social security reductions and discounts applicable to young self-employed workers under 30—or 25 in the case of women—ranging between

aforementioned Law takes an ambitious approach promoting a general application of its principles in order to encourage a global improvement of the service sector regulatory framework, as well as to achieve efficiency, productivity and employment gains for the relevant sectors, in addition to an increase in the variety and quality of the services available to businesses and citizens.

[18] Converted into Law 3/2012 of 6 July 2012, [2012] BOE 7 July.

[19] Servicio Público de Empleo (SEPE), 2nd quarter 2015.

30 per cent and 80 per cent of the social security contribution for common contingencies. It was basically an economic measure included in the 2013–2016 Youth Entrepreneurship and Employment Strategy approved by the Government, resulting, with different legal changes approved later, in a minimal increase of the number of self-employed workers registered in the RETA of 0.8 per cent in the 2014–2015 reference period.[20] Articles 2 to 5 of Law 11/2013 also allowed combining unemployment benefits and self-employed work,[21] as well as receiving all unemployment benefits in a single payment to start self-employed work, which has eased the transition from unemployment to self-employment for workers under 30. However, the figures of this transfer, some 15,000 to 20,000 unemployed workers became self-employed in 2014–2015, are not overly encouraging.

In the third stage of promotion of self-employment and redirecting unemployed workers to self-employment, it is also necessary to highlight the driving role of Law 14/2013, of 27 September, on support to entrepreneurs and their internationalisation. Taking into account the importance of the external sector—exports—in our economy, the purpose of this Law was to support self-employed workers in the internationalisation of their activities by creating the legal figure of entrepreneur, defined in Article 3 as the individual or legal person carrying out a business or professional activity in the terms set forth by this Act. This means that the legislator has differentiated the traditional self-employed worker from the now called limited liability entrepreneur, a new legal figure that limits the civil liability for debts on the entrepreneur's home to 300,000 euros, establishes the possibility of an out-of-court settlement with creditors,[22] and regulates a whole series of tax and social security benefits.[23] In this way, a new figure of self-employed worker has emerged, characterised by a selective legal economic regime, with a clearly defined business projection in research and technological development essentially, and with a legal business framework which is closer to company law that to labour law.

Finally, this last period concludes with the enactment of Law 5/2015, of April 27, on promotion of corporate finance. Article 1 allows self-employed workers subject to the 2007 Self-Employed Work Statute to defend their rights in case of cancelation or reduction of the financing of their business by banking institutions. This is a further step in the readdressing of self-employment in Spain, inasmuch as legislative measures have been approved to equate the financial and economic treatment of self-employed workers to that of companies. This means that, in this stage, the Government is establishing legal structures to strengthen the financial position of self-employment, which is a clear invitation for the traditional self-employed workers to professionalise and move towards to legal corporate structures, which are much stronger and closer to the traditional concept

[20] Federación Nacional de Asociaciones de Trabajadores Autónomos (ATA), 2nd quarter 2015.

[21] Amendment of Article 228 of the General Social Security Law 1/1994. Articles 7 and 8 of Law 11/2013, BOE 27 July, have also established tax incentives for the incorporation of micro-enterprises.

[22] Article 21 of Law 14/2013, [2013] BOE 28 September.

[23] Article 23 of Law 14/2013, [2013] BOE 28 September.

of a company. To this end, Article 12 of Law 14/2013 establishes the figure of limited liability company with successive incorporation, which is a clear invitation to the conversion of the individual operating as self-employed worker into a legal person, in the above terms followed by Law 5/2015.

IV. Self-Employed Work as Regulated Work

Law 20/2007, of June 11, on the Statute of Self-Employed Work, intended some form of squaring the circle between Article 38 of the Spanish Constitution (CE) (freedom of enterprise), Article 25.1 CE (free choice of profession and trade, advancement through work and sufficient remuneration), Article 40.2 CE (professional training and retraining, occupational safety and hygiene, and paid holidays) and Article 41 CE (maintaining a public Social Security system).[24]

At the time it was approved, the over 3 million self-employed workers registered with the Social Security were classified into four Special Schemes (Special Scheme for Self-Employed Workers, Special Scheme for Agricultural Workers, Special Scheme for Offshore Workers and Special Scheme for Domestic Workers). Among them, 1,755,703 self-employed workers did not have any employees or had just one (50 per cent). Nowadays, after the amendment of Law 28/2011, of 22 September, the Special Scheme for Agricultural Workers has disappeared and all self-employed workers have been transferred to the General Scheme and the Special Scheme for Domestic Workers has disappeared too with Law 27/2011, of 1 August, with the same effect. The justification for these reforms approved in 2011 has been rationalising and simplifying the management of Social Security benefits. Therefore, their integration and regrouping into the General Scheme should not be interpreted as an assimilation of these workers with employees, but rather as a mechanism to reduce the system's management structures, with a merely economic purpose to reduce public expenditure in management.

Together with these self-employed workers in the classical sense (manager of a commercial establishment, farmers and various professionals), other heterogeneous figures are listed in Article 1.2 of Law 20/2007, such as: (1) industrial partners of general and limited partnerships; (2) economically dependent self-employed workers (TAED); (3) members of joint-property entities and irregular civil partnerships not limited to the mere administration of property; or (4) managers of commercial companies holding effective control of them, according to the twenty-seventh additional provision of the General Social Security Act. Law 20/2007 excludes employees, employment relationships of a special nature and CEOs of companies with a merely representative function.

In summary, Law 20/2007 includes a list of the activities that are characteristic of employers as mentioned in Article 1.2 ET, which in many cases find their

[24] See Explanatory Memorandum (I) Law 20/2007, [2007] BOE 12 July.

legal framework in the Civil or Commercial Codes, or have not even been legally defined, such as in the case of 'entrepreneurs' or individuals starting an economic or professional activity.[25] Likewise, the Eleventh Additional Provision of Law 20/2007 classifies as Economically Dependent Self-Employed Workers (TAED) all workers excluded from the scope of application of Article 1.1 ET (employees) by Article 1.3.g. i.e. hauliers driving an owned vehicle holding a transport licence and working regularly for the same carrier or operator.[26]

All these categories do really exist in the Spanish labour market and can be grouped into three general categories, i.e. the true self-employed worker (with no employees), the self-employed employer (with one or more employees), and the self-employed worker working for someone else or 'false self-employed worker'. The law designates the latter as economically dependent self-employed worker (TAED)[27] and this term poses great difficulties in terms of definition. It is very hard to find any valid legal reason to justify how the diverging interests of these three categories should be regulated by the same legal norm.[28]

This is especially visible in the case of the TAED. While in the case of true self-employed workers and self-employed employers there are clear common interests, since their professional rights and duties (Article 4 and following of Law 20/2007), as well as their social protection and risk prevention guarantees are the same, this is not the case for TAED, since they are characterised by Law in a manner so similar to the definition of employee in the Workers' Statute that it is hard to understand the legal rationale that has led legislators to draw this delicate balance between the scope of Article 1.1 ET and Article 11 of Law 20/2007 we will try to describe below.[29]

V. Concurrence of Legal Sources in the Regulation of Self-Employment

One of the most important new developments incorporated by Law 20/2007 was the introduction of a new system of legal sources, as well as the establishment of

[25] See second paragraph, Preamble II, Law 20/2007, [2007] BOE 12 July.

[26] Insurance brokers meeting the requirements set forth in chapter III of Law 20/2007 shall enjoy the consideration of TAED. Likewise, sales representatives acting as independent intermediaries without assuming the risk and venture of operations shall also be considered TAED, and they shall enter into the appropriate TAED agreement.

[27] See, Chapter II, Law 20/2007, [2007] BOE 12 July.

[28] See, J García Murcia, 'Trabajo autónomo' in J García Murcia (ed), *El trabajo autónomo y otras formas de trabajo no asalariado* (Pamplona Thomson, -Aranzadi, 2007) 21-24; J López Gandía, *Contrato de trabajo y figuras afines* (Valencia, Tirant lo Blanch, 1999); A Selma Penalva, *Los límites del contrato de trabajo en la jurisprudencia española* (Valencia, Tirant lo Blanch, 2007); J Cruz Villalón, 'Trabajo subordinado y trabajo autónomo en la delimitación de fronteras del Derecho del Trabajo' in AaVv, *Homenaje al profesor Cabrera Bazán* (Madrid, Tecnos, 1999).

[29] See the reflections on the intentions of the legislator in J Luján Alcaraz, *El Estatuto del Trabajo Autónomo. Análisis de la Ley 20/2007, de 11 de julio* (Murcia, Ediciones Laborum, 2007) 17.

a new source of the self-employed work relationship. An interesting debate has emerged in Spain on the legal nature of this source and it is far from being settled, among other reasons because there is still little practical experience and the economic crisis has generated new phenomena, such as the readdressing of self-employment in Spain, which makes assessments in quantitative terms extremely difficult.

Article 3 of Law 20/2007 establishes that the professional regime of self-employed workers shall be governed: (i) by the Law itself, provided that it does not enter into conflict with the regulations applicable to the worker's specific activity; (ii) the civil, commercial and administrative regulations applicable to the legal relationship applicable to the worker; (iii) the individual work contract; and (iv) to local and professional uses and traditions. This hierarchical legal blend of regulations of different scopes, in which the specialisation principle has been altered by the legal hierarchy principle, is quite surprising. We understand that this rationale poses clear legal certainty problems, inasmuch as it is not possible to select the applicable regulation when the typology of legal orders does not coincide.[30]

In turn, Article 3.3 excludes the possibility of applying labour legislation, except where otherwise specifically provided by law, to work performed on one's own account (former First Additional Provision of ET). This specification of Law 20/2007 in addition to being unnecessary is quite indicative of the idea the legislator itself has on the nature of this Law and the purpose of its legal amendment.

We cannot say that Law 20/2007 is a civil or commercial regulation, but it is not a labour regulation either. Its essential content is the recognition of rights to a series of groups of people that cannot be included in labour legislation but do not belong entirely to the subjective scope of the civil or commercial regulation framework. Law 20/2007 is not a labour regulation and it is not a Social Security regulation, but it grants labour and insurance rights to self-employed workers. Moreover, it does so to the extent that the borders between work as employee and self-employed work, which were clearly laid down in our legal system end up blurred by a dense fog. New rights, new legal figures for workers, new problems.

On the other hand, professional interest agreements do not fit into this list of sources for self-employed workers other than TAED. Article 3.2 of Law 20/2007 just determines that:

> 'any clause in the individual contract of a TAED who is member of a trade union or a self-employed workers association that may apply to such worker for having entered into such contract, will be null and void if it infringes the terms of the professional interest agreement entered into by such trade union or association.'

Law 20/2007 establishes a unique exception to Spanish collective law, which is the possibility of TAEDs to become either members of a trade union—and be

[30] ibid 59; J García Murcia, 'El sistema de fuentes de la relación laboral' in J García Murcia (ed) *Estudios ofrecidos al profesor Martín Valverde* (Oviedo, Universidad de Oviedo, 2007) 19; J Cruz Villalón, 'Propuestas para una regulación del trabajo autónomo' (2005) *Documentación Laboral* no 73, 9.

subject to the terms of Article 28.1 CE and the Freedom of Association and Right to Organise Act[31]—or being members of a professional organisation—under the legal scheme of Article 22 CE and the Law regulating Freedom of Association.[32] This is simply unheard-of and evidences that the legislator has attributed to TAEDs the double condition of employees and employers in terms of freedom of association and right to organise.

The problems in determining the legal nature of these professional interest agreements arise precisely from this vagueness. Are they collective agreements or business agreements of a public legal nature? What is the content of such agreements? Labour, commercial, both? Can a norm-agreement regulate collective working conditions arising from a civil or commercial agreement? What is the normative effectiveness of this new source? Is it a new source of labour rights? Who determines the legitimacy rules to negotiate a professional interest agreement? Is it civil legislation or labour legislation? Moreover, Law 20/2007 grants a large amount of labour rights to self-employed workers, especially TAEDs, which renders ineffective the labour-related contents of such professional interest agreements.[33]

The Law includes a series of statements in Article 13.4 that must be analysed in detail. To begin with, it determines that professional interest agreements must be negotiated under the provisions of the Civil Code. We understand that under the clauses of formation and defects of willingness to contract, since the civil regulations do not include any procedure to enter into agreements. This is in sharp contrast and contraposition with the rules on representativeness and legitimacy to negotiate collective agreements, which partially apply to these agreements. Therefore, we are facing a negotiation procedure that is hybrid too in which civil, labour and trade union regulations converge. How can the industrial action rules on representativeness and legitimacy to enter into collective agreements be compatible with the civil law principles regulating the execution of agreements? What would happen if a party with sufficient representativeness and legitimacy refuses to negotiate a professional interest agreement based on the freedom of negotiation derived from the Civil Code? What instance could force the negotiation of agreements with legal-labour effects subject to the civil procedural law?

In terms of effectiveness, the same Article 13.4 of Law 20/2007 establishes that it will be restricted to the signing parties, and where appropriate, to the self-employed workers' associations and trade unions that have given their explicit consent. Civil agreements with effects on labour with limited effectiveness that are binding for trade unions in Spain? The immediate consequence would be the appearance of real closed-shop clause, which are constitutionally banned in our system, and will

[31] Law 11/1985 of 2 August.

[32] Organic Law 1/2002 of 22 March.

[33] See, M R Martínez Barroso, *Régimen profesional, prevención de riesgos y derechos colectivos de los trabajadores autónomos* (Madrid, Centro de Estudios Financieros, 2006) 135.

determine that for some employers only the workers that are members of the trade unions that have previously signed the agreement will be eligible to enter into agreements. This is a true revolution in our trade union system, and obviously, will place self-employed workers unions in a worse position regarding guaranteed rights than the rest of trade unions made up by employees.

We understand that the Spanish legislator has not taken sufficiently into account the reach of the suppression of the erga omnes effectiveness of the collective agreement by a regulation that has a huge impact on labour relationships. It is true that professional interest agreements cannot be technically labelled as collective agreements. It is likewise true that trade unions can enter into such agreements, and to this end, they do not have to demonstrate any given representativeness. Moreover, the negotiation of professional interest agreements becomes an indicator of representativeness—sufficient presence, says Article 21.1 of Law 20/2007—of the self-employed workers union, whereas in the employee trade union sphere, agreements may be entered into only by unions that are sufficiently representative. It is the world upside down. Therefore, this regulation model can generate clearly discriminatory practices among groups, and of course, the implementation of exclusion practices based on closed-shop clauses that even from the point of view of right to free competition, may lead to major legality problems.

The reality is that Title III of Law 20/2007, on the collective rights of self-employed workers does not provide any rules of any kind for the negotiation of professional interest agreements.[34] It just establishes the sufficient presence criterion to recognise the representativeness of professional associations of self-employed workers (Article 21 of Law 20/2007), without establishing any minimum thresholds or determining who holds the legitimacy to enter into such agreements. Moreover, these organisations, which are subject to the Freedom of Association Law (Article 20 of Law 20/2007), are also subject too, regarding the institutional representativeness typical of trade unions, to Articles 6 and 7 of the Freedom of Association and Right to Organise Act. This means that these professional associations have a hybrid legal nature, which is also unique in our legal system. Moreover, if we consider the fact that self-employed workers can join the trade union or professional association of their choice (Article 19.1.a of Law 20/2007), it is easily understandable that it will be difficult for self-employed workers to find out on which side of the negotiation table they must sit to negotiate such agreements.[35]

[34] ibid, 277; J Tárraga Poveda, 'Los derechos colectivos del trabajador autónomo' in J Luján Alcaraz (ed) *El Estatuto del Trabajador Autónomo* (Murcia, Editorial Laborum, 2007) 207.

[35] See M A Castro Argüelles, 'Los Acuerdos de Interés Profesional: un balance de la negociación llevada a cabo al amparo del Estatuto del Trabajo Autónomo' (2011) *Anales de Derecho* no 29, 20; B Gutiérrez-Solar Calvo and J. Lahera Forteza, 'Ámbito y fuentes de regulación del trabajo autónomo' in AaVv, *El Estatuto del Trabajo Autónomo*, (Madrid, La Ley, 2008) 110; J LLuis y Navas, 'Los acuerdos de interés profesional de los trabajadores autónomos' (2010), *Actualidad Laboral* no 4; S del Rey Guanter, 'Introducción: trascendencia, función y características esenciales de la LETA' in S del Rey Guanter (ed), *Comentarios al estatuto del trabajo autónomo* (Madrid, Lex Nova, 2007) 32.

VI. Civil, Economic and Labour Rights of Self-Employed Workers

Law 20/2007 grants a series of civil, economic and labour rights to self-employed workers in its chapter II. The basic individual rights are free choice of profession or trade, free economic initiative and free competition and right to intellectual property on their work (Article 4.2 of Law 20/2007). Then it lists a series of rights of a mixed nature, civil and labour, which are connected to the performance of a professional activity, among them the right not to be discriminated on any grounds, right to personal privacy and dignity, to training and retraining, to safety and health, to effective judicial protection, to Social Security benefits, and to a working and family life balance (Article 4.3 of Law 20/2007).[36]

The last two are especially relevant. The right to healthcare and sufficient social benefits in case of need, including right to protection in case of maternity, paternity, risk during pregnancy, risk during breastfeeding and adoption or fostering, including pre-adoption and permanent or simple, according to civil regulations, provided that the latter is for a period of not less than one year (Article 4.3.h of Law 20/2007) has been partially regulated by Law 26/2003, of 11 November, on Economic Reform Measures. It includes benefits for temporary disability from the fourth day of sick leave, the possibility of enjoying benefits for occupational accidents and occupational diseases, and the reduction of contributions to individuals under 30 registering with the RETA for the first time and for women over 45. In conclusion, the Law moves forward in equating the social protection of self-employed workers and employees, in line with Recommendation no 4 of the Toledo Covenant.[37]

Regarding the working and family life balance, the Law establishes the right to the activity in the following situations: maternity, paternity, risk during pregnancy, risk during breastfeeding and adoption or fostering, including pre-adoption and permanent or simple, according to civil regulations, provided that the latter is for a period of not less than one year, even if they are provisional, in the terms set forth in Social Security legislation. The absence of ulterior details in the Law leads us to understand that in the matter of suspension, the employment rule of the ET regulating this type of situations, i.e. Article 48,[38] shall apply in suppletive capacity.

In addition to these rights, a series of professional duties are listed in Article 5. Among them, we should highlight the generic duty to fulfil all the obligations resulting from the contracts they have entered into, to comply with all occupational

[36] See, FA González Díaz, 'Régimen profesional del trabajador autónomo' in J Luján Alcaraz (ed), *El Estatuto del Trabajador Autónomo* (Murcia, Editorial Laborum, 2007) 69; J Cruz Villalón, 'El trabajo autónomo: nuevas realidades, nuevos retos' (2005) *Revista Temas Laborales*, no 81, 16.

[37] Decision of 6 April 1995 of the Congress of Deputies, renewed by Decision of 2 October 2003.

[38] See Martínez Barroso, *Régimen profesional* (n 33) 147.

health and safety regulations, registration with and communication of all Social Security registrations and de-registrations and compliance with all tax obligations. Subjection to occupational risk prevention regulations poses likewise the problem of the subjective location of the responsible subject. For the purposes of the Prevention Act, are self-employed workers employees or employers? Are they active or passive subjects regarding safety obligations?

Article 8 of Law 20/2007 tries to give an answer to this important problem but does not add anything new to the provisions of Law 31/1995 of 8 November, on Occupational Risk Prevention. Where, at the same worksite, self-employed workers are working together with employees of other companies, as well as where self-employed workers perform their activity in the facilities of the companies they provide services to, the co-operation, information and training duties set forth in paragraphs 1 and 2 of Article 24 of Law 20/2007 shall apply to all of them. At this level, self-employed workers act as employers and, therefore, their relationship with the manager of the facilities where they perform their activities must be one of co-operation.[39] There is an in vigilando responsibility on the side of the companies contracting with self-employed workers for the performance of works or services that are part of their own activity, and that take place at their facilities; and they shall monitor compliance with occupational risk prevention regulations by these self-employed workers (Article 8.4 of Law 20/2007).

Where self-employed workers must operate with machinery, equipment, products, materials or tools supplied by the company for which they perform their professional activity, but do not carry out such activity within the facilities of such company, the company shall assume the obligations set forth in the last paragraph of Article 41.1 of Law 31/1995, according to which the company must deliver to self-employed workers all the information available from manufacturers, importers and suppliers of the products, machines, equipment, etc they will have to use to perform their work. Therefore, it cannot be assumed that self-employed workers will have an especially protective treatment from the system in terms of occupational risk prevention, and Law 20/2007 just gives them the same treatment as any other employer.

Only paragraph e of Article 8 of Law 20/2007 establishes that non-complying companies shall be liable for any compensation for any damages caused, provided there is a direct relationship between such non-compliance and the damages caused. In these cases, the liability, which will be held by the offending employer, will be so regardless of whether the self-employed worker is paying contributions covering occupational accidents. Therefore, the only real case in which

[39] See A Ceinos Suárez, 'Autónomos Económicamente Dependientes' in J García Murcia (ed), *El Trabajo Autónomo* (2007) 71; FA González Díaz, 'La prevención de riesgos laborales del trabajador autónomo' in J Luján Alcaraz (ed), *El Estatuto del Trabajador Autónomo* 97; S González Ortega, 'El tratamiento de los riesgos de los trabajadores autónomos' (2005) *Temas Laborales* no 81, 152; J Fernández Costales Muñiz, 'Los trabajadores autónomos en la Ley de Prevención de Riesgos Laborales' in AaVv, *La Seguridad Social de los Trabajadores Autónomos* (Granada, Editorial Laborum, 2007) 186.

self-employed workers are treated similarly to employees in the field of occupational risks is the right to stop working and leave the workplace when they consider that the activity they are carrying out entails a severe and immediate risk for their life or health. Therefore, it cannot be said that Law 20/2007 has meant any change or improvement in the recognition of occupational risk prevention rights for self-employed workers. If at all, the right to stop their activity, but in no case the regulation specifies the contractual consequences at civil or commercial level such interruption may cause, since the nature of this right, despite being based on Article 21 of Law 31/1995 is by no means related to labour.

The hybrid—civil, commercial, labour—nature of this Law 20/2007 becomes evident in the recognition of a series of economic guarantees (Article 10 of Law 20/2007) which is a mere reminder of the battery of civil and commercial provisions guaranteeing credits in operations of this nature.[40] Indeed, it is with these types of provisions that this Law evidences its most positive aspects. It is a regulation that brings together different regulatory sources and orders; it is just a regulation compiling and systematising other legal provisions. It is indeed a Statute, but a Statute that does not create a new legal framework, it just delimits it formally, probably creating specific problems that did not exist before.

VII. The Economically Dependent Self-Employed Worker (TAED): Core Worker or Contingent Worker?

Article 11.1 of Law 20/2007 defines the TAED as a worker performing an economic or professional activity for profit and in a regular, personal, direct and predominant manner for an individual or legal person called client, from which they are economically dependent, since they receive from such client at least 75 per cent of their total income from employed work and economic and professional activities. There is, therefore, a quantitative assessment element, which makes this figure very unstable, because such 75 per cent of total income—is it gross income, net income, income subject to taxation?—in addition to having been randomly defined, may change based on the specific economic situation at any time of the contracts entered into by such TAED with the main employer.[41]

[40] Especially, Law 3/2004, of 29 December, establishing measures to fight late payments in commercial operations, or Insolvency Law 22/2003 of 9 July, or Insolvency Law in the matter of privileges and preferences of credits of these workers, and Articles 605 to 607 of Law 1/2000, of 7 January, on Civil Procedures. See, C Tolosa Treviño, 'Comentarios a la Ley 20/2007, del Estatuto del Trabajador Autónomo' (2007) *Información Laboral-Jurisprudencia* no 8, 2007.

[41] See A Ceinos Suárez, 'Autónomos Económicamente Dependientes' (n 39) 57; A Selma Penalva, 'El Trabajador autónomo económicamente dependiente' in J Luján Alcaraz (ed), *El Estatuto del Trabajador Autónomo* (Murcia, Editorial Laborum, 2007) 125; C Tolosa Treviño, 'Comentarios a la Ley 20/2007' (n 40) 9.

The Law intends to correct this situation by establishing a series of objective requirements that can be met simultaneously for a worker to be classified as TAED. In this regard, Article 11.2 establishes (a) that he shall not have any employees or contract or subcontract all or part of his activity to any third party. This applies both for the activity contracted with the client from which he is economically dependent and for any other activity contracted with other clients. Moreover, (b) he shall not carry his activity in a manner that is not different from the workers under any type of employment contract with the client; and shall (c) have his own production infrastructure and materials, as required for the performance of his activity and independent from those of his client whenever they are economically relevant for such activity. The last two conditions required are: (d) carrying out his activity according to his own organisational criteria, subject to any technical directions received from the client; and (e) receive a financial compensation based on the outcome of his activity according to the terms agreed with his client on his own risk and venture. It is obvious that the main concern of the legislator is to ensure a series of traits that clearly identify the employer, which may turn out to be a paradox, since in conclusion, the ultimate purpose is to provide the greatest possible labour protection to someone who is required to show unequivocal signs of being an employer in the legal commercial sense.

The determination of the percentage with its natural fluctuations will be that the condition of TAED will be alternatively granted or denied to these workers, resulting in the generation of an extremely high legal uncertainty regarding their status and obligations. This can be verified by just reading the list of individual rights that will derive from the recognition of the TAED conditions, a recognition that shall take place for each specific activity the TAED may perform. Article 12 sets forth that the condition of TAED shall be determined by means of a contract regarding the performance of the productive activity of the TAED, which must be executed in written and shall be registered at the relevant public office. These issues have been regulated by Royal Decree 197/2009, of 23 February, regulating the Self-Employment Statute regarding contracts of economically dependent self-employed workers and their registration, and establishing the National Register of professional associations of self-employed workers.

Hence, the TAED must state specifically in the contract his condition of economic dependence from the client who is party to the contract, as well as any changes that may occur in this respect. Article 12.2 determines that the condition of TAED can be held with one single client. There is an extreme difficulty derived from establishing whether the amount of the consideration the self-employed worker shall receive from his main client will exceed 75 per cent of his total income or not. It may happen that this is not initially the case, but the Law (Article 12.3) establishes that when subsequent circumstances occur, leading to the threshold being exceeded, that would allow the self-employed worker to be classified as TAED, the contract signed by the parties shall remain in force unless the parties agree to change it in order to update it to the new conditions that would correspond to an economically dependent self-employed worker.

Moreover, if such TAED contract has not determined a specific term or service, it shall be assumed, unless there is proof to the contrary, that such contract has been agreed for an indefinite term. Article 1583 of our Civil Code established that any lifelong lease of services is null and void. The only guidance we have in order not to consider such provision of Law 20/2007 as invalid is understanding that a TAED contract is not a civil contract. We may consider that it is a contractual hybrid of a civil-commercial nature with legal-labour effect, but the truth is that the Law does not contain any provision on the legal nature of such contract. The baseline problem is that the content of such contract assumes the existence of a special legal relationship with evident labour effects, which places this relationship in a vagueness environment.

To make the situation brought about by this TAED contract even more complex, Article 13 of Law 20/2007 establishes the rules of articulation between professional interest agreements and such contract, completing the regulation of the normative hierarchy principle of Article 3.3 Law 20/2007. According to it, the conditions agreed in the professional interest agreement prevail over the terms of the individual TAED contract. If both, the individual contract and the professional interest agreement have contractual effects, why does the legislator grant the role of hierarchical superior source to the professional interest agreement, with derogative effects on the clauses of the individual contract? What type of effectiveness is this which faced with two equal contracts, one individual and on collective, grants preference to the collective agreement? Is this a civil effectiveness or a labour effectiveness? It is obviously another hybrid in our system and additionally, it does not guarantee the rights of the TAED, this new and mysterious class of workers/employers.

VIII. The TAED as Holder of Labour Rights

Articles 14 to 18 of Law 20/2007 establish a series of rights of an unquestionably labour nature for economically dependent self-employed workers. To start with, Article 14 grants the right of TAEDs to holidays, establishing 18 working days, without prejudice to an eventual extension agreed by the parties or by means of professional interest agreements. Nothing is said about whether such days of 'interruption' shall be paid, interruption is the euphemism used by the legislator to label what is obviously a holiday period. Could it be agreed that such holidays be paid? Of course, since it will depend on the professional interest agreements, rather than on the individual contract. Is it possible that there are TAEDs with paid holidays and TAEDs with unpaid holidays working for the same company? Without a doubt, since it will depend on whether there is an agreement or not. Therefore, the holiday regulation model is subject to potential situations of discrimination.

The same happens with the weekly rest period, bank holidays, maximum working hours and weekly distribution of working hours over the year. Article 14.2

leaves their determination to the individual contract and the professional interest agreement. Only Article 14.3 attempts to set by contract of collective agreement the limits of overtime work, which is euphemistically called 'performance of work for longer time than agreed'. In the absence of such regulation of limits, the additional working hours, regardless of the method of calculation, shall not exceed 30 per cent of the initially agreed standard activity time. After all, this is an expression of the legislator's state of mind. On the one hand, it wants to grant a level of protection to the working conditions of TAEDs equivalent to that of employees, at least in formal terms. On the other hand, it realises that the setting of limits for working hours, their distribution, or of minimum weekly rest periods cannot be too interventionist, it cannot invade the field of freedom of enterprise, of free competition.

The consequence is that regarding working hours, there would be no impediment for an appropriate regulation through individual contracts of interest agreements of working hours at all levels, daily and weekly working hours, distribution of working time, daily and weekly rest periods, holidays, etc to establish for TAEDs the same working conditions enjoyed by the employees of the main contractor.

Regarding termination of contracts, it is surprising that Article 15 of Law 20/2007 establishes a list of legal causes of termination, which are remarkably similar to the generic causes for termination of employment contracts listed in Article 49 ET. Since they are not employment contracts, the general clauses for contract termination established in the Civil Code (Article 1290 CC) would have sufficed to regulate this matter, but the legislator has opted for introducing details of a labour nature, that add little in terms of protection of rights of self-employed workers. Mutual agreement of the parties and any valid clause included in the contract are the two general clauses; in addition to death, retirement or disability incompatible with professional activities according to Social Security regulations, withdrawal with prior notice by the TAED, decision of the worker based on serious breach of contract by the other party, or decision of the client based on justified reasons.

Since the client's justified reasons are not specified, it is really a free unilateral withdrawal by the client what the regulation provides, which in our opinion is incompatible with the supposed guarantees the regulation should provide. Moreover, it is so although in these cases the TAED is entitled to compensation for damages. Therefore, there is little protection in case of termination of the TAED contract. When a contract is terminated by a decision of either party based on breach of contract by the other party, the party terminating the contract shall be entitled to receive the appropriate compensation for damages (Article 15.2 of Law 20/2007).

Regarding compensation for termination of contract, paragraph 3 of Article 15 establishes that when the TAED is the party entitled to compensation, the amount of such compensation shall be the one established by the individual contract or the applicable professional interest agreement. Where such compensation has not been regulated, the factors that shall be taken into account to calculate such compensation are the following: time remaining of contract duration, seriousness of breach by client, investments and expenses made by TAED in connection with the performance of the professional activity under contract, and prior notice period given to client from contract termination date.

The provision for justified interruptions of professional activity (Article 16 of Law 20/2007) includes a heterogeneous list of causes, some of them directly related to the suspension of the employment regulated in Articles 45 to 48 ET, the leaves listed in Article 37 ET and other ones are fully new, such as the one allowing self-employed women suffering gender-based violence to make protection effective or their right to integrated social care. This list includes the need to take care of urgent, sudden and unexpected responsibilities (Article 8.7 of Law 20/2007), force majeure (without specifying whether it affects the client of the TAED) or temporary disability, maternity or paternity (which in principle excludes all other situations arising from taking over parenting duties). This list can be extended by personal contract of professional interest agreement; these causes cannot justify a decision to terminate by the client, except in the case of force majeure, where such termination causes severe damages or stops or alters the normal performance of the activity.

Hence, the labour bias is clearly defined in this list of causes for termination or suspension of the TAED contract. Indeed, Article 17 of Law 20/2007 sets forth that labour courts shall hear all claims related to contracts entered into by a TAED and his client. Labour courts are also competent to hear any demand resulting from the application and interpretation of professional interest agreements, subject to the terms of competition law.

The designation of law courts to settle controversies is a more than indicative element of the strong labour bias existing in the legal definition of the TAED figure. There is no question that in the future we will face a series of major problems when it comes to judicial consideration of individual contracts and professional interest agreements. Their non-labour nature being hybrid, if at all, will force judges to decide on the legal-labour consequences of contractual clauses with a strong civil or commercial nature. Indeed, competition law, Law 15/2007, of 3 July, designates the National Competition Commission to resolve all litigation and arbitration on all issues related to the matters addressed in the text of the regulation, which gives rise to conflicts of jurisdiction with the labour courts.[42]

Another factor that does not contribute to clarifying this situation is the fact that Article 18 establishes that administrative or pre-judicial conciliation are mandatory prior to the filing of any legal action regarding the professional regime of TAEDs. A further element that does not help either is the possibility to establish, through professional interest agreements, specific conflict settlement bodies,

[42] See J Tárraga Poveda, 'Cuestiones procesales' in J Luján Alcaraz (ed), *El Estatuto del Trabajador Autónomo* (2007) 291; P Aramendi Sánchez, 'La competencia de la jurisdicción social en el anteproyecto de la Ley del Estatuto del Trabajo Autónomo' (2006) *Documentación Laboral*, no 77, 22; C Tolosa Triviño, 'Comentarios a la Ley 20/2007' (n 40) 14.

as Article 97 ET establishes for collective agreements. Indeed, since professional interest agreements lack regulatory effectiveness, paragraph 3 of Article 18 of Law 20/2007 sets forth that the decisions of such conflict settlement bodies shall be enforceable for the parties, without the need of ratification before the course, and be enforced through judgment enforcement proceedings.[43]

Such proceedings shall take place before the labour courts; however, we wonder whether it is possible that the present labour mediation, arbitration and conciliation bodies be the best suited ones to take over these new conciliation competences. It might seem that this is the case; moreover, it would not make much sense establishing the duplicity of such bodies when what is actually intended is to settle controversies, which at the end have a social and labour content, and their settlement will ultimately depend from a labour court. Regarding the specific arbitration procedure, arbitral awards will be considered equivalent to final judgments. Voluntary arbitration proceedings shall fall under the scope of Law 60/2003 on Arbitration, Law 16/1987 on Regulation of Inland Transport or any other specific or sectoral regulations.

IX. Social Security Rights of TAEDs

Title IV of Law 20/2007 is entirely devoted to the regulation of the social protection of self-employed workers, but its content is largely programmatic and laws and special regulations on registration, contributions and benefits regulate the material content of such social protection. The reference in Article 23 of Law 20/2007 to Article 41 CE is especially significant, since this constitutional provision establishes the right of individuals performing an economic activity on their own or self-employed to maintain a public Social Security system, which guarantees the sufficient social care and benefits in situations of need, allowing additional voluntary benefits.[44]

In Spain, the protection of workers on their own account or self-employed will be instrumented after the approval of this Law through one single scheme, called Special Social Security Scheme for Workers of their Own Account or Self-Employed. The legislator's idea is systematically stated in the Second Final Clause of Law 20/2007, according to which all necessary measures shall be progressively implemented, according to the principles inspiring this Law to achieve the confluence in contributions and rights of self-employed workers and with those established for employees in the General Social Security Scheme. Registration with the

[43] See, P Aramendi Sánchez, 'La competencia de la jurisdicción social' (n 42) 25.

[44] See J Tárrega Poveda, 'La protección social del trabajador autónomo' in J Luján Alcaraz (ed), *El Estatuto del Trabajador Autónomo* 253; F Cavas Martínez and A Cámara Botía, *La acción protectora del Régimen Especial de la Seguridad Social de los Trabajadores por Cuenta Propia o Autónomos* (Pamplona, Thomson-Aranzadi, 2005) 40.

Social Security system is mandatory for all self-employed workers, and one single one for their entire professional life, without prejudice to the registrations and deregistrations with the different schemes integrating the system. Together with this Special Scheme, only the schemes for Offshore Workers and Coal Miners survive.[45]

Article 25 of Law 20/207 reminds us that according to Article 15 of the General Social Security Act, contribution to the RETA is mandatory, although different contribution bases for TAEDs can be established by law. Likewise, it provides for legal reductions or discounts in the contribution bases for specific groups of self-employed workers in accordance with their individual characteristics or the professional characteristics of the activity they perform.[46]

The protective action of the RETA has been extended thanks to the enforcement of Law 20/2007. According to its Article 26, such action shall include, in all cases, healthcare in the cases of maternity, common or occupational disease and occupational and other accidents. Likewise, self-employed workers are entitled to economic benefits in case of temporary disability, risk during pregnancy, maternity, paternity, risk during breastfeeding, permanent disability, retirement, death, survival and child allowance. Social Service benefits shall be as established by law and, in all cases, shall comprise benefits for re-education, rehabilitation for disabled people, care for the elderly and professional recovery.

After the coming into force of Law 20/2007, TAEDs must pay Social Security contributions to cover temporary disability and occupational accidents and diseases.[47] For the purposes of such coverage, occupational accident shall be construed as any bodily injury suffered during or as a result of professional activities, comprising also accidents on the way to work. Unless proven otherwise, it shall be assumed that an accident has no relationship to work when it takes place outside of the relevant professional activity.

[45] Regulated by Decree 3772/1972, of 23 December, Decree 2346/1969, of 25 September, Decree 2864/1974, of 30 August and Decree 298/1973, of 8 February, respectively. In addition to these framework regulations, there are multiple legal and regulatory provisions regulating their basic rules and protective action. The plethora of rules and their highly specific nature makes a simplification process necessary. The Government is already working in it.

[46] The Second Additional Provision of Law 20/2007, [2007] BOE 12 July, defines the groups of workers entitled to reductions and rebates: (a) workers that because of another activity pay contributions accounting for a total sum above the maximum General Social Security Scheme base; (b) self-employed disabled workers; (c) self-employed workers engaged in itinerant trade and doorstep sales; and (d) any other groups established by law or regulation.

[47] The Third Additional Provision of Law 20/2007, [2007] BOE 12 July, established that as from 1 January 2008, self-employed workers having decided not to contribute to temporary disability benefits shall do so mandatorily, provided that they are not entitled to such benefit based on activities performed under a different Social Security Scheme. The only exception to this obligation is self-employed workers under the Special Scheme for Agricultural Workers that join the General Social Security Scheme, for whom temporary disability and professional contingencies coverage will remain voluntary. A further regulation shall establish professional activities with a higher occupational accident risk, for which occupational accident and professional disease coverage shall be mandatory.

Article 26.4 of Law 20/2007 is also programmatic where it proclaims that public powers shall promote policies encouraging continued exercise of the trade, work or economic activity of self-employed workers beyond the standard retirement age. Early retirement is also provided for in hazardous and arduous activities in the same cases established for employees. In a clear statement of the general intention of the legislator, Article 26.5 finally proclaims that the protective action of the public Social Security scheme for self-employed workers shall converge in terms of contributions, rights and benefits with the scheme in place for employees in the General Social Security Scheme. The economic crisis and budget situation of the Social Security System in Spain has prevented this convergence so far.

In turn, the Fourth Additional Provision of Law 20/2007 introduced a benefit for end of activity, which turns out to be a euphemism to speak about the unemployment benefits for self-employed workers. Provided that the principles of contributiveness, solidarity and financial sustainability can be guaranteed, and that it meets the needs and preferences of self-employed workers, the Government shall propose the legal regulation of a specific protection system in case of end of activity based on the workers' personal characteristics or on the nature of the activity performed. Public Authorities may, for duly justified economic policy reasons, co-finance end of activity plans for specific groups or economic sectors. According to Law 32/2010, of August 5, from January 2012 it is possible to pay contribution for cessation of activity establishing benefits for a minimum of 2 months and a maximum of 12 months with a contribution of 48 months.

X. Towards A 'Soft' Labour Law for TAEDs and Contingent Workers?

The concept of core worker is reserved in our labour law to employees who are included in the scope of the 'Estatuto de los Trabajadores'. Its characterisation includes the application of collective agreements with general effectiveness and the existence of a permanent or temporary contract regulated by law. They are also characterised by general coverage of the social security regime. The TAEDs are clearly contingent workers. Their regulatory framework can be characterised as soft labour law, with supplementary application of the 'Estatuto de los Trabajadores' and a very precarious regime of social security. The group of contingent workers in Spain is growing at an enormous speed, especially in the last five years. This situation is exacerbated as a result of several factors. The first is redirecting workers and unemployed workers into self-employment. Active employment policies focus their efforts on easy drive entrepreneurship, as we have seen. The second factor has to do with the reform of collective bargaining. This reform has led to a very sharp devaluation of wages and other working conditions in Spain. The possibility of small companies to declare the non-application of the industry collective agreement when the economic, technical, organisational or production circumstances are unfavourable, leaves the regulation of working conditions in the hands of the free market.

But contingent workers in Spain are also characterised by other circumstances. The abuse of contractual formulae of part-time work, 'zero hours' contract, and the concatenation of temporary work contracts also contribute to the precariousness of working conditions. There is currently a generalised debate about the figure of the 'poor worker', that is the one that has a full-time, fixed or temporary work contract rewarded with the national minimum wage (less than 700 euros/month). Trade unions estimate that there may be 2 million workers in Spain in these conditions. Contingent workers are also young people and women. In the past five years, more than 200,000 workers under 30 years have left Spain to find work. These are qualified workers, with higher education. Young workers without professional qualifications and no possibility of working abroad are accessing now more easily the labour market, but their working conditions are much more precarious. Gender also characterises contingent workers in Spain, who are mostly women.

To conclude, we could say that the segmentation between core and contingent workers in the Spanish labour market is growing in leaps and bounds after the labour reforms of 2010, 2012 and 2013. There is an accelerated process of 'escape of the labour law framework' in which redirection towards self-employment is only one of its manifestations. The debate on the single contract is currently part of all political programmes in Spain. If we want to combat the gap between core and contingent workers through this contract, things will surely evolve for the worse. The levels of protection of labour rights are under minimum in Spain, and that can be a bad starting point to initiate this debate.

10

Inverting the Flexicurity Paradigm: The United Kingdom and Zero Hours Contracts

JEFF KENNER

I. Introduction

If the United Kingdom has, to quote one former Prime Minister, 'the most lightly regulated labour market of any leading economy in the world',[1] the phenomenon that has become known as the 'zero hours contract' (ZHC) is a meme that has entered into societal discourse as connotative of the ultimate form of the legalised commodification of labour. The ZHC, as a label, is colloquial and legally specious, in the absence of an accepted cognisable normative definition for the types of contract to which it is applied. As there is no single typology, it is best to understand ZHCs as encompassing a 'wide spectrum' of casual work contracts,[2] under which, in essence, 'an employer agrees to pay for work done but makes no commitment to provide a set number of hours of work per day, week or month'.[3] Zero hours arrangements can simply be described as a mix between casual labour and part-time work.[4] Nevertheless, despite the absence of a 'clear or overarching category or organising principle',[5] the widespread use of these types of contract in the UK makes a study of ZHCs pertinent in the context of the core/contingent dichotomy as, firstly, in many cases, zero hours workers (ZHWs) perceive

[1] Tony Blair MP, Introduction, *Fairness at Work* (White Paper, Cm 3968, 1998): webarchive.nationalarchives.gov.uk/+/http:/www.berr.gov.uk/files/file24436.pdf.

[2] See A Adams, M Freedland and J Prassl, *The 'Zero-Hours Contract': Regulating casual work, or legitimating precarity?* (European Labour Law Network Working Paper No 5, March 2015) 5.

[3] Z Adams and S Deakin, *Re-regulating Zero Hours Contracts* (Institute of Employment Rights, 2014) 6.

[4] *Mailway (Southern) Ltd v Wilsher* [1978] ICR 511 (Kilner Brown J).

[5] A Adams, M Freedland and J Prassl (n 2) 7.

themselves as having no contract for continuing employment, and secondly, these workers often do not have access to the firm's 'internal labour market' of collective agreements, pensions and security.[6] It is necessary, however, when analysing the zero hours phenomenon, and proposing reforms of the law, to take heed of the warning that any attempt at regulation 'must … be approached most cautiously, so as not to become merely an exercise in normalising a wide array of precarious arrangements'.[7]

The rise in ZHCs is a feature of globalisation and, throughout the EU, various forms of zero hours contracting are multiplying often in the form of 'on call' working but, in several EU Member States, subject to specific minimum standards' requirements to protect workers.[8] In the UK, however, where zero hours working is part of a long-term trend towards more flexibility and diversity in working arrangements,[9] these forms of contract have become synonymous with the 'most extreme form'[10] of precarious employment that the EU's most casualised labour market has spawned. Within the boundaries set by UK law for permissible employment contracts, ZHCs offer total flexibility to the employer to choose if and when to offer work,[11] so as minimise cost and maximise profitability, and, conversely, total insecurity for the worker, who has no guarantee of a stable income or social security. ZHCs represent contingency max, an inversion of the European 'flexicurity' paradigm of an inclusive labour market that meets the need of workers for both flexibility and security throughout their working lives.[12]

In part two of this chapter, the emergence and rise of the culture of zero hours working in the UK's flexible labour market is explored in the light of increasing concerns about the use of ZHCs by some companies and organisations as part of their business model. Part three assesses the legal status and employment rights of workers on ZHCs. Part four discusses the lawfulness of ZHCs and proposals for reform of the law to end exploitation of ZHWs. Part five concludes with some suggestions for widening the scope of employment protection.

[6] See Ch 3 by Lo Faro in this volume.

[7] A Adams, M Freedland and J Prassl (n 2) 4.

[8] Z Adams and S Deakin (n 3) 28.

[9] Chartered Institute of Personnel and Development (CIPD), 'Zero Hours Contracts: Myths and Reality' (November 2013) 6, see www.cipd.co.uk/binaries/zero-hours-contracts_2013-myth-reality.pdf.

[10] Z Adams and S Deakin (n 3) 3.

[11] See part III of this chapter below.

[12] See further, European Commission Communication, *Towards Common Principles of Flexicurity: more and better jobs through flexibility and security*, COM(2007) 359 final; and J Kenner, 'New Frontiers in EU Labour Law: From Flexicurity to Flex-Security' in M Dougan and S Currie (eds), *50 Years of the European Treaties: Looking Back and Thinking Forward* (Hart Publishing, 2009) 279–310.

II. The Culture of Zero Hours Work in the UK

A. Zero Hours Work: The Raw Facts

According to estimates from the UK Office for National Statistics (ONS), 801,000 people, 2.5 per cent of those in employment, had a ZHC as their main employment contract in the period from October to December 2015.[13] This was an increase of 15 per cent from the same period in 2014, when the total was 697,000 or 2.3 per cent of people in employment. However, because many people have more than one ZHC, or have a ZHC in addition to a standard full-time or part-time employment contract, and the numbers of ZHCs vary seasonally, the total number of ZHCs at the mid-point of the survey period stood at a much higher 1.7 million, or 6 per cent of all employment contracts.[14] The ONS also identified a further two million ZHCs where no work was carried out either because workers were not accepting work for personal reasons or, due to fluctuating demand, no work was available in the reference period.[15] 10 per cent of businesses as a whole make use of ZHCs with a much larger 40 per cent of businesses that employ 250 or more people.[16] For the purpose of these statistics, the ONS defines ZHCs broadly as contracts 'that do not guarantee a minimum number of hours', based on a survey of businesses.[17]

People on ZHCs are more likely to be young, part-time, women, and students in full-time education, when compared to the UK workforce as a whole.[18] This is hardly surprising as jobs on the periphery 'tend to be taken by people who are already disadvantaged in the labour market for other reasons'.[19] The statistics reveal that 38 per cent are aged 16 to 24 compared with 12 per cent for all people not on a ZHC.[20] Such contracts are most prevalent in low paid sectors such as hotels, catering, retail and leisure.[21] 63 per cent of ZHWs work part-time with an

[13] Office for National Statistics (ONS), *Contracts that do not guarantee a minimum number of hours* (9 March 2016): www.ons.gov.uk/employmentandlabourmarket/peopleinwork/earningsandworkinghours/articles/contractsthatdonotguaranteeaminimumnumberofhours/march2016.

[14] ibid Summary. The figures are for the fortnight beginning 9 November 2015. Indeed, in the fortnight beginning 11 May 2015, 2.1 million contracts were recorded.

[15] ibid part 3.

[16] ibid.

[17] ibid Summary.

[18] ibid.

[19] A Davies, *Employment Law* (Pearson, 2015) 95.

[20] ONS report 2016 (n 13) part 4. It is also notable that 23% of people on ZHCs are in full-time education compared to 3% of all people in employment. This suggests that many young people find ZHCs flexible for combining work with study.

[21] ibid part 3. In accommodation and food services, one in four companies, 26%, make use of ZHCs when compared with around one in twenty companies, 5%, in construction. Seasonal factors may accentuate these variations.

average of 26 weekly hours, with 17 per cent working no hours in the surveyed week.[22] More than one in three, 37 per cent, would like to work more hours with most wanting those additional hours in the same job.[23]

Research by the Resolution Foundation reveals that the growth in the number of workers employed on ZHCs is a factor in the general 'squeeze' on low wages as ZHWs receive lower gross weekly pay, an average of £236 per week, compared with £482 per week for those who are not on ZHCs.[24] Moreover, because workers on ZHCs work fewer hours than workers on standard contracts, the growing use of ZHCs is a contributory factor in rising rates of under-employment.[25] Many ZHWs have the experience of being 'zeroed-down' when the amount of work on offer reduces week by week and eventually dries up altogether.[26]

One side-effect of the fluctuations in working hours and pay, which go hand in hand with ZHCs, is a negative impact for the workers concerned when they are required to interact with the UK welfare system. As earnings fall, workers on ZHCs may revert to claiming Jobseeker's Allowance (JSA) to supplement their income. Under the JSA system, a claimant can be disqualified from benefit, or sanctioned, for refusing a direction to take work and may face the loss of all social security benefits for a certain period.[27] Under the new system of Universal Credit, which is gradually replacing JSA and other benefits,[28] even more stringent conditionality will be applied, which 'will increase the pressure on individuals to accept casualised forms of employment'.[29] In practice, this might mean that a worker in such a predicament, who refuses to accept an offer of zero hours work because they are seeking more regular hours, could be subjected to a sanction and loss of benefits.[30] The UK Government does not accept that ZHCs are, by default, unsuitable and is prepared to 'mandate' ZHCs for job-seekers on Universal Credit.[31] Overall, as Zoe Adams and Simon Deakin note, the cumulative effect of these and other social security changes has made the UK system of unemployment compensation 'one of the least protective in the developed world'.[32] There is no doubt that the threat

[22] ibid part 4. The 17% not working in the surveyed week compares with 12% of the workforce as a whole who are not working.

[23] ibid Summary.

[24] M Pennycock, G Cory and V Alakeson, *A Matter of Time: The rise of zero-hours contracts* (Resolution Foundation, 2013) 3, see www.resolutionfoundation.org/publications/matter-time-rise-zero-hours-contracts/.

[25] ibid.

[26] ibid 4.

[27] Jobseeker's Allowance Regulations 2013, SI 2013/378. See further, Z Adams and S Deakin (n 3) 19–27.

[28] Introduced by the Welfare Reform Act 2012 and due to become fully effective in 2017.

[29] Z Adams and S Deakin (n 3) 24.

[30] D Pyper and A Dar, *Zero-hours contracts* (House of Commons Briefing Paper Number 06553, 10 November 2015) 13.

[31] Letter from Esther McVey MP, then Minister for Employment, to Sheila Gilmore MP, dated 1 March 2014. Cited, ibid 13.

[32] Z Adams and S Deakin (n 3) 20.

of the removal of the safety net of social security is a key driver in the growth of ZHCs and other forms of precarious work in the UK labour market.[33]

Many of the most vulnerable ZHWs now form part of an increasing 'precariat' in the UK, described by Guy Standing as 'a multitude of insecure people, living bits-and-pieces lives, in and out of short-term jobs, without a narrative of occupational development'.[34] Such workers, denied the certainty of work, are under constant pressure because they simply do not know, from week to week, whether they can pay the rent or household bills or clothe their children.[35]

Nevertheless, it is argued by some that ZHCs are 'unfairly demonised' because many ZHWs benefit from the flexibility that such arrangements offer.[36] These workers prefer adaptable working hours' contracts because they do not wish to work at fixed and regular times from week to week. Flexible hours contracts suit many students, single people, carers and older or retired workers, who wish to use zero hours work to 'blend paid work with other domestic commitments, education or other personal, family or community interests'.[37] According to a survey by the Charter Institute of Personnel and Development (CIPD), ZHWs are more likely to be satisfied with their work-life balance (65 per cent) when compared to all employees (58 per cent), and have similar overall job satisfaction levels with those working on more standard employment contracts.[38] This is somewhat at odds with the findings of research conducted by the Resolution Foundation that, for the majority of people employed on these types of contract, the freedom and choice they ostensibly offer is 'more apparent than real'.[39]

The immediate question, therefore, is whether such an uncertain but flexible form of working, desirable for some, should be permitted for those for whom it is convenient, when others, for whom ZHCs are not a matter of choice, seek, and indeed need, regular hours, secure employment and an end to a vicious cycle of personal and financial precariousness. Additionally, we must ask, when such uncertainty inexorably leads to exploitation, what steps should be taken to prevent the abuse of such contractual arrangements or indeed to outlaw them altogether if no other solution can be found. In seeking to find answers to these questions, we first need to understand the motivation and the method of those employers who have made ZHCs a central part of their business model.

[33] ibid 19.

[34] G Standing, *The precariat—the new dangerous class* (Policy Network 2011) 1, see www.policy-network.net/uploads/media/154/7468.pdf.

[35] See P Fleming, 'There's nothing good about the rise in zero-hours contracts—ban them now', *The Guardian* (London, 7 September 2015), see www.theguardian.com/commentisfree/2015/sep/07/nothing-good-about-zero-hours-contract-abolish-them.

[36] Chartered Institute of Personnel and Development (CIPD), *Consultation on zero-hours employment contracts: submission to the Department for Business, Innovation and Skills* (March 2014) para 7.

[37] CIPD (n 9) 6.

[38] ibid 14.

[39] Resolution Foundation (n 24) 4.

B. Zero Hours Contracts—'Demutualising' the Employment Relationship

According to research by the Resolution Foundation, there are four main reasons why ZHCs are attractive for UK employers.[40] First, they allow employers to maximise the flexibility of their workforce to more easily adjust to variations in demand, which may help them cope with an economic downturn. As the authors put it bluntly: 'zero-hours contracts allow an employer to transfer the burden of varying demand onto the workforce'.[41] This process of burden shifting is an example of what Freedland and Kountouris have aptly described as 'demutualisation', a term used to describe the many ways in which employers may seek to transfer economic risks that they would normally have to bear onto the workforce.[42] Of course, it is also sometimes the case that such workforce flexibility may be introduced to provide flexibility for individual staff.[43] Second, ZHCs allow employers to better manage costs, keeping wages down, and reduce risk. If a major contract falls through, ZHWs hours can be zeroed down 'at a stroke'.[44] Third, recruitment and training costs are reduced because ZHWs are, in practice, a pool of trained workers ready to bring in as and when required and, therefore, save the employer the cost of hiring and training new workers or using an agency. Fourth, some employers may, anecdotal evidence suggests, use ZHCs to avoid employment obligations such as maternity leave and redundancy pay.[45] The extent to which ZHCs actually enable employers to evade employment protection laws will be considered further in part three below.

In the CIPD survey, 45 per cent of employers reported using ZHCs as part of a long-term strategy.[46] Many public sector organisations in the UK have made ZHCs a central part of their business model. In the public and non-profit sectors, the use of ZHCs is common in order to respond to fluctuations in demand to meet needs, such as education and health care, and to manage tight budgets. Many organisations, such as Moorfield Eye Hospital National Health Service (NHS) Foundation Trust and Outlook Care, have introduced 'staff banks' of ZHWs to be called in to meet unpredictable demand for care, reduce the need for agency staff, cut overtime and fill in for sickness absence and holidays.[47] Such practices are

[40] ibid 13.

[41] ibid.

[42] M Freedland and N Kountouris, *The Legal Construction of Personal Work Relations* (OUP, 2011) 433–446.

[43] CIPD (n 9) 12.

[44] Resolution Foundation (n 24) 13.

[45] ibid.

[46] CIPD (n 9) 13.

[47] ibid case studies at 22 and 26. In the case of Outlook Care, a non-profit organisation, 330 permanent staff are employed to meet basic needs with an extra 200 on casual contracts to meet variations in demand for services.

increasingly common in the care sector where 23 per cent of the adult social care workforce are on ZHCs.[48]

In the private sector, significant users of ZHCs include major retailers (Tesco, Sports Direct, Amazon), hotel chains (Holiday Inn), vehicle hirers (Hertz), food outlets (Subway, McDonalds), pub chains (Wetherspoons), and entertainment businesses (Cineworld).[49] For example, all 300 of Hertz UK's drivers are ZHWs. In a highly competitive market, the use of ZHWs meets fluctuating customer demand, varying from season to season. While this causes uncertainty for the workers, Hertz classifies its ZHWs as employees and provides them with contracts similar to those of its permanent staff.[50] In other cases, such as Holiday Inn, 15 per cent of ZHWs typically progress to permanent contracts.[51] Nevertheless, a study by the Work Foundation found that 44 per cent of ZHWs have had the same employer for two years and 25 per cent have been with the same employer for five years or more.[52]

The media, sometimes using undercover investigations, have revealed many examples of alleged abuses. For example, an exposé by Channel 4 News found heavy reliance on ZHWs at Amazon's massive packing warehouse at Rugeley in Staffordshire. According to former workers, staff were 'forced to make themselves available for work with no guarantee they will be offered a shift on a particular day'.[53] Claims were made of GPS tracking of staff to monitor their movements and airport-style security searches of staff for stolen goods during meal breaks.[54]

Much of the media coverage has focused on Sports Direct, one of the UK's largest sportswear retailers, which has developed a business model that is almost totally reliant on zero hours contracting and other 'demutualising' or burden shifting practices. More than eight in ten of the company's 27,000 workers are on ZHCs.[55] Following a lawsuit over its use of ZHCs in November 2014, Sports Direct, as part of a settlement, agreed to make clear in its job advertisements and employment contracts that there would be no guarantee of work and also to produce clear written policies on the entitlement of staff to sick pay and holiday pay.[56] Further legal action has been brought by unions against the company's policy of

[48] Skills for Care, *The State of the Adult Social Care Sector and Workforce in England* (March 2015) para 3.5, see www.skillsforcare.org.uk/Document-library/NMDS-SC,-workforce-intelligence-and-innovation/NMDS-SC/State-of-2014-ENGLAND-WEB-FINAL.pdf.

[49] Examples given by Z Adams and S Deakin (n3) 10; CIPD (n 9) case studies.

[50] CIPD (n 9) 10.

[51] ibid 31.

[52] I Brinkley, *Flexibility or insecurity? Exploring the rise in zero-hours contracts* (The Work Foundation, 2013) www.theworkfoundation.com/Research/Socio-Economic/Zero-hours-contracts.

[53] Channel 4 News, *Anger at Amazon working conditions*, see www.channel4.com/news/anger-at-amazon-working-conditions.

[54] ibid.

[55] See J Kellowe, 'Sports Direct chief defends zero-hours contracts', *The Guardian* (London, 29 October 2015) www.theguardian.com/business/2015/oct/29/sports-direct-chief-defends-zero-hours-contracts.

[56] Leigh Day Solicitors, *Sports Direct agree major changes for zero hours staff following legal battle* www.leighday.co.uk/News/2014/October-2014/Sports-Direct-agree-major-changes-for-zero-hours-s.

excluding ZHWs from its bonus schemes.[57] Sports Direct have hit back arguing that ZHCs 'work well for the vast majority of our casual staff as well as it does for the company'.[58] Under mounting pressure from a UK Parliamentary enquiry over allegations of paying its warehouse staff less than the National Minimum Wage,[59] 'zeroing out' staff who fail to keep up with sales targets, and 'naming and shaming' workers using loudspeakers, the company has agreed to carry out a review of its processes.[60]

Evidence from the CIPD suggests that zero hours contracting is increasing as 'employers seek more variable or contingent forms of work to manage business uncertainty in the face of fierce competition and tight budget constraints'. The CIPD advises that employers should only use them when the inherent flexibility of the arrangement 'suits both the organisation and the individual'. This leads us to consider, in the next part, the employment status of this growing army of ZHWs and the contractual rights of these most contingent workers for whom 'demutualisation' has pushed them to the outermost boundaries of labour law.[61]

III. Zero Hours Working—Legal Status and the Scope of Employment Protection

> 'Contracts of service must not be turned into contracts of slavery'
> (*De Francesco v Barnum* [1890] 45 Ch D 430 (Fry LJ))

A. Introduction

As outlined in the introduction of this chapter, ZHCs are 'enormously varied'[62] and, as such, there is no 'unitary notion of the Zero Hours Contract'.[63] The term ZHC may include various types of 'work arrangements … for which there are no fixed or guaranteed hours of remunerated work'.[64] It is not just the heterogeneity of these contracts, but their intangibility, that poses challenges both for the common law tribunals and courts in the UK and also for the legislator. For the

[57] *The Guardian* (n 53).
[58] ibid.
[59] Now relabelled the National Living Wage with effect from 1 April 2016. See The National Minimum Wage (Amendment) Regulations 2016, SI 2016/68.
[60] 'Sports Direct comes out fighting on zero hours contracts' (*The Yorkshire Post*, 18 December 2015) www.yorkshirepost.co.uk/business/retail/sports-direct-comes-out-fighting-on-zero-hours-contracts-1-7632334.
[61] See A Davies (n 19) 94–95.
[62] Dr Vince Cable MP (HC Deb 16 Oct 2013, vol 567, col 756).
[63] A Adams, M Freedland and J Prassl (n 2) 5.
[64] M Freedland and N Kountouris (n 42) 318–319.

judiciary, the main challenge is to interpret each individual contractual arrangement in its specific employment law context, while for the legislator, the main task is to draft laws that provide, at least, for the outlawing of abuses of ZHCs and which may go further to provide ZHWs with the minimum standard of employment protection normally available to core workers. In order to frame this discussion, in this part, we must address the employment status of ZHWs and identify the scope and limitations of employment protection afforded to them.

B. Employment Status of Zero Hours Workers

Employment status in the UK is determined by the operation of what Anne Davies has identified as the 'main organising concepts' of employment law,[65] specifically, in this context, the concepts of 'employee' and 'worker'. We must first seek to determine whether the ZHW is an 'employee' with a 'contract of employment'.[66] This prioritisation is important because the existence of a contract of employment, which is the foundation for 'employee' status, operates as a passport for the individual to be afforded the fullest protection that is available under employment law. Formally, as emphasised by the use of suffixes, an 'employee' is a counterpart to an 'employer', suggesting a certain kind of relational equilibrium between the contracting parties, but this notional sense of equality is illusory because the statutory 'contract of employment' is defined as a 'contract of service',[67] directly drawn from the common law hierarchical relation of master and servant. It is the common law tests evolving from this relation that have become the benchmark for UK Employment Tribunals[68] to establish, on a case by case basis, the existence of a contract of employment.

The common law tests are somewhat fluid but require evidence of elements of: 'control', indicating a measure of subordination of the employee to the employer; 'risk', or economic reality, identifying the employer as the person who takes the economic risk in the relationship; and 'mutuality of obligation', a variant of the control test, whereby the employee is obliged to accept work when it is offered to him or her by the employer.[69]

Among these tests, it is mutuality of obligation that is the most problematic for those working under ZHCs. The mutuality of obligation test is founded on the notion that the contract of employment is more than a mere wage/work bargain between the parties but rather, as Mark Freedland has explained, there is a second

[65] A Davies (n 19) 96–120.

[66] Employment Rights Act 1996 s 230(1).

[67] ibid s 230(2).

[68] Strictly speaking there is a separate system of tribunals in, respectively: England and Wales; Northern Ireland; and, Scotland.

[69] See A Davies (n 19) 101–108; S Deakin and G Morris, *Labour Law* (Hart Publishing, 6th edn, 2012) 159–169.

level of obligation of mutual promises of future performance.[70] These are 'the mutual undertakings to maintain the employment relationship in being which are inherent in any contract of employment so called'.[71] The problem with this test for ZHWs arises from the weight it places on a promise made by the worker to be available to serve the employer when required, on an ongoing basis, even where there is uncertainty about whether, if at all, the employer will promise future work and for how long. It is even more difficult in cases where ZHWs are dependent on a series of short 'spot contracts', sometimes with more than one employer, in which there is no contract in force between engagements.[72] Is it possible for each of these separate wage/work bargains, if they are with the same employer, to be joined together into what is known as a 'global contract' if there is evidence of an ongoing mutuality of obligation during and between each hiring?[73]

Two late twentieth century court judgments illustrate how the mutuality of obligations test has been elaborated in cases involving casual or intermittent workers who might nowadays be described as 'zero hours workers'. The first case, *O'Kelly*,[74] concerned a group of hotel wine waiters described as 'regular casuals' in the contractual documents. Under the arrangement, the wine waiters were available for hire periodically to cater at functions and were expected to offer their services. The waiters could turn down an offer of work but, under a preferential list system, those who refused work would be removed from the list. In practice, many worked long hours in the hotel most weeks and had not refused offers of work. Nevertheless, the Court of Appeal of England and Wales upheld the finding of an Employment Tribunal that, under the arrangement, there was no obligation for the hotel to provide work and no obligation on the waiters to offer their services. This meant that, according to the Court, each individual hiring of the waiters for a function was a singular wage/work bargain without the necessary mutuality of obligation and, further, there was no global contract of employment spanning these bargains. Without the necessary mutuality, the waiters were merely independent contractors choosing to work for the hotel as a client. To the extent that there was an exchange of promises between the parties, these promises were not strong enough to amount to mutual obligations to maintain the relationship on an ongoing basis.[75] There was also interplay between the absence of mutuality of obligation and the 'risk' test because, by being able to exercise a choice to work, rather than having an obligation, the waiters 'bore the risk of the absence of work'.[76]

[70] M Freedland, *The Contract of Employment* (Clarendon Press, 1976) 21–22.
[71] ibid.
[72] See Z Adams and S Deakin (n 3) 12.
[73] See A Davies (n 19) 104.
[74] *O'Kelly v Trusthouse Forte Plc* [1984] QB 90 (CA).
[75] A Davies (n 19) 105.
[76] H Collins, *Employment Law* (OUP, 2nd edn, 2010) 40.

In the second case, *Carmichael*,[77] two tour guides at a power station were hired on a 'casual as required' basis. Like the waiters in *O'Kelly*, these women had no minimum hours of work and were simply offered work and performed it whenever the employer decided that they were needed. Each party bore a risk of the unavailability of labour.[78] When the case reached the House of Lords,[79] Lord Irvine, in the leading judgment, observed that the documentation signed by the parties pointed to an absence of the 'irreducible minimum' of mutual obligation necessary to create a contract of service. He noted that, in practice, both tour guides had not been available for work on several occasions when it had been offered indicating an absence of mutuality. Lord Irvine approved of what we would understand today as zero hours contracting, commenting, with gendered undertones, that '[t]his flexibility of approach was well suited to their family needs. Just as the need for tours was unpredictable so also were their domestic commitments. Flexibility suited both sides.'[80] The price that these women paid for this 'domestic' convenience and 'flexibility' for their 'family needs' was to be denied the right to seek some of the most basic protection afforded by UK employment law, including the right to claim unfair dismissal, the right to a redundancy payment and the right to take maternity leave and parental leave, all of which are reserved exclusively for those granted the status of 'employee'.[81] If the same conclusion were reached today in a similar case, such workers would even be denied the right to request flexible working, which is also confined to 'employees'.[82]

In more recent cases, however, the courts have made 'much less aggressive use'[83] of the strict mutuality of obligation approach laid down in *O'Kelly* and *Carmichael*. In *Wilson*,[84] it was held that absence of mutuality means there is no obligation on either party to perform work. Therefore, if, as in many zero hours arrangements, an employer is not obliged to offer work but, when it is offered, it must be accepted by the worker, that worker would have the necessary obligation required for a contract of employment. In such a case, there might not be a positive mutual obligation but there would not be an absence of mutuality. Further, in *Williams*, it was found that a refusal to accept work was not fatal to being awarded 'employee' status 'if there is some obligation upon an individual to work, and some obligation upon the other party to provide or pay for it'.[85]

The mutuality of obligation test will be applied on the basis of the facts, which gives considerable latitude to an Employment Tribunal (ET) hearing a particular

77 *Carmichael v National Power Plc* [1999] 1 WLR 2042 (HL).

78 See H Collins, 'Employment Rights of Casual Workers' (2000) 29 ILJ 73, 73.

79 Now replaced by the UK Supreme Court.

80 *Carmichael v National Power Plc* [1999] 1 WLR 2042 (HL).

81 In each case, statute limits the protection to 'employees'; see for example the Employment Rights Act 1996 s 94(1) concerning unfair dismissal.

82 Employment Rights Act 1996 s 80F.

83 A Adams, M Freedland and J Prassl (n 2) 15.

84 *Wilson v Circular Distributors Ltd* [2006] IRLR 38 (EAT).

85 *Cotswold Developments Ltd v Williams* [2006] IRLR 181 (EAT) [55].

case. For example, in *Haggerty*,[86] a worker who was on a list of casuals was found to be under a contract of employment for each shift she worked and, although there was no guarantee of minimum hours of work, on the facts, it was shown that the claimant had an expectation of a reasonable amount of work. As in *O'Kelly*, it was understood that refusal to accept offers of work would lead to her removal from the employer's list of casuals. On appeal, the Employment Appeal Tribunal (EAT) approved the emphasis given by the ET on the need to deduce the intention of the parties from their conduct over a long period of time. This evidence was 'just sufficient' to point to an ongoing mutuality of obligations between shifts.[87] *Haggerty* suggests that, in the case of a ZHW who is 'on call', and thus required to be available to work, the obligation on the employer to offer work can be inferred as a reciprocal obligation.[88]

After *O'Kelly*, it was common for employers to put 'no mutuality of obligations' clauses into contracts with casual or intermittent workers. How strictly should such clauses be interpreted and how much scope is there for a broader contextual interpretation of the parties' statements? The traditional 'contract' approach to interpretation is very strict indeed as typified by the majority of the Court of Appeal in *Kalwak*, which held that an express 'no obligations clause' could only be shown to be a 'sham' if 'at the time of the contract, both parties [must have intended the term] to misrepresent their true actual relationship'.[89]

More recently, however, the higher courts have preferred an alternative 'employment' approach to interpretation that looks beyond the content of any promises.[90] Smith LJ in *Szilagyi* stressed that the task of the ET was to put such clauses in a wider employment context, to look at 'the substance not the label' and recognise that 'in the field of work … the reality may be that that the principal/employer dictates what the written agreement will say and the contractor/employee must take it or leave it'.[91] The Supreme Court in *Autoclenz*[92] went further, expressly rejecting the notion in *Kalwak* of 'common intent' to misrepresent because it implied a degree of equality between the parties that did not normally exist in an employment contract. Lord Clarke observed that:

> '[T]he relative bargaining power of the parties must be taken into account in deciding whether the terms of any written agreement in truth represents what was agreed and the *true agreement* will often have to be gleaned from all the circumstances of the case, of which the written agreement is only a part.'[93]

[86] *St Ives Plymouth Ltd v Mrs D Haggerty* [2008] UKEAT 0107/08/MAA.
[87] ibid [9].
[88] See S Deakin and G Morris (n 69) 167.
[89] *Consistent Group Ltd v Kalwak and Others* [2008] EWCA Civ 30 (Rimer LJ) [51].
[90] A Davies (n 19) 105.
[91] *Protectacoat Firthglow Ltd v Szilagyi* [2009] IRLR 365 (CA) [52] and [61].
[92] *Autoclenz Ltd v Belcher* [2011] UKSC 41. For comment, see A Bogg, 'Sham Self-Employment in the Supreme Court' (2012) 41 ILJ 328.
[93] ibid [35]. Emphasis added.

Autoclenz matters because, for the most precariously situated workers, such as those on various forms of ZHCs, it is vital for tribunals to recognise that, whatever the formal terms, the contract of employment is to a large extent, as Kahn-Freund put it, 'a figment of the legal mind' that conceals a 'condition of subordination'.[94] The more the worker needs work, any work, however infrequently it is offered, the more likely it is that he or she will have 'take it or leave it' and accept the employer's contractual terms.[95]

The importance of *Autoclenz* is illustrated by *Pulse Healthcare*.[96] The case concerned the transfer of a contract for 24-hour care provision for a woman with severe physical disabilities in the context of the Transfer of Undertakings (Protection of Employment) Regulations 2006, known as TUPE. Under TUPE, any employees performing the relevant contract are normally transferred to the new contractor and their acquired employment rights are protected. Pulse, the transferee company, refused to agree to the transfer of the care workers responsible for the care package from the transferor, Carewatch, on the basis that there was no mutuality of obligation. The workers had signed a document provided by Carewatch entitled 'Zero Hours Contract Agreement'. Apart from the title, many of the other provisions in the document referred to typical requirements of a contract of employment such as annual leave and sickness leave entitlements. The document even set out 'particulars of employment' as required for employees.[97] It did not exclude the workers from working for another employer but this was only possible when 'unassigned' to Carewatch. Against the heading, 'Hours of Employment', the document stated 'Zero hours'. In practice, however, it was shown that each of the carers worked an agreed number of hours per week varying from 24 to 36. Not surprisingly, the Employment Judge found that the document 'did not reflect the true position'.[98] Once the work rota was fixed the workers were required to work and the employer was required to provide that work. This was sufficient to show mutuality of obligations. On appeal, the EAT found that the judgment was wholly in accord with *Autoclenz*.[99]

What is interesting about *Pulse Healthcare* is not so much the application of *Autoclenz*, but the approach of the EAT to the wage-work bargain. Each of the care workers were rostered for individual shifts. Such individual wage/work bargains can be regarded as 'miniature contracts of employment' so long as, firstly, there are the necessary requirements of control and risk,[100] and, secondly, if the employer is obliged to pay the worker for the whole of the agreed shift.[101] This is important

[94] P Davies and M Freedland, *Kahn-Freund's Labour and the Law* (Stevens, 3rd edn, 1983) 18.
[95] See further, H Collins, *Employment Law* (OUP, 2nd edn, 2010) 7.
[96] *Pulse Healthcare Ltd v Carewatch Care Services Ltd and 6 Others* [2012] UKEAT/0123/12/BA.
[97] Employment Rights Act 1996 s 1(1)-(2).
[98] *Pulse Healthcare Ltd v Carewatch Care Services Ltd and 6 Others* [2012] UKEAT/0123/12/BA [21].
[99] ibid [35].
[100] A Davies (n 19) 106. For example, see *McMeechan v Secretary of State for Employment* [1997] ICR 549 (CA).
[101] A Davies ibid. See *Little v BMI Chiltern Hospital* [2009] UKEAT/0021/09/DA.

because duration is not a decisive factor in establishing a contract of employment. If there is an absence of mutuality between each contract that will mean that the contract is legally unenforceable at common law, as in *O'Kelly* and *Carmichael*, but it does not mean that the worker has not acquired any statutory rights.[102] For example, certain employment rights, such as the right to a statement of employment particulars, or the right not to be dismissed for trade union membership, do not require a long period of continuity of employment.[103]

In *Pulse Healthcare*, these conditions were met and, moreover, in the interpretation of the EAT, the care workers were employed under a global contract which required mutual obligations to subsist for the entire period leading up to the transfer and no problem of lack of continuity of employment arose.[104] The EAT reached this conclusion because, although each worker was rostered for specific shifts, there were mutual obligations for the delivery of the whole care package on an ongoing basis including to cover for holidays and sickness. It followed that the care workers had global contracts of employment to work a certain number of hours each week in relation to the care package.

On the one hand, the outcome of *Pulse Healthcare* can be seen as a positive for the employment protection of ZHWs. Workers designated by their employer as ZHWs may be found, on the particular facts, to be 'employees' not just for specific engagements but on an ongoing basis, satisfying the mutuality of obligations. If it is possible to 'join up' each shift, or miniature contract, a global contract can be established. This is important because, in order to access many employment rights in the UK, it is necessary to fulfil a lengthy qualifying period of continuous employment. Continuity requirements are thus 'an important filter for employment protection'.[105] For example, two years of continuous employment is required to bring a claim for unfair dismissal.[106]

On the other hand, *Pulse Healthcare* was a relatively straightforward case where the designation of the workers as 'zero hours' was shown to be a rather obvious sham. Indeed, it is not the case, even after *Autoclenz*, that the written agreement, if there is one, can simply be disregarded. In other cases, even if the worker can

[102] H Collins (n 76) 77.

[103] See S Deakin and G Morris (n 69) 167. The right to a written statement of particulars of employment requires one month's continuous employment, Employment Rights Act 1996 s 1(2). No qualifying period is required for an employee to bring a claim for the right not to be dismissed for reasons related to trade union membership or activities under the Trade Union and Labour Relations (Consolidation) Act 1992 s 152.

[104] *Pulse Healthcare Ltd v Carewatch Care Services Ltd and 6 Others* [2012] UKEAT/0123/12/BA [40].

[105] S Deakin and G Morris (n 69) 199.

[106] Employment Rights Act 1996 s 108. See, for example, *Borrer v Cardinal Security Ltd* [2013] UKEAT/0416/12/GE, a case involving a supermarket security guard with a contract stipulating that his working hours 'will be specified' by his line manager. He received a text message each week informing him of his working hours. In practice, he regularly worked 48 hours a week for two years. He resigned when his hours were drastically reduced. It was held, applying *Autoclenz*, that the true agreement was a contract of employment for 48 hours a week. As an employee with two years' continuous employment, he was entitled to bring a claim for unfair dismissal.

establish a series of contracts of employment, unless it is possible to convert those separate contracts into a global contract, casual or intermittent ZHWs will be filtered out of important areas of employment protection because they will not have the necessary continuity to bring claims. This is precisely what happened in the subsequent case of *Saha v Viewpoint Field Services Ltd*,[107] in which a telephone interviewer who worked on an ad hoc basis for between seven and 43 hours almost every week for a year was found not to have mutuality of obligations because she was not obliged to work each week when work was offered and the employer was not obliged to offer her work. Even though she had been referred to by the employer as an 'employee' and, during her shifts she had spot contracts of employment, she did not have mutuality of obligation and, therefore, was filtered out of protection against unfair dismissal because she had no global contract of employment.[108]

UK legislation provides limited protection against filtering in cases that, on the facts, satisfy the requirements of 'statutory continuity' under s. 212 of the Employment Rights Act 1996. Under this provision, any week 'during the whole or part of which an employee's relations with his employer are governed by a contract of employment counts in computing the employee's contract of employment'.[109] If, however, there is a gap in employment on account of, inter alia, 'a temporary cessation of work', that gap does not break the period of continuous employment.[110] In this way, as Anne Davies explains, statutory continuity provides the 'glue' to stick a series of short contracts of employment together to create one whole period of what is deemed to be continuous employment.[111]

For example, in *Prater*,[112] a teacher who taught pupils at their homes was given a different assignment lasting a varying period of time for each pupil she taught. There were gaps between teaching assignments including for holidays. The Court of Appeal held that there was a mutual obligation for each assignment in the sense that Ms Prater was obliged to teach the pupil and the Council was obliged to pay her.[113] Mummery LJ noted that the question as to whether each engagement was an individual work contract in which there were mutual obligations was not addressed in *O'Kelly* and *Carmichael*.[114] In *Prater*, there were a succession of individual work contracts in each of which there was mutuality of obligation. Once this was established, s 212 'took care of the gaps between the individual contracts and secured continuity of employment' for the purposes of employment protection.[115] The significance of the judgment is that, for the purpose of establishing

[107] [2014] UKEAT/0116/13/DM.

[108] Miss Saha was therefore denied the opportunity to bring a claim for unfair dismissal. At the time of her claim, in 2012, the period of continuous employment for bringing such a claim under the Employment Rights Act 1996 s 108 was one year.

[109] Employment Rights Act 1996 s 212(1).

[110] ibid s 212(2)(c).

[111] See A Davies (n 19) 107.

[112] *Cornwall County Council v Prater* [2006] EWCA Civ 102.

[113] ibid [33] (Mummery LJ).

[114] ibid [34] and [36].

[115] ibid [40].

statutory continuity, if there is a temporary cessation, there is no need to consider the contractual position between each contract or whether there is ongoing mutuality of obligation.[116]

There is no doubt that statutory continuity does solve some problems for certain casual or intermittent ZHWs, who will have a series of capsuled contracts of employment that can be linked together, but may not be able to establish ongoing mutuality or a global contract. However, statutory continuity is not a golden bullet to solve all problems for ZHWs. Many cases will be unlike *Prater*. For example, where no work is available from week to week because the work has already been allocated to other casual workers, the week will not count as a 'temporary cessation' and continuity will be broken.[117] In other cases, as in *Saha*,[118] individual shifts, which may be erratic and unpredictable, will be found to lack mutuality of obligation and be distinguishable from *Prater*. Such ZHWs will either have the status of 'worker', in which case they will have access to a more limited menu of employment rights, or, if they take on the risk of profit and loss in the relationship,[119] they will be deemed to be autonomous and self-employed.

The statutory term 'worker' is defined in s 230(3)(b) of the Employment Rights Act 1996 as including contracts where 'the individual undertakes to do or perform personally any work or services for another party to the contract whose status is not by virtue of the contract that of a client or customer of any profession or undertaking carried on by the individual'.[120] 'Worker' is an intermediate category lying between an 'employee' who is dependent on the employer and an independent contractor who is self-employed. The statutory concept of the 'worker' is designed to protect those who do not have sufficient mutuality of obligation to be 'employees' but are, unlike the self-employed, 'semi-dependent'[121] on an employer and are normally in a subordinate position in the employment relation, although a relation of subordination is not necessarily essential.[122]

Simon Deakin and Gillian Morris have explained the rationale for the 'worker' concept in the following terms:

> '... the legislature has in essence taken the view that casual workers who would not necessarily fall within "employee" status should not, for that reason, be denied basic protections which do not depend, for their effective functioning, upon the employment relationship in question being regular or long-term'.[123]

116 See A Davies (n 19) 108.

117 ibid. See *Byrne v Birmingham City Council* [1987] ICR 519 (CA).

118 *Saha v Viewpoint Field Services Ltd* [2014] UKEAT/0116/13/DM.

119 See *Quashie v Stringfellows Restaurants Ltd* [2012] EWCA Civ 1735.

120 Employees are also included in the definition of a 'worker' in s 230(3)(a) of the Employment Rights Act 1996. This ensures that statutory references to rights for every 'worker' cover all those in both the 'employee' and 'worker' categories.

121 See M Freedland, *The Personal Employment Contract* (OUP, 2003) 30–33.

122 *Clyde & Co v Bates van Winkelhof* [2014] UKSC 32 [39] (Baroness Hale).

123 S Deakin and G Morris (n 69) 175.

These 'basic protections' include, inter alia, the right to be paid the National Living Wage,[124] paid holidays and limits on working hours,[125] and protection against unauthorised pay deductions.[126] Those in 'employment', who have 'a contract personally to do work',[127] are also protected under the Equality Act 2010 against discrimination on the grounds, inter alia, of age, sex, racial or ethnic origin, religion or belief, disability or sexual orientation. The Equality Act definition, although it does not use the term 'worker', is increasingly regarded as similar in meaning to the definition of 'worker' in the Employment Rights Act.[128]

To establish 'worker' status it must be shown that the individual has a contract to perform work or services personally. Also, to more clearly distinguish workers from the wholly self-employed, an individual must not be a 'client or customer', which means that it is possible that an individual can run a business and be a worker 'provided that the recipient of the business's services cannot be described as a customer'.[129]

As with the concept of 'employee', following *Autoclenz*, the ET must look at the 'true agreement' taking into account the conduct of the parties. In *Buckborough*,[130] for example, a bricklayer who had signed a document stating that he was self-employed was found to be a 'worker' on the facts.

Early case law on the 'worker' concept tended to blur the tests for 'employee' and 'worker' by suggesting that some, more limited, degree of mutuality of obligation between the parties was required for 'worker' status.[131] More recently, the courts have developed a distinctive interpretation of 'worker', emphasising the need for an obligation on the part of the 'worker' to perform work or services personally.[132] This will cover most situations where there is a personal work relationship with an employer except where the true agreement includes an unqualified clause under which, when a worker is not required to provide a personal service, he or she can nominate a substitute.[133] As Anne Davies has succinctly put it: '"Worker" is not a "low-fat" version of employee: it is a different concept altogether'.[134] It follows that, a broad approach to the 'worker' concept, untied to the common law tests for 'employee', will encompass many zero hours arrangements, including intermittent working, so long as there is an obligation on the part of the ZHW to perform work or services for another person on each occasion when they accept an offer of work.

[124] Formerly the National Minimum Wage. See The National Minimum Wage (Amendment) Regulations 2016, SI 2016/68.

[125] Working Time Regulations 1998, SI 1999/584.

[126] Employment Rights Act 1996 ss 13–14 and 17–22.

[127] Equality Act 2010 s 83(2)(a).

[128] *Clyde & Co v Bates van Winkelhof* [2014] UKSC 32 [31] (Baroness Hale); see also *Jivraj v Hashwani* [2011] UKSC 40.

[129] A Davies (n 19) 113. See *Hospital Medical Group v Westwood* [2012] IRLR 834 (CA).

[130] *Redrow Homes v Buckborough* [2009] IRLR 34.

[131] *Byrne Bothers (Formwork) Ltd v Baird* [2002] ICR 667 (EAT).

[132] *Community Dental Centres Ltd v Sultan-Darmon* [2010] UKEAT/0532/09/DA.

[133] See *Express & Echo Publications v Tanton* [1999] IRLR 367 (CA).

[134] A Davies (n 19) 114.

C. Employment Protection of Zero Hours Workers—Examples of Entitlements and Limitations

Even where the law does provide formal protection for workers on ZHCs, whether they have the status of 'employee' or 'worker', in practice it may be difficult for them to exercise their rights. For example, if the ZHW has a contract of employment, with at least one month's continuous employment, which would include many shorter wage/work bargains with mutual obligations, he or she is entitled to a statement of written particulars of employment.[135] The written statement must include 'terms and conditions relating to hours of work' including 'normal hours of work'.[136] On one reading, this might suggest that, where there is an opaque ZHC, the employer would be forced to reveal regular working hours to the employee in the statement. However, the statement is no more than a reflection of the employer's interpretation of the terms and conditions contractually agreed between the parties.[137] The contract itself does not have to be in writing.[138] The statement does not replace the contract, nor does it create an obligation on the employer to fix a set number of contractual hours per week or month, or to provide work on particular days or at certain times of the day. In a best case scenario, it could be argued, that if the employer has in practice offered fixed hours on a regular basis this 'crystallises' over time into a legal obligation that must be faithfully reflected in the statement.[139]

Bringing a claim for unfair dismissal will also be difficult for a ZHW. It may be possible to establish a global contract by linking together a series of contracts of employment and relying on the rule on temporary cessations to stick them together so as to establish the necessary qualifying period of two years' continuous employment.[140] However, there may be uncertainty over whether a temporary cessation, with no further work being offered, amounts to a 'dismissal' in law.[141] It is possible for the termination of a fixed-term contract to be deemed a 'dismissal',[142] but it would be relatively straightforward for the employer to show that such a dismissal is 'fair'[143] in the absence of compelling evidence that he or she has acted unreasonably when compared to the standard of the 'reasonable employer'.[144]

ZHWs, including those with 'worker' status, even if they are only offered work intermittently, will be entitled, when they are working, to the National Living Wage

[135] Employment Rights Act 1996 s 1(1)-(2).
[136] ibid s 1(4)(c).
[137] See *Southern Cross Healthcare Co Ltd v Perkins* [2010] EWCA Civ 1442.
[138] Employment Rights Act 1996 s 230(2).
[139] See Z Adams and S Deakin (n 3) 13.
[140] Employment Rights Act 1996 s 108.
[141] ibid s 95(1). See further, Z Adams and S Deakin (n 3) 13.
[142] ibid s 95(1)(b).
[143] ibid s 98.
[144] *Iceland Frozen Foods Ltd v Jones* [1983] ICR 17 (EAT).

(NLW) at an hourly rate,[145] a limit on their maximum weekly working hours, rest periods and paid holidays calculated on a pro-rata basis.[146] The right to be paid the NLW is important, not only as a statutory wage floor, but also because the legislation can be used to clamp down on abuses, such as clocking on and clocking off during times of inactivity or only paying staff when they are serving customers.[147] It also covers many 'on-call' workers, such as care workers, who are required to be at, or close to, the workplace, and those who may have to sleep during part of their shift.[148] Under the legislation, hourly paid workers are entitled to the NLW not only for the time that they are actually working but also for time when they are 'available at or near a place of work'.[149] Travelling time while on business, such as between appointments, is also included.[150] While the NLW provides important protection, it is not payable in situations when casual workers turn up for work in the hope of being hired but are turned away without work.[151]

IV. Outlawing Abuses of Zero Hours Contracts and Proposals for Reform

A. Are Zero Hours Contracts Legal?

In this part, measures to outlaw abuses of ZHCs and proposals to reform the law will be discussed. As Shanks J observed in a recent case before the EAT, 'there can be no doubt that this is an area which is crying out for some legislative intervention'.[152] An immediate question, however, is whether ZHCs are legal.[153] According to the UK Government, in its December 2013 consultation on 'Zero Hours Employment Contracts', a ZHC 'is a legitimate form of employment contract drawn up between employer and individual, providing both parties freely agree to it'.[154] This is a fairly obvious reference to the well-rooted common law notion of 'freedom of contract', but this assumes that the contract is a 'freely negotiated agreement of two equal

145 National Minimum Wage (Amendment) Regulations 2016. With effect from 1 April 2016, the National Living Wage, formerly the National Minimum Wage is £7.20 per hour for workers aged 25 and over with lower rates for those under 25 and apprentices.

146 Working Time Regulations 1998, SI 1998/1833.

147 See A Adams, M Freedland and J Prassl (n 2) 6–7.

148 *Esparon v Slavikovska* [2014] UKEAT/0217/12/DA.

149 National Minimum Wage Regulations 1999, SI 1999/584, reg 15(1).

150 ibid reg 15(2).

151 See A Adams, M Freedland and J Prassl (n 2) 19.

152 *Saha v Viewpoint Field Services Ltd* [2014] UKEAT/0116/13/DM, 23.

153 See further, E McGaughey, 'Are Zero Hours Contracts Lawful?' (20 November 2014) SSRN ssrn.com/abstract=2531913.

154 Department for Business, Innovation and Skills, *Zero Hours employment contracts* (December 2013) www.gov.uk/government/consultations/zero-hours-employment-contracts.

parties in the market'.[155] In the absence of statutory protection, the conventional rule is that the parties' bargain is enforceable regardless of whether it is fair.[156] However, the courts have come to recognise that the employment contract is a special type of relational contract to be interpreted and applied in the context of the inequality of bargaining power between the parties.

One might ask, how can an employment contract be lawful if it does not guarantee that a worker will be provided with any work (or any further work) or, indeed, any specified hours of work? This is problematic because it is a basic tenet of the common law that the employee only has a right to be paid if he or she performs an obligation under the contract. It is the performance of this obligation that triggers the employer's corresponding obligation to pay.[157] As Greer LJ succinctly put it in *Browning v Crumlin Valley Collieries Ltd*: 'the consideration for work is wages, and the consideration for wages is work'.[158] The absence of a guarantee of work has the effect, therefore, of undermining the purpose of the minimum wage—to provide a basic income—but there is no statutory or common law guarantee of minimum working hours.[159] It is only possible to secure a right to work, or to be paid for work not provided, if a term can be implied based on the agreement of the parties. In *Devonald v Rosser and Sons Ltd*,[160] workers were laid off without pay but had no contractual provision specifying their hours of work. The contract did, however, specify a notice period to be applied before the employees could be dismissed. The Court of Appeal held that, during this contractual notice period, a term could be implied that the employer had a duty to offer a reasonable amount of work based on the hours normally worked. The employees were entitled to damages for the employer's failure to provide that work.

An alternative approach at common law would be for the courts to imply that, at least some regular work should be offered to provide employees with a subsistence income, even if the contract is formally described as 'zero hours', on the basis that this would represent the reasonable expectations of the parties.[161] McGaughey, relying on the 'true agreement' test in *Autoclenz*, suggests that express contract terms referring to 'zero hours' are one-sided and may 'lie in a shadowy recess of borderline legality'.[162] This is an argument that is compelling, particularly in cases where it can be shown that 'zero hours' clauses are a sham, as in *Pulse Healthcare*, but it would not apply in situations where a ZHC accurately reflects the agreement of the parties even if the ZHW would like to have more regular work.[163] This takes

[155] A Davies (n 19) 138.
[156] ibid.
[157] See S Deakin and G Morris (n 69) 318.
[158] [1926] 1 KB 522 [528] (CA).
[159] E McGaughey (n 153) 2.
[160] [1906] 2 KB 728 (CA).
[161] E McGaughey (n 153) 3.
[162] ibid 5.
[163] As in *Saha v Viewpoint Field Services Ltd* [2014] UKEAT/0116/13/DM, discussed in Part III.B above.

us back to the point that there is no single type of ZHC but, on a case by case basis, a contract dressed up as 'zero hours' may be shown, if regular hours of work are offered and accepted over an extended period, to be, in truth, a contract for a fixed number of hours per week.[164]

B. Proposals for Reform

Much of the discourse on ZHCs has been concerned with identifying ways to end the exploitation of these types of contracts or even to abolish them altogether. One possible solution to the problems of lawfulness of ZHCs, identified above, would be to create a statutory presumption of illegality of ZHCs that could only be rebutted by objective justification.[165] For example, if evidence shows that the contractual arrangement is flexible in a way that genuinely suits both parties taking into account their unequal power relations. The difficulty with proposals for reforming the law, by giving official blessing to 'fair' ZHCs, is that ZHCs have to defined and to an extent legitimised whilst simultaneously minimising abuse and setting core standards of protection for ZHWs.[166]

This very specific focus on ZHC-specific legislative proposals is an understandable, and to an extent inevitable, short-term response to media reporting of abuses and the public demand for action. The danger is that a targeted approach leads to piecemeal measures that 'legitimate precarity'[167] but do not address the wider challenge of meeting needs of contingent workers in the UK for security in working life.

i. Exclusivity Clauses

The UK Government consulted in 2013 on abuses of ZHCs and problems with how they were operating.[168] In the consultation, the underlying assumption of Government was that ZHWs were a positive phenomenon because they 'support business flexibility, making it easier to hire new staff and providing pathways to employment for young people'.[169] From this standpoint any action would be

164 *Borrer v Cardinal Security Ltd* [2013] UKEAT/0416/12/GE. See n 106 for fuller details.

165 See E McGaughey (n 153) 7, who suggests that such a presumption 'leaves room for development of the law by the courts'. See also, House of Commons Scottish Affairs Committee, *Zero-Hours contracts in Scotland: interim report, Tenth Report of session 2013–14*, HC 654 (9 April 2014) www.publications.parliament.uk/pa/cm201314/cmselect/cmscotaf/654/654.pdf.

166 Department for Business Innovation and Skills (BIS), *Zero-Hours Employment Contracts* (December 2013), Foreword by the Secretary of State, 4; see www.gov.uk/government/consultations/zero-hours-employment-contracts.

167 A Adams, M Freedland and J Prassl (n 2).

168 BIS (n 166).

169 ibid Foreword by the Secretary of State, 4.

targeted as a 'crack down on any abuse and exploitation' by a small number of employers who were not behaving responsibly.[170]

One of the main areas of concern identified by the Government was 'exclusivity clauses', which prevented a ZHW from working for another employer, even if their current employer was not guaranteeing any hours of work. Even without legislation, such clauses, known as restrictive covenants, would be of doubtful legality at common law because of their coercive nature.[171] In the absence of a global contract maintaining mutuality of obligation, exclusivity clauses are unenforceable in periods in between individual 'spot contracts' as they amount to a restraint on the individual's freedom to work.[172] Such clauses are deemed antithetical to the concepts of 'choice and flexibility' that provide the rationale for zero hours contracting.[173]

CIPD evidence presented in 2013 found that 9 per cent of ZHWs reported that they had an exclusivity clause or believed that they were restricted from exercising their choice to take up work with additional employers.[174] After further consultation, which revealed that 83 per cent of 36,000 respondents supported an outright ban on exclusivity clauses in ZHCs,[175] the Government, wishing to be seen to be doing something in the wake of considerable public outrage over the exploitation of ZHWs, concluded that 'exclusivity clauses were used to the detriment of individuals'[176] and introduced legislation banning them. The Small Business, Enterprise and Employment Act 2015 inserted a new section 27A into the Employment Rights Act 1996. The provision is the first explicit statutory reference to the ZHC. It defines a ZHC as:

> '(1) … a contract of employment or other worker's contract under which
>
> (a) the undertaking to do or perform work or services is an undertaking to do so conditionally on the employer making work or services available to the worker, and
>
> (b) there is no certainty that any such work or services will be made available to the worker.
>
> (2) For this purpose, an employer makes work or services available to a worker if the employer requests or requires the worker to do the work or perform the services'.

On the one hand, this provision is sufficiently broad to include both 'employees' and 'workers'. It recognises that all forms of employment, other than genuine

[170] ibid.

[171] See *De Francesco v Barnum* [1890] 45 Ch D 430.

[172] Z Adams and S Deakin (n 3) 16; *Faccenda Chicken Ltd v Fowler* [1986] IRLR 69.

[173] BIS, *Zero-Hours Employment Contracts. Banning Exclusivity Clauses: Tackling Avoidance* (August 2014) 8 www.gov.uk/government/consultations/zero-hours-employment-contracts.

[174] CIPD (n 9) 23.

[175] BIS (n 173) 12; and, see also, BIS, *Zero Hours Employment Contracts. Government Response to the 'Banning Exclusivity Clauses: Tackling Avoidance'* (March 2015).

[176] BIS (n 173) 12.

self-employment, involve a degree of dependency. On the other hand, it endorses exploitation of that dependency by permitting contracts rooted in uncertainty over working hours or even the very availability of work. The benign language of s 27A(2) implies a genuine choice on the part of the worker to accept or refuse work whenever it is made available by an employer. As has been shown in Part II.A above, the new system of Universal Credit creates a pressure on the ZHW to accept offers of work, however uncertain the hours and however low the pay, so as to avoid punitive welfare sanctions.

Exclusivity clauses are defined in s 27A as follows:

> '(3) Any provision of a zero hours contract which—
>
> (a) prohibits the worker from doing work or performing services under another contract or under any other arrangement, or
> (b) prohibits the worker from doing so without the employer's consent,
>
> is unenforceable against the worker'.

An exclusivity clause is thus deemed to be an automatically unfair contract term without reference to whether the individual who is subject to it is an employee or a worker.[177] The law is stronger, in certain respects, than parallel legislation concerning unfair terms in consumer contracts which outlaw some 'unfair' terms whilst allowing others based on satisfying a test of 'reasonableness'.[178] The legislation also provides scope, in a new s 27B, inserted into the Employment Rights Act 1996, for the Secretary of State to make further regulatory provisions to penalise employers for using exclusivity clauses or to tighten the law if there is evidence of workers who ignore an exclusivity requirement being refused further work.[179] Under this provision, new Regulations have been issued to provide for individual redress in cases when an 'employee' is dismissed or a 'worker' is subjected to a detriment for breaching an exclusivity clause as defined in s 27A(3) above.[180] The introduction of a redress mechanism provides protection to all ZHWs who are adversely affected by being refused work by an employer relying on an exclusivity clause. In the case of 'employees', dismissals for this reason will be regarded as automatically unfair.[181] Moreover, claims can be brought without the need to satisfy a qualifying period of employment.[182] Individuals seeking redress can bring a complaint before an ET and, if the complaint is well founded, they will be entitled to compensation for the infringement and any loss attributable to it.[183]

177 Employment Rights Act 1996 s 27A(4).
178 Unfair Contract Terms Act 1977.
179 D Pyper and N Dar (n 30) 18.
180 The Exclusivity Terms in Zero Hours Contracts (Redress) Regulations 2015, SI 2015/2021. Effective from January 2016.
181 ibid reg 2(1).
182 ibid reg 2(5).
183 ibid regs 3 and 4.

Compensable losses may include expenses incurred and loss of benefits that the complainants might be reasonably expected to receive.[184]

Banning exclusivity clauses is welcome, from a protective labour law standpoint, because the new law provides clarity in striking out a particular form of exploitation affecting an estimated 125,000 ZHC workers and also remedies for violations. This group of ZHWs are now free to seek additional work to boost their income.[185] However, bearing in mind the protection against trade restrictive clauses at common law, and the relative paucity of these types of exclusivity clauses, this measure provides, at best, a statutory gloss on the law without addressing the fundamental problems for the worker arising from the inherent ambiguity and unpredictability of no minimum hours contracting. Moreover, there is a danger that providing a statutory definition offers yet further scope for 'rogue employers' to find a way of evading the exclusivity ban by, for example, shaping contract terms that may fall outside of the definition.[186]

Further measures are anticipated in s 27B, which allows the Secretary of State to take additional regulatory steps to modify ZHCs and confer rights on ZHWs.[187] Several suggestions, made independently of Government, are discussed below.

ii. Increasing Transparency in ZHCs

Lack of transparency in ZHCs was highlighted as an issue in the UK Government's consultation exercise in 2013.[188] The provisions banning exclusivity clauses included a definition of ZHCs but it does not necessarily cover all arrangements where there is a lack of certainty about the number of hours of work arising from a dearth of information, or conflicting information, about the contract terms. In turn, an information vacuum leads to uncertainty for the worker about present and future earnings and entitlement to welfare benefits.[189]

Under the law as it stands, statutory provisions concerning the right to a written statement of particulars of employment, including information about hours and pay, are only applicable to employees with two months' continuity of employment.[190] Eligible employees can demand a written statement from their employer and seek to rely on it, if it precisely reflects the essential elements of their contract of employment, or challenge any inaccuracies, by bringing a claim before an ET.[191]

[184] ibid reg 4(3).

[185] BIS press statement, *Government crackdown on zero hours contract abusers* (25 June 2014) www.gov.uk/government/news/government-crackdown-on-zero-hours-contract-abusers.

[186] ibid.

[187] Employment Rights Act 1996 s 27B(5)(a) and (e).

[188] BIS press statement, *Cable announces plans to boost fairness for workers* (16 Sept 2013) www.gov.uk/government/news/cable-announces-plans-to-boost-fairness-for-workers.

[189] ibid.

[190] Employment Rights Act 1996 s 1(1)-(2).

[191] See J Kenner, 'Statement or Contract?—Some Reflections on EC Employee Information (Contract or Employment Relationship) Directive after *Kampelmann*' [1999] 28 ILJ 205.

The right to a written statement is a modest measure first introduced in 1963.[192] It does not fundamentally affect the balance of power between the employer and the employee but it does help to demystify the terms of their relationship. Sir John Hare MP, the Minister of Labour when the original legislation was introduced, explained that its purpose was to enforce the principle that 'workers' obligations and rights should be clear and in writing'.[193] At the time, the concept of a ZHC, as we understand it today, was unknown. More than 50 years later, those ZHWs and other casual workers categorised as 'workers' without employee status, or whose contracts of employment are too short and lack mutuality of obligation, are denied this basic right of information. It would, therefore, be straightforward and relatively unburdensome for employers to be obliged by law to issue an accurate written statement of contract particulars, including hours of work and rates of pay, to all 'workers' employed by them, regardless of the type of contract, at the commencement of their employment.[194] It has also been suggested that employers should confirm employment status in the statement and be required to state their policy on when the worker should be notified that work is available.[195] Such an extension of legal scope would necessarily cover all ZHCs, except in cases of genuine self-employment, and would give some measure of certainty about the terms of employment. It would not, however, guarantee minimum hours of work or any guarantee of future work.

iii. Sharing the Risk of Insecurity and Income

One of the main drivers of ZHCs, identified in Part II.B above, is the 'demutualisation' of the employment relationship whereby the risks of insecurity and income are placed on the worker who can be 'zeroed out' and 'zeroed in' to maximise flexibility.[196] This kind of one-sided flexibility puts huge pressure on ZHWs and other casual workers who will face uncertainty over paying bills and entitlement to welfare benefits. In an independent report for the opposition Labour Party, Norman Pickavance, recommended a sharing of this risk of insecurity between the employer and the ZHW.[197] Pickavance proposed, inter alia, that employers should only be able to require availability in direct proportion to the amount of work they offer. For example, employers would only be able to require additional availability for a maximum of 50 per cent of contracted hours.[198] This would ensure that workers would normally not be required to be available when there is no

[192] Contracts of Employment Act 1963.

[193] HC Deb, vol 671, col 1511 (1962). See further, J Kenner (n 191) 207–208.

[194] See Z Adams and S Deakin (n 3) 34.

[195] *Zeroed Out: The place of zero-hours contracts in a fair and productive economy: An independent report by Norman Pickavance* (The Labour Party 2014) 18 www.yourbritain.org.uk/uploads/editor/files/ZHCs_report_final_FINAL_240414.pdf.

[196] See further, A Adams, M Freedland and J Prassl (n 2) 23.

[197] Pickavance Report (n 195) 16. Pickavance is a former human resources director at the supermarket chain, Morrisons.

[198] ibid.

guarantee of work. Legislation could be introduced to make clauses to that effect unenforceable. In order to maintain some flexibility, additional availability might be possible for on-call staff if they are paid a retention fee by employers.

Another example of sharing the risk of insecurity would be to implement the proposal of the UK House of Commons Scottish Affairs Committee for employers to compensate workers for the inconvenience of arriving for work but finding that none is available.[199] Such a compensation scheme would discourage, but not eradicate, a particularly inimical exploitative practice. The Committee also proposed a rule requiring an employer to give a minimum notice period of work.[200] Along similar lines, legislation has been adopted in New Zealand, requiring notice to be given to the worker when a shift is cancelled.[201] The introduction of such requirements would shift the burden of risk in the employment relation back onto the employer, albeit that neither measure would be as strong as the former National Dock Labour Scheme which guaranteed work for dockers and effectively ended *On The Waterfront*[202] style casual working at ports before its abolition in 1989 during the first phase of labour market deregulation in the UK.[203]

iv. Guaranteeing Regular Working Hours

Whilst each of the proposals discussed above would mitigate some of the worst abuses of ZHCs none of them adequately addresses the precariousness of working under a contract with no guaranteed working hours. The Pickavance Report suggested a highly convoluted measure to convert a ZHC into a more standard employment contract.[204] It proposed that, after six months on a ZHC, workers who are in practice working 'regular hours' should have the right to request a contract other than a ZHC which would provide a minimum amount of work.[205] Employers would only be able to refuse such a request 'if they can demonstrate that their business needs cannot be met by any other form of flexible contract'.[206] The concept of a 'right to request' a change of contract is modelled on the 'right to request flexible working' for employees with six months' continuous employment.[207] The proposal would appear to offer considerable scope for an employer to refuse such a request on business grounds.[208]

[199] HC Scottish Affairs Committee (n 165). A similar scheme was proposed by Pickavance, ibid 17.

[200] ibid.

[201] Employment Relations Amendment Bill (No 3) 2016 s 67G, www.legislation.govt.nz/bill/government/2015/0053B/latest/DLM6774103.html.

[202] Columbia Pictures, 1954.

[203] *Dockers' Job for Life Scrapped* (BBC, 6 April 1989). news.bbc.co.uk/onthisday/hi/dates/stories/april/6/newsid_2522000/2522787.stm.

[204] Pickavance Report (n 195) 17.

[205] ibid. For example, a contract for seasonal work.

[206] ibid.

[207] Employment Rights Act 1996 s 80F-I, as amended by the Flexible Work Regulations 2014, SI 2014/1938.

[208] See Z Adams and S Deakin (n 3) 33.

As a fall back, Pickavance proposed that, after 12 months of continuous employment, workers on regular hours (suggested as a minimum of eight hours per week over the reference period) would have the right to be offered a contract other than zero hours which would provide a minimum amount of work. The law would ensure that this happened automatically and reflect the actual hours being regularly worked. The proposal allows for an individual opt-out from conversion to a regular hours contract subject to independent advice and freely given consent by the worker.[209] This proposal is quite similar to the law in the Netherlands under which a contract of employment guaranteeing minimum hours is implied after three months working on-call.[210]

Pickavance anticipated that such rules would be liable to abuse by 'unscrupulous employers' who might lay people off to break continuity of employment or 'game' the hours during the reference period by using fixed one or two hour contracts. Bridging provisions, similar to the rules on 'temporary cessation', discussed in Part III.B above, would be introduced to overcome this problem.[211]

Pickavance's fall back proposal represents the most serious attempt to devise a solution to the maximum flexibility/minimum security conundrum that is a typical feature of ZHCs in the UK even in cases where the worker is working regular hours. However, despite the proposed safeguards, there would be a twofold problem if it were implemented. Firstly, the right to end the ZHC after 12 months would be dependent on satisfying mutuality of obligations at least during each individual engagement, as in *Prater*.[212] This may be difficult to prove over a 12-month period unless, as in *Pulse Healthcare*,[213] there is strong evidence that a zero hours clause in the contract is a sham. Secondly, the proposal would not assist the many ZHCs who work irregular hours, as in *Saha*,[214] and who are, in practice, the most vulnerable ZHWs in the greatest need of a standard employment contract to provide them with more certainty as to working hours, pay and benefit entitlement.

In New Zealand, a more radical proposal has been introduced, effective from 1 April 2016,[215] stipulating that employers must specify the number of guaranteed hours of work when the worker is required to be available.[216] Workers can refuse extra hours without being subjected to any detriment. What it does not do, contrary to some reporting, is set a default minimum number of hours per week.[217] It does not ban zero hours working in contracts where there is no mutuality of

[209] Pickavance Report (n 195) 17.

[210] See Z Adams and S Deakin (n 3) 29–30 and 33.

[211] ibid.

[212] *Cornwall County Council v Prater* [2006] EWCA Civ 102, see Part III.B above.

[213] *Pulse Healthcare Ltd v Carewatch Care Services Ltd and 6 Others* [2012] UKEAT/0123/12/BA, see Part III.B above.

[214] *Saha v Viewpoint Field Services Ltd* [2014] UKEAT/0116/13/DM, see Part III.B above.

[215] Employment Relations Amendment Bill (No 3) 2016 (n 201) ss 67E-H.

[216] Eleanor Ainge Roy, 'Zero-hour contracts banned in New Zealand', *The Guardian* (London, 11 March 2016) www.theguardian.com/world/2016/mar/11/zero-hour-contracts-banned-in-new-zealand.

[217] As suggested by E McGaughey (n 153) 7.

obligation, to offer and accept work, but it does prohibit ZHCs that require availability without a guarantee of work. Protection is reinforced by a provision that prevents an employer from requiring the worker to perform additional hours without showing reasonable grounds and, where such grounds are shown, compensates the employee for being available.[218] If imported into the UK, it would provide a simpler, more effective mechanism to provide some certainty about working hours requiring the availability of the worker but it would not end no minimum hours contracting.

V. Conclusion—Towards 'Horizontal Equity' for all Workers

Each of the proposals for labour law reform discussed in the previous part has merit in addressing and, to an extent, rectifying some of the worst abuses of ZHCs. Fundamentally, however, what this study has revealed is that, even if some 'light-touch' measures are introduced to regulate the practice of zero hours contracting,[219] the dynamic of casualisation in the UK labour market is set to continue with the ZHW situated at the extreme end of the arc of precariousness. Other factors, such as social security reform, following the introduction of Universal Credit, further privatisation, and outsourcing of services, will tend to increase reliance on the ZHC model.[220] Low paid sectors more dependent on ZHWs, such as hotels and catering, retail and social care, can be expected to continue to segment from the rest of the labour market.

As was shown in part III of this chapter, many ZHWs are situated in a twilight zone of employment status hovering somewhere between 'employee' and 'worker' with cases falling either side of the distinction based on the weight given to particular facts gleaned from the contractual documentation, the labels used by the employer to describe the relationship, and the conduct of the parties. Even if a ZHW passes the common law tests for recognition as an 'employee', his or her fortunes may founder on the 'archaic rules'[221] of continuity of employment. Indeed, it is somewhat ironic that several of the published proposals for reform of ZHCs require the worker to cross the threshold of a continuity period. The use of continuity provisions only serves to highlight the divide between core and contingent workers in the UK's two-tier labour market.

[218] See D Newman, 'New Zealand bans zero hours contracts? Not exactly …' (A Range of Reasonable Responses, 13 March 2016), see darrennewman.wordpress.com/2016/03/13/new-zealand-bans-zero-hours-contracts-not-exactly/.

[219] A Adams, M Freedland and J Prassl (n 2) 25.

[220] See Z Adams and S Deakin (n 3) 35.

[221] ibid 33.

Against this backdrop, workers on ZHCs will remain contingent in the absence of more stringent measures placing a duty on the part of the employer to provide a default minimum hours' requirement and a guaranteed regular income for workers who have made themselves available for work. Targeted measures aimed at regularising ZHCs will not be sufficient, however, to bring about a less segmented and more inclusive labour market in which the dignity of the worker is respected. We must understand the issue of ZHCs to be totemic for social actors seeking to respond to the challenges arising from the surge in many different types of flexible working which have transformed the expectations of employers and workers about flexibility and security.[222] For this reason, it is necessary to extend the personal scope of employment protection legislation to include all those in diverse non-standard but dependent relationships of which ZHCs are one small part.[223] This does not mean that divergences in protection between core and contingent workers can be easily eradicated but certain changes can be made to achieve more of an equilibrium.

Two reforms would serve as starting blocks for the development of a more inclusive system of labour law in the UK.

First, the application of continuity rules impacts most harshly on intermittent workers, such as ZHCs, who often work for the same employer for long periods. These workers will usually have contracts of employment when working, but continuity of employment will be broken when they are 'zeroed-out' or laid off between engagements. In order to overcome this problem, the law could be modernised straightforwardly, as Zoe Adams and Simon Deakin suggest, to add together all periods of employment with the same employer while disregarding 'breaks' in continuity.[224] This would minimise abuses designed to take advantage of the continuity rules and widen access to rights, such as maternity pay, which require a qualifying period of continuous employment.[225]

Second, a statutory presumption of employment could be introduced.[226] It would allow for essential employment protection laws to be applicable more widely. The present system in the UK no longer fits the reality of the employment relationship. As has been shown in part III.B above, much of the litigation on the status of casual workers has concerned sham labels and bogus terms in employment contracts. What is required is more transparency, and therefore certainty, about both the scope and the content of the employment relationship. Guidance can be found in ILO Recommendation No 198, which is designed to ensure that workers whose contractual position is uncertain are not deprived of the legal

[222] See J Kenner (n 12) 279.

[223] For a wider exploration of the modalities of how this might be achieved see J Kenner, ibid.

[224] See Z Adams and S Deakin (n 3) 33.

[225] The qualifying period is 26 weeks under the Social Security Contributions and Benefits Act 1992 s 164(2)(a).

[226] See further, J Kenner (n 12).

protection to which they are entitled.[227] It seeks to encourage transparency and effectiveness of laws concerning the existence of an employment relationship.[228] The Recommendation suggests a range of indicators as a basis for a legal presumption of an employment relationship. The indicators include 'control' and 'integration of the worker in the organisation of the enterprise' which are drawn from the common law tests for 'employee'.[229] Other indicators fit the broader 'worker' definition in UK law,[230] specifically where 'work … is performed solely or mainly for the benefit of another person' and 'carried out personally by the worker'.[231] The Recommendation also identifies socio-economic indicators such as 'the fact that [payment of] remuneration constitutes the worker's sole or principal source of income'. It does not include factors that negate proof of employment such as the absence of mutuality of obligation.

If the UK was serious about updating its employment law to be more inclusive, consistent with the 'flexicurity' paradigm, it would consult about the content of the most appropriate indicators to form the point of reference for a new proof of employment law or, if a normative measure is not the preferred route, a Code of Practice on establishing an employment relationship might be a first step. Consultation might extend to suggestions about the material scope of employment protection to be afforded to all those with proof of employment based on the indicators. For example, this could include core rights to, inter alia, a minimum wage, safe working conditions, paid holidays, maximum working hours, maternity leave and pay and other family leave rights, non-discrimination, joining a union, taking collective action and protection against arbitrary dismissal. The logic of reaching an agreement on these matters might lead to a decision to have a single category of 'employee' for all those in a position of economic subordination or dependency by reference to the indicators. Alternatively, the separate categories of 'employee' and 'worker' could be retained but the indicators would help to clarify the essential elements of 'employee' or 'worker' status and form a basis for deciding on the detailed content of the employment protection afforded to every 'worker'.

To conclude, the zero hours culture has flourished in the UK's increasingly flexible and 'demutualised' labour market.[232] For some employers, zero hours contracting has become an art form for exploitation by means of transferring the burden of insecurity and risk to the worker. ZHWs are further disadvantaged by benefit rules that increase pressure on them to be available to accept offers of work even when there is no guarantee of minimum hours. In the absence of a uniform

[227] Para 3 of the preamble. The Recommendation was adopted at the 95th session of the International Labour Conference in June 2006 www.ilo.org/dyn/normlex/en/f?p=NORMLEXPUB:12100:0::NO::P12100_ILO_CODE:R198.

[228] ibid point 4(a)-(g).

[229] ibid point 13(a).

[230] Employment Rights Act 1996 s 230(3)(b).

[231] ILO Recommendation No 198 [1996] point 13(b).

[232] See M Freedland and N Kountouris (n 42).

definition of ZHCs, workers who are working, often irregularly, over a period of time for the same employer are faced with uncertainty about their legal status and the scope of employment protection afforded to them. It is, therefore, essential for coercive ZHCs to be challenged to test their lawfulness on a case by case basis. Some of the most egregious abuses of ZHCs could be stamped out, or at least minimised, by adopting proposals that have been put forward or using the New Zealand legislation as a blueprint for further regulation. More stringent measures are needed to guarantee minimum hours and income security. Ultimately, however, the divide between core and contingent work in the UK will only be bridged if measures are initiated to widen access to employment rights for intermittent workers like ZHWs and create a statutory presumption of employment to which a minimum standard of employment protection can be attached.

In the UK, the majority of employers do not use ZHCs as part of their business model or, to the extent that they do offer them, there is evidence that flexibility often suits both parties. An alternative vision of a competitive, more productive, social market economy is possible in which workers' dignity is respected, more legal certainty is provided in the employment relation, and there is greater opportunity for full engagement of all workers in the enterprise. As Judy Fudge has observed, the most important shift in the discipline of labour law has been towards individualisation.[233] The task of labour law in the twenty-first century is to regulate for flexibility by providing 'horizontal equity' between workers in ever more diverse working relationships.[234]

[233] J Fudge, 'Labour as a 'Fictive Commodity': Radically Reconceptualizing Labour Law' in G Davidov and B Langille (eds), *The Idea of Labour Law* (OUP, 2011) 120-136, 124.

[234] ibid. See also, M Link, 'Labour Law and the New Inequality' (2009) 59 UNBLJ 14–47.

11

Collective Regulation of Contingent Work: From Traditional Forms of Contingent Work to Crowdwork—A German Perspective

THOMAS KLEBE AND JOHANNES HEUSCHMID

I. The Notion of Contingent Work—Focus from A Collective Perspective

The working environment faces immense changes at present in the context of globalisation and digitalisation. Self-evidently, this will also affect the standard employment relationship. In other words, recent developments are putting at risk the common understanding of the employment relationship.[1] The gradual abandonment of the core employment relationship with a move towards contingent forms—also known as detached employment—is nothing new for labour law.[2] However, what is new are certain dynamics leading to new forms of contingent work, questioning the very foundations of our existing understanding of the functioning of labour law.

In this chapter we will approach several forms of contingent work—both traditional and new—from the perspective of the labour movement or, in other words, from the perspective of the collective actors operating on the labour side.

Our discussion of traditional forms of contingent work focuses on temporary agency work (Section II) and service contracting (Section III). Both types of contingent work, known also as Fremdfirmenarbeit (external contractor work), have featured heavily in national debates and in the regulatory activities of the collective actors in Germany. According to a 2013 survey by the metalworkers union

[1] C Summers, 'Contingent Employment' (1996-97) 18 *Comparative Labor Law Journal* 503; recently the National Labour Relations Board (NLRB) acknowledged a 'dramatic growth in contingent employment relationships', see NLRB, 27 August 2015, Case 32-RC-109684.

[2] Summers (n 1) 505 and 514–18.

(IG Metall), temporary agency workers (230,000) and workers supplied through service contracting (800,000) accounted for some 22 per cent of those working in the metalworking and electrical engineering sector. The share taken by these two forms of work was particularly high in the automotive industry (31 per cent) and shipbuilding (35 per cent).[3] The research and development departments of the automotive industry made even greater use of these forms, with between 40 per cent and 60 per cent of the workforce engaged on this basis. According to analysis by IAB, the research institute allied to the German public employment service, during the follow up to the economic and financial crisis, 200,000 new jobs created on the basis of temporary agency work have replaced 100,000 regular jobs.[4] Similar findings are reached by the employers' association for the metalworking industry, Gesamtmetall, which assumes that 30 per cent of the new jobs are simply replacements for regular jobs that previously existed.[5] And these are just the figures for temporary agency work. Other forms of contingent employment are not included. This underlines how crucial the problems are that trade unions now face. Indeed, the matter was considered sufficiently important that, on coming to power in 2013, the parties in Germany's governing coalition (Christian democrats and social democrats) agreed to legislate for stricter regulation of these forms of contingent work.

Following this discussion of traditional forms of contingent work, our attention shifts in Section IV to the development of new forms of contingent work, taking the example of crowdwork. This type of work raises many questions requiring regulatory responses both from collective actors and the legislative authorities.

II. Temporary Agency Work

A. The Legal Situation in Germany

Olaf Deinert's chapter has already analysed in detail the legal situation in Germany. Therefore, it suffices to stress, here, simply the two major shortcomings of German law in this area. According to various writers, these shortcomings mean that German law is incompatible with EU law.[6] First, in the context of section 1(1) of the Act on Temporary Agency Work (Arbeitnehmerüberlassungsgesetz), which provides on the basis of the EU Directive on Temporary Agency Work (2008/104/EC) that 'the supply of workers to an end user shall be effected on a temporary

[3] M Dettmer et al, 'Mittendrin und nicht dabei' *Der Spiegel* (Hamburg, 18 November 2013) 78.

[4] E Jahn and E Weber, 'Zusätzliche Jobs, aber auch Verdrängung' (2013) 2 *IAB-Kurzbericht* 5.

[5] Arbeitgeberverband Gesamtmetall, *Arbeiten im Herz der Wirtschaft* (Berlin, Arbeitgeberverband Gesamtmetall, 2012) 17.

[6] P Sansone, 'Leiharbeit' in U Preis and A Sagan (eds), *Europäisches Arbeitsrecht* (Köln, Otto Schmidt, 2015) § 8 par 32 and 82.

basis', many writers criticise the lack of definition of what is meant by 'temporary' in this situation. The courts have declined to clarify this point.[7] Does temporary really mean eternally minus one day? That cannot be right. Some writers[8] expected the European Court of Justice (ECJ) to provide some clarification in its judgment in *AKT*.[9] However, the Court's judgment refrained from any detailed examination of this issue. Nonetheless, following the judgment, it would appear that EU law does not impose any serious limitations on restrictions of temporary agency work through actors on the national level.[10] The other main shortfall in the German legislation results from the broad possibility to derogate by way of collective agreement to the detriment of employees from the equal treatment principle established in the Act on Temporary Agency Work. In practice, this has led to numerous collective agreements concluded with yellow—ie employer dominated—unions which derogated from the equal treatment principle to the detriment of employees and putting collective agreements establishing decent terms and conditions under considerable pressure. As will be explained later, it was quite a difficult job for the collective actors to tackle these problems.

B. Regulation Through Collective Agreements Negotiated by Trade Unions

Against this background, trade unions faced an increasingly difficult task to deal with the increasing use of temporary agency workers in the German economy, with the number of temporary agency workers reaching 860,000 at the end of 2014.[11] Two main strategies can be identified in the bargaining policy. The first strategy has been to re-establish the equal pay principle, which is the main principle of the Act on Temporary Agency Work as well as the underlying EU Directive. The second strategy is to contain the extent to which agency work is used. Collective agreements have followed both of these routes.

i. Re-establish the Equal Pay Principle

The idea of re-establishing the equal pay principle through collective agreements can be subdivided into two further strategies. The first is to conclude collective agreements with the employer associations on the agency side on supplements to the basic remuneration. Before the collective actors started to deal with the

[7] Federal Labour Court 10 December 2013, 9 AZR 51/13.

[8] G Thüsing, 'Dauerhafte Arbeitnehmerüberlassung: Neues vom BAG, vom EuGH und auch vom Gesetzgeber' (2014) *Neue Zeitschrift für Arbeitsrecht* 10 and 12.

[9] Case C-533/13 *Auto- ja Kuljetusalan Työntekijäliitto AKT ry v Öljytuote ry and Shell Aviation Finland Oy* EU:C:2015:173.

[10] J Heuschmid, 'Leiharbeit kann durch TV eingeschränkt werden' (2015) *Arbeit und Recht* 279.

[11] G Deter, 'Zahl der Leiharbeiter steigt wieder' (2015) *Arbeit und Recht* 268.

issue, the average hourly wage of temporary agency workers was 8.91 euros compared with an average hourly wage among regular workers in the metalworking sector of 17.09 euros.[12] Negotiating experience over recent years has shown that this is probably the most successful way to improve the working conditions of temporary agency workers, at least as regards the re-establishment of the equal treatment principle. To date, eleven collective agreements have been concluded between the relevant employer organisations, Bundesarbeitgeberverband der Personaldienstleister (BAP) and the Interessensverband Deutscher Zeitarbeitsunternehmen (iGZ) and DGB trade unions on the labour side establishing awards for different industries (known in German as Branchenzuschläge (industry supplements)).[13] One example is the collective agreement for the metalworking and electrical engineering industry, concluded with the IG Metall trade union.[14] This collective agreement provides for the remuneration of temporary agency workers to advance in stages to the regular rates of remuneration in the metalworking and electrical engineering industry during the loan period. After six weeks of employment in the metalworking and electrical engineering industry, a temporary agency worker is entitled to a supplement of 15 per cent in addition to his basic remuneration based on the collective agreement in the temporary agency work sector. The supplement increases after three months to 20 per cent, after five months to 30 per cent, after seven months to 45 per cent and finally after nine months to 50 per cent. A similar pattern can be found in other industries, albeit with different figures. As many temporary agency workers remain only for a relatively short period in the user undertaking,[15] this solution is not perfect, but at least a starting point.[16] However, especially in the metalworking and electrical engineering industry, the loan period is increasing.[17]

The second strategy is to conclude agreements with the hirers' side, aimed at ensuring agency workers' right to equal treatment in the user undertaking.[18] The most well-known example is the 2010 collective agreement for the steel industry

[12] T Klebe and T Jacquemin, 'Die Zukunft der Betriebsratsarbeit 2.0' (2014) 11 *Arbeitsrecht im Betrieb* 33.

[13] R Krause, *Tarifverträge zur Begrenzung der Leiharbeit und zur Druchsetzung von Equal Pay* (Frankfurt am Main, Bund-Verlag, 2014) 38; A Bissels and F Mehnert, 'Tarifverträge über Branchenzuschläge in der Zeitarbeit—ein Rechtsprechungsüberblick' (2014) *Der Betrieb* 2407. In Austria, a similar approach has been followed in cases where the equal treatment principle does not apply, see Kollektivvertrag für das Gewerbe der Arbeitskräfteüberlassung IX No 3 and No 4.

[14] Tarifvertrag über Branchenzuschläge für Arbeitnehmerüberlassungen in der Metall- und Elektroindustrie, 22 May 2012.

[15] Statistics show that, in 2011, half of all work assignments of temporary agency workers were for periods of less than three months, D Schumann, 'Tarifverträge zur Leiharbeit in der Metall- und Elektroindustrie' (2012) *Arbeitsrecht im Betrieb* 423–24.

[16] J Schubert and U Zachert, in O Kempen and U Zachert (eds), *Tarifvertragsgesetz*, (5th edn, Frankfurt am Main, Bund-Verlag, 2014) § 1 par 779.

[17] Schumann (n 15) 424.

[18] J Heuschmid and M Hensche in W Däubler (ed), *Tarifvertragsgesetz mit Arbeitnehmer-Entsendegesetz*, (3rd edn, Baden-Baden, Nomos, 2012) § 1 par 793.

in north-western Germany.[19] This agreement lays down the rule in section 2 of the agreement that the user undertaking must ensure that temporary agency workers have a right to equal pay enforceable against the temporary work agency. If the hirer (user undertaking) fails to ensure that such an equality clause is inserted in the hire agreement, it will be liable to compensate the worker for the shortfall in wages resulting from the unequal treatment.[20]

ii. Containment of the Extent to Which Agency Work is used in the User Undertaking

The second main strategy has been to contain the extent to which agency work is used. Here, too, there are different strategies in place. One approach is to establish a maximum loan period, as was done, for example, in the collective agreement for the steel industry in the Saarland.[21] The parties to this agreement established, as a general rule, a maximum loan period of three months, extended in exceptional circumstances to six months. Another means of containment is to agree quotas for the use of temporary agency workers in the relevant plant.[22] One example is the 'future agreement' with Airbus, signed in October 2011, which anticipated, starting from January 2012, a maximum share of 20 per cent temporary agency workers reducing to a maximum share of 15 per cent from January 2015. A further technique used in these collective agreements has been to strengthen the participation rights of works councils. The effect of these provisions will be examined below in Section II.C.

C. Regulation Achieved at the Works Council Level

Our focus now shifts to the other important collective actor in Germany at plant level, namely, the works council. These provide an additional channel for the workers' voice and, in practice, are closely connected with the trade unions. Several works council agreements (Betriebsvereinbarungen) exist establishing quotas for the use of temporary agency workers. For example, in the shipbuilding industry, several companies reached works council agreements establishing a 20 per cent limit.[23] Similar examples can also be found in the car industry. Daimler

[19] Heuschmid and Hensche (n 18) § 1 par 793; Krause (n 13) 40.

[20] Heuschmid and Hensche (n 18) § 1 par 793.

[21] Tarifvertrag über den Einsatz von Leiharbeit für die Arbeitnehmer der eisenschaffenden Industrie des Saarlandes, 24 January 2012; Krause (n 13) 36f.

[22] These provisions are also common in the Netherlands, see N Zekic, *Werkzekerheid in het arbeidsrecht* (Deventer, Kluwer, 2014). Moreover, in its *AKT* judgment, the CJEU accepted a Finnish collective agreement which lays down the situations in which temporary agency workers may be hired and restricts the reasons for which such workers may be used, see Heuschmid (n 10) 279f.

[23] Betriebsvereinbarung Nr. 01/2013 zwischen der Geschäftsführung und dem Betriebsrat der Lürssen-Kröger Werft GmbH & Co. KG über den Einsatz von Zeitarbeit, 29 July 2013. In Austria, too, works council agreements exist specifying quotas. In addition, they provide for financial sanctions where those quotas are breached.

(Mercedes-Benz) concluded an agreement with its works council as early as 2004 setting a limit of 8 per cent.[24]

A widespread feature in the metalworking and electrical engineering industry are agreements known as Besservereinbarungen.[25] These are works council agreements on a voluntary basis. Besservereinbarung means literally better than the law. More than 1,400 agreements of this kind have been agreed in the metalworking industry. The construction used to achieve this goal is to lay down obligations in the Besservereinbarung requiring the user undertaking to ensure that in the hire contract between the temporary employment agency and the user undertaking there is an obligation to pay equal pay during the loan period.

In addition to these arrangements, agreed in legal terms on a voluntary basis, the German Works Constitution Act (Betriebsverfassungsgesetz) lays down a series of co-determination rights for the works council in the user undertaking. According to a 2013 decision of the Federal Labour Court (Bundesarbeitsgericht), the strongest participation rights, namely, those contained in points 1, 2, 3, 6, 7, 8, 12 and 13 of section 87(1) of the Works Constitution Act also apply with regard to temporary agency workers.[26] This opens a huge area in which works councils can contribute to the regulation of temporary agency work. Some writers go further, arguing that section 95 of the Works Constitution Act on criteria for staff selection also applies with regard to the hiring of agency workers.[27]

Following another judgment of the Federal Labour Court, it is now clear that temporary agency workers are relevant for the thresholds of the Works Constitution Act, eg, regarding the size of the works council.[28] Likewise, legislation provides that temporary agency workers have voting rights in the plant of the user undertaking where they are deployed (section 7 of the Works Constitution Act).

Another important means of containment for the works council is the participation right established by section 14(3) of the Act on Temporary Agency Work in conjunction with point 1 of section 99(2) of the Works Constitution Act.[29] This concerns the right of the works council in the user undertaking to participate in the context of human resources operations. Before an agency worker can start working in the plant, the employer has to obtain the agreement of the works council. If the employer does not fulfil obligations laid down in legislation or other regulations, such as collective agreements, the works council is entitled to refuse. As a consequence, the employer cannot employ the relevant employee. One of the reasons for refusing could be, for example, contravention of the temporary workers quota established in the collective agreement. Further examples of

[24] This included also the use of fixed-term work in actual vehicle production.

[25] Krause (n 13) 41; Schumann (n 15) 424.

[26] Federal Labour Court 13 March 2013, 7 ABR 69/11; for details, see T Klebe in W Däubler et al (eds), *Betriebsverfassungsgesetz*, (14th edn, Frankfurt am Main, Bund-Verlag, 2014) § 87 par 8.

[27] Klebe (n 26) § 95 par 32.

[28] Federal Labour Court 13 March 2013, 7 ABR 69/11; J Homburg (n 26) § 9 par 16.

[29] Krause (n 13) 37.

collectively agreed rules that a relevant employer must comply with can be seen in the May 2012 collective agreement for the metalworking and electrical engineering industry in Baden-Württemberg which only allows temporary agency workers to be deployed in the user undertaking if there are no dangers for the working conditions of the regular employees.[30] In addition, it clarified that only a temporary use of temporary agency workers is allowed. Alongside these rules, other provisions of the collective agreement strengthened the participation rights of the works council in the user undertaking.[31] This illustrates how the combination of collective bargaining and works councils can be a powerful tool for containing temporary agency work.

D. The Coalition Agreement of the Present Government and Temporary Agency Work

The sections above have demonstrated that there are numerous examples of how the collective actors, namely the trade unions and the works councils, have reacted to the problems that arose with the expansion of temporary agency work following deregulation in the context of the 2003 labour market reforms (known as the Hartz reforms). On coming to power, the newly-elected German Government was also aware of the problems this form of contingent work causes for society as a whole, committing to address this issue in their coalition agreement of 17 December 2013.[32] Interestingly, the solutions found by the collective actors have served as a role model for the regulatory proposals set out in the coalition agreement.

The Government plans to establish by law a maximum loan period of 18 months and offer equal pay after nine months. These are two important steps forward. The first draft legislation on this issue is anticipated in late 2015. As far as one can tell, the Government appears unwilling to regulate for the legal consequences where the assignment of an agency worker is not temporary. On the other hand, several proposals exist that academic commentators have developed.[33] It will be interesting to see what the final outcome of the legislative activities will be. The main beneficiaries of these legislative activities will be workers in sectors with fewer works councils and poor collective agreement coverage.

[30] Tarifvertrag Leih-/Zeitarbeit Metall- und Elektroindustrie Baden-Württemberg, 19 December 2012; Schumann (n 15) 424.

[31] Schumann (n 15) 424.

[32] *Deutschlands Zukunft gestalten. Koalitionsvertrag zwischen CDU, CSU und SPD 18. Legislaturperiode* (Berlin, 2013).

[33] M Franzen, 'Neuausrichtung des Drittpersonaleinsatzes—Überlegungen zu den Vorhaben des Koalitionsvertrags' (2015) *Recht der Arbeit* 141; P Schüren and C Brors, 'Neue gesetzliche Rahmenbedingungen für den Fremdpersonaleinsatz' (2014) *Neue Zeitschrift für Arbeitsrecht* 569; J Ulber and D Stang, 'Die geplante Neuregelung der Leiharbeit' (2015) *Arbeit und Recht* 250.

III. Service Contracting

Service contracting is another (traditional) form of Fremdfirmenarbeit. In the German context, it is important to emphasise that a significant increase in service contracting, in the form of outsourcing operations, has taken place also with a view to circumventing the stricter regulation of temporary agency work achieved through the collective actors. This development has led to another cheap labour force, which automatically increased the pressure on the regular workforce. Unlike regular employees who benefit from generous collective agreements, these employees usually do not receive any Christmas allowance, holiday bonus, overtime pay, etc. At the same time, there has been a sharp rise in the number of solo self-employed (ie self-employed individuals who do not employ another person) from 1.8 million in 2000 to 2.6 million in 2011.[34] In this context, the earnings spread is extremely large. Alongside some jobs for highly qualified people, in 2013, around one third of the solo self-employed earned less than 8.50 euros per hour. Average earnings were around 13 euros per hour.

A. The Legal Situation in Germany

The typical form of contract used for service contracting of this kind is a contract known as the Werkvertrag governed by section 631 of the German Civil Code (Bürgerliches Gesetzbuch). One can define the Werkvertrag as a special kind of contract for services in which the contractor has a duty to produce a work and is responsible for the result. Not far away from the Werkvertrag is the Dienstvertrag (contract of service), governed by section 611 of the Civil Code. However, in contrast to the Werkvertrag, under a Dienstvertrag the contractor is required to perform a certain activity but is not responsible for the result. The labour contract is a special form of Dienstvertrag under which the employee has to follow the managerial authority of the employer whereas under other forms of a contract of service (known as 'free' contracts of service) the supplier is free to decide how to perform his work. There is an important distinction between labour provided under a Werkvertrag and temporary agency work. In the case of agency work, the user undertaking has managerial authority (Direktionsrecht). In the case of service contracting in the form of a Werkvertrag, managerial authority remains with the contractor, which could be a company or a solo self-employed individual.

B. Types of Service Contracts

As one might imagine, the phenomenon of service contracting is quite heterogeneous and not easy to capture in legal terms. Therefore, it appears sensible to

[34] Klebe and Jacquemin (n 12).

undertake some form of categorisation to arrive at a common understanding of the phenomenon. In practice, three types of service contract dominate.

- The first type is a contract for the provision of sporadic services. From a labour law perspective, this does not present any problems. One typical example is the contracting out of renovation works in a car manufacturing company.
- Another widespread phenomenon is service contracting with the solo self-employed. This is one of the problematic aspects of recent developments. In many cases, solo self-employed individuals are used to undercut regular labour contracts. In other words, this could result in bogus self-employment. This type of service contracting is also quite common in the context of new forms of contingent work such as crowdwork (see Section IV below).
- Finally, and also importantly, there are service contracts with other companies as subcontractors especially in the context of outsourcing operations. This type of contracting is heavily used in the German car industry, especially in collaboration with industrial service providers. These operations are mainly driven by dumping strategies. If, for example, an industrial service provider is included in the outsourcing operation, wage costs are up to 40 per cent lower than under the comparable collective agreement for the metalworking and electrical engineering sector.[35] One example of this practice is the BMW factory in Leipzig. Of the total workforce of 6,950 employees on the BMW factory site, in 2013, only 3,000 were employees with a direct labour contract with BMW. Working alongside these were 2,200 workers employed by industrial service providers holding a service contract with BMW and, finally, 1,750 of the workers were temporary agency workers.[36] In many situations, it is questionable whether the contract with the service provider is a genuine service contract or, in fact, a contract to supply temporary agency work.

C. Regulation Through Collective Agreements Negotiated by trade Unions

A breakthrough in regulating service contracting through collective agreements in the metalworking and electrical engineering industry occurred in September 2013 with the conclusion of a company-level collective agreement with the northern German shipbuilder Meyer Werft.[37] The background to this development was a major accident that occurred on the Meyer Werft site. In this accident, two Romanian workers employed by a service contracting company (subcontractor) died.

[35] ibid.

[36] ibid.

[37] Haustarifvertrag in Ergänzung der getroffenen Bündnisvereinbarungen zur Regelung von Arbeitsbedingungen bei der Vergabe von Aufträgen an Werkvertragsunternehmen, 12 September 2013.

It turned out that their working conditions had been quite scandalous. According to a Romanian newspaper, the workers of the subcontractor were required to work very long hours, between 200 and 300 hours per month, for low wages, with monthly earnings of between 1,200 and 1,800 euros, which is far removed from the German wage level.[38] After the accident, this leading German shipbuilder was very keen to conclude a collective agreement with the trade union IG Metall to regulate the working conditions of the workers in subcontracting companies. The collective agreement of 12 September 2013 deals with several important issues including working time, health and safety, housing and remuneration in the context of subcontracting. For example, the parties agreed that workers in the subcontracting companies must be entitled to a minimum wage of 8.50 euros per hour, which, since January 2015, is now the official national minimum wage. Following this agreement at company level, the IG Metall trade union concluded the first sectoral agreement of this kind in July 2014, establishing similar regulations for workers of subcontracting companies in the steel sector.[39] More agreements may follow soon.

D. Regulation Achieved at the Works Council Level

Just as in the agency work context, there are also possibilities to regulate service contracting at the works council level through works council agreements. Particularly well known is the works council agreement concluded in July 2013 at Lürssen Werft, also a leading shipbuilder.[40] In this agreement, the parties agreed, in a similar manner to the later collective agreement with the Meyer Werft, on the minimum wage, housing conditions and health and safety of the workers of subcontracting companies working at the plant.

In addition, in several car manufacturing companies, works council agreements, known as 'make or buy' agreements, have been established on a voluntary basis. Under such agreements, in the case of outsourcing operations, the employer is obliged to follow a certain procedure. Before the outsourcing takes place, the works council has a right to make a final call, proposing alternatives to the outsourcing. Arrangements of this kind have been common in the automotive industry for many years.[41] A similar approach can be found in 'fair owner' agreements, which exist, for example, in the Thyssen company (steel industry). According to these agreements, outsourcing is only possible if the contract is awarded to a fair owner who ensures certain minimum working conditions such as compliance with relevant collective agreements. Recently, BMW has announced that it

[38] M Romalo, 'Muncitori români dezvăluie abuzurile unei reţele de subantreprenori turci din Constanţa şi din Germania' *Observator* (Constanţa, 29 August 2013) 8.

[39] Tarifvertrag über den Einsatz von Werkverträgen,8 July 2014.

[40] Betriebsvereinbarung zur Regelung der Arbeitsbedingungen bei der Vergabe von Aufträgen an Werkvertragsunternehmen.

[41] Klebe and Jacquemin (n 12).

will only outsource if the subcontractor has a collective agreement with the trade union IG Metall.[42] Similar provisions are in place at VW.

Moreover, the works council has some information and participation rights with regard to employees of subcontractors. These are the rights laid down in section 80(2), point 3 of section 90(1) and sections 92 and 92a of the Works Constitution Act.[43] However, it remains unresolved whether the co-determination rights in section 87 of the Works Constitution Act also apply in relation to workers of subcontracting companies. Some writers take the view that this should be the case.[44] This applies in particular where the workers of the subcontractor are closely integrated in the client company plant.[45]

E. The Coalition Agreement of the Present Government and Service Contracting

Compared to the plans for regulation with regard to temporary agency work, the coalition agreement plans dealing with service contracting are rather poor. This reluctance to act results from the Christian Democrats who are not very keen to regulate these kinds of issues. On the coalition's agenda is, firstly, better monitoring of service contracting by public authorities, better compliance with health and safety regulations, perhaps involving works councils, and, finally, greater specification of works council rights with regard to information and consultation. However, given that service contracting is seemingly the most serious problem currently facing the workforce and collective actors in traditional industrial sectors, these proposals clearly do not go far enough. To take the problem seriously, much more would be necessary.[46]

IV. Crowdwork—(New) Contingent Work Under Platform Capitalism

Now we will turn to the most recent developments. Currently, new forms of work are emerging in the context of internet platforms, otherwise known as the world of platform capitalism or the gig economy.[47] The basic thrust of these labour market developments is that the standard employment relationship becomes

[42] 'Bewegung bei BMW' *Mittelbayerische Zeitung* (Regensburg, 20 July 2015) 14.
[43] B Karthaus and T Klebe, 'Betriebsratsrechte bei Werkverträgen' (2012) *Neue Zeitschrift für Arbeitsrecht* 419.
[44] Klebe (n 26) § 87 par 10 f.
[45] Karthaus and Klebe (n 43) 424 ff.
[46] Karthaus and Klebe (n 43) 425.
[47] Sometimes, somewhat disingenuously, this is also referred to as the 'sharing economy'.

increasingly marginalised coupled with an expansion of (solo) self-employment and similar activities.[48] In more general terms, this is just another feature of the wider trend towards individualisation and deregulation. The variety of services offered by these new companies in the context of platform capitalism is very broad. The range includes self-employed shoppers who deliver groceries for your fridge offered at Instacart, local transportation services from Uber and lawyers on-demand available from Axiom. According to the global consulting firm PwC, platform capitalism firms in the five key sectors will achieve sales of 335 billion US dollars by 2025.[49] One of the most important new developments in this context is a new form of outsourcing known as crowdsourcing, which we will now examine more closely.

A. First Empirical Findings on Crowdwork

Crowdwork is a new form of outsourcing of tasks to a large, possibly unlimited, pool of online workers.[50] Tasks are advertised on (internet) platforms and the crowd is invited to apply to perform the tasks. This process is referred to as crowdsourcing. Under this system, the employers are the 'crowdsourcers' for whom the crowdworkers provide services. An important feature of this system is that the relationship between crowdsourcers and crowdworkers is usually managed through an intermediary: the crowdsourcing platform.[51] In principle, crowdsourcing can take place internally or externally, depending on the composition of the crowd, in other words whether the crowd consists of the company's internal workforce[52] or external individuals.[53] Our analysis will focus on this latter group, examining their position from the labour (law) perspective. In contrast, in the case of internal crowdwork, the crowdworkers are regular employees.

The range of crowdsourced tasks is quite wide. At one extreme, there are so-called micro tasks. Usually larger tasks are divided into several smaller tasks for this purpose.[54] One example is the cataloguing of craters on a moon or planet. At the other end of the spectrum, there are more complex tasks, mostly in the

[48] The German Federal Statistical Office calculates that in 2013 around 7% of those in work were solo self-employed persons, in figures, 2.97 million individuals.

[49] A Peterson, 'The FTC wants to talk about the "sharing economy"' *The Washington Post* (Washington, 17 April 2015) www.washingtonpost.com/news/the-switch/wp/2015/04/17/the-ftc-wants-to-talk-about-the-sharing-economy.

[50] JM Leimeister et al, 'Crowdwork—digitale Wertschöpfung in der Wolke' in C Benner (ed), *Crowdwork, zurück in die Zukunft* (Frankfurt, Bund Verlag, 2014) 9; M Risak and J Warter, 'Decent Crowdwork—Legal Strategies towards fair employment conditions in the virtual sweatshop', (Regulating for Decent Work Conference, Geneva, 8-10 July 2015) 1; W Däubler and T Klebe, 'Crowdwork: Die neue Form der Arbeit—Arbeitgeber auf der Flucht?' (2015) *Neue Zeitschrift für Arbeitsrecht* 1032.

[51] Leimeister (n 50) 15; Risak and Warter (n 50).

[52] Däubler and Klebe (n 50) 1033.

[53] Leimeister (n 50); Risak and Warter (n 50) 2.

[54] Leimeister (n 50) 15.

context of project-oriented work, eg, in the field of research and development. This form of crowdwork may also be contest-based.[55] In principle, crowdwork can be applied to every part of the value creation chain.

The contractual relationships between the related parties vary according to the platform involved.[56] One model, which is used at Amazon Mechanical Turk (AMT), leads to a direct contractual relationship between the crowdsourcer and the crowdworker and, at the same time, to contractual relationships with AMT. The same model can be found on the platforms operated by Freelancer, InnoCentive or, in Germany, Twago. In contrast, there is a different model that only leads to contractual relationships between the platform and the crowdworker. This model can be found on the platforms operated by Clickworker and CrowdFlower.[57]

At the start of 2015, some 2,300 crowdworking platforms were in existence worldwide, including 65 in Germany.[58] AMT has 500,000 crowdworkers working for it on a regular basis. The German platform, Clickworker, 'employs' more than 700,000 crowdworkers from 136 different countries. The recently published World Bank report, *The Global Opportunity in Online Outsourcing*, estimates that, by 2020, the business will generate revenues of up to 25 billion dollars.[59] Others estimate that the volume will reach 46 billion dollars.[60]

B. Protection of Crowdworkers—The Applicable Labour Law and Beyond

Attention should also be paid to the working conditions of crowdworkers. Just as the tasks and contractual relationships differ, there is also a considerable spread in wages. Micro tasks are generally compensated with average wages of two dollars per hour.[61] Very experienced workers can make more, with wages of up to eight dollars per hour.[62] Higher skilled work such as software engineering or design is paid better. In Germany and the United States, the average wage in this segment was around 33 dollars per hour in 2013, whereas worldwide the average wage was 24 dollars per hour according to a statement by the platform Upwork.[63] These are, of course, gross wages from which workers must also pay all their taxes and social security contributions.

[55] Risak and Warter (n 50) 3; Leimeister (n 50) 15.

[56] M Risak, 'Crowdwork' (2015) *Zeitschrift für Arbeits- und Sozialrecht* 11, 13 ff.

[57] Däubler and Klebe (n 50) 1033.

[58] ibid.

[59] World Bank, *The Global Opportunity in Online Outsourcing* (Washington DC, World Bank, 2015) 24.

[60] ibid 25.

[61] Eurofound, *New forms of employment* (Luxembourg, Publications Office of the European Union, 2015) 115.

[62] M Marvit, 'How Crowdworkers became the Ghosts in the Digital Machine', *The Nation* (New York, 5 February 2014), see www.thenation.com/article/how-crowdworkers-became-ghosts-digital-machine.

[63] N Dittberner, 'Fünf Fragen an Nicolas Dittberner' in C Benner (ed), *Crowdwork, zurück in die Zukunft* (Frankfurt, Bund Verlag, 2014) 94.

In addition to these poor rates of remuneration, the more general question arises as to how far the traditional protection provided by labour law is applicable to crowdworkers.[64] We will examine this more closely below. However, one thing is already clear, crowdwork has a major potential to undermine the established system of worker protection. This is supported by the words of Lukas Biewald CEO of CrowdFlower who said:

> 'Before the Internet it would be really difficult to find someone, sit them down for ten minutes and get them to work for you, and then fire them after these ten minutes. But with this technology, you can actually find them, pay them the tiny amount of money, and get rid of them when you don't need them anymore.'[65]

This statement emphasises in a nutshell the precariousness of the working conditions of crowdworkers.

The diversity in the contractual relationships, existing in this decentralised model of work distribution, is matched by the broad range of possible approaches for the protection of crowdworkers. The greatest difficulties arise in cross-border contexts.

i. Application of Labour Law

The first question to tackle is whether crowdworkers are employees. If this is the case, the crowdworker is protected by the complete system of labour law. Under the German approach, there is no statutory definition of an employee. Instead, the notion of an employee is defined in accordance with a typology developed by case law. This relies on identifying certain characteristics, the most important of which are integration in the organisation of the employer and a relationship of personal dependency.[66] According to the Federal Labour Court (Bundesarbeitsgericht), this must be assessed taking into account all the circumstances of the individual case.[67] In the case of subordinate and simple tasks, employee status is more likely to be found.[68] This approach is very similar to that applied by the ECJ in identifying the notion of a worker for the purposes of free movement of workers under Article 45 TFEU.[69]

Given this background, it is absolutely conceivable that crowdworkers are employees notwithstanding the very short duration of the employment relationship.[70] Indicators for an employment relationship could be found, for example, if

[64] T Klebe and J Neugebauer, 'Crowdsourcing: Für eine handvoll Dollar oder Workers of the crowd unite?' (2014) *Arbeit und Recht* 4.

[65] Marvit (n 62).

[66] Federal Labour Court 26 May 1999, 5 AZR 469/98; for greater detail, see O Deinert in M Kittner et al (eds), *ArbeitsrechtHandbuch für die Praxis* (8th edn, Frankfurt am Main, Bund-Verlag, 2015) § 3 par 23ff.

[67] Federal Labour Court 26 May 1999, 5 AZR 469/98.

[68] ibid.

[69] Deinert (n 66) § 3 par 9.

[70] Risak (n 56) 17.

the contract defines very specific conditions of the action the crowdworker has to fulfil. This could be the case if there are clear specifications concerning the work timetable and providing for control through screenshots.[71] Furthermore, there is often the possibility to discipline crowdworkers through ratings on the platform. Taken together, these mechanisms could equate to the degree of personal dependency necessary to find that an employment relationship exists with the platform or crowdsourcer.[72] As a consequence, the crowdworker would be entitled to the minimum wage, paid annual leave, statutory sick pay, etc. In those circumstances, the question then arises how the rules on fixed-term work will impact on crowdwork.[73] Moreover, in the case of employee status, full social security protection must be provided. Therefore, it will be very interesting to see how the Federal Labour Court deals with the definition of employees in the context of these new forms of work. Quite clearly, there is considerable scope to apply labour law to crowdworkers.

ii. Application of 'Employee-like' Status to Crowdworkers

If, in a specific situation, crowdworkers cannot be categorised as employees, the next question is whether they meet the conditions for 'employee-like' status (Arbeitnehmerähnlichkeit). This is an intermediate status lying between full employee status and self-employment—to which some provisions of labour law apply. Just as there is no statutory definition of an employee, employee-like status is also not defined in legislation. Despite this fact, several laws refer to employee-like status.[74] Thus, it has fallen to the Federal Labour Court again to define employee-like status. There are two main criteria: economic dependency and a need for protection similar to that of an ordinary employee.[75] One shortcoming is that minimum wage legislation does not apply to employee-like persons. However, this could be tackled easily by extending the legislation to this category.[76] For the purposes of collective bargaining, the German legislation specifically authorises trade unions to bargain for employee-like persons (section 12a of the Collective Agreements Act (Tarifvertragsgesetz)). On the other hand, in the case of social security, employee-like persons are basically considered self-employed persons. However, by way of exception, specific provision is made to include these individuals in the context of the state pension scheme (point 9 of section 2 of the Sixth Book of the Social Security Code (Sozialgesetzbuch VI)) and statutory accident insurance scheme (the first sentence of section 2(2) of the Seventh Book of the Social Security Code

[71] Däubler and Klebe (n 50) 1034 f.

[72] Risak (n 56)16.

[73] Risak (n 56) 17.

[74] For an overview see O Deinert (n 66) § 3 par 175.

[75] Federal Labour Court 16 July 1997, 5 AZB 29/96.

[76] W Däubler, 'Der gesetzliche Mindestlohn—doch eine unendliche Geschichte?' (2014) *Neue Juristische Wochenschrift* 1924, 1926; with particular reference to crowdworkers: M Cherry, 'Mindestlohn für Crowdarbeit' in C Benner (ed) n 50.

(Sozialgesetzbuch VII)).[77] Employee-like status is a category that can also be found in several other legal orders.[78]

In Germany, like in other jurisdictions, there is an important subcategory of employee-like status of particular interest in the context of crowdwork: this is known as homework (Heimarbeit). The concept is rooted in the early years of industrialisation and is regulated in Germany in the Homeworking Act (Heimarbeitsgesetz). As a general rule, the provisions of labour law do not apply to homeworkers. However, there are some important exemptions. Ultimately, homeworkers could be entitled to some of the protection specified in the Works Constitution Act, Statutory Sick Pay Act (Entgeltfortzahlungsgesetz), Parental Leave Act (Elternzeitgesetz), Paid Leave Act (Urlaubsgesetz), Safety and Health at Work Act (Arbeitsschutzgesetz) and the Dismissal Protection Act (Kündigungsschutzgesetz). Moreover, section 17 of the Homeworking Act makes special provision for collective bargaining in this area. Germany is not alone in having such rules. A specific legal regime governing homework can be found in several jurisdictions.[79] For the purposes of social security, homeworkers in Germany are generally protected (section 12(2) of the Fourth Book of the Social Security Code (Sozialgesetzbuch IV)).[80] Although certain frictions exist in applying the 'old school' rules on homework to the new phenomenon of crowdwork,[81] Risak and Warter argue that there are many parallels between the original notion of homework and the new phenomenon of crowdsourcing/crowdwork.[82] Therefore, in their view, it should be possible to apply the rules governing homework, at least by way of analogy, to many crowdworkers.[83] To the extent that the legislation appears outdated, now is the time to adapt it to the new challenges.[84]

iii. Crowdworkers as (Solo) Self-employed

If crowdworkers cannot be considered employees or employee-like persons, under current German rules, they have to be classified as self-employed persons. In this case, crowdworkers have significantly less social protection. This lack of protection, in particular in terms of social security, could result in major problems for future generations. Thus, if the phenomenon of crowdwork cannot be tackled by qualifying these workers as employees or employee-like persons, the legislature

[77] For details, see Deinert (n 66) § 3 par 191ff.

[78] O Deinert, *Internationales Arbeitsrecht* (Tübingen, Mohr Siebeck, 2013) § 4 par 40 ff.; R Rebhahn, 'Arbeitnehmerähnliche Personen—Rechtsvergleich und Regelungsperspektive' (2009) *Recht der Arbeit* 236.

[79] Austria: Heimarbeitsgesetz; Italy: Law No 877/1973 on homework (lavoro a domicilio); France: Loi sur le travail à domicile. For further details, see Risak and Warter (n 53).

[80] H Volgelsang in G Schaub (ed), *Arbeitsrechts-Handbuch*, (16th edn Munich, Beck, 2015) § 163 par 61.

[81] Däubler and Klebe (n 50) 1036.

[82] Risak and Warter (n 50).

[83] ibid.

[84] Risak (n 56) 18.

should act and extend social security coverage to crowdworkers in general. In this regard, examples exist from other EU jurisdictions where social security coverage has already been extended to self-employed persons.[85]

Aside from the possibility to develop labour law or social security solutions, some basic protection is provided by consumer protection laws dealing with the general terms and conditions of the platform or crowdsourcer.[86] In Germany, these provisions are laid down in sections 305 to 310 of the Civil Code (Bürgerliches Gesetzbuch). As is widely apparent, the terms and conditions applied in the market are heavily one-sided in favour of the platform. Indeed, they are completely unfair. Therefore, in some cases, it seems to be correct to talk about digital sweatshops.[87] Consequently, consumer protection law could play an important role.[88] Däubler has examined in detail some of the most recent terms and conditions applied by these platforms. He concludes that many of them are contrary to German consumer protection law.[89] This means that special legal provisions can be invoked in challenging these wrongful terms and conditions.[90]

iv. The Cross-Border Dimension

The situation gets more complicated where the contractual relationships have a cross-border dimension, which is not uncommon since the competition takes place worldwide through the internet. For crowdworkers who deliver their work on German or European territory, the rules on conflicts of law laid down in the Rome I Regulation[91] might apply. This would mean, in the case of employees or employee-like persons,[92] a certain minimum protection under Article 8 of that Regulation.[93] However, this might result in disadvantages for crowdworkers from high-cost countries when compared to those in low-cost countries in other parts of the world.

This illustrates how important it is to have an internationally co-ordinated approach to the regulation of these new forms of labour.[94] At the ILO level, regulation already exists in the form of the Home Work Convention No 177, ratified, however, by only ten States. The definition of homework in Convention No 177 could also apply to crowdwork. Consequently, it would make sense to support the ratification process of this Convention, since it could serve as a basis for the

[85] Däubler and Klebe (n 50) 1041.

[86] Däubler and Klebe (n 50) 1037.

[87] In this vein: T Klebe, 'Workers of the crowd unite' *Die Tageszeitung* (Berlin, 29 July 2015) 12.

[88] Klebe and Neugebauer (n 64) 5ff.

[89] W Däubler, 'Crowdworker—Schutz auch außerhalb des Arbeitsrechts?' in C Benner (ed), *Crowdwork, zurück in die Zukunft* (Frankfurt, Bund Verlag, 2014) 248ff.

[90] Däubler and Klebe (n 53) 1037.

[91] Regulation (EC) No 593/2008 of the European Parliament and of the Council of 17 June 2008 on the law applicable to contractual obligations (Rome I) [2008] OJ L177/1.

[92] Heuschmid (n 66) § 139 para 16.

[93] For more detail, see Heuschmid (n 66) § 139 para 16.

[94] Risak and Warter (n 50).

regulation of crowdwork. A first step might be to obtain a clear commitment from the European Commission supporting the ratification process in the EU context. In parallel, the Commission should turn its hand to developing a regulatory framework in this context. This is likely to be more useful than simply proposing to recast existing directives without any added value.

C. Possible Approaches for Collective Actors

As has been outlined above, the regulation of crowdwork is quite a huge task, also requiring some collective action on the part of crowdworkers and trade unions involved. The first step could be to establish some self-help systems leading to greater transparency from the platforms as far as the interests of the workers are concerned. Practical examples already exist, eg, Turkopticon,[95] a site that allows workers to review crowdsourcers in the context of AMT, or the new platform provided by the IG Metall trade union: www.faircrowdwork.de.

Trade unions can also take action to organise crowdworkers. In Germany, section 12a of the Collective Agreements Act specifically permits collective agreements governing the working conditions of crowdworkers, provided that they are employee-like persons or employees. This is also the case in several other EU countries. Only recently, the ECJ clarified that competition law does not apply to collective agreements dealing with the working conditions of the (solo) self-employed who are in a similar situation to regular employees.[96] In common law countries too, collective bargaining for crowdworkers is possible even when they are self-employed.[97] This is in accordance with numerous opinions issued by ILO bodies, which presuppose that ILO Conventions No 87 and No 98 are also applicable to self-employed workers.

Another important means of dealing with crowdsourcing in Germany are the rights of works councils established in the Works Constitution Act. Important information and consultation rights set out in sections 80, 90, 92, 92a, 106 and 111 of the Works Constitution Act require the works council to be informed about planned changes in good time.[98] Moreover, section 95 of the Works Constitution Act provides for co-determination rights in dealing with the extent of outsourcing. In addition, the works council may seek to negotiate Besservereinbarungen to

[95] LC Irani and MS Silberman, 'Turkopticon' in C Benner (ed) (n 50).

[96] Case C-413/13 *FNV Kunsten Informatie en Media v Staat der Nederlanden* EU:C:2014:2411; J Heuschmid and D Hlava, 'Keine Anwendung des europäischen Kartellrechts auf TV, die Regelungen für Selbstständige enthalten' (2015) *Arbeit und Recht* 193.

[97] For examples from Australia and Canada, see S McCrystal, 'Designing Collective Bargaining Frameworks for Self-Employed Workers: Lessons from Australia and Canada' (2014) 30 *International Journal of Comparative Labour Law and Industrial Relations* 217.

[98] Klebe and Neugebauer (n 64) 6; T Klebe, 'Workers of the crowd unite?' in C Benner (ed) (n 50) 277.

improve on the statutory position, as has happened in the context of the regulation of temporary agency work.[99]

Another regulatory avenue could be the regulation of crowdwork via international framework agreements.[100] In this context, ILO Convention No 177 could play an important role.

V. Conclusion

Our focus in this chapter was the question of how collective actors have dealt with several forms of contingent work. In relation to temporary agency work, we illustrated that, especially in the metal working industry, the collective actors have been very successful in regulating the use of this form of work. The situation is much more difficult in relation to service contracting. Here, there is still a lot of work ahead for both the collective actors and for the legislature. Finally, we examined the upcoming challenges in the context of crowdwork. Here, developments are in their infancy. Nonetheless, there are several regulatory options for both the collective actors and for the legislature.

99 Klebe and Neugebauer (n 64) 7.

100 R Krause, 'International Framework Agreements as Instrument for the Legal Enforcement of Freedom of Association and Collective Bargaining? The German Case' (2012) 33 *Comparative Labor Law & Policy Journal* 749; R Zimmer, *Soziale Mindeststandards und ihre Durchsetzungsmechanismen: Sicherung internationaler Mindeststandards durch Verhaltenskodizes?* (Baden-Baden, Nomos, 2008).

12

Does Age Matter? Sweden, Younger and Older Workers and the Intergenerational Dimension of Contingent Work

MIA RÖNNMAR*

I. Introduction

Younger and older workers face different challenges in today's labour market, and an ageing population, economic crisis, austerity and youth unemployment increase the risk of intergenerational conflict.

This chapter aims at a discussion and analysis of contingent work from the perspective of younger and older workers and intergenerational solidarity or conflict. Swedish law, including its interplay with EU law, serves as the main national example, but reference is also made to general European developments. The focus is age discrimination law and the scope provided for age-related and intergenerational regulation and measures; fixed-term work and temporary agency work; employment protection; and intergenerational bargaining. The legal analysis covers statutory, collective bargaining and case law developments, and is set against the backdrop of a discussion of the labour market situation faced by both younger and older workers.[1]

* Professor of Private Law and Dean at the Faculty of Law at Lund University, mia.ronnmar@jur.lu.se. Member of the Norma Research Programme, www.jur.lu.se/norma.

[1] This chapter draws upon earlier research in the fields of age discrimination law and intergenerational collective bargaining, see especially M Rönnmar, 'Age Discrimination and Labour Law: A Comparative Analysis' in A Numhauser-Henning and M Rönnmar (eds), *Age Discrimination and Labour Law. Comparative and Conceptual Perspectives in the EU and Beyond* (Alphen aan den Rijn, Kluwer Law International, 2015), B ter Haar and M Rönnmar, 'Intergenerational Bargaining, EU Age Discrimination Law and EU Policies—an Integrated Analysis. Report for the project iNGenBar', 2014, and M Rönnmar, 'Intergenerational Bargaining in Sweden. Report for the project iNGenBar', 2014 (the two reports are available at intergenerationalbargaining.eu, and the research project was co-ordinated by AIAS at Amsterdam University and funded by the European Commission).

The flexibilisation of work is often discussed in terms of labour market segmentation, externalisation and the legal tension between permanent employment—which is associated with employment protection—and precarious, atypical and flexible employment. Atkinson's early model of the flexible firm is frequently referred to in this regard. The flexible firm is made up of three different labour force segments: the core group of workers with firm-specific skills, typically offered high-quality working conditions and employment protection; the peripheral group of workers with a looser connection to the firm, often employed on fixed-term or part-time employment contracts; and the external group of workers, workers who are utilised, but not employed by the firm, such as temporary agency workers or self-employed persons.[2] In a similar way, core work can be contrasted with contingent work.[3]

According to the model of the flexible firm, the employer typically makes use of different flexibility strategies with regard to these labour force segments. Numerical flexibility relates to both the form and duration of the employment contract and to working-time arrangements, and primarily serves the purpose of achieving greater flexibility in the number of workers employed. In focus, for example, are fixed-term, part-time and temporary agency work and employment protection. Functional flexibility is a matter of adaptability and versatility within permanent employment relationships, and it primarily affects the core group of workers. The aim of functional flexibility is to vary the content of work in relation to the changing demands of production.[4] This chapter focuses mainly on contingent work and numerical flexibility and, throughout, the chapter the notions of contingent and flexible work will be used basically interchangeably, and in contrast to core work.

The EU law flexicurity discourse is not seldom criticised; it is inspired by national developments in Denmark and the Netherlands and by Wilthagen's flexicurity research, which develops the model of the flexible firm into a flexibility-security nexus.[5] The EU law flexicurity discourse encompasses the Part-Time

[2] See J Atkinson, 'Manpower Strategies for Flexible Organisations', (1984) 28 *Personnel Management*.

[3] Contingent work is originally an American notion (linked to the employment-at-willdoctrine and a general lack of employment protection) referring to work without an implicit or explicit contract for ongoing employment (according to the U.S. Bureau of Statistics) and to diverse forms of non-standard work, see KVW Stone, 'Appendix. The Decline in the Standard Employment Contract: A Review of the Evidence', in KVW Stone and H Arthurs (eds), *Rethinking Workplace Regulation. Beyond the Standard Contract of Employment* (Russell Sage Foundation, 2013) 367 ff. See also the chapter by Lo Faro in this volume for a theoretical and conceptual discussion of the notion of contingent work, and similarities with and differences from flexible work.

[4] For an analysis of Swedish, UK and German law from the perspective of functional flexibility, see further M Rönnmar, 'The Managerial Prerogative and the Employee's Obligation to Work: Comparative Perspectives on Functional Flexibility', (2006) 35(1) *Industrial Law Journal* 56–74.

[5] See T Wilthagen, 'The Flexibility-Security Nexus: New approaches to regulating employment and labour markets',Flexicurity research paper FXP 2003-2, OSA/Institute for Labour Studies (Tilburg, Tilburg University, 2002).

Work, Fixed-Term Work and Temporary Agency Work Directives.[6] Furthermore, in 2007, following a report by the European Expert Group on Flexicurity (led by Wilthagen), the Council adopted Common Principles of Flexicurity, which have been integrated into the European Employment Strategy and the Europe 2020 Strategy.[7] The aim of flexicurity is to reduce labour market segmentation, but also to increase economic growth and Europe's competitiveness in a global perspective. Flexicurity is an integrated strategy to enhance, at the same time, both flexibility and security in the labour market, and contains these components: flexible and reliable contractual arrangements; comprehensive life-long learning; effective active labour market policies; and modern social security systems. Flexible and reliable contractual arrangements—clearly linked to labour law regulation and contingent work—aim at reduced labour market segmentation and equal treatment of permanent employees and flexible workers. Such equal treatment can be achieved through principles of non-discrimination and equal treatment proper, and reforms to the regulation of employment protection and fixed-term work.

The concepts of younger and older workers must be defined in a contextual way. EU statistics often cover the age groups of 15–24 and 55–64. National and EU legislation, policy initiatives and collective bargaining measures may have a broader or more limited scope. In age discrimination law, the concept of age is central, and in EU non-discrimination law, age refers to all chronological ages. In this chapter, intergenerational bargaining refers to the integration of policies and strategies for younger and older workers through collective bargaining and social dialogue.[8]

Swedish industrial relations are characterised by self-regulation, co-operation between the social partners, and autonomous collective bargaining. Wages and terms and conditions of employment are generally set by collective bargaining, but labour law legislation is also frequent. Most labour law legislation is so-called semi-compelling, and allows for collectively bargained deviations, both to the advantage and detriment of employees.

The outline of the chapter is as follows. Part II provides a discussion of the labour market situation of younger and older workers. Part III presents an analysis of labour law regulation linked to contingent work, younger and older workers,

[6] Council Directive 97/81/EC of 15 December 1997 concerning the Framework Agreement on part-time work concluded by UNICE, CEEP and ETUC; Council Directive 99/70/EC of 28 June 1999 concerning the Framework Agreement on fixed-term work concluded by the ETUC, UNICE and CEEP; and, Directive 2008/104/EC of the European Parliament and of the Council of 19 November 2008 on temporary agency work.

[7] See European Expert Group on Flexicurity, T Wilthagen (rapporteur), 'Flexicurity Pathways. Turning hurdles into stepping stones' (Brussels, 2007); European Commission, Communication from the Commission to the European Parliament, the Council, the European Economic and Social Committee and the Committee of the Regions. 'Towards Common Principles of Flexicurity: More and better jobs through flexibility and security', COM(2007) 359 final; and, European Commission, Communication from the Commission, 'Europe 2020. A strategy for smart, sustainable and inclusive growth', COM(2010) 2020 and COM(2010) 682 final.

[8] See further the iNGenBar research project (intergenerationalbargaining.eu) and M Rönnmar, 'Intergenerational Bargaining in Sweden. Report for the project iNGenBar', 2014.

and intergenerational solidarity or conflict. Part IV discusses intergenerational bargaining, and Part V provides concluding remarks.

II. Contingent Work, Younger and Older Workers and the Labour Market

Many of the trends influencing demographical development and the labour market situation of younger and older workers are global, and equally relevant for Sweden and other EU Member States and developed countries. Such trends refer, for example, to an average reduction of the time spent on market work across the life-course due to earlier exit from the labour force, increased life expectancy and an increase in leisure time and time spent on education. More young persons are in higher education, periods of education are prolonged and the entry into the labour market is delayed. Despite this, younger workers' lack of necessary education is also a problem.[9]

In many countries, in and beyond the EU, the global financial crisis has led to increased youth unemployment rates, and younger workers are overrepresented when it comes to flexible and precarious employment, such as fixed-term work and part-time work. Across all 28 EU Member States (EU28), the average youth unemployment rate (15–24) in 2013 was about 23 per cent, twice as high as the overall unemployment rate. The situation is particularly difficult in some countries, such as Portugal, Italy, Spain and Greece, where in 2013 the youth unemployment rates were 38, 40, 56 and 59 per cent, respectively. The economic crisis has increased the 'North-South gap' in Europe and has given rise to social unrest and increased intergenerational conflict. The vulnerability, social exclusion and labour market disengagement of young people is also analysed in terms of NEET rates—the share of young people aged 15–24 years who are not in employment, education or training. In the EU28, the NEET rate in 2013 was 13 per cent.[10]

An ageing population is a shared concern for the EU Member States. Life expectancy will increase, as will the dependency ratio. The EU Active Ageing Policy aims to promote a healthy and active ageing population, increase the labour market participation of older workers (55+) and prolong working life.[11] However,

[9] See D Anxo, 'Entry and Exit Patterns from the Labour Force: A European and Life-Course Perspective' in A Numhauser-Henning and M Rönnmar (eds), *Age Discrimination and Labour Law. Comparative and Conceptual Perspectives in the EU and Beyond* (Alphen aan den Rijn, Kluwer Law International, 2015) 1748.

[10] The NEET rate is receiving increased attention in public debate due to the difficulties of measuring youth unemployment.

[11] See Decision No 940/211/EU of the European Parliament and of the Council of 14 September 2011 on the European Year for Active Ageing and Solidarity between Generations (2012) (OJ [2011] L246/5).

there are differences among the EU Member States when it comes to the labour market situation of older workers. Nevertheless, since the mid-1990s, there has been a trend towards increasing employment rates among older workers as well as increasing retirement ages.[12]

The Swedish labour market is characterised by high employment rates and high employment continuity over the life course.[13] The employment rate in Sweden in 2013 for the age group 20–64 reached 79.8 percent. In 2013, the employment rate of older workers in the age group 55–64 was 73.6 percent.[14] About 15 to 17 per cent of all employees in Sweden have a fixed-term employment contract, and this figure has been relatively stable for several years. The corresponding rate for younger workers in the age group 20–24 is 50 per cent and for older workers in the age group 65–74 it is also 50 per cent.[15] Temporary agency workers account for about 1.5 per cent of all employees in Sweden.

The average unemployment rate in Sweden in 2014 was about 7 per cent. The youth unemployment rate (15–24 years) in Sweden in recent years has been about 24 per cent. However, this way of measuring youth unemployment is debated in Sweden (for example, some question the way in which it includes students.[16] In Sweden, the NEET rate is about 8 per cent.

The overall trade union organisation rate in 2012 was about 70 per cent and the employers' organisation rate was about 90 per cent. The collective bargaining coverage is about 90 per cent. Among younger workers, however, the trade union organisation rate is lower. In 2012, the trade union organisation rate in the age group 16–24 was 36 per cent, and in the age group 25–29 it was 57 per cent.[17]

Sweden has a strong tradition of active labour market policies for all workers, including younger and older workers. A number of labour market initiatives are specifically designed to combat youth unemployment and increase labour market inclusion of younger workers, and reforms have also been made to systems of education, social security and taxes.[18]

[12] See D Anxo, 'Entry and Exit Patterns from the Labour Force' (n 9).

[13] D Anxo, 'Towards an Active and Integrated Life Course Policy: the Swedish Experience' in D Anxo, G Bosch and J Rubery (eds), *The Welfare State and Life Transitions: a European Perspective* (Cheltenham, 2010) 113.

[14] See Eurostat, Labour Force Survey. Cf also P Záková, 'Sun spots on the Swedish labour market?', *EC Fin Country Focus*, May 2013.

[15] Among younger workers in the age group 15–19, 80% had a fixed-term employment in 2013. See J JulénVotinius, 'Age Discrimination and Labour Law in Sweden', in A Numhauser-Henning and M Rönnmar (eds), *Age Discrimination and Labour Law. Comparative and Conceptual Perspectives in the EU and Beyond* (Alphen aan den Rijn, Kluwer Law International, 2015). The part-time employment rate in Sweden in recent years has been about 24 to 25%.

[16] See, eg, E Oscarsson, *Ungdomsarbetslöshet—Mått, orsaker och politik* (Stockholm, SACO, 2013).

[17] See National Mediation Office, *Avtalsrörelsen och lönebildningen 2013. Medlingsinstitutets årsrapport* (Stockholm, National Mediation Office, 2014) 31 ff.

[18] See, eg, Regeringskansliet, *Insatser på arbetsmarknaden för unga* (Stockholm), *Sweden's national reform programme 2014*; Europe 2020—the EU's strategy for smart, sustainable and inclusive growth; and, J JulénVotinius, 'Age Discrimination and Labour Law in Sweden' (n 15).

Interviews with leading representatives of Swedish social partners about the labour market situation of younger and older workers within the research project iNGenBar highlighted important problems and issues (Part IV).[19] As regards younger workers, basically all interviewees pointed to the problematic situation of high youth unemployment, and younger workers' difficulties in entering the labour market and establishing themselves there more firmly. Many were concerned about young persons who lack necessary, relevant education. Several trade unions pointed to the lower trade unionisation rate among younger workers as an important problem that they were trying to address. As regards older workers, many interviewees pointed to the need for active ageing and to prolong working life. However, the situation differs between different sectors and between blue-collar and white-collar employees. In some sectors, such as the industry sector and the municipal and regional sector, it is difficult—especially for blue-collar employees—to continue working until 'normal' retirement age. This is related to heavy, strenuous and stressful work tasks and increased demands for productivity. As a result, employees retire early (often with low pensions), reduce their working time, or go on sick leave. At the same time, several interviewees also emphasised that older workers are more attractive to the labour market today than before. A common key theme in the interviews was the central role played by competence, qualifications and education, and the urgent need to secure future competence provision.

III. Contingent Work, Younger and Older Workers and Labour Law

A. Age Discrimination

The Employment Equality Directive 2000/78/EC introduced the ban on age discrimination in secondary EU law.[20] The Directive bans discrimination on the grounds of religion or belief, disability, age or sexual orientation, as regards employment and occupation. The Employment Equality Directive encompasses

[19] For more information on the research project iNGenBar, the interviews and methodology, see M Rönnmar, *Intergenerational Bargaining in Sweden. Report for the project iNGenBar*, 2014.

[20] In addition, Article 21 of the EU Charter of Fundamental Rights contains an open list of discrimination grounds and states that '[a]ny discrimination based on any ground such as sex, race, colour, ethnic or social origin, genetic features, language, religion or belief, political or any other opinion, membership of a national minority, property, birth, disability, age or sexual orientation shall be prohibited'. The Court of Justice of the European Union (CJEU) has also held that EU law encompasses a general principle of non-discrimination on grounds of age, see Case C-144/04 *Werner Mangold v Rudiger Helm* [2005] ECR I-09981 and Case C-555/07 *SedaKücükdeveci v SwedexGmBH& Co* [2010] ECR I-00365. Furthermore, solidarity between generations is one of the main aims of the EU (Art 3(3) TEU).

prohibitions on direct and indirect discrimination, harassment, and instruction to discriminate, as well as provisions on positive action and active measures, and a rule on a reversed burden of proof. The protection against age discrimination covers all chronological ages and, thus, both younger and older workers are protected. According to the preamble to the Employment Equality Directive, the prohibition of age discrimination is an essential part of meeting the aims set out in the European Employment Strategy and the Employment Guidelines and for encouraging diversity in the workforce. The prohibition of old-age discrimination helps to reduce ageism, and is also an important aspect of the EU Active Ageing Policy.

EU age discrimination law is characterised by the tension between a human rights rationale and market rationale. Likewise, the tension between an individual-rights approach and a collective-interest approach—the so-called 'double-bind'—influences the development of age discrimination law and the case law of the Court of Justice of the European Union (CJEU) in this field.[21] Age has traditionally been given a key role in labour market organisation and labour law, and has, thus, served as a legitimate social and economic stratifier. In general, age discrimination can be justified to a larger extent than discrimination on other grounds.[22] This difference has been discussed in terms of age being a less 'suspect' or 'forbidden' ground.[23]

According to Article 6(1) of the Employment Equality Directive, differences of treatment on grounds of age do not constitute discrimination if they are objectively and reasonably justified by a legitimate aim, including legitimate employment policy, labour market, and vocational training objectives, and if the means of achieving that aim are appropriate and necessary. The Member States and the social partners enjoy a broad margin of appreciation when it comes to justifying differential treatment on grounds of age. Since the adoption of the Employment Equality Directive, some thirty cases related to age discrimination have been decided by the CJEU. A large part of the cases has dealt with compulsory retirement and premature retirement. The absolute majority of cases have dealt with old-age discrimination, and only a few cases with young-age discrimination.

The CJEU applies different standards of justification. The most lenient standard is applied as regards more general systems of compulsory retirement, while a stricter standard is applied when it comes to compulsory retirement for specific

[21] See S Fredman and S Spencer (eds), *Age as an Equality Issue* (Oxford, Hart Publishing, 2003) and F Hendrickx, 'Age and European Employment Discrimination Law' in F Hendrickx (ed), *Active Ageing and Labour Law. Contributions in Honour of Professor Roger Blanpain* (Cambridge, Intersentia Publishing Ltd, 2012).

[22] With the exception of part-time and fixed-term work, see the non-discrimination principle in the Part-Time Directive 1997/81/EC and Fixed-Term Work Directive 1999/70/EC.

[23] See, for example, the chapters by C O'Cinneide and D Schiek in A Numhauser-Henning and M Rönnmar (eds), *Age Discrimination and Labour Law. Comparative and Conceptual Perspectives in the EU and Beyond* (Alphen aan den Rijn, Kluwer Law International, 2015).

professional groups or premature retirement.[24] Likewise, a stricter standard seems to be applied in cases related to collective dismissals and the age discrimination of younger workers.[25] When it comes to compulsory retirement, the CJEU has found the differences of treatment on grounds of age to be objectively and reasonably justified by the legitimate aims, such as intergenerational fairness in terms of access to employment, prevention of humiliating forms of employment termination, and a reasonable balance between labour market and budgetary concerns.[26]

The Swedish Non-Discrimination Act (2008:567), a so-called single non-discrimination Act, implements the Employment Equality Directive and other EU equality directives. The Act not only gathers different discrimination grounds but is also applicable in part outside the realm of working life; for example, it is applied for goods and services, and in public employment services, education, health care, social services, and social security.[27] The Non-Discrimination Act covers protection against discrimination on grounds of sex, ethnicity, religion and other belief, sexual orientation, disability, age and transsexual identity/expression, and contains prohibitions on direct and indirect discrimination, harassment, and instruction to discriminate, as well as provisions on a reversed burden of proof, positive action and active measures. Chapter 2 Section 2 p. 4 of the Act contains the provision for justification of age-related differences.[28],[29]

EU and Swedish age discrimination law—through a large scope for justification of age-related differential treatment, specific exemptions and a broad margin of appreciation for Member States and social partners—in principle enables directly and indirectly age-related regulation as well as intergenerational bargaining and collective bargaining on age-related measures for younger and older workers.[30]

[24] See Case C-411/05 *Palacios de la Villa v CortefielServicios SA* [2007] ECR I-8531; Case C-45/09 *Rosenbladt v OellerkingGebaudereinigungsgesmbH* [2010] ECR I-09391; and, Case C-341/08 the *European Commission v Hungary*, EU:C:2012:687.

[25] See Case C-152/11 *Johann Odar v Baxter Deutschland GmbH*, EU:C:2012:772 and Case C-555/07 *SedaKücükdeveci v SwedexGmBH& Co* [2010] ECR I-00365. See also, eg, D Schiek, 'Age Discrimination Before the ECJ—Conceptual and Theoretical Issues' (2011) 48 *Common Market Law Review*, 777–99; M Schlachter, 'Mandatory Retirement and Age Discrimination under EU Law' (2011) 27 *International Journal of Comparative Labour Law and Industrial Relations*; C Kilpatrick, 'The Court of Justice and Labour Law in 2010: A New EU Discrimination Law Architecture' (2011) 40(3) *Industrial Law Journal*; and, E Dewhurst, 'Intergenerational balance, mandatory retirement and age discrimination in Europe: How can the ECJ better support national courts in finding a balance between the generations' (2013) 50 *Common Market Law Review* 1333.

[26] See, eg, Case C-45/09 *Rosenbladt v Oellerking GebaudereinigungsgesmbH* [2010] ECR I-09391 and Case C-141/11 *Hörnfeldt v PostenMeddelande AB* EU:C:2012:421.

[27] See Governmental Bill Prop 2007/08:95 and Governmental Inquiry Report SOU 2006:22.

[28] Up to this point, case law from the Swedish Labour Court has been limited regarding age discrimination; see, eg, Labour Court judgments AD 2013:64 and AD 2014:28.

[29] When it comes to age discrimination, Swedish law goes further than EU law, and extends the ban on age discrimination beyond working life, for example for goods, services, social security and health care; see Government Bill Prop. 2011/12:159.

[30] See B ter Haar and M Rönnmar, *Intergenerational Bargaining, EU Age Discrimination Law and EU Policies—an Integrated Analysis* (Amsterdam, AIAS—iNGenBar, 2014).

B. Fixed-term Work And Temporary Agency Work

Fixed-term work and temporary agency work are contingent forms of work, which have increased in Sweden as in other EU Member States. There is a particularly close relationship between fixed-term work and employment protection. Regulation of fixed-term employment contracts serves to prevent circumvention of the employment protection linked to permanent employment contracts.[31]

The Fixed-Term Work Directive was adopted in 1999 and its purpose is to improve the quality of fixed-term work by ensuring the application of the principle of non-discrimination, and to establish a framework to prevent abuse arising from the use of successive fixed-term employment contracts or relationships.[32] When it comes to the measures to prevent abuse stemming from the use of successive fixed-term employment contracts or relationships, the Member States shall introduce one or more of the following measures, in a manner which takes into account the needs of specific sectors and/or categories of workers: objective reasons justifying the renewal of such contracts or relationships; the maximum total duration of successive fixed-term employment contracts or relationships; or the number of renewals of such contracts or relationships. However, the Directive does not introduce any requirement for objective reasons for the parties' first entry into a fixed-term employment contract.[33]

Fixed-term work is regulated in the Employment Protection Act (LAS) (1982:80). In Sweden, permanent employment is the main rule and fixed-term employment contracts are permitted only when agreed upon, and when specifically provided for by law or collective agreements. In order for a fixed-term employment contract to be legal, the detailed rules in Sections 4, 5 and 6 of LAS must be adhered to. These provisions are semi-compelling, and collective agreements regulating fixed-term contracts in specific, narrower or broader ways are frequent.[34] The regulation of fixed-term work was amended in 2007, and this reform partly represents a new standpoint on fixed-term employment contracts. A long list of fixed-term employment contracts has been replaced by a new form of fixed-term employment contract—the general fixed-term employment, Section 5 of LAS—supplemented only by temporary substitute employment, seasonal employment,

[31] In Sweden, for example, the regulation of fixed-term employment contracts first became an important issue in the beginning of the 1970s. Statutory employment protection, first established through the Employment Protection Act (1974:12), required regulation of fixed-term employment contracts to prevent circumvention of the employment protection linked to permanent open-ended employment contracts.

[32] Clause 1.

[33] The CJEU has developed substantial case law in relation to Clause 5 of the Directive; see, for example, Case C-212/04 *Adeneler and Others* [2006] ECR I-6057; Joined Cases C-378/07 to C-380/07 *Angelidaki and Others* [2009] ECR I-3071; and, Case C-596/10 *Kücük*.

[34] In addition, provisions on fixed-term employment contracts in specific statutes or regulations, for example for universities and higher education, have priority before the provisions in the Employment Protection Act (1982:80).

fixed-term contracts for employees above the age of 67 years, and probationary employment.[35] Thus, the scope for fixed-term employment contracts has broadened. The employer is free to conclude general fixed-term employment contracts, and there is no requirement for objective reasons. However, when an employee has been employed under a general fixed-term employment contract or as a temporary substitute by one employer for a total of two years during the last five years, the contract is automatically converted into an indefinite permanent employment contract, Section 5(2) of LAS.[36]

As early as 2007, the Swedish Trade Union TCO (The Swedish Confederation for Professional Employees) made a complaint to the European Commission as regards the failure in Sweden to correctly implement the Fixed-Term Work Directive. TCO criticised the content of the 2007 reform of the regulation on fixed-term employment contracts, inter alia the vast scope for general fixed-term employment without any need for objective reasons and the effects of the non-cumulative calculation in the periods of employment spent in general fixed-term employment and temporary substitute employment. The European Commission has issued two reasoned opinions (in 2013 and 2014), where the Commission claims that Sweden has failed to correctly implement Clause 5.1 on measures to prevent abuse arising from the use of successive fixed-term employment contracts or relationships. In the course of the process, the Swedish Government (first the centre-right, and then the social-democratic-green Government) has put forward three different legislative proposals to address the situation. The most recent proposal (which has been sent out for remit) includes a new provision by which general fixed-term employments will be converted into indefinite employments in more cases than at present.[37]

On-call or on-demand work—sometimes also referred to as zero-hours contracts—does not constitute a separate form of employment in Sweden. An on-call worker is employed either on a permanent contract for an indefinite period or on a fixed-term employment contract (and then often on a separate fixed-term employment contract for each working day/working period, often a general fixed-term employment contract). The specific arrangements as regards the employee's working time, workload and obligation to be 'on call' are explicitly or implicitly agreed between the parties to the employment contract. Problems related to zero-hours contracts and the vulnerability of on-call workers are increasingly the subject of critical debate in Sweden, as in other European countries such as the UK.[38]

Younger workers are over-represented when it comes to fixed-term work in Sweden. During interviews in the research project iNGenBar, the trade unions

[35] See Government Bill Prop. 2006/07:111.

[36] The non-discrimination principle in the Fixed-Term Work Directive 1999/70/EC was implemented through the creation of a new Act, the Prohibition of Discrimination of Employees Working Part-Time and Employees with Fixed-Term Employment Act (2002:293).

[37] See Government Inquiry Reports Ds 2011:22, Ds 2012:25 and Ds 2015:29.

[38] See further Ch 10 by J Kenner in this volume. See also, eg, A Adams, M Freedland and J Prassl, *The 'Zero-Hours Contract': Regulating casual work, or legitimating precarity?*, ELLN Working Paper 5/2015.

emphasised that this is a big problem and that younger workers are 'caught' in flexible forms of work, such as fixed-term work and temporary agency work. This creates insecurity, results in low income and makes it difficult for younger workers to establish themselves in the labour market, start families, acquire appropriate housing etc. The employers' organisation in the municipal and regional sector, SKL, declared that they did not entirely share the trade union's view of the situation of fixed-term employment in their sector, and emphasised that it is important to take the age structure into account when evaluating the situation and the statistics. In the age group 16–24, many are fixed-term employees and students at the same time. In the age group 63+ many have retired, and the fixed-term employment with wages per hour is not the main source of income. The parties in this sector have handled the problem of successive fixed-term employment contracts by concluding a collective agreement with a solution that is more favourable for employees, and especially for younger workers who are in the beginning of their careers, than the solution contained in LAS. The provision provides for a quicker conversion of the fixed-term employment contract into a permanent employment contract (after more than three years in temporary substitute employment or general fixed-term employment within a five-year period).

In many of the EU Member States and in countries beyond the EU, specific fixed-term employment contracts for younger and older workers are used as a means to promote the entry into the labour market for younger workers and the prolonging of working life for older workers. The seminal *Mangold* case concerned the German regulation providing a broader scope for successive fixed-term employment contracts for older workers and its relation to the Fixed-Term Work Directive and the Employment Equality Directive and the ban on age discrimination.[39] Swedish law provides for an unlimited access to fixed-term employment for employees above the age of 67 years (the compulsory retirement age), as a way of promoting work after compulsory retirement and a prolonged working life.

Fixed-term employment contracts for younger workers sometimes have an emphasis on training, in line with an apprenticeship tradition (which is strong in countries such as Germany). In Sweden, for example, recent collective agreements—so-called introduction agreements (discussed further in Part IV on intergenerational bargaining)—provide introduction employment contracts for younger workers combining work with education, training and supervision. In the wake of the economic crisis, some countries—like Greece, Italy, Portugal and Spain—have also seen the emergence of fixed-term employment contracts specifically aimed at younger workers, less focused on training and skills development and more directed at de-regulation, cost-cutting and a 'levelling-down' of employment rights, in order to promote younger workers' entry into the labour market (sometimes in combination with a more general deregulation of employment protection and industrial relations, as in the case of Greece). Similar fixed-term

[39] See Case C-144/04 *Mangold v Helm* [2005] ECR I-09981.

employment contracts have been introduced in Latin America, and are also supported by the International Labour Organisation (ILO) in their efforts to promote the Decent Work Agenda. The critique and debate in Latin America is similar to the one in Europe, and fears of deregulation, flexibilisation and precariousness are expressed; and efforts to develop good job opportunities and skills, training and education have been called for.[40]

In Sweden, in 2012, a Government Inquiry Report on a new form of statutory fixed-term employment contract, the education employment contract was presented.[41] The education employment contract was aimed at making labour market establishment easier for younger persons and to provide an incentive for smaller companies to employ. This new fixed-term employment contract was meant to complement existing measures and employment contracts for workplace-based education and training and labour market policies for younger persons. Many collective agreements already contain provisions on employment contracts linked to introduction, education and apprenticeship—such as the introduction agreements (Part IV). An education employment contract would be available to persons under the age of 23, for a maximum of 18 months, and presuppose an agreement concluded between the employer and the employee regarding a training element. An education employment contract would (as probationary employment) automatically be converted into a permanent employment contract after 18 months. Up until that point, however, the employer would be free to terminate the contract, without showing just cause or objective reasons. This proposal was criticised, for example by the trade unions, for intervening in existing collective agreements and social partner autonomy, and for expanding the scope for fixed-term employment, and has not resulted in any legislative changes. Thus, Sweden has not introduced specific labour law reforms aimed at combating youth unemployment through the 'levelling-down' of employment rights for younger workers.

The Temporary Agency Work Directive 2008/104/EC was adopted in 2008 and its purpose is to ensure the protection of temporary agency workers and to improve the quality of temporary agency work while taking into account the need to establish a suitable framework for the use of temporary agency work with a view to contributing effectively to the creation of jobs and to the development of flexible forms for working.[42]

Temporary work agencies (and private employment agencies) were prohibited in Sweden between 1935 and 1991. This prohibition was not fully implemented in practice, though. Temporary agency work was legalised in 1991, and more effectively

[40] See for a critical analysis, see J Julén Votinius, 'Young Employees—Securities, Risk Distribution and Fundamental Social Rights' (2014) 5(3–4) *European Labour Law Journal* 387–410. See also SCF Gamonal and Rosado Marzán, 'Age Discrimination and Labour Law in Latin America: The Challenges of Equality Law in Light of Underdevelopment', in A Numhauser-Henning and M Rönnmar (eds), *Age Discrimination and Labour Law. Comparative and Conceptual Perspectives in the EU and Beyond* (Alphen aan den Rijn, Kluwer Law International, 2015) 357–78.

[41] See Government Inquiry Report SOU 2012:80.

[42] Article 2.

liberalised in 1993. Today, temporary agency work is regulated in the Agency Work Act (2012:854), which also transposes the Temporary Agency Work Directive.[43]

The temporary agency work sector is principally covered by collective bargaining, and all collective agreements ensure a guaranteed wage, between assignments, of about 80 to 85 per cent of normal wages. The principle of equal treatment is regulated in Section 6 of the Act, which states that:

> '[a] temporary-work agency shall, for the duration of the worker's assignment at a user undertaking guarantee the worker at least the same basic working and employment conditions as would apply if they had been recruited directly by that undertaking to carry out the same job.'

Exceptions to the principle of equal treatment are permissible with regard to pay in accordance with Article 5(2) of the Directive, and Section 8 of the Act provides that the equal treatment principle does not apply to temporary agency workers who have a permanent contract and receive pay between temporary assignments. In addition, the Act states in Section 3 that deviations from the principle of equal treatment may be made through a collective agreement concluded or approved by a central trade union, on the condition that the agreement respects the overall protection of workers within the meaning of the Directive.[44]

According to Swedish law, a temporary agency worker is an employee of the temporary work agency, who within the framework of his/her employment relationship performs work for a third party (the user undertaking). Labour law provisions, eg on employment protection, working time, annual leave, and information and consultation generally apply to all employees, including temporary agency workers. Permanent employment and open-ended contracts are the main form of contract for temporary agency workers as well (Sections 4–6 of LAS). Fixed-term work is somewhat more common for temporary agency workers.[45]

A controversial issue in the Swedish context has been the use of temporary agency work as a circumvention of employment protection regulation, especially the priority right to re-employment, based on seniority, following dismissal for reasons of redundancy (Section 3.3). This amounts to a practice that aims at increasing the use of contingent work in the company, and undermining the rights and protection of dismissed core workers. It follows from the case law of the Swedish Labour Court that an employer may dismiss employees for reasons of redundancy, and thereafter, even during the time period when former employees have a priority right to re-employment, make use of temporary agency work.[46]

[43] See Government Inquiry Report SOU 2011:5 and Government Bill Prop. 2011/12:178.

[44] However, also the implementation of the Temporary Agency Work Directive is disputed. The employers' organisation, Bemanningsföretagen, has made a complaint to the European Commission, claiming that Article 4 regarding the review of restrictions or prohibitions has not been implemented correctly.

[45] About 80% of temporary agency workers are permanently employed, see Government Inquiry Report SOU 2011:5.

[46] See Labour Court judgments AD 2003:4 and AD 2007:72.

The priority right of re-employment is relevant only when the employer hires employees—not when the employer engages temporary agency workers. In the 2010 collective bargaining round and onwards, to address this issue, provisions on a re-enforced priority right to re-employment and restrictions on the employer's possibilities to use temporary agency work following dismissals for reasons of redundancy have been introduced in some collective agreements.

C. Employment Protection

The content and strength of employment protection influences the scope for contingent work. Weak or deregulated employment protection provides a larger scope for contingent work and numerical flexibility. At EU level, employment protection is only partly regulated, for example by Article 30 of the EU Charter of Fundamental Rights, the Fixed-Term Work Directive, the Transfers of Undertakings Directive 2001/23/EC[47] and the Collective Redundancies Directive 98/59/EC,[48] as well as by the different non-discrimination directives.[49]

Swedish employment protection is traditionally viewed as relatively strong.[50] The statutory employment protection and LAS apply to all employees, whether in private or public employment, from the first day of employment.[51] Small companies are not exempted. The employer may dismiss a permanent employee for personal reasons or for reasons of redundancy. The employer must have just cause or objective grounds) for dismissal (Section 7 of LAS). Coupled with this basic just-cause requirement are different rules obliging the employer (depending on whether the dismissal relates to personal reasons or reasons of redundancy) inter alia to negotiate with trade unions, give notice, provide the employee with alternative work, warn the employee, retrain the employee, apply seniority rules, and if necessary conditions are met, re-employ dismissed employees. Thus, in line with an ultima ratio principle, the employer must make an effort to avoid dismissing employees by first taking less radical measures.

The vulnerability of older workers has influenced the content of employment protection in many EU Member States and special protection for older workers has been afforded.[52] In some EU Member States, such as Sweden, there is a general and

[47] Council Directive (EC) 2001/23 of 12 March 2001 on the approximation of the laws of the Member States relating to the safeguarding of employees' rights in the event of transfers of undertakings, businesses or parts of undertakings or businesses.

[48] Council Directive (EC) 98/59 of 20 July 1998 on the approximation of the laws of the Member States relating to collective redundancies.

[49] See J Kenner, 'Article 30' in S Peers et al (eds), *The EU Charter of Fundamental Rights: A Commentary* (Oxford, Hart, 2014) 805–832.

[50] Sweden has ratified ILO Convention No 158 Termination on Employment Convention 1982.

[51] Some minor groups of employees, however, such as employees in upper management and the employer's family members, are excluded.

[52] In Sweden, for example, an important background to the first Employment Protection Act from 1974 was the need for social protection of especially vulnerable workers due to old age or sickness; see Governmental Bill Prop. 1973:129, 126.

important rule that sickness or old age does not constitute just cause for dismissal. In Sweden, the employer has extensive obligations to rehabilitate the employee and to adjust the working environment and the job duties or tasks. An employee can be dismissed only after such measures have been taken, and the employee can no longer perform work of any importance for the employer. However, the extent to which sickness or reduced working capacity constitutes just cause for dismissal differs in the Member States.

According to Swedish law, redundancy is a broad concept, encompassing different reasons of an economic, organisational or other business-related character. The legislator and the courts give the employer a unilateral right to decide when and if a redundancy situation exists. Redundancy per se amounts to just cause.[53]

Seniority rules (such as the last-in-first-out principle, LIFO) and different forms of directly or indirectly age-related differential treatment still influence redundancy regulation in many countries in the EU. In Sweden, the statutory seniority rules imply that the priority and selection of employees is to be made according to the last-in-first-out principle, ie according to each employee's total period of employment with the employer (and in the event of equal periods of employment, giving priority to senior age, Section 22 of LAS). The employee has to have sufficient qualifications for the tasks, which remain after the redundancy. In principle, the order of dismissals encompasses all employees in the same production unit and who are covered by the same collective agreement (redundancy unit). However, the seniority rules are semi-compelling and the employer and the trade union may deviate from the statutory rules when determining the order of dismissals by concluding a local collective agreement (avtalsturlista).[54] If the employee is actually dismissed, this employee has a priority right to re-employment—a rule that facilitates access to employment for older workers. Any employment opening within nine months from the expiry of the former employment should be offered to employees dismissed by redundancy, on the condition that the employees are sufficiently qualified and have been employed for a total of more than 12 months by the employer during the last three years (Section 25 of LAS). The order of employees being offered employment is decided in accordance with the last-in-first-out principle.

Seniority rules are thus potentially indirectly age-discriminatory.[55] These rules have not yet been explicitly tried by the CJEU against the ban on age discrimination.

[53] See for example Labour Court judgments AD 1993:61, AD 1993:101 and AD 1995:152.

[54] The principal restriction is that the decided order of dismissals must not go against so-called good labour market practice, or be blatantly discriminatory or offensive, see Labour Court judgements AD 1983:107, AD 1996:114 and AD 2002:37. An employer with at most ten employees may, before the order of dismissals is determined, exempt at most two employees who, in the opinion of the employer, are of particular importance for future activities (s 22(2) of LAS).

[55] In Sweden, some directly age-discriminatory elements, such as providing extra protection for employees above the age of 45, were removed from the Employment Protection Act (1982:80) in 2007.

However, there are signs that such rules may be found acceptable and justifiable according to EU law.[56]

Transition agreements provide an important, collectively-bargained complement to employment protection in redundancy situations. There is no statutory severance pay in Sweden. In Sweden and several other EU Member States, such as France, Germany, the Netherlands, Poland and the UK, severance pay and other forms of compensation in redundancy situations, set by legislation or collective bargaining or negotiation with works councils, are seniority-based and linked to length of service. At the same time, older workers, having reached pre-retirement or retirement age, sometimes receive less or no compensation in such situations, with reference to their access to pensions and social security benefits.

Employment protection and seniority rules are seen by some as affording necessary protection for older workers, while others view them as barriers for the entry of younger workers into the labour market and the cause of potential intergenerational conflict. This was confirmed by the interviews in the iNGenBar research project. The employers' organisations Svenskt Näringsliv and Teknikföretagen emphasised the problems caused by the employment protection regulation, for example by way of, insider-outsider problems and lock-in effects, and advocated a reform of LAS. They argued that the design and content of the Act provide an advantage for older workers. The trade unions were generally in favour of the existing employment protection regulation. According to TCO, it is difficult to prove the claim that employment protection and seniority rules favour older workers at the expense of younger workers. Other trade unions agreed that the design and content of the employment protection may in part favour older workers. According to Unionen's analysis, it would be easier for younger persons to enter the labour market if the employment protection regulation were removed, but at the same time many older workers would be removed from the labour market and would not be able to re-enter. IF Metall and Kommunal pointed to a general acceptance among their members of the seniority rules, and to perceptions that it is fair that a person who is older and has worked longer gets to stay, as he or she may find it more difficult to get another job.

Perhaps surprisingly, the age-discriminatory character of the seniority rules has not been the subject of much debate in Sweden. Instead the discussion has revolved around the need for protection against arbitrary dismissals, the need for increased labour market flexibilisation and a right for employers to choose which employees to retain in a redundancy situation, based on the needs of the business and the qualifications of the employee, and the links between the seniority rules and youth unemployment and the inclusion of younger workers and their entry into the labour market.

[56] Compare the Opinion of Advocate-General Bot in Case C-555/078 *SedaKücükdeveci v SwedexGmBH& Co. KG*, para 43 and C O'Conneide, *Age Discrimination and European Law* (European Commission, 2005) 40.

Rules on compulsory retirement reflect important links between employment protection and pension systems, and the substantial amount of case law from the CJEU in this area reveals that such schemes prevail in a number of EU Member States. However, compulsory retirement is not a general norm, and many different compulsory retirement rules can be found in the EU Member States.[57] In some Member States, such as the UK, rules on compulsory retirement have been abolished as a result of the introduction of a ban on age discrimination.

In Sweden compulsory retirement is regulated through the '67-year rule', in Sections 32a and 33 of LAS.[58] An employee has a right to stay in employment up until the age of 67, when the employer may terminate the employment relationship after one month's notice and without having to provide objective grounds for dismissal. If the employer does not make use of this possibility, the permanent employment relationship continues; however, it does so with limited employment protection (for example, the employee has one month's notice, and is given no right of priority in accordance with seniority rules or rules on re-employment in redundancy situations). Thus, coupled with this is unlimited access to fixed-term employment contracts after 67 years. In the Hörnfeldt[59] judgment, the CJEU found that the '67-year rule' is allowed according to Article 6(1) of the Employment Equality Directive, because that measure is objectively and reasonably justified by a legitimate aim relating to employment policy and labour-market policy and constitutes an appropriate and necessary means by which to achieve that aim. The CJEU referred, for example, to intergenerational redistribution and the need to avoid a humiliating end to the employment relationship.

IV. Intergenerational Bargaining

A. Introduction

In Sweden, as in the EU more generally, there is thus a need to advance the inclusion of both younger and older workers in the labour market, to combat youth

[57] See D O'Dempsey and A Beale, *Age and Employment*, Report from the Network of Legal Experts in the non-discrimination field to the European Commission, 1 July 2011.

[58] The Swedish pension reform in the late 1990s was an early attempt to adapt to demographical developments and an ageing population. Now, the pension system is built on a lifetime earnings principle and flexible retirement, and provides freedom to combine work with pensions. In 2013 a Government Inquiry Report proposed a number of measures to promote active ageing and increase the actual retirement age in the areas of environment, skills and training etc. The Inquiry Report also proposed the introduction of a recommended retirement age (related to the development of average life expectancy), to which other pension-related age limits could be linked; see Government Inquiry Report SOU 2013:25.

[59] Case C-141/11 *Hörnfeldt v Posten Meddelande AB* EU:C:2012:421.

unemployment and to promote active ageing and longer and healthier working lives for older workers. The iNGenBar research project aimed at a comparative and interdisciplinary analysis of intergenerational bargaining in EU law and a number of EU Member States. Intergenerational bargaining refers here to the integration of policies and strategies for younger and older workers through collective bargaining and social dialogue, and the integration can be both direct and indirect. This section provides a synthesis of the key content and conclusions of the study, aimed at an analysis of intergenerational bargaining in Sweden.[60] Focus was on collective bargaining and three case studies on introduction agreements for younger workers, collective agreements on partial retirement for older workers, and transition agreements, respectively—all linked in different ways to the issue of contingent work, and the balance between numerical and functional flexibility. The study combined a legal-analytical method with a socio-legal approach, and an integration of industrial relations perspectives. In the case studies, analysis of the specific collective agreements was complemented by interviews with leading representatives of social partners and other actors in the labour market, to gain further insights into the context, goals, content and implementation of collective agreements and the views and strategies of the trade unions and employers' organisations.

Swedish labour law, industrial relations and collective bargaining lack a clear intergenerational dimension, as well as an articulated debate on intergenerational solidarity or conflict. The interests of younger and older workers, and the labour market inclusion of these groups, are to a large degree dealt with separately and in parallel. The strategies to combat youth unemployment and to promote active ageing and a prolonged working life for older workers, respectively, are largely seen as separate, equally important and non-conflicting strategies.

The dominant Swedish public-policy stance towards the position of older workers in working life—and intergenerational redistribution of employment—is reflected in the following quotes from the recent Government Inquiry Report on pensionable age:

> 'Many people still consider that early retirement, or by 65 at the latest, increases welfare. These values are largely based on old ideas and myths. The belief is that older people become healthier, happier and live longer if they stop working early. There is also, even among otherwise educated people, a widespread and fixed belief that older people should give way to young people in the labour force, in order, among other things, to reduce youth unemployment … [S]tudies that are designed to seek to establish causal relationships do not provide any clear support to show that early retirement on average improves health, reduces mortality or increases the quality of life for older people. Nor do economic theory or empirical studies provide any support to show that people who

[60] M Rönnmar, *Intergenerational Bargaining in Sweden. Report for the project iNGenBar*, 2014. See generally this report for further information and details, for example on methodology, the interviewees and the content and interpretation of the collective agreements (available at www.intergenerational-bargaining.eu).

continue to work crowd out younger people from the labour market. … Early retirement can be regarded as a historical remnant that entails a waste of human capital. It is out of keeping with the times for well-educated and healthy people in their sixties to permanently leave the labour market with a public pension, occupational pension or retirement pension'.[61]

The idea that older workers (for example, through early retirement) should make room for younger workers is alien to the Swedish context. The interviews confirmed that in Sweden, the perspective of intergenerational solidarity or conflict is not clearly in focus. The discussion is more complex, and revolves around other questions. What is needed to enable younger workers to enter and establish themselves in the labour market? What is needed to prevent older workers from retiring early or going on sick leave? What is needed to persuade older workers to work until the 'normal' retirement age of 65, and beyond?

Given the lack of direct intergenerational bargaining in the Swedish context, it was not possible to select only the case studies that displayed a direct and central intergenerational element. Instead, collective agreements that address the interests and situation of younger workers—the introduction agreements—and older workers—the collective agreements on partial retirement—were included. The transition agreements were also included because they are central to labour market restructuring and company reorganisation, and are fundamentally linked to employment protection and redundancy, when the interests and inclusion or exclusion of younger and older workers may be competing.[62]

In Sweden, collective agreements are entered into at different levels. Nationwide collective agreements are concluded at sectoral level, and supplemented by local collective agreements concluded at workplace level. In addition, some master agreements are concluded at national top level. In recent decades, there has been a trend towards individualisation and (organised) decentralisation of industrial relations and wage negotiations. Today, wages are set mostly through local bargaining within the framework of national sectoral bargaining.[63]

B. Case study: Introduction Agreements for Younger Workers

In recent years, a number of national sectoral collective agreements, so-called introduction agreements for younger workers (yrkesintroduktionsavtal), have been concluded in Sweden, and have attracted a lot of attention. Youth unemployment

[61] See English summary to Government Inquiry Report SOU 2013:25.

[62] All three types of collective agreements are recently concluded or the subject of re-negotiations; they are topical and debated. Within each type of collective agreement, one or a few collective agreements were studied more closely. The collective agreements cover both the private and public sector of the labour market and blue-collar and white-collar/professional employees.

[63] In 2013, there were about 670 national sectoral collective agreements in force. See National Mediation Office, *Avtalsrörelsen och lönebildningen 2013. Medlingsinstitutets årsrapport* (Stockholm, National Mediation Office, 2014).

and labour market inclusion of younger workers form a background, and the introduction agreements regulate employments for younger workers, combining work with education, training and supervision.[64] In 2010, Teknikföretagen and IF Metall concluded a 'pioneer' introduction agreement, and introduction agreements have since been concluded, for example in municipal/regional healthcare and care, the retail sector, and the wood and graphical sector.[65]

In 2012, the Government started negotiations with the social partners on a tripartite job pact, aimed at tackling youth unemployment. One of the aims was to provide young persons with employment through introduction agreements, partly financed by the State. In January 2014, a Government regulation (2013:1157) entered into force for a Government scheme to support and subsidise introduction employments for younger workers.[66]

The introduction agreement concluded by Teknikarbetsgivarna and IF Metall declares initially that the industry is facing a large generational renewal in coming years, which increases the need for new employees. Today, work entails greater requirements on theoretical education and qualified professional experience. Recruitment measures are, therefore, vital to secure the future long-term competence provision of industry. The aim of the introduction agreement is to stimulate companies in the industry sector to offer specific introduction employments to younger people so they can work and develop in their professional life in the Swedish labour market. Introduction employments are aimed at younger persons under the age of 25 who lack relevant professional experience. The introduction employment contract is a fixed-term employment contract, which may last for 12 months, with a possibility for an extension of up to 12 months. Every introduction employment shall be combined with supervision and an individual training plan regarding work tasks and educational and introductory elements. The employer and the employee are free to terminate the introduction employment contract with one month's notice. If there is no termination, the introduction employment contract is converted into a permanent employment contract.

A common theme in the interviews with the social partners was that in general, the introduction agreements are not labour market measures that can be expected to grow quickly into large volumes (contrary to the declarations of the Government). The introduction agreements are only one way of combating youth

[64] However, already prior to these agreements, a number of collective agreements have regulated employments, linked to introduction, education and apprenticeships, for example in sectors such as construction and painting; see National Mediation Office (n 63) 149 ff.

[65] See Arbetsförmedlingen, *Återrapportering 2014, Yrkesintroduktionsanställningar, 1 augusti 2014* (Stockholm, 2014); cf also Regeringen, *Yrkesintroduktionsanställningar—en ny väg till jobb för unga*, 2014 (www.regeringen.se/sb/d/17361/a/223949).

[66] The Government scheme has been authorised by the European Commission under EU state aid rules, see decision C(2013)4053 final. According to the scheme, an employer who hires a young person within the framework of a collectively bargained introduction agreement can be awarded financial support corresponding to ordinary employers' social-security contributions and a monthly supervisor grant. See also Government Inquiry Report Ds 2013:20.

unemployment and promoting younger workers' entry into the labour market. Another important aim of the agreements is to ensure provision of current and future competence. The introduction agreements are about securing the future core group of employees and building up competence.[67]

C. Case Study: Collective Agreements on Partial Retirement

In the Swedish labour market, several collective agreements, for both blue-collar and white-collar employees, offer possibilities for employees to apply for partial retirement from the age of 60 or 62.[68] Here the focus is on provisions on partial retirement for older workers, recently included in collective agreements in the industry sector, Teknikavtalen, between Teknikarbetsgivarna and the blue-collar trade union IF Metall and the white-collar and professional employees' trade unions Unionen/SverigesIngenjörer, respectively. According to Teknikavtalet, IF Metall employees can apply for a right to partial retirement from the age of 60 years. If partial retirement is granted, the employment contract is transformed into a part-time employment contract. The employer can deny the application for partial retirement if, from an objective perspective, the partial retirement in question could cause a considerable disturbance in the business or activity. In the contracting parties' 'Common Commentary' to these provisions, they clarify that their starting point is that employees in the future must work longer and up to a higher age than today. For many employees, this will result in pressures that make it necessary to work somewhat less at the end of working life by decreasing the degree of activity from full-time to part-time. The aim of the provisions of partial retirement is, thus, to provide an opportunity for a longer working life and create fruitful conditions for generational renewal.[69]

The background to the agreements on partial retirement is found in the systems on working-time reduction, where a part of the growth and productivity increase has been taken out as working-time reduction. Some of the productivity increase is now used for partial retirement instead of wage increases. The funds set aside can also be used for ordinary occupational pension benefits. The employers' organisations and trade unions involved in these agreements all agree that it will take a long time before adequate funds are built up to finance partial retirement, fully or to a large degree.

[67] The introduction agreements from the municipal and regional sector do not clearly address younger workers or reserve introduction employments for them.

[68] See National Mediation Office (n 63) 137.

[69] The provisions on partial retirement in *Teknikavtalet Unionen/Sveriges Ingenjörer* are, in principle, the same.

D. Case study: Transition Agreements

Transition agreements (earlier often called employment security agreements, trygghets- ochomställningsavtal) cover all sectors (private and public, blue-collar, white-collar and professional employees) and large parts of the labour market. They constitute a key feature of Swedish labour law and collective bargaining, and an important complement to the statutory employment protection regulation on redundancy dismissals—but also to active labour market policies and unemployment insurance. The first transition agreements were concluded in the 1970s.[70] The transition agreements provide employees facing dismissal, owing to reasons of redundancy, different rights to severance pay and economic compensation and active transition support measures, by way of coaching, job-searching services, training and re-education etc.[71] The agreements also provide support for employers in re-organisations and redundancy situations. The transition agreements are administered by transition foundations, set up by the social partners and collective bargaining, and the severance pay and transition support are financed by the employers, often through an insurance and premium-based scheme.

Here the focus is on the leading transition agreement between Svenskt Näringsliv (SN) and PTK (Council for Negotiation and Co-operation, a joint negotiation organisation of trade unions representing private-sector white-collar and professional employees): Omställningsavtalet, covering private-sector and white-collar and professional employees. The SN-PTK Transition agreement initially declares that the main idea of the agreement is that the company continuously sets aside economic funds to be used in connection with redundancy situations. Thereby, in a redundancy situation, the company's needs can be accommodated as regards the composition of the workforce as well as the dismissed employees' demands for economic compensation and assistance in getting a new job. In a redundancy situation, this in turn implies an obligation for the parties involved to seek, at either party's request, to reach a local collective agreement on the selection of employees to be dismissed (avtalsturlista). The parties have a common responsibility to ensure that the remaining workforce enables the company to achieve productivity, profit and competitiveness. The companies pay a fee to the transition fund, TRR Trygghetsrådet, to cover their activities, severance pay (avgångsersättningen, AGE) and the transition support (omställningsstödet).

The aim of the transition agreement is to mitigate the transition problems experienced by both employees and companies in redundancy situations, due to reorganisation, restructuring, rationalisation and economic loss. The employees made redundant shall receive financial aid during a transition period and help in

[70] See Sebardt for a historical account of the early agreements and the developments in this area, G Sebardt, *Redundancy and the Swedish Model. Swedish Collective Agreements on Employment Security in a National and International Context* (Uppsala, Iustusförlag, 2005).

[71] Additional income insurances may follow from the membership in a trade union.

finding a new job. Companies facing redundancy shall be provided with staffing conditions that, to the greatest extent possible, enable their future activity. Severance pay is awarded to an employee if the employee has: worked for a company connected to Trygghetsrådet and has been dismissed for reasons of redundancy; is at least 40 years old; has been permanently employed for a continuous period of five years in the company; and becomes unemployed when the employment relationship is terminated. Transition support can be offered to an employee who has worked at least 16 hours per week for one year with one and the same company and who has been dismissed for reasons of redundancy by a company connected to Trygghetsrådet.

In recent years, Svenskt Näringsliv and PTK have been in the process of renegotiating their transition agreement. Svenskt Näringsliv, for example, wanted to set aside the statutory seniority rules and the last-in-first-out-principle, and link the selection of employees in redundancy situations entirely to the employee's competence and qualifications. PTK wanted to broaden the scope of the agreement to include fixed-term employees and employees who have to leave their employment due to sickness or health problems, and to strengthen the right to education and competence development for all employees, also during an existing employment relationship. However, these renegotiations failed in September 2015.

At first glance, the transition agreements appear to apply to all employees. However, the agreements (such as the SN-PTK Transition Agreement) establish different qualification criteria related to a certain age or period of employment for the granting of severance pay and transition support in a way that favours older workers and disfavours younger workers (and is potentially directly and indirectly age-discriminatory). In addition, younger workers are more often fixed-term employees, and suffer from being excluded from the scope of the transition agreements. At the same time, the way in which the SN-PTK Transition Agreement presupposes, in redundancy situations, the conclusion of local collective agreements (avtalsturlistor), adapting or setting aside the statutory seniority rules based on length of employment and age only (with a requirement for sufficient qualifications), may favour younger workers in relation to older workers, compared to the application of the statutory employment protection regulation.

E. Analysis

In Sweden, the strong emphasis on collective bargaining and social partner autonomy and strong trade unions and employers' organisations create favourable basic conditions for intergenerational bargaining. Wages, terms and conditions of employment and other working-life issues are generally collectively bargained. In principle, labour law and collective bargaining in Sweden have a uniform scope. As we have seen, in Sweden, some age-related regulation does exist in legislation and collective bargaining. In general, the introduction agreements are targeted at younger workers, while the collective agreements on partial retirement are targeted at older workers. The transition agreements regulate restructuring, redundancy and transition in general (but their scope and benefit coverage is often seniority-based). This age-related regulation is linked to the traditional and legitimate role afforded to age in labour law and in the organisation of the labour market more generally.

The case study on introduction agreements highlights the fact that apart from combating youth unemployment and promoting labour market inclusion of younger workers, an important aim of the agreements is to secure current and future competence provision. The social partners involved in the introduction agreements subjected to study here emphasised that there are no direct intergenerational elements in the aim or content of the agreements. However, there are indirect intergenerational implications of the introduction agreements linked to generational renewal, competence provision, supervision, training and education. Supervision and education are likely to be provided by older workers, who will then be able to transfer their knowledge and experience to younger workers. Being supervisors may also help individual older workers to stay longer in the job and in working life. The introduction agreements, to different degrees, are age-related and tied to a specific group of younger workers. The case study also highlights the challenges and difficulties of combining a social partner initiative and collective agreements with a governmental financial support scheme and the activities of a public employment service.

The case study on collective agreements on partial retirement for older workers emphasises that the aim of the provisions of partial retirement is to provide an opportunity for a longer working life and create fruitful conditions for generational renewal. In line with the strategy on active ageing, this right to partial retirement is not about early retirement or about making room for younger workers. Instead, it is a question of prolonging working life from the individual (older) employee's perspective. Thus, these collective agreements also have some, more indirect, intergenerational elements. Apart from prolonging working life for older workers, it is hoped that the partial retirement of older workers will also lead to a corresponding recruitment of younger workers. A crucial question for the realisation of the right to partial retirement is of course the level of economic compensation. Here, a long-term perspective must be applied in relation to the build-up of adequate funds for partial retirement pension benefits.

The case study on transition agreements highlights that in general, the transition agreements complement the statutory employment protection regulation in important ways, focus on employability and transitions, and offer redundant employees both severance pay and active transition support. One indirect intergenerational element of the transition agreements relates to the interplay between the transition agreements, employment protection regulation and seniority rules. Some transition agreements (such as the leading SN-PTK Transition Agreement) enable and promote the conclusion of local collective agreements that set aside or adapt the last-in-first-out-principle, and may, therefore, favour younger workers in relation to older workers. At the same time, the scope and content of the transition agreements seem to favour older workers in several other respects.

Furthermore, the recent renegotiations of the SN-PTK Transition Agreement, and the trade unions' attempt to expand the scope of the agreement beyond redundancy to include employees who have to leave their employment due to sickness or health problems, contribute to a 'blurring' of the boundary between redundancy and personal reasons. I have previously questioned this 'conceptual dichotomy' which characterises Swedish employment protection.[72]

Collective bargaining developments and the case studies display a lack of direct and explicit intergenerational bargaining in the Swedish context. However, several indirect and implicit intergenerational elements can be found in the introduction agreements, the collective agreements on partial retirement, and the transition agreements. These indirect intergenerational elements relate to such concepts as generational renewal in terms of future competence provision, competence development and transfer of knowledge and experience between older and younger workers, and older workers' participation in education and supervision of younger workers, as a way of adapting the working environment to enable a longer working life.

Intergenerational redistribution of employment between older and younger workers is alien to Swedish public policy and collective bargaining. Thus, Swedish developments are in line with economic research on the 'lump of labour fallacy', and oppose propositions that compulsory or premature retirement schemes will help combat youth unemployment or that older workers crowd younger workers out of the labour market.[73]

The case studies, and interviews with social partners, imply that there is limited integration or synergy among the three different types of collective agreements. This seems to be the case even though some collective agreements, such as introduction agreements and collective agreements on partial retirement for older workers, are concluded by the same collective bargaining partners. However, fruitful linkages can be found and developed, not least in the practical application of these agreements—for example, when it comes to the educational element and the supervision of younger workers.

V. Concluding Remarks

It follows from the analysis of fixed-term and temporary agency work, employment protection and intergenerational bargaining that Swedish law provides a scope for contingent work and numerical flexibility—and that the regulation of

[72] See, eg, M Rönnmar and A Numhauser-Henning, 'Swedish Employment Protection in Times of Flexicurity Policies and Economic Crisis' (2012) 28(4) *International Journal of Comparative Labour Law and Industrial Relations* 443–67.

[73] On the links between the 'lump of labour fallacy' and labour law and industrial relations, see E Dewhurst, 'Intergenerational balance, mandatory retirement and age discrimination in Europe: How can the ECJ better support national courts in finding a balance between the generations' (2013) 50 *Common Market Law Review* 1333, with further references.

contingent work, by way of legislation and collective bargaining, has an age-related and intergenerational dimension. In principle, despite the ban on age discrimination, EU law and Swedish age discrimination law enable directly and indirectly age-related regulation as well as intergenerational bargaining.

The Swedish labour market is generally characterised by high employment rates. In comparative European terms, the labour market situation of older workers in Sweden is good. The employment rate among older workers is high and the average retirement age is about 65 years. Still, in some sectors, it is difficult for employees (especially blue-collar employees) to stay in working life until 'normal' retirement age. Thus, there is a need for an adaptation of the work and working environment. There is also a general need for prolonging working life for older workers beyond 'normal' retirement age to cover future costs for pensions and the healthcare system. Here, the collective agreements on partial retirement become relevant. High youth unemployment and younger workers' difficulties in entering and establishing themselves on the labour market are a fundamental problem, from both an individual and a societal perspective. In Sweden, the debates on ways to combat youth unemployment and promote labour market inclusion of younger workers revolve around such factors as lower entry wages for younger workers, the scope for contingent work and flexible employment contracts, the strength of employment protection, and implications of seniority rules.

The regulation of fixed-term work is closely connected to employment protection, and younger workers are over-represented when it comes to contingent forms of work. Swedish law provides for specific fixed-term employment contracts for younger and older workers as a means to promote entry into the labour market and prolong working life—by way of collectively bargained introduction employment contracts and fixed-term contracts for employees above the age of 67 years and beyond compulsory retirement. These forms of fixed-term work are not clearly linked (as are general fixed-term employment contracts and zero-hours contracts, for example) to precariousness and vulnerability. An important theme in the study on intergenerational bargaining (in line with the EU law flexicurity discourse and its emphasis on employability) is the key role played by competence, qualifications and education and the urgent need to secure future competence provision for the Swedish labour market. In this context, generational renewal is central to collective bargaining developments, introduction agreements and agreements on partial retirement. Thus, the introduction agreements aim not only at addressing youth unemployment but also at recruiting and educating future core workers and building up competence. Similarly, temporary agency work is not only a form of contingent work aimed at increasing numerical flexibility, but can also increase functional flexibility in the user company and simplify recruiting of future core workers. Thus, competence and qualifications serve as a dividing line between core and contingent work.

Previous studies have shown that the Swedish labour law and industrial relations system provide a rather wide scope for functional flexibility, and favourable conditions for the implementation of functional flexibility strategies linked to the employee's obligation to work, the employer's right to direct and allocate work and a tradition of social partnership and strong mechanisms for information, consultation and co-determination.[74]

Swedish employment protection has traditionally been viewed as relatively strong. However, in relation to fixed-term work and dismissals for reasons of redundancy, the statutory employment protection (and accompanying collective bargaining) leaves much room for managerial prerogative. The employer has a principal right to decide when reorganisation and reduction of the workforce is needed, opening up a possibility for flexible adjustment of the number of workers and access to numerical flexibility.[75] From an intergenerational perspective, employment protection is seen as both providing necessary protection for older workers and hindering the entry of younger workers into the labour market.

Swedish labour law, industrial relations and collective bargaining lack a clear intergenerational dimension, as well as an articulated debate on intergenerational solidarity or conflict. One challenge is to address the interests of both younger and older workers, and the strategies to combat youth unemployment and promote a prolonged working life, in appropriate and effective ways. Another challenge—and opportunity—is to promote further integration and co-ordination between these interests and strategies.

[74] See M Rönnmar, 'The Managerial Prerogative and the Employee's Obligation to Work: Comparative Perspectives on Functional Flexibility' (2006) 35(1) *Industrial Law Journal*, 2006, 56–74.

[75] See further M Rönnmar and A Numhauser-Henning, 'Swedish employment protection in times of flexicurity policies and economic crisis' (2012) 28(4) *International Journal of Comparative Labour Law and Industrial Relations*, 443–67.

13

Social Protection of Contingent Work: Austria and the Full Coverage Social Insurance System

FRANZ MARHOLD

I. Introduction—The Development of the Austrian Social Security System

The Austrian social security system has been historically grown, and still partly preserves some traditional features, such as the distinction between the different professions. However, the social security system faces similar troubles to those in other European countries. The major common challenge is to guarantee its long-term sustainability and at the same time to cover all those persons who need to be protected by the statutory insurance. To serve this latter goal, the protection of statutory insurance has been progressively extended.

Austria has followed a clear concept of gradual extension of its social protection system to cover also those performing work in the framework of a non-standard employment. The gaps in the protection in terms of personal scope have been mainly closed in the last couple of decades. Recently, a very broad group of people has been covered by the social security system, independently of the specific form of employment including also the economically dependent persons (eg freelancers).

Initially, the social insurance coverage was bound to the membership of the Chamber of Commerce and, thus, self-employed persons were not covered. In 1998, the system was changed fundamentally by linking the protection to the income tax with the consequence that nearly everybody who is subject to income tax enjoys social security protection. Consequently, compulsory insurance is linked to gainful activity in terms of producing income and therefore being subjected to income tax, whereas a uniform social security system for all those performing work in a legal sense does not exist.[1] Great differences exist regarding the content and the organisation of social security based on the kind of gainful activity undertaken. An exception to this general rule is the occupational accident insurance, which is basically uniformly regulated for all groups. On the other hand, in the health and pension systems, there are major differences build on the traditional differentiation of the activity performed. Different groups have separated funding based on the idea that every group shall care for the social security of its own members.[2]

The Allgemeines Sozialversicherungsgesetz (ASVG) or General Social Security Statute which regulates the statutory health and occupational accident insurance as well as the public pension scheme, applies to all employees. Self-employed persons fall under the scope of the Gewerbliches Sozialversicherungsgesetz (GSVG) or Trade Social Security Statute which regulates the health and pension insurance provisions for this group.[3] A special statute, namely the Bauern-Sozialversicherungsgesetz (BSVG) applies to self-employed persons in the agriculture and forestry sectors.

II. Social Coverage of the Core Workforce

A. The Scope of Insured Persons—The Definition of 'Employee'

The term 'employee' (Dienstnehmer) has slightly different meaning depending on whether it is used in the context of labour, social security or tax law. Recent legislative developments have sought to unify the meaning of this term in the different fields of law. Since 1998, the ASVG refers to the slightly broader scope of the term 'employee' in the sense of the Statute on Income Tax.

The same definition of 'employee' (Dienstnehmer) applies across all social insurance sectors. The term covers those persons who are employed in a personally and economically dependent relationship for a remuneration.[4] The statute emphasises that the prevalence of these criteria is decisive, ie the personal and economic dependency shall dominate against the characteristics of an independent activity carried out by a self-employed person.[5]

[1] Social security protection is extended in certain cases beyond the group of persons performing a gainful activity; eg persons receiving statutory pension are partly insured. The same rule applies to persons doing military service or, instead of it, community service and to those receiving childcare allowance. Article 8(1) Allgemeines Sozialversicherungsgesetz (ASVG), General Social Security Statute.

[2] WJ Pfeil, *Österreichisches Sozialrecht* (Wien, Verlag Österreich, 2014) 10.

[3] Separate statutes apply to freelancers, artists, notaries, civil servants, etc.

[4] § 4 par 2 ASVG.

[5] See in detail, S Auer-Mayer, 'Die Grenze zwischen selbständiger und unselbständiger Tätigkeit aus sozialversicherungsrechtlicher Sicht' (2015) in *Zeitschrift für Arbeits- und Sozialrecht* 4–5.

The most important characteristic of personal dependency is that the employee's freedom to determine the way work is performed is limited and, thus, s/he is bound to the instructions of the employer. It means less technical or subject-specific guidance, but rather instructions regarding the behaviour of the employee. The main feature of personal dependency is the exclusive performance of work in person. The duty of personal performance is not fulfilled, if the person can regularly represent himself, or can assign the task to a third person, or if he can refuse to work without fear of sanction.[6] The case law and literature have identified some further criteria for personal dependency: integration into the corporate structure, which means predetermined working time and place; integration into the working process; being bound to instructions or directives of the principal; supervision and control by the principal; the employee owes a certain endeavour and has to carry out the work to the best knowledge and belief but not success in work; work equipment is provided by the employer; the work's output benefits the employer. Not all of these criteria have to be fulfilled, but there has to be a qualitative majority of the mentioned criteria in order to qualify someone as an employee.[7]

The legal definition requires also economic dependency for the qualification as an employee. Pursuant to the prevailing opinion, economic dependency does not only mean that the employee needs the remuneration to make ends meet.[8] This criterion covers also the circumstances where the employee cannot choose where to work or what equipment to use.[9] In this sense, economic dependency is also the consequence of personal dependency.

Contrary to the term of employee in labour law, where remuneration is not required for being qualified as an employee, it is considered as an important part of the definition in the context of social security. The right to remuneration is decisive, whereas the fact of whether the employee actually receives the pay does not affect the insurance coverage.

B. Blue-Collar and White-Collar Workers

The historically grown distinction between blue-collar (Arbeiter) and white-collar (Angestellte) workers dates back to the time of the Austro-Hungarian monarchy and still exists today under Austrian labour and social security law. Whereas white-collar workers are characterised by accomplishing intellectual services, blue-collar workers undertake physical work.

[6] T Tomandl, *Wesensmerkmale des Arbeitsvertrages in rechtsvergleichender und rechtspolitischer Sicht* (Wien, Springer Verlag, 1971) 40.

[7] F Marhold and M Friedrich, *Österreichisches Arbeitsrecht* (Wien, Springer Verlag, 2012) 33–38. C Kietaibl, *Arbeitsrecht I—Gestalter und Gestaltungsmittel*, (Wien, new academic press, 2013) 23–28.

[8] Pfeil, *Österreichisches Sozialrecht* (n 2) 16–17.

[9] Tomandl, *Wesensmerkmale des Arbeitsvertrages* (n 6) 39.

While the most significant law applicable to the blue-collar workers are the Austrian Civil Code and the Trade Act (Gewerbeordnung), white-collar workers are subject to the Employees Act (Angestelltengesetz). White-collar workers are privileged in certain fields of labour law, such regulations regarding payment, continuation of payment in case of illness, length of notice period, etc. Collective agreements regularly make a difference between the two categories of persons. This distinction raises serious concerns, as it might be unconstitutional and probably harm the right to equal treatment.

The distinction still plays a role in social security law as well, even if the earlier marked differences have been mainly abolished. The notion of white-collar workers in social security law is basically linked to the term in labour law, but slightly extends this group.[10] In the public pension scheme, there are some differing provisions left regarding the incapacity of the person to work. However, the pension funds of the two groups have been united and the contribution rate to the health system has been unified, as well.

III. The Social Inclusion of Self-Employed Persons

A. The Recent Regulation

Self-employed persons have been gradually included in the statutory insurance, but there is no uniform social security system for all self-employed persons. Self-employment in a social security sense includes several groups and, consequently, different statutes apply to different groups. The GSVG, which regulates the health and pension insurance applies to most of them.

The obligatory insurance of self-employed persons differs in comparison to employees due to the different way work is performed. In case of self-employment, it is not possible to link the insurance to a certain type of contract, as with employees, but only to the profession. Therefore, the insurance is bound to the membership in the Chamber of Commerce (Wirtschaftskammer) and to the entitlement to practise a certain profession. Statutory insurance applies automatically to the members of the Chamber of Commerce by the acquisition of a trading licence.[11] However, the possession of the licence does not exclude the qualification of the person concerned as a dependent employee, if the circumstances of the performance of work determine the relationship as one of employment.[12] As self-employed individuals can have very volatile income, the start and end of

[10] Article 14 ASVG.
[11] Article 2 (1) No 1 GSVG.
[12] See also Auer-Mayer, 'Die Grenze zwischen selbständiger und unselbständiger Tätigkeit' (n 5) 4.

the insurance until recently used to depend exclusively on the membership and not on the income. These were structural differences between self-employed and employees.[13]

Since 1997, the statutory insurance has been extended also to those self-employed persons, who either do not need to possess a licence (eg writers, artists) or the licence has not been required or not received. They are the so-called 'new self-employed', who have not been covered by statutory insurance until 1997. Following recent legislative amendments, Article 2(1) point 4 GSVG provides that all self-employed are covered by the GSVG independently of the existence of a licence.[14]

B. Perception of Self-Employed Persons in the Early Social Security System

The early Austrian social security system was based on the idea that within the group of individuals performing a gainful activity, differences in contributions and thus in benefits were justified, as these individuals had different interests and needs as far as the social security protection was concerned. Self-employed are in another life situation, than employees and therefore they do not need the same social security protection like employees.

Moreover, the Constitutional Court declared in a decision in 1969 that the principle of equal treatment does not require a uniform federal regulation of health insurance.[15] Territorial differences can be justified due to the actual historical, geographic and economic differences between different areas. The Court pointed out that the factual circumstances of the various categories of persons are so different that distinct regulations are not only allowed, but under certain objective conditions circumstances are even necessary. Such objective conditions have to be assessed in light of the fact, whether the individual is performing work as an employee or as a self-employed as well as due to the large variety of professions. Based on this reasoning the Court concluded that employees and self-employed have different life and financial situation and thus different interests regarding social security provisions and, therefore, differences in contributions and social benefits were allowed between these groups.[16]

[13] See T Tomandl, 'Rechtsprobleme einer umfassenden Sozialversicherung' (1998) *Zeitschrift für Arbeits- und Sozialrecht* 9, 11.

[14] However, as indicated earlier, different rules apply to independent pharmacists, doctors and notaries and a separate statute applies to farmers.

[15] VfGH Erk v 27 Juni 1969, B 157/68 Erk Slg Nr 6004/1969 Band Nr 34 S 478–482. [Decision of the Constitutional Court of 27 June 1969, published in Collection of Verdicts Nr 6004/1969 Nr 34 issue, 478–482.] and also VfGH Erk v 4 März 1961, B 193/60 Erk Slg Nr 3897/1961. Band Nr 26 S 66-69 [Decision of the Constitutional Court of 4 March 1961 published in Collection of Verdicts Nr 3897/1961 Nr 26 issue, 66–69].

[16] Decision No 6004/1969 p 481.

The Constitutional Court confirmed this reasoning in its judgment in 1983,[17] where the major question was, whether the regulation of statutory health insurance complies with the principle of equal treatment, as in the case of employees, the statute used the principle of multiple insurance, but in the case of self-employed, members of free professions and farmers it used the principle of subsidiarity. The Constitutional Court declared that the difference was justified because of the diverging situations of the insured persons. The Court argued that the professional's life situation shall be decisive to answer the question whether double (multiple) insurance coverage is to be accepted or not. Self-employed and farmers are less interested in cash benefits, than in measures serving the continuation of their trades, therefore, the double insurance of these groups is not desirable. Completely different, however, is the life situation of a public servant who has an additional employment as self-employed. For that person, the high cash benefits constitute an essential financial aid in case of illness or maternity.[18] Following the decision of the Constitutional Court, the self-employed remained resistant to their integration within the system of social security and, particularly, to the organisation of their social security system based on the model of blue-collar workers. The Court pointed out that this group of people faces different economic risks and opportunities. Therefore, the Court held that it is reasonable to provide self-employed with a statutory health insurance only in the case that they otherwise would not be protected at all (principle of subsidiarity).

C. Shift in Approach

In the last decades, a shift in approach to the statutory insurance of self-employed and persons belonging to the intermediary category between employees and self-employed can be noticed. The tendency is clear and brings about the inclusion of these groups into the statutory insurance system and the replacement of the link of statutory insurance to the professions to a link to income. The ideological background for this change is the assumption that self-employed persons need the protection of statutory insurance.[19] In the European labour law literature, the prevailing view is that the majority of self-employed persons face greater social and economical challenges and require special protection from the State. Particularly sensitive is the situation of self-employed individuals who have been pushed into self-employment by employers reluctant to offer them an employment contract. It is now understood, in line with the European tendencies, that quasi self-employed individuals are particularly worth protecting. The need to protect self-employed

[17] VfGH Erk v 1 Juli 1983 Erk Slg Nr 9753/1983. See *Zeitschrift für Arbeits- und Sozialrecht* (1985)146–151.

[18] ibid 147.

[19] M Gleitsmann and M Kircher, 'Soziale Errungenschaften für Selbständige aus rechtspolitischer Sicht' in P Aschauer and E Kohlbacher (eds), *Sozialversicherungsrecht—Jahrbuch 2014* 87, 89.

persons means a clear change of approach and a major shift of values in the Austrian social security law.

However, this ideologically backed reform also has a significant financial objective, namely to guarantee the financial feasibility of the social security system. A tax-financed social security system can follow this aim better than the one based on professions. The shift of values has also brought about the extension of the basis of contributors.

A clear sign of adapting the legal situation of self-employed persons to the one of employees is the unification and simplification of the contributions. As of late, all categories of persons performing a gainful activity pay nearly the same percentage to the insurance funds independently of the fact of whether they are dependently or independently employed. The difference between employees and self-employed lies, therefore, not in the different level of protection, but in the amount of contribution which a person has to pay for social security. The employees, self-employed and persons having an intermediary status pay overall the same percentage to the funds, only in case of employees and those persons in the intermediary category, the employers are obliged to pay for half of the contributions. In case of self-employed individuals, a small percentage of the contributions still come from the State, but this is continuously being abolished. Therefore, the health, pension and occupational accident insurance companies receive basically the same percentage of contributions from all categories of individuals performing work.[20]

D. The Extension of the Protection in 1997

Landmark regulation in the extension of the social security system to self-employed was the Arbeits- und Sozialrechts-Änderungsgesetz 1997 (ASRÄG 1997) which came into force in 1998. This statute marked a clear shift in approach.

The major goal of the reform was to include the largest possible group of all those people who perform gainful activity into the social security system. This brought about the decline of the traditional breakdown by occupations and led to the increasing unification of the three big statutes on insurances (ASVG, GSVG and BSVG). The reform included a set of amendments to the law.

The notion of employee in Article 4 (2) ASVG has been extended and clarified so that persons performing a gainful activity in a relationship of dependency who are obliged to pay income tax in line with the Statute on Income Tax (Einkommensteuergesetz 1988) are considered as employees (Dienstnehmer) in the social security sense. This had the effect of reconciling distortions between the regulation of social security and tax law.

[20] A special rule applies to the self-employed regarding the occupational accident system, as they have to pay a fixed monthly amount rather than a certain percentage of their income. Another difference is that unemployment insurance is not compulsory for self-employed, but they can opt-in to pay the same contribution as the employees.

The centrepiece of the amendments to ASRÄG 1997 was the inclusion of the so-called 'new self-employed' into the statutory health and pension insurance according to the GSVG and into the occupational accident insurance according to the ASVG.[21]

The GSVG was extended also to those self-employed persons, who have no trade licence and, thus, are not members of the economic chamber, provided they earn a certain amount of income. These persons are regarded as being employees. The distinction between self-employed covered by the GSVG and employees covered by the ASVG is based on the type of their income. The main goal of the new rule was to reduce the possibility of evading social security contributions. This is a great risk for the sustainability of the social security system and the legislator wanted to put an end to the possibility of evading such an obligation. The term 'employee' now broadly has the same meaning under both tax and labour law.[22]

As a result of these legislative changes, certain professions, such as for instance lawyers, vets, architects, independent journalists have been integrated into the health and pension insurance of GSVG. However, the statute provided the possibility for their respective chamber to make an application to the competent minister to opt-out from the statutory insurance, as long as the members of a particular chamber have their own compulsory self-insurance in terms of health and pension, which is equivalent with the benefits of the GSVG.[23] Most of the chambers took advantage of this possibility and opted out from the health insurance of GSVG. Chambers representing lawyers and engineers also opted out also from the pension system of GSVG. Such opt-outs have contributed to the survival of professionally based differences in the system.

E. Recent Tendencies

Since 2008, self-employed are involved in the system of severance pay,[24] which is also regarded as a second pillar in the old age insurance system.[25] The participation is compulsory for all self-employed, but persons performing a free profession and farmers can opt-in to this system. At the time this obligation was introduced, the contribution of self-employed to the health insurance was reduced in order not to burden self-employed unduly. The self-employed person can get the paid

[21] 22. Novelle zum GSVG—Art 8 ASRÄG 1997 and 54. Novelle zum ASVG—Art. 7 ASRÄG 1997. See in detail, W Schrammel, 'Vom "Werkvertragserkenntnis" zur umfassenden Sozialversicherungspflicht' (1997) *Arbeits- und SozialrechtsKartei* 333, 335.

[22] Tomandl, '*Rechtsprobleme einer umfassenden Sozialversicherung*' (n 13) 9, 12.

[23] Article 5 (1) GSVG.

[24] Betriebliches Mitarbeiter- und Selbständigenvorsorgegesetz, BMSVG, [Statute on Enterprise Precaution for Entreprise Employees and Self-employed Persons] § 49–61 apply to self-employed and § 62–67 apply to persons performing a free profession and farmers.

[25] Gleitsmann and Kircher, 'Soziale Errungenschaften' (n 19) 95.

contributions back after three years of payment in case of two years break in the exercise of the trade or after two years termination of the trade or following retirement; in the last case, independently of the length of the duration of payment.

Since 2009, self-employed persons have the possibility of voluntarily joining the unemployment insurance. Such access has the consequence that the person enjoys a full protection and entitled to all the benefits of the unemployment insurance system. Entry into and withdrawal from the voluntary insurance is only allowed in every ninth year in order to avoid misuses.[26]

Self-employed persons have various kinds of benefits to which they are entitled in case of illness. One of the alternative instruments to the traditional health insurance is the so-called 'enterprise aid' (Betriebshilfe) which can be provided to self-employed in case of illness, accident or pregnancy. The goal of this kind of assistance is to maintain the operation of small enterprises in such situations. In case of maternity, this enterprise aid is provided eight weeks before and eight weeks after the birth. Only members of the Economic Chamber who have health insurance can make use of this aid. Conditions of entitlement are that the incapacity to work lasts longer than 14 days, the annual income of the insured person does not exceed €19,666 (amount in 2015) and the aid has to be essential for the maintenance of the enterprise. An important feature of the enterprise aid is that usually it is an allowance in kind; ie for the duration of the incapacity to work—for the maximum duration of 70 days in a calendar year—a workforce is provided free who performs the work instead of the ill self-employed. In certain cases, the social security authority provides real cash subsidy towards the remuneration of the employed person. The enterprise aid is an excellent illustration for the statement that self-employed persons have different interests from employees and the continuation of the activity of the small enterprise can be more important than receiving a lump sum financial support.

An important trend regarding self-employed persons in the last decade was the gradual decrease in the percentage of their social insurance contributions to the health and pension systems in order to reduce the financial burden on this group.[27]

Taken as a whole, self-employed persons enjoy a broad and comprehensive social protection against the main risks in life. According to a comparative study in this field, which analysed the level of social protection of self-employed persons in 18 European states, Austria provides the highest level of protection compared to other countries.[28]

[26] See in detail, J Pacic, 'Arbeitslosenversicherung für Selbständige' (2008) *Zeitschrift für Arbeits- und Sozialrecht* 156.

[27] Gleitsmann and Kircher, 'Soziale Errungenschaften' (n 20) 90.

[28] S Traub and S Finkler, *Soziale Absicherung von Selbständigen im internationalen Vergleich*, Scientific study by order of the Austrian Economic Chamber and the Social Insurance Institution of the Commercial Economy (Sozialversicherungsanstalt der gewerblichen Wirtschaft), Universität Bremen, Zentrum für Sozialpolitik, 2013, www.wko.at/Content.Node/kampagnen/Soziale_Absicherung_von_Selbstaendigen_im_internationalen_V.pdf.

IV. Contingent Workers

A. Intermediary Category Between Employees and Self-Employed

The Austrian labour law recognises an intermediary category of workers between employees and self-employed persons, who are called 'persons with a similar status to the employee' (dienstnehmerähnliche Personen).[29] Such persons are personally and legally independent, but economically dependent on one or a few clients. The main characteristic of the persons belonging to this group is that they do not fulfil all criteria of an employment relationship. The work, however, is determined by a third person, eg an important client, to a certain extent.[30]

The term used in social security law is not the same as the one used in labour law. In particular, those persons called 'free employees' (*freie Dienstnehmer*) can be regarded as belonging to the intermediary category.[31] Free employees generally belong to the social security system of dependent persons, whereas self-employed belong to the system of independent persons.

In 1996, the Government attempted to include this intermediary group of workers into the ASVG.[32] This was the first regulation which aimed to bring also those persons who earn their income in the context of a contract for services (Werkvertrag) within the statutory social security protection system. This amendment has been heavily criticised[33] as it intended to cover all persons performing a free profession, also those who run a business and employ other employees. A major criticism was that the situation of these persons is more similar to the situation of self-employed persons than to employees and, therefore, it is not appropriate to include them into the ASVG, which is tailored to the needs of employees with personal dependency.

The Constitutional Court declared that the proposed rule violated the Constitution.[34] The only formal criterion set down in the original provision was that in order to qualify as belonging to this group, the worker had to be in regular employment. The criterion would be met as long as a person had concluded

[29] See in detail, G Wachter, *Wesensmerkmale der arbeitnehmerähnlichen Person* (Berlin, Duncker & Humblot, 1980).

[30] Marhold and Friedrich, *Österreichisches Arbeitsrecht* (n 7) 53–56; Kietaibl, *Arbeitsrecht I* (n 7) 39–41.

[31] To the distinction between employee, free employee and self-employed in the social security and tax law see: H Blasina, *Dienstnehmer—Freier Dienstnehmer—Selbständiger, Begriffe und Abgrenzungen im Sozialversicherungs- und Steuerrecht* (Wien, Facultas AG, 2007).

[32] § 4(5) ASVG. Introduced by the statute BGBl 1996/441 and suspended by BGBl I 1997/39 after the decision of the Constitutional Court.

[33] H Krejci, 'Das Werkvertragserkenntnis' (1997) *Verwaltungsrundschau* 81–85. and Schrammel, 'Vom "Werkvertragserkenntnis" zur umfassenden Sozialversicherungspflicht' (n 21)_334.

[34] Decision of the Constitutional Court, VfGH G 392, 398, 399/96, 14.3.1997.

more than three agreements with a client in the last six months or the activity lasted more than two months. In these cases, it should have been assumed that the employment was regular and the person had a status similar to that of an employee.

The Constitutional Court was critical of the law which does not give any indication whether, in addition to the mentioned regular activity, other criteria should be included in the assessment of the decision. The Court pointed out that usually a number of other circumstances should be taken into consideration, such as the economic dependency, the structure of the establishment where work is performed and the number of the principals, with whom he has a contact. Whether the person performing the activity has a similar status to that of an employee needs to be decided on a case-by-case basis.[35]

Following the decision of the Constitutional Court, the term has been changed. Some members of this intermediary group have been put on an equal footing with the employees by Article 4(4) ASVG. The scope of persons included is, however, very limited and not all who belong to this group in a labour law sense are covered by ASVG. Only those people who receive remuneration (above the level of marginal work), perform their work in person, do not possess significant own equipment and are not compulsory insured by other regulation are integrated within the statutory insurance scheme. The aim of this regulation was to exclude from the scope of ASVG, those persons who do not perform the work in person and who possess an own entrepreneurial structure (significant working tools, personnel etc). Another condition is that these people need to be employed on the basis of a freelance contract of service which constitutes an obligation to work for a client for the time as agreed on in the contract but the remuneration does not depend on a specific business performance. The differentiation between a contract of service and contract for service is based on the real content of the relationship.

The regulation is problematic when it comes to persons who perform mainly intellectual activities with high professional expertise in the framework of free contract of services, for example consultation. In such situations, the disposal of significant own work equipment does not work as a criterion for distinction. In case of intellectual work, the significance of own working tools is relatively low and should not be necessarily regarded as a sign of economic dependency.[36]

Important to note is that people who possess a trade licence are excluded from the scope of ASVG. The conditions mentioned above radically limit the range of people belonging to this intermediary category from the scope of ASVG and

[35] For the background of this decision see T Tomandl and W Aigner, 'Verfassungsprobleme bei der Sozialversicherung dienstnehmerähnlicher Beschäftigungsverhältnisse' (1997) *Zeitschrift für Arbeits- und Sozialrecht*, 1 and W Aigner, 'Das VfGH-Erkenntnis zur sog "Werkvertragsregelung"' (1997) *Zeitschrift für Arbeits- und Sozialrecht* 129.

[36] U Runggaldier, 'Probleme der Einführung einer alle Erwerbseinkommen umfassenden Sozialversicherungspflicht' (1998) *Österreichische Juristen-Zeitung* 494, 496.

open the door for the statutory provisions to be evaded. The borderline between so-called 'free employees' belonging to this intermediary category and 'new self-employed' is a floating one and, consequently, clients could urge their service provider to become self-employed in order to avoid the high contributions.[37]

All those persons, who perform work in a personally independent, but economically dependent relationship and do not fulfil the conditions described above—eg they possess a trade licence—are insured by the GSVG. The most important difference in the protection of self-employed and employed persons concerns the protection in case of invalidity. Employees qualify for invalidity pensions in case, as a result of their invalidity, they earn less than 50% of what a comparable worker with the same qualification in a comparable profession would earn. Self-employed persons have to accept any forthcoming economic activity prior to pension and, therefore, are not protected by reference to their last professional activity. Besides, illness benefit is only granted to self-employed persons after the 43rd day of illness.

B. Employees with Fixed-Term Contract

Employees with a contract for a definite period are employees in social security term and, as such, have full social protection independently from the length of their employment. Only a few distinctions between employees with definite and indefinite term of contract can be noticed.

Employees with fixed-term contracts are treated adversely regarding the continuation of payment of remuneration in case of illness after the termination of employment contract. Employees with an indefinite contract are entitled to the continued payment of their remuneration even after the end of the relationship, if the relationship was terminated during the illness by ordinary dismissal or summary dismissal of the employer due to the illness or premature resignation of the employee caused by the fault of the employer.[38]

This rule on the continued payment of remuneration in case of illness even after the end of the employment relationship is a good example of the ambiguity of the norms under Austrian law with regard to employee protection. Such norms are counterproductive, as they often achieve the opposite result aimed at.[39] In practice very often, terminations are agreed in order to transfer the burden of illness to the social security institution. Such agreements are valid, unless there is an agreement

[37] Ibid 497–98.

[38] § 9 par 1 AngG for white-collar employees and § 5 EFZG for blue-collar workers include basically the same regulation.

[39] See on this topic in detail, P Aschauer and E Kohlbacher, 'Einvernehmliche Auflösung im Krankenstand—Deckmantel zur Umgehung sozialversicherungsrechtlicher Beitragspflicht?' in B Karl and K Marko-Herzeg and P Aschauer (eds), *Sozialversicherungsrecht—Jahrbuch 2011* (Wien, NWV Verlag, 2011) 93–101.

of reinstatement. Therefore, these clauses of reinstatement, which have been quite common earlier, are avoided nowadays.

In the case of fixed-term contracts, the continued payment of employees in case of illness ends with the expiry of the fixed-term contract.[40] However, in this case, the employee knows that her/his employment relationship—and consequently all benefits related to it—will end at the date of the expiry of the contract. Furthermore, the continuation of payment also ends in case of open-ended contracts, if the employer has given notice already before the insured event happened. In the latter case, the employer is obliged to continue to pay only until the end of the employment relationship. In order to make use of this rule and avoid the obligation of continuation of payment, the parties often agree on the—at least temporary—termination of the employment relationship. In practice, in case of expected longer illness, the employer and employee have often mutually agreed on the termination of the employment relationship and unsubscribed the employee from the compulsory health insurance. In spite of the elimination of the compulsory insurance, the employee would be entitled to sick pay from the health insurance. The question arose in such cases as to whether the mutually agreed termination constitutes an abuse of law in order to evade the unilaterally cogent labour and social law rules.[41]

The Austrian Administrative Court (Österreichischer Verwaltungsgerichtshof, VwGH) declared that in this case, if the termination of the employment relationship cannot be explained by any other purpose than the evasion of the mentioned statutory obligation, an abuse of law has to be assumed. The crucial point was that the parties have mutually agreed on the termination of the contract and the re-employment after the recovery at the same time. In the specific case, there was only one month between the two acts. As the termination was a bogus act, it was held that it should remain without any legal effect.

Pregnant women having a fixed-term contract enjoy special protection, as § 10a Mutterschutzgesetz (MSchG), Statute on the Protection of Mothers, sets the rule that the expiry of a fixed-term employment contract will be delayed from the date of the notification to the employer of the pregnancy until the beginning of the prohibition of employment (eight weeks before the expected date of childbirth).[42] The goal of this rule is to guarantee that pregnant women are entitled to maternity benefit during the compulsory maternity leave of eight weeks respectively before and after the childbirth. However, the statute also provides an exception.

[40] § 9 par 3 AngG and § 5 EGFZ.

[41] Particularly, VwGH 14.4.2010, 2007/08/0327; See E Kohlbacher, 'Fortbestehen der SV-Beitragspflicht bei einvernehmlicher Auflösung im Krankenstand mit gleichzeitiger Wiedereinstellungszusage' (2011) *Arbeits- und SozialrechtsKartei* 15. P Aschauer and E Kohlbacher, 'Einvernehmliche Auflösung im Krankenstand—Deckmantel zur Umgehung sozialversicherungsrechtlicher Beitragspflicht?' in *Jahrbuch Sozialversicherungsrecht 2011*, B Karl and K Marko-Herzeg and P Aschauer (eds) 93–102 (Wien, Neuer wissenschaftlicher Verlag, 2011).

[42] Marhold and Friedrich, *Österreichisches Arbeitsrecht* 59; B Karl in F Marhold and G Burgstaller and H Preyer, *AngG, Angestelltengesetz—Kommentar*, § 19 mn. 24–34.

If the time limitation is based on a ground objectively justifiable or ordered by statute, the contract will expire by its end date. The statute specifies the objective grounds of justification as follows: the time limitation of the contract serves the interests of the employee; the contract was concluded for the replacement of another employee, who was prevented from performing work; the employment serves an apprenticeship; the employment contract was concluded for the season or on probation, if in the last instance, based on the special qualification of the employee, a longer probationary period is necessary than allowed in the statute or in the collective agreement.

C. Part-Time and Marginal Employees

i. Definition and Social Coverage of Marginal Employment

From the view of the social security coverage of part-time workers, the crucial question is, whether it is lawful to set a limit on income, below which the part-time employed person is not covered by social security. The answer to this question is affirmative, as the CJEU confirmed in its judgment that the exclusion of minor employment—in the contested German case, less than 15 hours' work a week—from compulsory invalidity and old-age insurance does not constitute discrimination on grounds of sex, even if the relevant provisions affect considerably more women than men.[43] The Court accepted that this exclusion can be justified by legitimate social policy aims, particularly that there is a social demand for minor employment and the coverage of such employments by compulsory insurance would only increase the unlawful employment, black market work and evading instruments, such as false self-employment. Furthermore, the judgment also reiterates the argument that contributory schemes, such as the Austrian or German schemes, 'require equivalence to be maintained between the contributions paid by employees and employers and the benefits paid in the event of the materialization of one of the risks covered by the scheme.'[44] The structure of the scheme could not be maintained if the marginal workers had to be covered by compulsory insurance. Serious problems would arise in particular in the statutory old-age insurance scheme. The scheme would no longer be able to function on a contributory basis.

Based on this financial consideration, the marginal feature of an employment in Austria is only linked to the earned income, but not to the working hours. Consequently, casual workers are also considered as being marginal part-time workers, if their income is below the statutory limit. Accordingly, marginal part-time workers (geringfügig Beschäftigte) are those employed persons whose income does not

[43] Case C-317/93 *Nolte v Hannover*[1995] ECLI:EU:C:1995:438 and Case C-444/93 *Megner v Innungskrankenkasse* [1995] ECLI:EU:C:1995:442.

[44] Case C-317/93 *Nolte v Hannover* [1995] ECLI:EU:C:1995:438, par 30.

exceed the monthly amount of €405.98 or the daily limit of €31.17 (in 2015).[45] Marginal workers enjoy only limited social protection, reduced to the occupational accident insurance. Statutory health insurance and public pension scheme do not apply to them. However, they can opt to be in both schemes.[46]

ii. Extension of the Protection

In practice, the regulation of marginal employment could be misused to evade regular employment through the employment of several marginal part-time employees instead of a full-time employee. Therefore, in the ASRÄG 1997, the legislator tried to bring this practice to an end. It changed the law in order to reduce the use of this form of employment and made it less attractive for both the employer and the employee. For this reason, two major amendments have been introduced.

First, it stated that, if the overall remuneration given by the employer to all of his marginal part-time employees exceeds the 1.5-fold of the maximum admissible amount of one marginal employed person, the employer has to pay a lump sum contribution (16,4% of the remuneration) to the health insurance and pension scheme based on the aggregated wages of all of his marginal workers.[47] This obligation was criticised because it obliged the employer to pay an abstract contribution without the simultaneous insurance of the marginal workers.[48] As a result of such contribution, employees can be insured as long as they choose to opt into the social insurance scheme.

Second, if the employee cumulates more marginal part-time jobs and earns in total over the limit of marginal work, a duty has been introduced to be insured for health and pension insurance and the worker is obliged to contribute based on the entire sum of the part-time incomes. In this way, minimum income workers gain full health insurance cover.[49]

Furthermore, the reform introduced the possibility for marginal workers to voluntarily contribute to the health and pension insurance system. This is an

[45] Article 5 (2) ASVG in the context of Verordnung über veränderliche Werte (Regulation on variable values). The gross and net incomes are the same in case of marginal workers, as they do not have to pay social insurance contributions and taxes from their wages.

[46] § 19a ASVG.

[47] E Zehetner, § 5, mn. 26, in Martin Sonntag (ed) *ASVG—Allgemeines Sozialversicherungsgesetz, Jahreskommentar* (Wien, Linde Verlag, 2015).

[48] See Schrammel who is critical of the fact that the employer's obligation to pay the contribution is independent from the insurance of the employee. In these cases, contributions do not lead to parallel entitlements, and so there is no functional connection between contribution and entitlement. Such contributions serve exclusively the funding of other insured persons and this regulation is consequently not a rule of the social security in terms of the distribution of competences. See Schrammel, 'Vom "Werkvertragserkenntnis" zur umfassenden Sozialversicherungspflicht' (n 22) 336. See also in support of this opinion, B Karl, 'Die Einbeziehung geringfügig Beschäftigter in die Sozialversicherung' (1997) *Arbeits- und SozialrechtsKartei* 383, 385.

[49] See B Karl, 'Die Sozialversicherungspflicht geringfügig Beschäftigter nach der 55. ASVG-Novelle' (1998) *Arbeits- und SozialrechtsKartei* 357, 358.

attractive possibility for workers, as they only have to pay EUR 57.30 to get full insurance under both systems, provided they are not entitled to any pension, are not compulsory insured and have their home address in Austria.[50]

iii. Maternity Benefit

Different regulations apply to marginal workers and regular workers regarding their benefit during maternity leave. As marginal workers usually do not have health insurance, they are not entitled to maternity benefit (Wochengeld) usually granted to workers. Subsidiary § 8 par 4 Angestelltengesetz (AngG), Employees Act, can be applied which states that female white-collar employees maintain the right to continued payment of their remuneration for six weeks after childbirth. However, even the application of this rule does not guarantee either the maintenance of a payment or entitlement to an adequate allowance for marginal workers in line with Article 11(2) of Directive 92/85/EEC, as payment is limited to six weeks after childbirth. Consequently, female marginal workers do not have the right either to continued payment of remuneration or maternity benefit during the absolute prohibition of employment before childbirth. In Austria, this period lasts eight weeks before the expected date of childbirth.

However, with the aim of receiving maternity benefit during the period of prohibition of employment, the marginal worker can at any time choose to contribute to the health insurance scheme. By doing so, the worker is entitled to maternity benefit, even if she has only been insured for one month before the prohibition of employment. § 19a par 6 ASVG expressly states that concerning the granting of social security benefits, self-insurance has the same legal effect as compulsory insurance. Bearing in mind this opportunity to opt-in, it would be wrong to say that the regulation of marginal workers regarding maternity benefit and continued payment is in violation of Article 11 of the Directive.[51]

The situation is different after the expiry of the period of absolute prohibition of employment after childbirth (usually eight weeks, but 12 weeks in case of a Caesarean section). If a parent takes parental leave, s/he is entitled to childcare benefit (Kinderbetreuungsgeld) independently of the fact of whether or not s/he has had earlier employment. Usually, the parent who stays home can choose between a lump sum or income-related childcare benefit. In case the person has not had prior employment for at least six months before the childbirth, s/he is only entitled to the lump sum childcare benefit, which varies from €14.53/day to €33/day

[50] M Freudhofmeier and W Höfle, 'Geringfügige Beschäftigungsverhältnisse' in *ASoK-Spezial: Sozialversicherung kompakt 2015*, 51.

[51] See, eg, K Burger-Ehrnhofer, 'Mutterschutz bei geringfügiger Beschäftigung' (2004) *Recht der Wirtschaft* 746; K Burger-Ehrnhofer, *Mutterschutzgesetz und Väter-Karenzgesetz*, § 14 Erl. 307 (Wien, ÖGB Verlag, 2013); M Drs in M Neumayr and P Reissner, ZellKomm, § 8 AngG, mn. 161. Against the compliance with the EU Directive see A Gerhartl, 'Geringfügig entlohnte Beschäftigungen—Arbeits- und sozialversicherungsrechtliche Besonderheiten' (2010) *Arbeits- und SozialrechtsKartei* 394–95.

depending on the length of the parental leave. Starting with 01.03.2017, the four existing models are going to be merged into one "childcare benefit account" which will be provided with a total of €15,499 for each parents couple. At the beginning of the entitlement to childcare benefit, parents may decide for how long the benefit is to be paid out within a period from 12 up to 35 months.[52]

iv. Unemployment Benefit

Marginal workers are not insured against unemployment. An unemployed person is allowed to perform dependent work up to the income limit for marginal workers without losing his unemployed status, so usually unemployed persons can take up marginal employment. The legislator wants to avoid the situation where the employer terminates the employment relationship of her/his employee and immediately after employs her/him as a marginal worker.[53] Therefore, the marginal worker is not considered to be unemployed, if s/he takes up a marginal employment with the same employer, s/he worked for before. However, this rule applies only if between the prior employment and the new marginal work there is less than a one-month period.[54]

v. Marginal Domestic Workers

In 2006, the Government introduced a new, simplified method for domestic workers, who are employed on a marginal basis, the so-called 'household service voucher' (Dienstleistungsscheck). According to the law, persons paid by means of this voucher are qualified as employees in the social security sense (Dienstnehmer) and as such fully insured (health, accident and pension).[55] Private household workers can be paid for their work with this voucher, if the service is marginal part-time and fixed-term up to one month—recurrence is, however, expressly allowed without any limitation. Only simple domestic work may be carried out within the framework of this legal relationship, not activities that require a special qualification like home healthcare.[56] Since the vast majority of household workers are illegally engaged foreign nationals who are explicitly and deliberately excluded from this model, there is a very low demand for the household service cheque. Private household workers are not covered by a collective bargaining agreement, but there are regional minimum wage rates covering them.

[52] Hess-Knapp, 'Das neue pauschale Kinderbetreuungsgeld als Konto und der neue Familienzeitbonus (17. Novelle des KBGG)'(2016) *Das Recht der Arbeit infas—Aktuelle Informationen aus dem Arbeitsrecht und Sozialrecht* 240.

[53] Gerhartl, 'Geringfügig entlohnte Beschäftigungen' (n 52) 398.; Gerhartl, 'Geringfügige Beschäftigung im Arbeitslosenversicherungsrecht' in *Zeitschrift für Arbeits- und Sozialrecht* (2012) 167.

[54] § 12 par 3 lit h Arbeitslosenversicherungsgesetz (Unemployment Insurance Act).

[55] § 4 par 2 sentence 2 ASVG.

[56] E Zehetner, § 4, mn. 71, in M Sonntag (ed) *ASVG—Allgemeines Sozialversicherungsgesetz, Jahreskommentar* (Wien, Linde Verlag, 2015).

vi. *Employment on a Case-by-Case Basis*

The ASVG contains special regulation on employees, who are employed only occasionally, but not permanently.[57] Pursuant to the definition in § 471b ASVG, 'occasionally employed' (fallweise beschäftigte Personen) are those persons, who are employed by the same employer irregularly on a daily basis, provided the employment is agreed for a shorter period than a week.[58] The latter constraint in terms of time limitation should not prevent the parties of an employment contract from concluding a framework contract for a longer period of employment on a case-by-cases basis, although the Austrian Supreme Court in such a case stated that, due to the framework agreement, several daily employments should be regarded as one permanent employment, even if the worker concerned had the opportunity to refuse to work.[59] For the determination of a permanent employment relationship instead of an employment on a case-by-case basis, the decisive criteria are the following: regular working time (eg the same day in a week proves regularity); the working days are determined far in advance; the person cannot refuse to work without sanctions; the employee must be available on certain days.[60]

Occasionally employed persons enjoy full compulsory insurance, if the remuneration for one day exceeds the daily limit set for marginal workers; otherwise, they are only insured by the statutory accident insurance system. The idea is that these persons do not have a permanent employment that would entitle them to social insurance, as they can refuse at anytime the employment without sanctions. Consequently, the missing personal dependency between two assignments usually excludes the existence of a continuous employment. However, it does not exclude the statement of several daily employments which constitute the basis for compulsory insurance coverage.[61]

The notion of occasionally employed person will be eliminated from the legal order from 2017 onward. This may occur due to the application of Directive 1999/70/EC on fixed-term work.

D. Agency Workers

The social security coverage of temporary workers depends upon their status in employment law and entitlement to remuneration. Temporary workers are

[57] M Friedrich, 'Flexibilisierung durch Befristungen und Bedingungen in Vertragsklauseln und Betriebsvereinbarungen' (2011) *Zeitschrift für Arbeits- und Sozialrecht* 109, 112–13.

[58] See Blume § 471b, mn. 1 in M Sonntag (ed) *ASVG—Allgemeines Sozialversicherungsgesetz, Jahreskommentar* (Wien, Linde Verlag, 2015).

[59] OGH 22.12.2004. The CJEU also dealt with the case in Case C-313/02, *Wippel v Peek & Cloppenburg* [2004] ECLI:EU:C:2004:607. See M Friedrich, 'Rahmendienstvertrag und Arbeitszeit—Zugleich eine Entscheidungsbesprechung zu OGH 8 Ob A 116/04y' (2006) *Arbeits- und SozialrechtsKartei* 12.

[60] Freudhofmeier and Höfle, 'Geringfügige Beschäftigungsverhältnisse' (n 50) 64.

[61] A Blume § 471a, mn. 1-4 in M Sonntag (ed) *ASVG—Allgemeines Sozialversicherungsgesetz, Jahreskommentar* (Wien, Linde Verlag, 2015).

regarded as employees in terms of their labour law classification. The temporary work agency is considered to be the employer of the assigned worker and as such the worker is responsible for the payment of social contributions.[62] However, the user undertaking bears statutory joint liability for the payment of the remuneration and social contributions.

Agency workers enjoy equal treatment to a large extent in terms of remuneration, working time and leave during the assignment.[63] Pursuant to § 10 par 1 Arbeitskräfteüberlassungsgesetz (AÜG), Temporary Agency Work Statute, the worker is entitled to a decent remuneration, in line with accepted practice in the field concerned. For the assessment of the adequacy of the remuneration during the assignment, the payment that has to be taken into consideration is the one laid down in a collective agreement or in a statute which apply to comparable workers employed in the user undertaking. In order to comply with the EU Directive on Temporary Agency Work, this rule on comparable workers has to be interpreted in a broad way so as to also include individuals who only work hypothetically in the user undertaking.[64] Following this interpretation of § 10 AÜG, the equal treatment principle applies independently of whether or not the user undertaking has any core workforce. Furthermore, the other compulsory general rules must be applied to comparable workers in the user undertaking such as regulations laid down in works council agreements on remuneration.[65]

Regarding works council agreement, we have to keep in mind that the entitlement to a remuneration based on such an agreement puts an obligation on the user undertaking, whereas the usual obligation to pay a decent, commonly accepted remuneration binds the temporary work agency.[66] Article 5(3) of the EU Directive provides an exception to the rule that other general rules in the enterprise must be taken into account.[67] The internal general rules shall not apply, if the temporary-work agency is under the scope of a valid collective agreement and the user undertaking is bound by a collective agreement, an order or a statute regulating the payment.[68] Companies performing temporary employment are compulsory members of the respective branch association of the Economic Chamber. This association concluded two major collective agreements (one for white-collar and one for blue-collar workers) with the trade unions on the regulation

[62] W Brodil and M Windisch-Graetz, *Sozialrecht in Grundzügen* (Wien, Facultas Verlag, 2013) 47; A Blume § 35, mn. 29, 32 in Sonntag (ed) *ASVG* (n 61).

[63] See in detail, F Schrank, 'Die wichtigsten Neuerungen zur Arbeitskräfteüberlassung (Teil 1 und 2)' *Recht der Wirtschaft* 2013, 31, 84, 87.

[64] M Fuchs and F Marhold, *Europäisches Arbeitsrecht* (Wien, Verlag Österreich, 2014) 162; P Sansone in U Preis and A Sagan (eds) *Europäisches Arbeitsrecht* (Köln, Verlag Dr. Otto Schmidt KG, 2015) 457.

[65] Marhold criticised this possibility: F Marhold, 'Atypische Arbeitskräfteüberlassung?' (2008) *Arbeits- und SozialrechtsKartei* 162, 168.

[66] See generally F Schörghofer, 'Zur Umsetzung der Leiharbeits-RL im AÜG' (2012) *Zeitschrift für Arbeits- und Sozialrecht* 336, 341.

[67] Sansone, *Europäisches Arbeitsrecht* (n 64) 460–61.

[68] See in detail T Rauch, 'Angemessenes Entgelt bei Arbeitskräfteüberlassung' *ecolex* 2013, 676.

of the working conditions of temporary workers, so these agreements may be regarded as crucial for the determination of their remuneration.

E. Distance Work (Homework, Telework, Crowdwork)

i. Homework

The scope and level of labour and social protection for distance workers are not consistent. The main rule applies here as well: the labour law status of the person performing work defines her/his protection.

The work performed at home is regulated in a separate statute, the Statute on Homework (Heimarbeitsgesetz) since 1960. Pursuant to § 2 No 1.a, a homeworker is a person who is not a self-employed individual pursuant to the rules of the Trade Regulation Act (Gewerbeordnung) but produces, works on, processes or packs up goods in her/his own home or in a self-determined place by order and for account of other people. The literature clarified that only those performing work without an employment contract are covered by this specific regulation.[69] This statute applies only to this rather small group of workers, who in fact perform simple manual work on goods. It is conceivable that persons performing very simple work by PC—like typewriting of a text—are also covered by this statute.[70] However, the statute does not apply to those performing work by means of IT tools, such as teleworkers and crowdworkers, because normally these persons render services and do not produce goods. Some argue, therefore, that the statute is in urgent need of reform regarding its personal scope.[71]

According to the settled case law of the Austrian Supreme Court, homeworkers cannot be considered as being employees due to the failure of personal dependency, particularly the personal performance of work.[72] Consequently, they belong to an intermediary category between self-employed and employed persons. It is important to note, that labour law statutes in general do not apply to homeworkers and their protection is adjusted accordingly to their special situation. The Statute on Homework does not guarantee the same labour law protection to homeworkers as to regular employees, but at least the minimum protection (paid annual holiday, minimum wage, continued payment of wages, etc.) is provided. The Statute on Working Time and the Statute on Rest Period expressly exclude homeworkers from their personal scopes, whereas the Statute on Employee Liability explicitly applies to this group.

[69] See especially N Melzer-Azodanloo, *Tele-Arbeitsrecht—der virtuelle Arbeitsplatz: Formen, Bedingungen, Gefahren* (Wien, Linde Verlag, 2001) 57.

[70] ibid 60.

[71] Risak, 'Crowdwork—Erste rechtliche Annäherungen an eine "neue" Arbeitsform' in *Zeitschrift für Arbeits- und Sozialrecht* (2015) 18.

[72] OGH 6.4.1954, Arb 5957; OGH 3.7.1957, Arb 6689. See Marhold and Friedrich, *Österreichisches Arbeitsrecht* (n 7) 37–38.

However, from the view of social security coverage, the homeworkers possess full social security insurance pursuant to § 4 par 1 Nr 7 ASVG.[73]

ii. Telework

The Austrian statutes do not have any definition of telework, but in 1997, the first collective agreement on 'the employment in a workplace outside of the firm combined with new communication technologies' was concluded.[74] Recently, numerous collective agreements contain a definition and short regulation on telework. Teleworkers can perform their activities generally both in an employment and an employee-like relationship, as well as in form of self-employment conditional on the actual circumstances of the performed work. If the teleworker performs work in the frame of an employment relationship—which is usually the case—s/he falls under the personal scope of the labour law statutes and enjoys full social security protection. The so-called freie Dienstnehmer too, who are determined by their economic, but not personal dependency, are fully insured pursuant to § 4 par 4 ASVG.[75]

iii. Crowdwork

The situation is certainly more controversial regarding crowdworkers, as the qualification of their employment is significantly more difficult and this brings about the uncertainty of their status under social law. Crowdwork is the less commonly used form of distance work in Austria, but it has a great potential to get used more extensively. Crowdworkers are usually not personally, but economically dependent either from the crowdsourcing-platform or directly from the crowdsourcer, as they earn their living from it.[76] It is also conceivable, that in specific cases, the work is performed in personal dependency with the result of the qualification of the relationship as employment.[77] However, in my opinion, personal dependency usually cannot be noticed in case of crowdworkers. Basically, the labour law qualification of these workers determines the applicable scope of social security provisions. As the Statute on Homework does not apply to them, they can perform their work either as employee, employee-like person or self-employed with the appropriate labour and social law consequences. There is no special labour or social security regulation on crowdworkers.

[73] Zehetner, § 4 in Sonntag (ed), *ASVG* 114–15.

[74] N Melzer-Azodanloo, 'Erster Kollektivvertrag für Tele-Arbeit' (1997) *Arbeits- und SozialrechtsKartei* 349.

[75] See especially Zehetner, § 4 in Sonntag (ed) *ASVG* (n 61) 140–46.

[76] M Risak, 'Crowdwork' (n 71) 11, 13.

[77] ibid 16.

V. Conclusions

The traditional Austrian social security system based on professions is gradually being abolished and has been primarily replaced by an income-related social security system.[78] Instead of linking the insurance to a profession, the insurance is more and more bound to the income earned. This reflects the change of values regarding the protection of the self-employed persons, whose legal situation has been brought gradually into line with the regulation of employees. Recently, self-employed persons enjoy a comprehensive protection of high level fairly comparable with the one of employees.

The level of social protection of contingent workers depends dominantly on the labour law status of these workers. Austria has followed the clear concept of gradual extension of its social protection system to cover also those performing work in the framework of a non-standard employment. The gaps in the protection in terms of personal scope have been mainly closed in the last couple of decades.

The definition of employee in the Austrian social security law is broadly formulated and is similar to the term used in labour law. The two main conditions of being insured in the social security system are personal and economic dependency. As far as contingent workers fulfil these two criteria, they enjoy full protection. Even if they are regarded as persons belonging to an intermediary category between workers and self-employed persons or self-employed persons, they generally enjoy a profound social protection with only minor gaps.

[78] Tomandl, *Rechtsprobleme einer umfassenden Sozialversicherung* (n 13) 12.

14

The 'Risk Approach' in Occupational Health and Safety (with an Eye to Italy): Alternative or Complement to the 'Core/Contingent Approach'?

EDOARDO ALES

I. Occupational Health and Safety: Some Background Remarks on the Legal Aspects

Lawyers, labour lawyers in particular, do not always feel comfortable with the occupational health and safety (hereinafter OHS) discourse, which tends to be monopolised by the hard and social sciences approach. On the contrary, one has to be aware of the fact that the understanding of the legal framework is crucial in a domain in which (labour) law aims at preventing harmful events deriving from dangers and risks at work by imposing a security obligation on the entrepreneur.[1] In such a perspective, it could be useful to clarify some basic legal notions.

First, the notions of 'danger' in connection with 'risk' shall be separately investigated even though comparative analysis shows[2] that in many European countries they overlap, creating a super-concept of 'risk', which includes the concept of 'danger'.

In order to gain a better understanding it is worth looking at the distinction drawn by the Italian legislator. According to Italian Law, 'danger' has to be regarded as the capacity that a given entity has to cause harm to a worker, whereas 'risk' pinpoints the probability that a harmful event caused by that danger occurs to the worker.[3]

[1] On the use of the concept of entrepreneur instead of that of employer, with reference to the health and safety discourse, see below.

[2] E Ales (ed) *Health and Safety at Work. European and Comparative Perspective* (Alphen aan den Rijn, Kluwer Law International 2013).

[3] E Ales, L Miranda, A Giurini, 'Italy: From Occupational Health and Safety to Well-being at Work' in E Ales (ed) *Health and Safety at Work* (n 2) 195.

Therefore, in theory, any assessment by the entrepreneur should focus, first on danger and, then on risk. In practice, those assessments overlap. Indeed European legislators, including the Italian legislator, when establishing the entrepreneur's duties, focus on the evaluation (assessment) of risk assuming that a risk can be eliminated or reduced to a reasonable level, by means of protection tools, without the need for eliminating the relevant source of danger. From such a perspective, the overlapping of the notions as well as of the assessments of danger and risk is likely to put into question the current conception of safety which emphasises the preventative approach, looking at protection as last resort to be used only exceptionally.

Furthermore, such an overlapping approach to danger and risk, already hardly acceptable in case of physical risks, becomes even more questionable when referred to psychical and psychosocial risks[4] in which the source of danger is represented by a bad work organisation (excessive working time, hardness at work, monotonous and solitary work) or by a human behaviour (moral or sexual harassment).

Indeed, by making reference to the notion of 'health' provided by the World Health Organisation (WHO) as 'a state of complete physical, psychical and social well-being', national legislators and EU law[5] has widened the extent of the safety obligation. From the narrow perspective of the tangible harmful event which produces a physical ill-health to the worker, to a more comprehensive view, in which also psychical and psychosocial damages that can derive from a tangible harmful event or risks of the same kind or originating in the bad organisation of work or in a human misbehaviour, are taken into account.

From such a perspective, case law above all, but also legislators and doctrine have played a decisive role in updating the legal discourse by looking at already existing phenomena in terms of new factors of danger (risk) and of possible sources of harmful events.

This has been the case, for example, of musculoskeletal disorders deriving from an incorrect posture the worker is obliged to adopt during work. Musculoskeletal disorders have been held by case law to be covered by social insurance as occupational diseases or to injury compensation. In the same perspective, Italian case law has recently recognised the right to damages not related to the loss or the reduction of the working and earning capacity (so called danno biologico).[6] Consequently, the Italian legislator has decided to extend the scope of application of social insurance to the psychical and psychosocial consequences of occupational accidents or diseases, thus, going beyond the principle that only the worker whose working and

[4] On the notions of psychical and psychosocial risk see below.

[5] Case C-84/94 *United Kingdom v Council* [1996] ECR I-5793, point 15. See, on it E Ales, 'Occupational Health and Safety: a European and Comparative Legal Perspective', in *WP CSDLE "M. D'Antona".INT* (2015) 120/2015.

[6] AaVv, *Il danno alla persona del lavoratore* (Milano, Giuffré, 2007).

earnings capacity has been reduced or withdrawn can be entitled to social insurance benefits.[7]

As far as non-physical risks are concerned, the most recent health and safety debate has focused on the concept of psychosocial risk. Indeed, what happened with 'risk' as super-concept including the concepts of 'danger' and 'risk', has happened also with 'psychosocial risks' as super-concept which includes the concepts of 'psychophysical risk' and 'psychosocial risk'.[8]

In fact, comparative analysis shows[9] that a distinction is made in legislation and case law, between risks related to the work organisation, which are likely to produce negative consequences on the psychophysical sphere of the worker, and risks related to behaviour coming either from the employer or from other employees. The latter are likely to produce negative consequences on the emotional and relational sphere of the worker.

Therefore, in our view, the first should be defined as 'psychophysical' and the second as 'psychosocial risks'.

Practically speaking, according to this distinction, excessive working time, hardness at work (the French *pénibilité au travail*),[10] monotonous and solitary work and night-work fall within the scope of 'psychophysical risk' whereas moral

[7] E Ales, L Miranda, A Giurini, 'Italy: From Occupational Health and Safety to Well-being at Work', in E Ales (ed) *Health and Safety at Work* (n 2) 195.

[8] According to the 1984 Report of the Joint ILO/WHO Committee on Occupational Health ('Psychosocial factor at work. Recognition and control. Report of the Joint ILO/WHO Committee on Occupational Health Ninth Session Geneva, 18-24 September 1984'): 'The concept of psychosocial factors at work is difficult to grasp, since it represents worker perceptions and experience, and reflects many considerations. Some of these considerations relate to the individual worker, while others relate to the conditions of work and the work environment. Still others refer to social and economic influences, which are outside the workplace but which have repercussions within it ... Fundamental individual factors include the worker's capacities and limitations relative to job demands, and the fulfilment of needs and expectations. Working conditions and the work environment include the task itself, physical conditions at the jobsite, worker/co-worker/supervisor relations, and management practices. Factors external to the workplace but relevant to psychosocial concerns at work include familial or private-life concerns, cultural elements, nutrition, ease of transport, and housing. On psychosocial risks see, at least, GG Balandi and others, *Organisational and Psychosocial Risks in Labour Law. A Comparative Analysis* (2012) I Working Papers Di Olympus no 14/2012, http://ojs.uniurb.it/; S Leka and E Kortum, 'A European framework to address psychosocial hazards' (2008) 50 *J Occ Health* 228; S Leka and T Cox (ed), *The European Framework for Psychosocial Risk Management: PRIMA-EF* (Nottingham, I-WHO Publications 2008); S Leka and others, 'The development of the European Framework for Psychosocial Risk Management: PRIMA-EF' (2011) 53 *J Occ Health* 137; S Leka and others, 'The role of policy for the management of psychosocial risks at the workplace in the European Union' (2011) 49 *Safety Sci* 558; K Lippel, 'Regulation of psychosocial risk factors at work: An international overview' (2011) 49 *Safety Sci* 543.

[9] E Ales, 'Occupational Health and Safety: A Comparative Perspective', E Ales (ed) *Health and Safety at Work* (n 2) 411.

[10] C Sachs-Durand, 'Occupational Health and Safety in France: A Good Formal Protection, but a Problematic Efficiency', in E Ales (ed) *Health and Safety at Work* (n 2) 99.

harassment (called also mobbing in Italy[11] or victimisation in Sweden)[12] or sexual harassment fall within the scope of 'psychosocial risk'.

Indeed, in many countries, the legislature and the judiciary have adopted a very pragmatic approach towards 'psychophysical' and 'psychosocial' risks by regarding as unlawful, often in the name of OHS, certain organisational solutions and certain individual or collective behaviours. As a result, in addition to the penal and administrative sanctions which usually assist legislative provisions, such misconduct constitutes a breach of the safety obligation and as such gives rise to the right to compensation in favour of the affected worker.

Such a pragmatic approach to non-physical risks has also made it possible to get around the unsolved and perhaps unsolvable problem of the recognition of work-related stress as a psychophysical consequence of bad work organisation or of unlawful behaviour. Indeed, since no medical evidence proves yet the link among the work organisation or the behaviour,[13] the unease of the worker and her physical or psychical ill-health stress is mainly regarded (also by the European Social Dialogue)[14] as the product of a subjectively distorted perception of the work organisation or of the behaviour by the worker. In such a controversial perspective, the employer can hardly be held liable for the breach of the safety obligation since the reasons for the worker's ill health lie mainly with the worker.

On the contrary, the fact that already existing phenomena are now regarded as new factors of risk (or sources of danger) has obliged (legislators, above all) to define their very notion in order to make them subject to sanction and/or to compensation.[15]

II. Occupational Health and Safety and EU Law as it Applies to Core and Contingent Workers

Whatever its nature, the super-concept of risk is at the centre stage of OHS EU Law.[16]

[11] R Pellecchia, 'Il *Mobbing*: fattispecie e tutele', in G Natullo (ed) *Salute e sicurezza sul lavoro* (Torino, Utet, 2015) 958.

[12] M Steinberg, 'Occupational Health and Safety in a Diverse, Post-Industrial Society: A Swedish Dilemma', in E Ales (ed) *Health and Safety at Work* (n 2) 281.

[13] Y Curzi, T Fabbri (eds), *Lavoro e salute. Approcci e strumenti per la prevenzione dello stress e la promozione del benessere al lavoro* (Torino, Giappichelli, 2012).

[14] Th Prosser, 'The implementation of the Telework and Work-related Stress Agreements: European social dialogue through 'soft' law?' (2011) 17 *EJIR* 245.

[15] E Ales, 'Occupational Health and Safety' (n 2) 411.

[16] E Ales, 'Occupational Health and Safety' (n 5; B Valdés de la Vega, 'Occupational Health and Safety: A EU Law Perspective', in E Ales (ed) *Health and Safety at Work* (n 2) 1.

In fact, its major instrument, Directive 89/391/EEC (hereinafter, the Framework Directive),[17] when defining employers' obligations, focuses on this concept, providing that risks shall be: (i) avoided; (ii) combated at source (iii); assessed in case they cannot be avoided (the so called risk assessment);[18] mapped in a document,[19] emphasising the existence of particularly sensitive risk groups[20] (see below).

In such a perspective, the employer 'shall develop a coherent overall prevention policy which covers technology, organisation of work, working conditions, social relationships and the influence of factors related to the working environment'.[21]

Furthermore, subsequent to the assessment, the preventive measures and the working and production methods implemented by the employer must: (i) assure an improvement in the level of protection afforded to workers with regard to safety and health; (ii) be integrated into all the activities of the undertaking and/or establishment and at all hierarchical levels.

In the above-mentioned perspective, the employer shall designate one or more workers capable[22] of carrying out activities related to health and safety within the company. Designated workers may not be placed at any disadvantage because of those activities and they shall be allowed adequate time to fulfil their obligations. In case of lack of competent personnel within the company, the employer shall enlist competent external services or persons.[23] By doing that, the employer does

[17] Directive (EC) 89/391 on the introduction of measures to encourage improvements in the safety and health of workers at work [1989] OJ L183/1.

[18] Case C-49/00 *Commission v Italy* [2001] ECR I-08575.

[19] 'By failing to ensure that the obligation to be in possession of an assessment in documentary form of the risks to safety and health at work, as laid down by Council Directive 89/391/EEC..., applies to employers of 10 or fewer workers in all circumstances, the Federal Republic of Germany has failed to fulfil its obligations under Articles 9(1)(a) and 10(3)(a) of that directive': Case C-5/00 *Commission v Germany* [2002] ECR I-01350.

[20] See below.

[21] On the impact of a changing work environment on OHS see Th Koukoulaki, 'New trends in work environment—New effects on safety' (2010) 48 *Safety Sci* 936; G Papadopoulos and others, 'Occupational and public health and safety in a changing work environment: An integrated approach for risk assessment and prevention' (2010) 48 *Safety Sci* 963. See, in such a perspective, the idea of Systematic Health and Safety Management, in particular, K Frick and others (eds), *Systematic Occupational Health and Safety Management. Perspective on an International Development* (Amsterdam, Pergamon 2000); C Gallagher and E Underhill, 'Managing work health and safety: recent developments and future directions' (2012) 50 *APJHR* 227; N Gunningham, 'Integrating Management Systems and Occupational Health and Safety Regulation' (1999) 26 JL & Soc 192; LS Robson and others, 'The effectiveness of occupational health and safety management system interventions: A systematic review' (2007) 45 *Safety Sci* 329; M Zanko and P Dawson, 'Occupational Health and Safety Management in Organizations: A Review' (2012) 14 *IJMR* 328.

[22] It is for the Member State to define the capabilities and aptitudes necessary for the persons or services who are responsible for protection from and prevention of occupational risks in undertakings. The approach consisting of entrusting the employer with the responsibility to determine the capabilities and aptitudes necessary to ensure protection from and prevention of occupational risks, obviously does not satisfy the requirements of the Framework Directive: Case C-49/00 *Commission v Italy* [2001] ECR I-08575.

[23] The Framework Directive lays down an order of precedence between the two alternatives by reference to an objective criterion, namely the existence or absence within the undertaking and/

not discharge itself from its responsibilities in health and safety. In the same way, workers' obligations in this field shall not affect the principle of the responsibility of the employer.

Where the employer entrusts the tasks to a worker, it shall take into consideration the worker's capabilities as regards OHS. Consequently, the employer shall take appropriate steps to ensure that only workers who have received adequate instructions and training (duty/right to train) may have access to areas where there is serious and specific danger/risk. The employer shall ensure that workers from outside undertakings and/or establishments engaged in work in its undertaking and/or establishment have also in fact received appropriate instructions regarding OHS risks during their activities in its undertaking and/or establishment.

From such a perspective, the employer shall take 'appropriate measures' so that workers and/or their representatives within the company receive all the necessary information concerning OHS (duty/right to information). In the same perspective, the employer shall take 'appropriate measures' so that employers of workers from any outside undertakings and/or establishments engaged in work in its undertaking and/or establishment receive the same information.

Moreover, employers shall consult, in advance and in good time, workers and/or their representatives and allow them to take part in discussions on all questions relating to OHS (so called balanced participation).

Workers' representatives with specific responsibility for OHS shall have the right to ask the employer to take 'appropriate measures' and to submit proposals in order to mitigate risks for workers and/or to remove sources of danger. Workers and workers' representatives with specific responsibility for OHS may not be placed at a disadvantage because of their activities.

Employers must allow workers' representatives, with specific responsibility for OHS, adequate time off work, without loss of pay, and provide them with the necessary means to enable such representatives to exercise their rights and functions deriving from the Framework Directive.

Furthermore, workers and/or their representatives are entitled to appeal, in accordance with national law and/or practice, to the authority responsible for OHS if they consider that the measures taken and the means employed by the employer are inadequate for the purposes of ensuring OHS. Workers' representatives must be given the opportunity to submit their observations during inspection visits by the competent authority.

Where several undertakings share a workplace, the employers shall co-operate in implementing the OHS provisions and, taking into account the nature of the activities, shall co-ordinate their actions in matters of protection and prevention of occupational risks, and shall inform one another and their respective workers and/or workers' representatives of these risks.

or establishment of staff possessing the appropriate competence to carry out those activities: Case C-441/01 *Commission v The Netherlands* [2003] ECR I-05463.

Last but not least, particularly sensitive risk groups must be protected against the dangers, which specifically affect them. In the same perspective, individual directives shall be adopted.

In the perspective of core and contingent workers, an interesting question is that of the personal scope of application of the Framework Directive and of OHS EU Law in general, ie the definition of worker and employer.

The Framework Directive provides a very traditional answer to this question, defining worker as 'any person employed by an employer, including trainees and apprentices but excluding domestic servants' and employer as 'any natural or legal person who has an employment relationship with the worker and has responsibility for the undertaking and/or establishment'.[24]

Such definitions seem to restrict the personal scope of application to a direct employer-employee relationship. However, from the statement that the employer bears the responsibility for the undertaking and/or establishment, one may derive that it bears the responsibility for the work environment as a whole, and, therefore, for anyone who performs its activity there.

Such a conclusion is confirmed by the already mentioned assumptions that the employer shall: (i) develop a coherent overall prevention policy, which covers technology, organisation of work, working conditions, social relationships and the influence of factors related to the working environment; (ii) ensure that also workers from outside undertakings and/or establishments engaged in work in its undertaking and/or establishment have in fact received appropriate instructions regarding health and safety risks during their activity in the undertaking and/or establishment; (iii) take appropriate measures so that employers of workers from any outside undertakings and/or establishments engaged in work in its undertaking and/or establishment receive the same information.

Furthermore, where several undertakings share a workplace, ie none of the employers bears the responsibility as owner of that place, all the employers shall: (i) co-operate in implementing the OHS provisions and, taking into account the nature of the activities; (ii) co-ordinate their actions in matters of protection and prevention of occupational risks; and, (iii) inform one another and their respective workers and/or workers' representatives of these risks.

On top of that, comparative analysis[25] shows that, even though still referring to it formally, national legislators have gone beyond the notion of 'employer' in order to indicate who is bound by the OHS legislation. In Italy, for instance, 'worker' has to be understood as the 'person who, independently of the type of contract, carries out a remunerated or unremunerated working activity within a public or private employer's organisation, even for the sole purpose of learning a trade, art or profession, excluding domestic workers and family members' (see art 2(1)(a) Legislative decree n 81 of 2008).

[24] Article 3 par. 1(a) Directive (EC) 89/391 on the introduction of measures to encourage improvements in the safety and health of workers at work [1989] OJ L183/1.

[25] E Ales, 'Occupational Health and Safety' (n 2) 411.

Thus, an all-inclusive concept of 'worker' is embraced by the Italian legislator. This not only covers employed workers (regardless of the various types of contract) but also workers that, albeit not employed by the employer, are nevertheless subject to its managerial authority (agency workers). It also covers those workers who have drawn up a contract for services with an employer, provided (obviously) that the service that is the object of such contract potentially (insofar as its provision is within the employer's organisation) exposes them to health and safety risks deriving from the activity pursued by the employer.

In such a broader perspective, one may say that anyone who organises a productive activity and/or exercises managerial prerogatives falls under the scope of the OHS legislation in the sense that they will be held responsible for the application of the prescribed preventive and protective measures within the general framework of the safety obligation.

As already stated elsewhere,[26] practically speaking, this means: (a) arrangement of a healthy and safe work environment for anyone who works within the employer's premises even outside a traditional employment relationship (like temporary workers, self-employed, students in laboratories, interns, inmates, volunteers); (b) control of the respect of the OHS regulations by anyone who works within the employer's premises even outside a traditional employment relationship; (c) control of the application of the OHS legislation by contractors and subcontractors, being them companies or self-employed workers; (d) assessment and co-ordination of the prevention of risk of interference deriving from the simultaneous presence in the same site of various contractors and subcontractors performing different activities. Therefore, all workers, self-employed and contingent included, are covered by OHS regulations.

The expression 'anyone who organises a productive activity and/or exercises the managerial prerogatives' seems to be very much closer to that one of 'entrepreneur', thus covering all kinds of employers. The same can be said with reference to the expression 'anyone who works within the premises of somebody who organises a productive activity even outside a traditional employment relationship', which seems to be very much closer to 'worker' in a broad sense than to 'worker' as 'employee'. For sure, 'entrepreneur' and 'worker' are more far-reaching than 'employer' and 'employee', at least in the domain of OHS law that is consequently covering all core and contingent workers and those who may be held responsible for risks to them in the context of their work.

The reference to 'anyone who organises a productive activity and/or exercises the managerial prerogatives' explains also the fact that in addition to the entrepreneur, being it a legal or natural person, which has the ultimate responsibility for health and safety, the so-called hierarchical structure[27] can also be bound by and held liable for the application of health and safety legislation.

[26] ibid.

[27] F Dorssemont, K Naert and A Van Regenmortel, 'Well-Being at Work in Belgium: A Matter of Co-operation', E Ales (ed) *Health and Safety at Work* (n 2). *European and Comparative Perspective* (Alphen aan den Rijn, Kluwer Law International, 2013) 67.

To conclude on this point, one may argue that the concept of risk, together with that of organisation, finds itself at the centre stage of the OHS discourse at EU and comparative level, above all, when it comes to deciding who bears the responsibility for the safety obligation towards the worker. In view of the dichotomisation of the workforce—the phenomenon that the core/contingent worker theory tries to explain—the concept of risk is thus likely to offer an alternative interpretative path, inclusive and protective of all workers regardless of the core or contingent distinction that may apply in national labour law systems.

Truth be told, EU law goes even further, emphasising the presence of particularly sensitive risk groups whose members shall be distinguished from the rest of the workforce as far as the content of prevention and protection measures is concerned. Therefore, from the risk perspective, there is no contingent workforce but only a core one. To this, the part of the workforce that belongs to a particularly sensitive risk group and needs to be protected in a special way shall be added.

Furthermore, from the fact that more than one employer may operate within the same workplace without being uniquely responsible for it, derives a specific work environment, without core workers, one may say, in which the so-called interference risk shall be added to the risks usually connected to each activity. In the overall risk perspective, workers operating in such work environment shall enjoy the 'standard' prevention and protection measures as well as specific measures aimed at coping with that interference risk.

Both subjects, 'particularly sensitive risk groups' and 'interference risk', require a closer examination from the core/contingent perspective.

III. The 'Particularly Sensitive Risk Group' Approach

As already mentioned above, according to the Framework Directive (Article 15), particularly sensitive risk groups must be protected against the risks which specifically affect them. In the same perspective, individual directives shall be adopted (Article 16(1)). From the early 1990s, the European Community adopted several directives, also under the form of Individual Directives, with the view to introducing or supplementing the measures to encourage improvements in OHS of particularly sensitive risk groups. In this way, the legislator has indirectly defined those groups and the personal conditions on the ground of which they are meant to be exposed to risks that specifically affect them.

Stretching the Spanish definition that restricts itself to 'any worker whose personal characteristics lead to a condition or physical, mental or sensory impairment, which makes it particularly vulnerable to occupational hazards',[28]

[28] J Aparicio Tovar, 'Occupational Health and Safety in Spain: A Formidable Array of Employers' Liabilities', E Ales (ed) *Health and Safety at Work* (n 2) 249.

persons belonging to such risk groups may be defined as 'specially sensitive workers'.

According to EU Law, they are: (i) workers with a fixed-duration employment relationship or a temporary employment relationship; (ii) pregnant workers and workers who have recently given birth or are breastfeeding; (iii) young people at work; (iv) workers working at temporary or mobile constructions sites.

To those ones, may be added people with disability, defined by the CJEU as 'a limitation which results in particular forms of physical, mental or psychological impairments which in interaction with various barriers may hinder the full and effective participation of the person concerned in professional life on an equal basis with other workers'.[29] In fact, according to Article 5 of Directive 2000/78/EC,[30] 'employers shall take appropriate measures, where needed in a particular case, to enable a person with a disability to have access to, participate in, or advance in employment, or to undergo training, unless such measures would impose a disproportionate burden on the employer'. There is no reason to think that appropriate measures shall not be also referred to OHS.[31] On the other hand, the 'disproportionate burden' approach closely echoes the 'reasonably practicable' one, admitted by the same CJEU[32] as factors limiting the employer's security obligation.

A. Fixed-Term and Temporary Employment Relationships

From the core/contingent perspective, a crucial piece of legislation within EU OHS Law is Directive 91/383/EEC.[33] According to its Preamble,

> 'the specific situation of workers with a fixed-duration employment relationship [fixed-term workers] or a temporary employment relationship [agency workers] and the special nature of the risks they face in certain sectors calls for special additional rules, particularly as regards the provision of information, the training and the medical surveillance of the workers concerned'.[34]

[29] Cases C-335/11 and C-337/11, *HK Denmark*, CJEU, 11 April 2013.

[30] Council Directive 2000/78/EC of 27 November 2000 establishing a general framework for equal treatment in employment and occupation, [2000] OJ L303/16.

[31] E Ales, 'Diritti sociali e discrezionalità del legislatore nell'ordinamento multilivello: una prospettazione giuslavoristica' *Giornale di Diritto del Lavoro e delle Relazioni Industriali*, 147, 2015, 3, 468.

[32] Case C-127/05 *Commission v United Kingdom* [2007] ECR I-4619. Nevertheless, some Member States are more inclined to employers' quasi-objective responsibility: see E Ales, 'Occupational Health and Safety' (n 2).

[33] Council Directive (EC) 91/383 supplementing the measures to encourage improvements in the safety and health at work of workers with a fixed-duration employment relationship or a temporary employment relationship [1991] OJ L206/19.

[34] Generally speaking, objective features of the work relationship are taken into account while shaping the OHS legal system, whether they be termed atypical/contingent/precarious/casual: see B Barrett and M Sargeant, 'Health and Safety Issues in New Forms of Employment and Work Organization' (2008) 24 *IJCCLIR* 263; M Quinlan, C Mayhew and Ph Bohle, 'The global expansion of precarious employment, work disorganization, and consequences for occupational health: a review of recent

Although the Directive does not explicitly refer to Article 15 of the Framework Directive, it is clear that those workers are regarded as a risk group within the meaning of that article.

Furthermore, even though Directive 91/383/EEC cannot technically be seen as an Individual Directive within the meaning of Article 16(1) of the Framework Directive, the latter remains applicable to the specific sector covered by the former, without prejudice to more stringent and/or specific provisions contained within it. In such a perspective, Directive 91/383/EEC supplements the Framework Directive.

Directive 91/383/EEC applies to fixed-term[35] and temporary agency workers,[36] ie workers who, at least according to the EU legislator, do not belong to the core workforce being rather contingent to the undertaking, therefore needing to be made specifically acquainted with the environment in which they are going to operate. However, the existence of employment relationships of those kinds shall not justify different treatment of those workers with respect to working conditions inasmuch as OHS is concerned, especially as regards access to personal protective equipment.

Before a worker with an employment relationship of those kinds takes up any activity, she shall be informed (and trained) by her employer (if fixed-term) or by the user undertaking (if temporary agency worker) about the risks she faces. Such information covers, in particular, any special occupational qualifications or skills or special medical surveillance required and states clearly any increased specific risks that the job may entail. Workers or external services or persons designated to take care of OHS within the undertaking shall be informed of the assignment of workers with an employment relationship of those kinds to the extent necessary for them to be able to carry out adequately their protection and prevention activities for all the workers in the undertaking.

Without prejudice to the responsibility of the temporary work agency as laid down in national legislation, the user undertaking is responsible, for the duration of the assignment, for OHS of agency workers, thus confirming the conclusion we have already reached in the above concerning the all-inclusive definition of employer (entrepreneur) and employee (worker) within EU OHS Law.

research' (2001) 31 *Int J of H&S* 335; M Virtanen and others, 'Temporary employment and health: a review' (2005) 34 *Int J of Epid* 610; V Howes, 'Who Is Responsible for Health and Safety of Temporary Workers? EU and UK Perspectives' (2011) 2 *ELLJ* 379. As to the effect of job insecurity/precarious employment on health, see I-H Kim, 'Welfare states, flexible employment, and health: A critical review' (2012) 104 *Health Policy* 99.

[35] See now also Directive (EC) 2008/104 on temporary agency work [2008] OJ L327/9; see B Nyström, '2008/104/EC: Temporary Agency Work' in M Schlachter (ed), *EU Labour Law. A Commentary* (Alphen aan den Rijn, Kluwer Law International 2015).

[36] See now also Directive (EC) 1999/70 concerning the framework agreement on fixed-term work concluded by ETUC, UNICE and CEEP, [1999] OJ L175/43; see M Schlachter, '1999/70/EC: Fixed Term Contract' in M Schlachter (ed), *EU Labour Law. A Commentary* (Alphen aan den Rijn, Kluwer Law International 2015).

It is rather clear that 'the special nature of the risks they face', which moves the EU Legislator to regard fixed-term and agency workers as belonging to a particularly sensitive risk group, consists in their being contingent to the company. Their contingent status, therefore, 'calls for special additional rules', aimed at safeguarding them from being putting at a greater risk because of their being contingent.

B. Pregnant Workers and Workers who have Recently given Birth or are Breastfeeding

Pregnant workers and workers who have recently given birth or are breastfeeding are protected by Directive 92/85/EEC,[37] which, in general, is strictly intertwined with EU anti-discrimination law, mainly but not exclusively, on the ground of sex.

The link is of course self-evident but it has been strengthened by the fact that the delay in introducing EU legislation on maternity pushed the CJEU to elaborate a protection of pregnant women referring to the anti-discrimination directives, relying, above all, on the fact that pregnancy is an event which occurs only to women.[38]

Directive 92/85/EEC was adopted as a health and safety measure based on Article 15 of the Framework Directive, since pregnant workers, workers who have recently given birth or who are breastfeeding must be looked at as a specific risk group in many respects, and measures must be taken with regard to their OHS, avoiding however, to treat women on the labour market unfavourably or to work to the detriment of EU anti-discrimination law.

For the purpose of the Directive, pregnant workers, workers who have recently given birth or who are breastfeeding are regarded as those who have informed their employer about their status,[39] and who provide services to the company as an integral part of it, if their activity is carried out: (i) for a certain period of time;

[37] Council Directive (EC) 92/85 on the introduction of measures to encourage improvements in the safety and health at work of pregnant workers and workers who have recently given birth or are breastfeeding (tenth individual Directive within the meaning of Article 16(1) of Directive 89/391/EEC) [1992] OJ L348/1; see E Kovács and Ch Hießl, '92/85/EEC: Maternity Protection' in M Schlachter (ed), *EU Labour Law. A Commentary* (Kluwer Law International 2015).

[38] Directive 76/207/EEC on the implementation of the principle of equal treatment for men and women as regards access to employment, vocational training and promotion, and working conditions, as amended by Directive 2002/73/EC and consolidated by Directive 2006/54/EC; see C Barnard, *European Employment Law* (4th edn, OUP 2013) 253 ff.

[39] However, 'Article 2(1) of Council Directive 76/207/EEC is to be interpreted as precluding a requirement that an employee who, with the consent of her employer, wishes to return to work before the end of her parental leave must inform her employer that she is pregnant in the event that, because of certain legislative prohibitions, she will be unable to carry out all of her duties': Case C-320/01 *Busch* [2003] ECR I-2041 and Case C-421/92 *Habermann-Beltermann* [1994] ECR I-01657, the latter with reference to night work. Moreover, 'Article 2(1) of Directive 76/207/EEC is to be interpreted as precluding an employer from contesting under national law the consent it gave to the reinstatement of an employee to return before the end of her parental leave on the grounds that it was in error as to her being pregnant': Case C-320/01 *Busch* [2003] ECR I-2041.

(ii) under the direction or supervision of another body of that company; (iii) against a remuneration.[40]

For all activities liable to involve a specific risk of exposure to the agents, processes or working conditions of which a non-exhaustive list is given in the Annexes of the Directive, the employer shall assess the nature, degree and duration of exposure of workers belonging to the above mentioned risk group and decide what measures should be taken.

As a first and foremost prevention measure, the employer shall take the necessary measures to ensure that, by temporarily adjusting the working conditions and/or the working hours of the worker concerned, the exposure of that worker to the above mentioned risks is avoided. If the adjustment of her working conditions and/or working hours is not technically and/or objectively feasible or cannot reasonably be required on duly substantiated grounds, the employer shall take the necessary measures to move the worker concerned to another job.[41] If moving her to another job is not technically and/or objectively feasible or cannot reasonably be required on duly substantiated grounds, the worker concerned shall be granted leave in accordance with national legislation and/or national practice for the whole of the period necessary to protect her OHS.[42]

Secondly, Member States shall take the necessary measures (such as day work or leave from work or extension of maternity leave) to ensure that, subject to submission of a medical certificate stating that this is necessary for their OHS, workers belonging to the above mentioned risk group are not obliged to perform night work during their pregnancy and for a period following childbirth to be determined by the national authority competent for OHS.

Thirdly, Member States shall ensure that workers belonging to the above mentioned risk group are entitled to a continuous period of maternity leave of a least 14 weeks allocated before and/or after confinement, including a compulsory maternity leave of at least two weeks allocated before and/or after confinement in accordance with national legislation and/or practice.[43]

[40] Case C-232/09 *Danosa* [2010] ECR I-11405.

[41] 'A pregnant worker who … has been temporarily transferred on account of her pregnancy to a job in which she performs tasks other than those she performed prior to that transfer is not entitled to the pay she received on average prior to that transfer. In addition to the maintenance of her basic salary, such a worker is entitled … to pay components or supplementary allowances relating to her professional status, such as allowances relating to her seniority, her length of service and her professional qualifications': Case C-471/08 *Parviainen* [2010] ECR I-06533.

[42] 'It is contrary to Council Directive 76/207/EEC and to Council Directive 92/85/EEC for national legislation to provide that an employer may send home a woman who is pregnant, although not unfit for work, without paying her salary in full when he considers that he cannot provide work for her': Case C-66/96 *Høj Pedersen* [1998] ECR I-07327.

[43] But not 'a female worker who as a commissioning mother has had a baby through a surrogacy arrangement, even in circumstances where she may breastfeed the baby following the birth or where she does breastfeed the baby'. Furthermore, an employer's refusal to provide maternity leave to a commissioning mother who has had a baby through a surrogacy arrangement does not constitute discrimination on grounds of sex: Case C-167/12 *C D* [2014] not yet reported. The same applies to the 'refusal to provide paid leave equivalent to maternity leave'. Nor that refusal constitutes discrimination on the ground of disability because the CJEU does not regard as disabled 'a women who is unable to bear a child and who has availed of a surrogacy arrangement': Case C-363/12 *Z* [2014] not yet reported.

Employment rights, including the maintenance of a payment and/or entitlement to an allowance that guarantees an income at least equivalent to that which the worker concerned would receive in the event of a break in her activities on grounds connected with their state of health, must be ensured in accordance with national legislation and/or national practice.

Member States may make entitlement to pay or the allowance conditional upon the worker concerned fulfilling conditions of eligibility, which may provide, under no circumstances, for periods of previous employment exceeding 12 months immediately prior to the presumed date of confinement.

Last but not least, Member States[44] shall prohibit[45] the dismissal of workers during the period from the beginning of their pregnancy[46] to the end of the maternity leave, save in exceptional cases based on substantiated grounds which: (i) the employer shall duly cite in writing; (ii) are not connected with their condition; (iii) are explicitly permitted under national legislation and/or practice, provided that, if any, the competent authority has given its consent.[47]

Therefore, the belonging to a particularly sensitive risk group gives rise to a highly protected legal regime, in between anti-discrimination and OHS Law, protecting those workers from being pushed to the periphery of the company or even outside it because of their status.

C. Young People at Work

Crucial as well for the 'risk approach' is Directive 94/33/EC[48] dealing with the very sensitive issue of children's, adolescents' and generally speaking, young people's physical, psychical and psychosocial well-being at work, taking also into account their cultural development.

[44] It has to be stressed, that even in the absence of transposition measures taken by a Member State within the period prescribed, the Directive 'confers on individuals rights on which they may rely before a national court against the authorities of that State': Case C-438/99 *Jiménez Melgar* [2001] ECR I-6915.

[45] That prohibition refers not only to the notification of a decision to dismiss on the grounds of pregnancy and/or of the birth of a child during the period of protection but also to the taking of preparatory steps for such a decision before the end of that period: Case C-460/06 *Paquay* [2007] ECR I-08511.

[46] The prohibition of dismissal of pregnant workers does not extend to a female worker who is undergoing in vitro fertilisation treatment where, on the date she is given notice of her dismissal, her ova have already been fertilised by her partner's sperm cells, so that in vitro fertilised ova exist, but they have not yet been transferred into her uterus. On the contrary, 'Articles 2(1) and 5(1) of Council Directive 76/207/EEC preclude the dismissal of a female worker who is at an advanced stage of in vitro fertilisation treatment, that is, between the follicular puncture and the immediate transfer of the in vitro fertilised ova into her uterus, inasmuch as it is established that the dismissal is essentially based on the fact that the woman has undergone such treatment': Case C-506/06 *Mayr* [2008] ECR I-01017.

[47] Directive 92/85 is not to be interpreted as imposing on Member States any obligation to have a national authority giving its consent prior to the employer's decision to dismiss the worker: Case C-438/99 *Jiménez Melgar* [2001] ECR I-6915.

[48] Directive (EC) 94/33 on the protection of young people at work [1994] OJ L216/12; see P Končar, '94/33/EC: Protection of Young People at Work' in M Schlachter (ed), *EU Labour Law. A Commentary* (Alphen aan den Rijn, Kluwer Law International 2015).

Directive 94/33/EC applies, in general, to young people, meaning any person under 18 years of age having an employment contract or an employment relationship as defined by each Member State. However, it pays particular attention to children, meaning any young person of less than 15 years of age or who is still subject to compulsory full-time schooling under national law, and to adolescents, meaning any young person of at least 15 years of age but less than 18 years of age who is no longer subject to compulsory full-time schooling under national law.[49] In fact, children and adolescents are both regarded as specific risk groups within the meaning of Article 15 of the Framework Directive.[50]

First, Member States shall prohibit work by children. However, they may make legislative or regulatory provision for the prohibition of work by children not applicable to: (i) children performing in cultural or similar activities; (ii) children of at least 14 years of age working under a combined work/training scheme or an in-plant work-experience scheme, provided that such work is done in accordance with the conditions laid down by the competent authority; (iii) children of at least 14 years of age performing light work other than that performed in cultural or similar activities.[51]

Secondly, the employer shall adopt the measures necessary to protect OHS of young people, taking particular account of the specific risks to their safety, health and development, which are a consequence of their lack of experience, of the absence of awareness of existing or potential risks or of the fact that they have not yet fully matured. Consequently, risk assessment shall be provided paying particular attention to: (i) the fitting-out and layout of the workplace and the workstation; (ii) the arrangement of work processes and operations and the way in which these are combined (organisation of work); (iii) the level of training and instruction given to young people.

Finally, yet importantly, specific provisions apply to children, adolescents and young persons in general, as far as working time, night work, rest periods and breaks are concerned.

Once again, the belonging to a particularly sensitive risk group gives rise to a highly protected legal regime, with specific reference to OHS in its broadest meaning, with the aim of guaranteeing them a specific protection, preventing

[49] On the action of ILO against child labour, see G Nesi, L Nogler and M Pertile (eds), *Child Labour in a Globalised World. A legal Analysis of ILO Action* (Farnham, Ashgate, 2008).

[50] Empirical evidence, even though referring to workers up to 25 years, in S Salminen, 'Have young workers more injuries than older ones? An international literature review' (2004) 35 *J Safety Research* 513.

[51] Light work means all work which, on account of the inherent nature of the tasks which it involves and the particular conditions under which it is performed: (i) is not likely to be harmful to the safety, health or development of children; and, (ii) is not such as to be harmful to their attendance at school, their participation in vocational guidance or training programmes approved by the competent authority or their capacity to benefit from the instruction received. However, light work other than that in cultural or similar activities may be performed by children of 13 years of age for a limited number of hours per week in the case of categories of work determined by national legislation.

them from being pushed out to the periphery of the company because of their lack of experience.

IV. The Interference Risk and the Temporary and Mobile Construction Sites Directive

Directive 92/57/EEC[52] refers to any construction site at which building or civil engineering works are carried out, usually by more than one contractor, thus requiring specific protection measures in view of protecting workers from the above mentioned interference risk.

As a first and foremost protection measure, the client, meaning any natural or legal person for whom a project is carried out, or the project supervisor, meaning any natural or legal person responsible for the design and/or execution and/or supervision of the execution of a project, acting on behalf of the client, shall[53] appoint an OHS co-ordinator at the project preparation's stage and an OHS co-ordinator at the project execution stage, for any construction site on which more than one contractor is present.[54] The appointment of the OHS co-ordinators does not relieve the client or project supervisor of her responsibilities as far as the tasks of the co-ordinators are concerned.

As a second prevention measure, the client or the project supervisor shall ensure that prior to the setting up of a construction site, an OHS plan is drawn up, defining the rules applicable to the construction site concerned, taking into account, where necessary, the industrial activities performed on the site and including specific measures concerning work involving particular risks for OHS (Annex II of the Directive).

Furthermore, in the case of constructions sites: (i) on which work is scheduled to last longer than 30 working days and on which more than 20 workers are occupied simultaneously; or, (ii) on which the volume of work is scheduled to exceed 500 person-days, the client or the project supervisor shall communicate a prior notice to the competent authorities before work starts.

When the work is being carried out, the employers operating within the site, under co-ordination and supervision of the OHS co-ordinator at the project

[52] Council Directive (EC) 92/57 on the implementation of minimum safety and health requirements at temporary or mobile construction sites (eighth individual Directive within the meaning of Article 16(1) of Directive 89/391/EEC) [1992] OJ L245/6.

[53] Article 3(1) of Directive 92/57 precludes national legislation under which, for private works not subject to planning permission on a construction site, on which more than one contractor is to be present, it is possible to derogate from that requirement: Case C-224/09 *Commission v Italy* [2010] ECR I-09295.

[54] On the crucial issue of sub-contracting, see Phil James and others, 'Regulating Supply Chains to Improve Health and Safety' (2007) 36 *ILJ* 163; D Walters and Ph James, 'What motivates employers to establish preventive management arrangements within supply chains?' (2011) 49 *Safety Sci* 988.

execution stage, are, among and above all the others, to our mind, responsible for taking into account the interaction with industrial activities at the place within which or in the vicinity of which the construction site is located, ie the so called interference risks.

In the same perspective, consultation and participation of workers and/or of their representatives shall take place ensuring, whenever necessary, proper co-ordination between workers and/or workers' representatives in undertakings carrying out their activities at the workplace, having regard to the degree of risk and the size of the work site.

The presence in the same place of more than one contractor gives rise to a specific regulation aimed at making sure that the existence of a specific work environment, without core workers, will make them all contingent in the sense that they will be exposed to interference risks nobody can control.

V. Italy and the 'Particularly Sensitive Risk Group' Approach

An imposing body of legislation characterises the regulation of OHS in Italy. Initially meant to realise certain constitutional precepts,[55] this then formed the fulcrum for implementing the EU Law.

Recently, the adoption of Legislative Decree No 81/2008 has drastically modified the national law by pursuing the reorganisation and consolidation of the general and sectoral legislation on the subject.[56]

A first important feature of the current national legislation is its application, in line with EU Law, to all sectors of activity, whether private or public, and to all types of risk. This has led to a new formulation of the risk-assessment provisions.[57] In fact, by regulating risk-assessment in Article 28 of Legislative Decree No 81/2008, the legislator not only expressly refers to technical risks deriving from production processes but also widens the employer's duty by referring to all the risks to workers' health and safety. These include, by way of example, those linked

[55] See G Natullo, *Latutela dell'ambiente di lavoro* (Torino,Utet 1995); L Galantino (ed), *La sicurezza del lavoro* (Milano, Giuffrè, 1996); L Montuschi (ed), *Ambiente, salute e sicurezza,* (Torino, Giappichelli, 1998); M Rusciano and G Natullo (eds), *Ambiente e sicurezza del lavoro*, (Torino, Utet, 2007); P Albi, *Adempimento dell'obbligo di sicurezza e tutela della persona. Art. 2087 c.c.* (Milano, Giuffré, 2008).

[56] M Tiraboschi (ed), *Il testo unico della salute e sicurezza nei luoghi di lavoro. Commentario al decreto legislativo 9 aprile 2008, n. 81* (Milano, Giuffrè, 2008); L Zoppoli, P Pascucci & G Natullo (eds), *Le nuove regole per lasalute e lasicurezza dei lavoratori, Commentario al Dlgs 9 Aprile 2008, n 81* (Milano, Ipsoa-Wolter Kluwer, 2008); L Montuschi (ed), *La nuova sicurezza sul lavoro. D.lgs. 9 Aprile 2008, n 81 e successive modifiche* (Bologna, Zanichelli 2011); M Persiani (ed), *Il nuovo diritto della sicurezza sul lavoro* (Torino, Utet, 2012); G Natullo (ed), *Salute e sicurezza sul lavoro* (Torino, Utet, 2015).

[57] G M Monda, 'La valutazione dei rischi per lasicurezza e lasalute dei lavoratori' in L Zoppoli, P Pascucci & G Natullo (eds), *Le nuove regole per lasalute e lasicurezza dei lavoratori* (Milano, Ipsoa-Wolter Kluwer, 2008) 336.

to work-related stress, those regarding pregnant workers (in accordance with the provisions of Legislative Decree No 151/2001) and those linked to gender differences, age and provenance from other countries.

A second important feature of Legislative Decree No 81/2008 is the lack of importance attached to the size of a business. This aspect is closely linked to the legislation's applicability to all types of activity and all risks, as well as the innovative all-inclusive concept of 'worker'.[58]

Indeed, even in the only case in which the size of a business becomes important, the innovative concept of 'worker' has a decisive influence on the application of the related law. This occurs by virtue of Article 47(3), (4) and (7) of Legislative Decree No 81/2008. In specifying the threshold of 15 workers (which constitutes the dividing line between the election or designation of representatives from among a business's trade union representatives on the one hand and their direct election from among the workers, on the other), these no longer use the concept of 'employee' but, rather, that of 'worker'.

Thus, an all-inclusive concept of 'worker' is also embraced for the purposes of applying the provisions on the participation and consultation of workers' representatives. This has the effect that, at least at the formal level and, in the absence of any other legislative specification, representation includes parties not typically covered at the collective/trade union level.

The general applicability of Legislative Decree No 81/2008 does not exclude further legislation governing a 'specially sensitive group risk', such as pregnant workers and workers who have recently given birth or are breastfeeding, in relation to whom specific regulations apply. These are currently contained in Chapter II of Legislative Decree No151/2001, which implemented Directive 92/85/EC.[59]

More specifically and in compliance with Directive 92/85/EC, Legislative DecreeNo151/2001 requires employers to carry out a specific risk-assessment for pregnant workers and for workers who have recently given birth or are breastfeeding. It further expressly identifies the measures that employers must adopt in order to avoid the related risks.

In the first place, employers must temporarily alter such workers' working conditions or working time (Article 12(1)). Should that prove impossible for organisational reasons or reasons linked to production, they must assign them different work duties.

An analysis of the Italian legislation clearly reveals the complementary relationship between Legislative Decree No 151/2001 (Maternity, paternity and parental leaves) and Legislative Decree No 81/2008 (OHS).[60] The close continuity between

[58] P Pascucci, 'Il campo di applicazione soggettivo delle nuove regole sulla salute e sicurezza nei luoghi di lavoro', *Diritti lavori mercati* (2008) no 2, 297.

[59] See F Adinolfi and R Bortone, 'Commento alla direttiva europea sulla tutela della maternità' *Giornale di diritto del lavoro e di relazioni industriali* (1994) no 1 373; M Lai, 'Tutela della maternità nella legislazione europea' *Diritto e pratica del lavoro*,(1993) no 2, 77.

[60] L Calafà, 'Le lavoratrici madri', in M Rusciano & G Natullo (eds), *Ambiente e sicurezza del lavoro* (Torino, Utet, 2007) 394.

them is evidenced by a series of references that Legislative Decree No 151/2001 makes to Legislative Decree No 626/94,[61] primarily regarding risk-assessment and workers' right to information. This provision not only expresses the complementary relationship between Legislative Decree No 151/2001 and Legislative Decree No 81/2008 but also indicates the special nature of the law contained in the former vis-a-vis the general health and safety legislation.

Another important feature of the Italian legislation is the use it makes of wholly distinctive concepts of 'worker', 'employer' and 'commissioning entity'. Such use ensures that the prevention duties and the protection afforded to parties extend beyond the confines of the contractual relationship.

To such end, as we have already seen in the above, the concept of 'worker' contained in Article 2(1)(a) has a preliminary importance. For the intents and purposes of Legislative Decree No 81/2008, 'worker' is to be understood as the 'person who, independently of the type of contract, carries out a remunerated or unremunerated working activity within a public or private employer's organisation, even for the sole purpose of learning a trade, art or profession, excluding domestic workers and family members'.

The all-inclusive concept of 'worker' embraced by the Italian legislator not only covers employees (regardless of the various types of contract)[62] but also workers that, albeit not employed by the employer, are nevertheless subject to the employer's managerial authority (agency workers).[63] It also covers those workers who have drawn up a contract for services with an employer, provided (obviously) that the service that is the object of such contract potentially (insofar as its provision is within the employer's organisation) exposes them to OHS risks deriving from the activity pursued by the employer.[64]

As regards the self-employed, however, the said extended application is important in relation to certain specific duties. These include the duty to procure individual preventive and protective equipment personally and use it within the business organisation, over and above the general duty to equip themselves with personal identity cards.

[61] Subsequently absorbed by Legislative Decree No 81/2008.

[62] There included fixed-term workers and job on-call workers, although for the former no specific provision is laid down as far as OHS is concerned, whereas for the latter the safety measures adopted in relation to the activity that they will perform shall be indicated in written within their hiring contract (art 15 Legislative Decree n 81 of 2015). Actually, as for the former, art 20, par 1 lett d) provides that employers who have not carried out the risk-assessment cannot hire fixed-term workers. If they do so, the fixed-term employment relationship is transformed into an open-ended one.

[63] According to art 35 par 4 Legislative Decree n 81 of 2015, the Temporary Work Agency shall inform and train the agency worker as far as OHS by the user company is concerned. However, the agency work contract may provide that the user itself shall fulfil such obligation. In any case, the user shall guarantee to agency workers the same level of prevention and protection guaranteed to its employees. One may wonder whether by such a synthetic piece of legislation, Italy has fulfilled the obligation deriving from Directive 91/383/EEC. See, dubitative, on this, C Lazzari, 'L'obbligo di sicurezza nel lavoro temporaneo, tra ordinamento interno e diritto comunitario' (2009) *DLRI* 633.

[64] P Pascucci, 'Dopo la legge n. 123 del 2007. Titolo I del d.lgs. 9 aprile 2008, n. 81 in materia di tutela della salute e della sicurezza nei luoghi di lavoro', in *WP CSDLE "M. D'Antona". IT,—73/2008* 33 ff.

Following the same line of interpretation, the legislator has also embraced a broad concept of 'employer'. Focussing on the function of managing OHS, this figure is defined as the person who has full and effective power to organise the business.

To such end, Article 2(b) of Legislative Decree No 81/2008 identifies a private sector 'employer' as the party in charge of the working relationship with the worker or, in any event, the party that, according to the type and set up of the organisation in which the worker performs, bears the responsibility for the organisation itself or for the relevant production unit, insofar as they exercise the decision-making and spending power. In this respect, a recent judgment of the Criminal Division of the Corte di Cassazione[65] has upheld the macro-concept of 'employer' and included within the category whomsoever has, in all reality, the de facto role of employer. For safety purposes, therefore, the position of 'employer' vis-a-vis workers reaches well beyond the existence of a formal employment relationship, whatever the nature of the contractual relationship may be. It coincides with the full and effective exercise of an employer's powers.

Within the Italian public sector, however, the employer's duties regarding workplace safety fall on the public servant with managerial authority or on an officer without managerial rank, but solely in those cases where the latter is in charge of an autonomous office, has been appointed by the individual authority's governing body and enjoys autonomous decision-making and spending powers.

Lastly, the same need for certainty as to the figure responsible for work organisation is met by the distinctive concept of a commissioning entity. This extends preventive duties considerably in favour of self-employed workers, particularly people involved in co-ordinated project work and of agency workers.

To such end, Article 26 of Legislative Decree No 81/2008 generally identifies the 'commissioning entity' as the person who entrusts works to a contracting undertaking or to self-employed workers or who uses agency workers within his or her own business.[66]

For the purposes of extending these important responsibilities, the determining factor is, therefore, the fact that a person carries out a working activity on the 'commissioning entity's' premises. In such cases, as the Criminal Division of the Corte di Cassazione has confirmed,[67] it is the commissioning entity who must organise appropriate measures for guaranteeing the safety of workers not directly employed by him or her but operating within his or her business. This is when such measures are generic and not tied to the worker's specific activity.

[65] See *Corte di Cassazione (Penale, IV Sezione)*, Judgment no 36878/2009.

[66] O Bonardi, 'La sicurezza sul lavoro nel sistema degli appalti', in G Natullo (ed), *Salute e sicurezza sul lavoro* (Torino, Utet, 2015) 831; V Pasquarella, 'La tutela della salute e della sicurezza negli appalti' in M Aimo, D Izzi (eds), *Esternalizzazioni e tutela dei lavoratori* (Torino, Utet, 2014) 138.

[67] So held the Corte di Cassazione (Penale, IV Sezione) in its Judgment no 12348/2008.

A similar extension of the safety duty to those responsible for the business structure in which the work is performed relates specifically to the building sector. Here, pursuant to Article 89(1)(b), the commissioning entity is identified as the party on whose behalf the whole work is being realised. This is independently of possible sub-divisions of the work involved. In the case of public procurement, however, the commissioning entity is identified as the party vested with decision-making and spending power for the contract.

In such a context, the commissioning entity must, therefore, be identified as a physical person who will have duties carrying a criminal liability. In the case of public or private juristic persons, this person corresponds to the person authorised to sign procurement contracts for the execution of works.

One of the most important innovations in the national legislator's recent modifications to the Italian system governing OHS concerns risk deriving from interference ie those risks present when the activities of other undertakings or self-employed workers become part of an employer's organised production structure 'through outsourcing "within" the production process'.[68]

Legislative Decree No 81/2008, therefore, also includes 'risk deriving from interference' amongst the basic concepts in OHS. This particular concept gives rise to a series of stringent duties for the so-called commissioning entity, the most important of which is the duty to assess the situation and draw up a consolidated risk-assessment document.

The legislator's intervention is, thus, a response to the need to tackle a phenomenon constituting a considerable threat to the safety of workers operating in complex business structures. This is the contemporaneous presence of the specific risks attaching to individual undertakings' activities and risks deriving both from the concomitant presence of employees from different undertakings and from reciprocal interference with the various activities carried out in the same work environment.

The above assumes a particular importance with regard to the duties imposed on undertakings operating in the building sector. Risk deriving from interference constitutes one of the greatest sources of danger for these undertakings, by virtue of the potentially multiple forms of work that may be performed on worksites where there is contracting or sub-contracting and that involve a main undertaking, sub-contractors, self-employed workers and suppliers of materials.

The risk deriving from interference with the commissioning entity's workplace (and, possibly, workers) caused by the activity of workers from 'outside' undertakings, therefore, assumes a central importance in the building sector and one that the legislator has deemed necessary to refer to specifically. Legislative Decree 81/2008 explicitly creates the duty to draw up a specific document on the risk from

[68] As the Corte di Cassazione (Sezione lavoro) expressed it in its Judgment no 45/2009.

interference and requires such a document to be given to all contractors entrusted with works under procurement contracts and works contracts.[69]

VI. The 'Risk Approach' as a Complement to the Core/Contingent Approach

As a result of the analysis carried out above, it is rather clear that, as far as the personal scope of application of Italian as well as EU OHS Law is concerned, despite any formal reference to the 'employer', the 'risk approach' focuses on 'anyone who organises a productive activity and/or exercises the managerial prerogatives', ie the 'entrepreneur'. The same can be said with reference to 'anyone who works within the premises of somebody who organises a productive activity even outside a traditional employment relationship', ie the 'worker' instead of the 'employee'.

Moreover, the reference to 'anyone who organises a productive activity and/or exercises the managerial prerogatives' explains also the fact that in addition to the entrepreneur, be it a legal or natural person, which has the prime responsibility for OHS, the so-called hierarchical structure, can also be bound by and held liable for the application of the relevant legislation.

Therefore, one may wonder whether, within the OHS domain, the 'risk approach', as defined in the above, may deprive the dichotomy of core/contingent work, assumed in this book, of its explicative power.

This might be true from a formal point of view, since the 'risk approach' regards differences in the 'personal work nexus'[70] as irrelevant. However, by focussing on specifically sensitive risk groups and by qualifying them also according to the typology of work relationship they entertain with the entrepreneur (fixed-term and agency work, for instance), the 'risk approach' too recognises the existence of a dichotomy based either on some objective feature of the work relationship or on a personal character of the worker. In doing so, it enriches the core/contingent perspective, adding features that may echo the so-called 'margin approach',[71] in which gender and nationality play a decisive role in highlighting workers' specificities (weaknesses?) that should be taken into account within a labour law perspective.

[69] G Pipeschi, 'La responsabilità nei cantieri', in G Natullo (ed), *Salute e sicurezza sul lavoro* (Torino, Utet, 2015) 896.

[70] M Freedland, 'From the Contract of Employment to the Personal Work Nexus' (2006) 35 *ILJ* 1.

[71] See LF Vosko, *Managing the Margins. Gender, Citizenship, and the International Regulation of Precarious Employment* (Oxford, OUP, 2010).

Thus, only apparently, the 'risk approach' seems to reverse the 'core/contingent approach' as assumed in this book. Actually, it just shows a (positive) way to handle contingent workers, regarded as especially sensitive workers, to whom the entrepreneur shall guarantee a qualitative and quantitative level of protection, which takes into account their specificities.

The question is then rather, whether such a 'sensitivity' from the entrepreneur's side shall be limited to OHS or whether it should extend to the working conditions of contingent workers as a whole.

We will try to answer this question in the final chapter of this volume.

15

Contingent Work and Social Cohesion: Some Outcomes and One Proposal

EDOARDO ALES AND OLAF DEINERT

I. The Retrenchment of Core Workforce in the Company

As will be apparent from the preceding chapters, a drift towards contingent work is ongoing in all the countries considered in this book, although the form the drift takes differs from country to country. In France, for instance, the trend is towards outsourcing, while in Spain, self-employment is likely to replace employment relationships, and in Germany, temporary agency work has played and still plays a crucial role. Even if a certain variety of contingent work does exist, overall, the core workforce, defined as that one working under an open-ended employment contract with the 'core' company, is shrinking.

It goes without saying, that it is a matter of definition whether some kind of work arrangements can be described as contingent. In his chapter, for instance, Lo Faro has built a concept of contingent work by contrast to the employment relationship. Self-employment, and triangular employment relationships such as temporary agency work or service contracting-out are seen as typical cases of contingent work, while part-time and fixed-term contracts fall within the category of core work because, in those cases, work is performed under an employment contract. Therefore, following Lo Faro's concept, the core workforce is not, by definition, a group of employees who work under a standard employment relationship.

Nevertheless, even within Lo Faro's definition of core workforce, a diversification between different groups of employees has to be made, taking into account the fact that non-standard employment relationships may be a root of uncertainty and insecurity for the employee, put, anyhow, at the margin of the company organisation. The same European Social Partners have been aware of that. In fact, as expressly advocated in the 6th 'general consideration' of the Framework

Agreement on Fixed-Term Contract,[1] they have emphasised the fact that the contract is intended to open the way towards a standard employment relationship.

Consistently, the CJEU holds that an open-ended contract has to be regarded as the general form of employment contract,[2] while fixed-term contracts should be an exception, not to be abused.

Dorssemont has highlighted this point in his contribution, proposing Belgium as 'cognitive prototype' for making the use of fixed-term contract conditional. On the other hand, as he has clearly demonstrated by reference to part-time work, flexible work is not, per se, contingent.

Against such background, his chapter aims at analysing how the countries seen as 'cognitive prototypes' in this volume have reacted vis-a-vis the increase of contingent work and the subsequent retrenchment of core workforce, taking also into account the role Social Partners may play in this field. It also aims at making some proposals for a better regulation of the recourse to contingent workforce within the company.

II. Contingent Work and the Legal Order

As we have seen in previous chapters, EU legislation has already reacted to some typologies of what we understand as contingent work. However, this has happened only selectively, with reference to atypical work arrangements like part-time, fixed-term and temporary agency work.[3] Furthermore, this legislation has only partially dealt with the problem that contingent workers have to be regarded as part of a whole—the workforce of a particular company.

This has happened, for instance, from the equal treatment perspective, although with the relevant exception of temporary agency work, as confirmed by Deinert with reference to Germany, where, in the first years after the deregulation of temporary agency work, the new legislation opened up the way for a practice towards a 'two-classes-workforce' (once again core and contingent). Collective bargaining and case law have been instrumental in reshaping agency work to be used only in case of extraordinary production need.[4]

If, according to national law, a selection between workers is necessary before dismissal when it comes to the application of the collective redundancies

[1] Framework Agreement on Fixed-Term Work concluded by ETUC, UNICE and CEEP, as implemented by Council Directive 1999/70/EC of 28 June 1999 OJ L175/43.

[2] Case C-586/10, *Kücük*, ECJ, 26 January 2012, ECLI:EU:C:2012:39, para. 37; Case C-212/04, *Adeneler and others*, ECJ, [2006] ECR I-06057, para. 61.

[3] Directive 2008/104/EC of the European Parliament and of the Council of 19 November 2008 on temporary agency work, [2008] OJ L327/9.

[4] T J Bartkiw, 'Labour Law and Triangular Employment Growth: A Theory of Regulatory Differentials' 30 (2014) *Int J Comp LLIR* (2014) 413, provides a brief comparative overview on legal situations in triangular work relations.

directive[5] the "foreign workforce" is not included. In fact, since the Directive does not regulate that matter, no EU priority rule exists with reference to core and contingent work. Consequently, EU Law is not able to make any stipulation on the question of whether the dismissals of the core workforce should be preceded by the termination of the temporary agency work contracts in place. As Lokiec pointed out in his chapter, something similar happens with reference to the Transfer of Undertaking Directive.[6]

Of course, the lack of an EU legal framework on core/contingent work does not prevent Member States from elaborating national solutions aiming at guaranteeing a certain level of protection for contingent work. However, these solutions will not follow a common concept within the EU Law meaning, thus putting into question the same minimum requirements effect attached to EU Directives on atypical work as far as non-discrimination is concerned.

In any case, as the German experience on temporary agency work shows, it is not easy to find balanced solutions that take into consideration contingent workers' protection and companies' competitiveness.

In some countries, although no attention has been paid to contingent work as such, existing legislation has had an impact on it. As Lokiec stresses in his chapter, this has been the case of France, with reference to outsourcing, which has been made conditional upon the exercise of information and consultation rights by works councils. The outsourcing case also shows that other EU legislation may be applicable to (regulate) contingent work, eg the Posted Workers Directive[7] and, its Enforcement Directive.[8] In the same vein, in Germany, the use of zero-hours contracts, although not explicitly regulated, is subject to rule restrictions, as reflected in the rules on unfair contract clauses and on part-time and fixed-term contracts.[9]

On the other hand, with reference to self-employment as contingent work, Member States normally refrain from legislative protection. This is true in the United Kingdom, the 'paradise' of deregulated labour law. Germany too has no specific legislation on the service contract.[10] Spain, on the contrary, which seeks

[5] Council Directive 98/59/EC of 20 July 1998 on the approximation of the laws of the Member States relating to collective redundancies, [1998] OJ L225/98.

[6] Council Directive 2001/23/EC of 12 March 2001 on the approximation of the laws of the Member States relating to the safeguarding of employees' rights in the event of transfers of undertakings, businesses or parts of undertakings or businesses, [2001] OJ L82/16.

[7] Directive 96/71/EC of the European Parliament and of the Council of 16 December 1996 concerning the posting of workers in the framework of the provision of services, [1997] OJ L18/1.

[8] Directive 2014/67/EU of the European Parliament and of the Council of 15 May 2014 on the enforcement of Directive 96/71/EC concerning the posting of workers in the framework of the provision of services and amending Regulation (EU) No 1024/2012 on administrative co-operation through the Internal Market Information System ('the IMI Regulation') [2014] OJ L159/11.

[9] Cf U Preis, 'Flexicurity und Abrufarbeit' (2015) *Recht der Arbeit* 244; M Bieder, 'Der Nullstundenvertrag—zulässiges Flexibilisierungsinstrument oder Wegbereiter für eine modernes Tagelöhnertum?' (2015) *Recht der Arbeit* 388; also G Forst, 'Null-Stunden-Verträge' (2014) *Neue Zeitschrift für Arbeitsrecht* 998.

[10] Cf with reference to the legal situation of solo self-employed persons: O Deinert, *Soloselbsständige zwischen Arbeitsrecht und Wirtschaftsrecht* (Baden-Baden, Nomos Verlagsgesellschaft, 2015).

to promote self-employment as an alternative to the employment contract, provides a certain level of (social security) protection for economically dependent self-employed persons. As Gómez Muñoz pointed out, the idea of protecting self-employed persons, by giving them employee-like status, is not new from a comparative point of view. In fact, the employee-like concept is also known in Germany and in Austria where employee-like self-employed persons are well protected by social security law.

Other Member States have adopted specific pieces of legislation in order to fight social dumping deriving from the core workforce retrenchment. As reported by Del Conte, this is true for Italy, where the legislator, in recent times, has enacted provisions aiming at protecting self-employed persons whose performance is, in reality, organised by the contractor, as far as working time and working place are concerned. In a similar perspective, the French jurisprudence enacting the co-employment concept should be mentioned. In the UK, as Kenner notes, outrage over the abuse of zero-hour contracts has persuaded the Government to act to ban egregious exclusivity clauses that coerce a worker to remain attached to an employer even when no minimum hours of work are guaranteed.

Halfway between these two positions, we can place Germany, where the legislation did not react to the segmentation of the workforce into core and contingent. Nevertheless, case law has developed an approach that allows considering the horizontal connections between the different typologies of workforce operating within the company, whatever their juridical status.[11]

From what has been mentioned, we can conclude that none of the countries taken into account in this volume has developed an overall legislative strategy in order to deal with contingent work. Legislation, if any, normally focuses on specific issues. Only in the field of occupational health and safety, can one register an exception from this general remark, because of the 'risk approach' as proposed by Ales in his chapter. Indeed, the personal scope of application of health and safety law is not dependent upon the juridical qualification under which anyone performs their activity within and for the benefit of the company.

III. National Occupational Strategies and the Drift Towards Contingent Work

As described before, national legislators neither take the segmentation of the workforce into core and contingent as given nor establish a conceptual matrix for it. Indeed, although considered within the framework of the European Employment Strategy and of the flexicurity approach, national legislations promote different forms of work and/or restrict them for purposes of national employment policy.

[11] Cf W Linsenmaier H Kiel, 'Der Leiharbeitnehmer in der Betriebsverfassung—, Zwei-Komponenten-Lehre und normzweckorientierte Gesetzesauslegung' (2014) *Recht der Arbeit* 135.

With reference to fixed-term contract and to the temporary character of agency work Dorssemont has shown that national legislation may also proactively react to the potential abuse of contingent work, by making it conditional on meeting certain legislative criteria.

In recent times, national parliaments have focused on the 'simplification' and 'modernisation' of labour law in order to promote occupation (labour relations).[12] That is for instance, the case in Spain where the conclusion of self-employed arrangements has been promoted by tax and social security law after the economic crisis, as Gómez Muñoz highlights in his chapter. The same was true for the German experience with temporary agency work, liberalised in order to reduce the unemployment rate, and for Belgium, where temporary agency work has been understood as a stepping stone towards permanent employment in the user firm. Rönnmar reported on it for Sweden by reference to fixed-term contracts concluded with young and elderly people, while open-ended contracts with elderly workers have been terminated.

Whatever the intent, these examples show that the adoption of such occupational policies has the effect of increasing the number of unprotected work relationships. Bearing that in mind, national legislators can intervene to reduce the pressure on the core workforce resulting from the growth in competitive contingent work. A good example of this is the Italian experience with the Increasing Protection Contract, as described by Del Conte in his chapter. In fact, the Renzi reform aims at promoting open-ended employment contracts just in order to increase the core workforce, although with a reduced dismissal protection and, at the same time, at restricting the recourse to self-employment, by increasing its level of protection. As for the latter, the same is true in Austria, where self-employment is accompanied by a sound social security legislation, as illustrated by Marhold.

The idea behind these approaches seems to be that of contingent work becoming (more) acceptable if it is accompanied by some kind of social protection. This protection must be provided either by the legislator or by the courts: that is the case in France where 'umbrella' work has been adopted as to the former and that of co-employment as to the latter.

IV. The role of Social Partners

As Rönnmar points out in her chapter on intergenerational bargaining, using Sweden as 'cognitive prototype', social partners may be able to cope with the challenge of regulating a responsible use of contingent work at company or even at branch level.

[12] Cf for a comparative view, I Schömann S Clauwaert, 'Temps de travail et travail atypique au cœur des réformes du droit du travail en Europe' (2014) Revue de Droit de Travail 582.

In the same vein, Klebe and Heuschmid draw, with reference to Germany, a precise picture of how strong trade unions can bargain not only on re-regulation of agency workers' rights but also on the regulation of the use of temporary agency work or service contracts by user firms. In such a perspective, Social partners deal not only with the working conditions of contingent workers but, indirectly, also with those of the core workforce. This shows that it would be wrong to argue that such agreements tend just to regulate economic decisions of the user and not the working conditions of its employees.[13]

As Klebe and Heuschmid demonstrate in their chapter, the collective regulation of the work status of crowdworkers could also be a trade union goal since, as we have learned from the recent case law of the CJEU,[14] collective agreements for 'false' self-employed (as crowdworkers could be regarded) would not per se violate EU Competition Law. On top of that, it should be stressed, that the crowdworker issue shows how the collective defence of interests is not in its nature restricted to collective bargaining. In such a perspective, crowdworkers' platforms are a good example of other forms of self-protection of workers' rights. The Spanish experience too, with the professional interest agreements, which cannot be regarded as collective agreements, underlines this.

As the German case shows, works councils too could have an influence in shaping the workforce structure in the company if they are able to reach plant agreements on quotas for contingent work and to prevent its use when exceeding the quota agreed. Worth mentioning in this context are also the Besservereinbarungen that are intended to ensure the equal treatment principle for agency workers.

V. Contingent Work and the 'New Forms of Employment'

The example of crowdworkers shows that the segmentation of the workforce into core and contingent is likely to exceed the 'traditional' forms of work and of outsourcing. Although crowdwork might fall under different existing work typologies (employment, distance work, self-employment—real or 'false'), one should take view crowdworking as a new and independent type of contingent work.

As Klebe and Heuschmid have clearly pointed out, crowdworking has a new 'quality' because of two aspects: it entails, on the one hand, a potentially global labour market and on the other, rather short time periods for micro-tasks, both

[13] Cf in the same vein, R Krause, 'Tarifverträge zur Widerherstellung von Equal Pay' (2012) *Arbeit und Recht* 55.

[14] Case C-413/13, *FNV Kunsten, Informatie en Media*, CJEU, 4 December 2014, ECLI:EU:C:2014:2411.

supported by the possibility of using digital media for initiation of the contract and performance/delivery of the work. This is exactly in line with Kovács' observations on crowdwork.

The German legal system, as analysed in Klebe's and Heuschmid's chapter, does not provide any specific and appropriate rule for crowdworking. The same is true, for the time being, for other legal orders. We cannot look into the future but it is not hard to imagine that further new forms of contingent work will appear.

Indeed, both Lo Faro and Lokiec consider the *Uber* case which seems not to exemplify a typical crowdsourcing situation.

VI. How to Cope with the Drift Towards Contingent Work: A Combined Approach for a Specially Sensitive Social Group

A considerable number of answers to the question of how to cope with the drift towards contingent work stem from the chapters of this volume.

A first, in a way traditional, answer comes from the 'conditionality approach' namely as Dorssemont pointed out in his chapter using Belgium as 'cognitive prototype', the fact that the recourse to contingent work can be made conditional, by the legislator, to the fulfilment of certain qualitative and/or quantitative criteria defined by the law. This has been and still is the case in many countries as far as fixed-term work and agency work are concerned. The 'conditionality approach' is strongly linked to the fight against abuse of non-standard work and aims at avoiding an uncontrolled recourse to such forms of contingent work. By consequence, it does not influence outsourcing of companies' activities. An alternative, more flexible approach, suggested for the United Kingdom by Kenner would be to identify indicators drawn from ILO Recommendation No 198 to establish proof of the existence of a contract of employment. This would be useful for zero-hours workers who are often uncertain about their employment status.

The 'conditionality approach' has been followed also by workers' representatives, such as trade unions or works councils, in order to bargain, at any level (company, sectoral and inter-sectoral; local, national or transnational), conditions (limits) to the use of non-standard work and also to mitigate the social consequences of outsourcing. Where strong trade unions or works council operate, this could be, of course, the most effective way to cope with the drift towards contingent work, providing a shared balance between competitiveness and social protection and guaranteeing a reasonable degree of social cohesion within the company.

A second, social security related, answer comes from the 'tax payer approach', as elaborated by Marhold in his chapter, using Austria as 'cognitive prototype'.

Instead of being linked to a certain juridical status, social insurance in Austria is more and more bound to the income earned by the worker from his/her activity.

This mainly reflects the change of values regarding the economic and social condition of self-employed persons, who now enjoy a comprehensive protection of a level comparable to the one of employees. More generally, Austria has followed the clear concept of a gradual extension of its social insurance system to cover also persons operating within the framework of non-standard employment. Therefore, the gap in protection, in terms of personal scope, has been mainly closed in the last couple of decades.

The condition to be fulfilled in order to be insured within the social security system are personal and economic dependency. To the extent that contingent workers fulfil these two criteria, they will enjoy a substantive social protection.

From such a perspective, outsourcing should not present an obstacle to the 'tax payer approach' in producing its positive effects on contingent workers, as it remains unaffected by any changes from the management side.

A third, EU Law-rooted answer comes from the 'equal treatment approach', as illustrated by Deinert, using Germany as 'cognitive prototype'. The same EU Law root, however, allowing Member States to provide for relevant exclusions to the equal treatment principle, is likely to put its effectiveness into debate, as the temporary agency work example shows. Nevertheless, in many countries, this principle remains crucial, guiding the legislator as well as case law, although within the framework of the 'objective grounds' exception. On the other hand, one have to admit that the 'equal treatment approach' is strongly limited by the fact that a general principle of equal treatment, not linked to specific discrimination grounds or situations, such as being in a fixed-term contract, is not recognised as such.

A fourth, once again EU Law-rooted answer comes from the 'risk approach', as elaborated by Ales in his theoretical-practical chapter, using Italy as 'cognitive prototype'. According to his analysis, it is rather clear that, as far as the personal scope of application of EU as well as Italian Occupational Health and Safety Law is concerned, despite any formal reference to the 'employer', the "risk approach" focuses on 'anyone who organises a productive activity and/or exercises the managerial prerogatives', ie the 'entrepreneur'. The same can be said with reference to 'anyone who works within the premises of somebody who organises a productive activity even outside a traditional employment relationship', ie the 'worker' instead of the 'employee'.

Therefore, one may even wonder whether, within the Occupational Health and Safety domain, the 'risk approach' may deprive the dichotomy of core/contingent work, assumed in this volume, of its explicative power.

This might be true from a formal point of view, since the 'risk approach' regards differences in the 'personal work nexus'[15] as irrelevant. However, by focusing on 'specifically sensitive risk groups' and by qualifying them according to the typology of work relationship they entertain with the entrepreneur (fixed-term and agency work, for instance), the 'risk approach' too recognises the existence of a

[15] M Freedland, 'From the Contract of Employment to the Personal Work Nexus' (2006) 35 *ILJ* 1.

dichotomy based either on some objective feature of the work relationship or on a personal character of the worker. In doing so, it enriches the core/contingent perspective, adding features that may echo the so called 'margin approach',[16] in which gender and nationality play a decisive role in highlighting workers' specificities (weaknesses?) that should be taken into account within a labour law perspective.

Thus, only apparently, the 'risk approach' seems to reverse the 'core/contingent approach' as assumed in this volume. Actually, it just shows a (positive) way to handle contingent workers, regarded as especially sensitive workers, to whom the entrepreneur shall guarantee a qualitative and quantitative level of protection, which takes into account their specificities.

The question is then rather, whether such a 'sensitivity' from the entrepreneur's side should be limited to OHS or whether it should extend to the working conditions of contingent workers as a whole.

A fifth, innovative answer is one coming from what we can call the 'end beneficiary approach' which elaborates on Lo Faro's and Lokiec's chapters.

Both chapters deal with the question of who the employer is or, more precisely, of who is responsible for the definition and the guarantee of the economic and normative conditions under which the work is performed. In both chapters, by what seems a coincidence of thought, the concept of the 'end beneficiary' of the work performed has been raised, that is the person or the legal entity held responsible for the working conditions, not only of its core workforce but also for the contingent workforce, whatever the kind of direct or indirect relationship may exist between the parties involved.

From a technical point of view, the 'end user approach' is concretised by the joint-employer (co-employeur) juridical construction, elaborated by case law (France) or directly introduced by the legislator (Italy) and/or by the joint and several liability concept. Both underline the need to preserve or establish the link not only between core and contingent work but also between core and contingent employers (entrepreneurs), which represent, at least in case of outsourcing, the other side of the coin of the core/contingent dichotomy.

In view of what has been said so far, to cope with the drift towards contingent work, our proposal would be to adopt a combined approach that takes into account the different problematic aspects that the approaches mentioned in the above have emphasised. These are: (i) the fight against abuse of contingent work; (i) the struggle for equal treatment between core and contingent workers; (iii) the need for a full social security coverage for contingent workers; (iv) the recognition of contingent workers as a specifically sensitive risk group; (v) the preservation or the establishment of a link between core and contingent employers (entrepreneur).

[16] See LF Vosko, *Managing the Margins. Gender, Citizenship, and the International Regulation of Precarious Employment* (Oxford, OUP, 2010).

At its turn, such a combined approach includes both, the recognition of contingent workers as a specially sensitive social group on the one hand and the protection of social and economic cohesion within the company and within the society on the other hand. This might occur through the law (labour law) or, if strong enough, through collective bargaining, preserving or establishing links between core and contingent work and employership (entrepreneurship), above all.

In the view of the economic, social and territorial cohesion commitment enshrined within the Treaty on the Functioning of the European Union (Articles 174–178), the specific protection of contingent workers should, primarily, be a task for the European Institutions to provide and to stimulate legislation and social dialogue, at all relevant levels, in such a direction.

Indeed, social and economic cohesion is the right answer to social and economic exclusion which is likely, at present, not only to increase poverty but also to fuel extremism and radicalism among those put at the margin of European society.

BIBLIOGRAPHY

Adams, A, Freedland, M and Prassl, J, 'The "Zero-Hours Contract": Regulating casual work, or legitimating precarity? in *ELLN Working Paper* (2015) No 5

Adams, Z and Deakin S, *Re-regulating Zero Hours Contracts* (Institute of Employment Rights 2014)

Adinolfi, F and Bortone, R, 'Commento alla direttiva europea sulla tutela della maternità' in *Giornale di diritto del lavoro e di relazioni industriali* (1994) 361–381

Aigner, W, 'Das VfGH-Erkenntnis zur sog. "Werkvertragsregelung"' in *Zeitschrift für Arbeits- und Sozialrecht* (1997) 129–134

Alarcón Caracuel, MR, 'La ajenidad en el mercado como criterio definitorio del contrato de trabajo' in *Revista Española de Derecho del Trabajo* (1986) 495–544

Albi, P, *Adempimento dell'obbligo di sicurezza e tutela della persona. Art. 2087 c.c.* (Milano, Giuffré, 2008)

Ales, E, 'Diritti sociali e discrezionalità del legislatore nell'ordinamento multilivello: una prospettazione giuslavoristica' in *Giornale di Diritto del Lavoro e delle Relazioni Industriali*, (2015) 455–495

Ales, E, Miranda, L and Giurini, A, 'Italy: From Occupational Health and Safety to Well-being at Work' in E Ales (ed), *Health and Safety at Work. European and Comparative Perspective* (Alphen aan den Rijn, Kluwer Law International, 2013) 195–248

Ales, E 'Occupational Health and Safety: a European and Comparative Legal Perspective' in *WP CSDLE "M. D'Antona".INT* (2015) 120/2015

Ankersen, P, 'Neues AÜG seit 1.3.2003 bundesweit in Kraft' in *Neue Zeitschrift für Arbeitsrecht* (2003) 421–425

Anxo, D, 'Towards an Active and Integrated Life Course Policy: the Swedish Experience' in D Anxo, G Bosch and J Rubery (eds), *The Welfare State and Life Transitions: a European Perspective* (Cheltenham, Edgar Elgar, 2010) 113–127

Anxo, D, 'Entry and Exit Patterns from the Labour Force: A European and Life-Course Perspective' in A Numhauser-Henning and M Rönnmar (eds), *Age Discrimination and Labour Law. Comparative and Conceptual Perspectives in the EU and Beyond* (Alphen aan den Rijn, Kluwer Law International, 2015) 17–48

Aoki, K and Lennerfors, ThT, 'The new, improved Keiretsu' in *Harvard business review* (2013) 9 109–113

Aparicio Tovar, J, 'Occupational Health and Safety in Spain: A Formidable Array of Employers' Liabilities' in E Ales (ed), *Health and Safety at Work. European and Comparative Perspective* (Alphen aan den Rijn, Kluwer Law International, 2013), 249–280

Aramendi Sánchez, P, 'La competencia de la jurisdicción social en el anteproyecto de la Ley del Estatuto del Trabajo Autónomo' in *Documentación Laboral* (2006) 77 13–26

Areta Martínez, M and Sempere Navarro, AV, *La contratación laboral (especial) entre abogados* (Pamplona, Thomson/Aranzadi, 2006)

Arthurs, H, 'The Dependent Contractor: A Study of the Legal Problems of Countervailing Power' in *Toronto Law Journal* (1965) 16 1 89–117

Aschauer, P and Kohlbacher, E, 'Einvernehmliche Auflösung im Krankenstand—Deckmantel zur Umgehung sozialversicherungsrechtlicher Beitragspflicht?' in B Karl, K Marko-Herzeg and P Aschauer (eds.), *Sozialversicherungsrecht—Jahrbuch 2011* (Wien, NWV Verlag, 2011) 93–102

Asztalos, S and Czibere, I, *Az atipikus formában szervezhető munkalehetőségek feltárása és elterjesztésének lehetőségei, Kutatási zárójelentés* (Budapest, Konszenzus Alapítvány, 2011)

Atkinson, J, *Flexibility, Uncertainty and Manpower Management* (Brighton, Institute of Manpower Studies, 1985)

Atkinson, J, 'Manpower Strategies for Flexible Organisations' in *Personnel Management* (1984) 28–31

Auer-Mayer, S, 'Die Grenze zwischen selbständiger und unselbständiger Tätigkeit aus sozialversicherungsrechtlicher Sicht' in *Zeitschrift für Arbeits- und Sozialrecht* (2015) 4–5

Bailly, P, 'Le co-emploi: une situation exceptionnelle' in *Semaine juridique (JCP), édition sociale* (2013) n. 1441 1–4

Bankó, Z, 'Atypical Employment Relationships in the Hungarian Labour Law', (Saarbrücken, Lambert Academic Publishing, 2014) 74

Bankó, Z, *Az atipikus munkajogviszonyok* (Pécs, Dialóg Campus Kiadó, 2010)

Bankó, Z, and Ferencz, J, *Atipikus munkajogviszonyok* (Budapest, Wolters Kluwer Kft, 2015)

Barassi, L, *Il contratto di lavoro nel diritto positivo italiano*, (Milano, Società editrice libraria, 1901)

Barnard, C, *European Employment Law*, 4th edn (Oxford, Oxford University Press, 2012)

Barrett, B and Sargeant, M, 'Health and Safety Issues in New Forms of Employment and Work Organization' in *Int J Comp LLIR* (2008) 24 243–261

Bartkiw, T J 'Labour Law and Triangular Employment Growth: A Theory of Regulatory Differentials' in *Int J Comp LLIR* (2014) 30 413–433

Befort, S, 'Revisiting the Black Hole of Workplace Regulation: A Historical and Comparative Perspective of Contingent Work' in *Berkeley Journal of Employment and Labor Law* (2003) 24 153–178

Benjamin, P, 'Who Needs Labour Law? Defining the Scope of Labour Protection' in J Conaghan, RM Fischl and K Klare (eds), *Labour Law in an Era of Globalization. Transformative Practices & Possibilities* (Oxford, Oxford University Press, 2002) 75–93

Benner, C, *Crowdwork—zurück in die Zukunft? Perspektiven digitaler Arbeit* (Frankfurt am Main, Bund-Verlag, 2015)

Berchtold, J, 'Nachforderung von Sozialversicherungsbeiträgen bei Nichtigkeit von Tarifverträgen der CGZP' in *Soziale Sicherheit* (2012) 70–76

Berke, G, and Kiss, G (eds), *Kommentár a Munka Törvénykönyvéhez* (Budapest, Complex Kiadó Kft., 2012)

Berliner, D and Greenleaf, AR, *Labor standards in international supply chains: aligning rights and incentives* (Cheltenham, Edward Elgar Publishing Ltd, 2015)

Bieder, M 'Der Nullstundenvertrag—zulässiges Flexibilisierungsinstrument oder Wegbereiter für eine modernes Tagelöhnertum?' in *Recht der Arbeit* (2015) 388–399

Bissels, A, Mehnert, F, 'Tarifverträge über Branchenzuschläge in der Zeitarbeit—ein Rechtsprechungsüberblick' in *Der Betrieb* (2014) 2407–2415

Blanc-Jouvan, G, 'L'unité économique et sociale et la notion d'entreprise' in *Droit social* (2005) 68–79

Blanke, T, 'Der Gleichbehandlungsgrundsatz in der Arbeitnehmerüberlassung' in *Der Betrieb* (2010) 1528–1533

Blasina, H, *Dienstnehmer—Freier Dienstnehmer—Selbständiger, Begriffe und Abgrenzungen im Sozialversicherungs- und Steuerrecht* (Wien, Facultas AG, 2007)

Boemke, B and Lembke, M, *Arbeitnehmerüberlassungsgesetz*, 3rd edn (Heidelberg, Deutscher Fachverlag Fachmedien Verlag Recht und Wirtschaft, 2013)

Bogg, A, 'Sham Self-Employment in the Supreme Court' (2012) 41 ILJ 328

Böhm, W, 'Zeitenwende bei der Zeitarbeit—Start mit Irritationen' in *Neue Zeitschrift für Arbeitsrecht* (2003) 828–832

Bonardi, O, 'La sicurezza sul lavoro nel sistema degli appalti' in G Natullo (ed.) *Salute e sicurezza sul lavoro* (Torino, UTET, 2015) 831–895

Bouloc, B, 'Note on Cour de cassation. Chambre criminelle, 4 February 1985, no 84-91581' in *Rev. sociétés* (1985) 648–650

Brauneisen, KT and Ibes, JW (eds), 'Der Tatbestand der Arbeitnehmerüberlassung' in *Recht der Arbeit* (2014) 213–222

Brodil, W and Windisch-Graetz, M, *Sozialrecht in Grundzügen* (Wien, Facultas Verlag, 2013)

Brynjolfsson, E and McAfee, A, *The Second Machine Age* (New York, W.W. Norton & Company, 2014)

Buelens, J and Reyniers, K, 'Standard and Non-standard Work in Belgium', in J Buelens and J Pearson (ed), *Standard Work: An Anachronism?* (Antwerpen, Intersentia, 2013) 17–40

Burger-Ehrnhofer, K, 'Mutterschutz bei geringfügiger Beschäftigung' in *Recht der Wirtschaft* (2004) 746–749

Burger-Ehrnhofer, K, *Mutterschutzgesetz und Väter-Karenzgesetz* (Wien, ÖGB Verlag, 2013)

Calabresi, G and Melamed, AD, 'Property Rules, Liability Rules, and Inalienability: One View of the Cathedral' in *Harvard Law Review* (1972) 1089–1128

Calafà, L, 'Le lavoratrici madri' in M Rusciano and G Natullo (eds), *Ambiente e sicurezza del lavoro* (Torino, UTET, 2007) 391–402

Carinci, F and Tiraboschi, M (eds), *I decreti attuativi del Jobs Act: prima lettura e interpretazioni* (Bergamo, ADAPT University Press, 2015)

Carinci, F, 'Provaci ancora, Sam: ripartendo dall'art. 18 dello Statuto' in *Rivista italiana di diretto del lavoro* (2012) 3–58

Carinci, MT, Tursi, A (eds), *Jobs Act, Il contratto a tutele crescenti* (Torino, Giappichelli, 2015)

Caruso, B, 'The Employment Contract id Dead! Hurrah for the Work Contract!' in K Stone and H Arthurs (eds) *Rethinking Workplace Regulation Beyond the Standard Employment Contract* (New York, Russel Sage Foundation Press, 2013) 95–111

Casaux-Labrunée, L, 'Le portage salarial: travail salarié ou travail indépendant?' in *Droit social* (2007) 58–71

Castro Argüelles, MA, 'Los Acuerdos de Interés Profesional: un balance de la negociación llevada a cabo al amparo del Estatuto del Trabajo Autónomo' in *Anales de Derecho* (2011) 34–80

Cavas Martínez, F, Cámara Botía, F, *La acción protectora del Régimen Especial de la Seguridad Social de los Trabajadores por Cuenta Propia o Autónomos* (Pamplona, Thomson-Aranzadi, 2005)

Ceinos Suárez, A, 'Autónomos Económicamente Dependientes', in J García Murcia (ed), *El Trabajo Autónomo* (Pamplona, Thomson-Aranzandi, 2007) 57–95

Cesaro, JF, 'Le co-emploi' in *Revue de jurisprudence sociale* (2013) n. 1/13, 3–9

Cherry, MA, 'A Taxonomy of Virtual Work' in *Georgia Law Review* (2011) 951–1013

Cherry, MA, 'Mindestlohn für Crowdarbeit' in C Benner (ed), *Crowdwork, zurück in die Zukunft* (Frankfurt am Main, Bund-Verlag, 2014) 231–242

Coenen, M, and Kok, RAW, 'Workplace Flexibility and New Product Development performance: The Role of Telework and Flexible Work Schedules' in *European Management Journal* (2014) 564–576

Collins, H, 'Independent Contractors and the Challenge of Vertical Disintegration to Employment Protection Laws' in *Oxford Journal of Legal Studies* (1990) 10 353–380

Collins, H, 'Employment Rights of Casual Workers' (2000) 29 ILJ 73

Collins, H, *Employment Law* (OUP, 2nd edn, 2010)

Combrexelle, JD, *La négociation collective, le travail et l'emploi*, Rapport au Premier ministre, France Stratégie, 2015

Corazza, L, *Contractual Integration e rapporti di lavoro* (Padova, CEDAM, 2004)

Coutrot, Th, *Critique de l'organisation du travail* (Paris, La Découverte, 1999)

Couturier, G, 'Comment on Vittel Perrier, Cour de cassation, Chambre sociale, 12 July 2000' in *Droit social* (2000) 845–846

Cruz Villalón, J, 'Trabajo subordinado y trabajo autónomo en la delimitación de fronteras del Derecho del Trabajo', in *Estudios en homenaje al profesor Cabrera Bazán* (Madrid, Tecnos, 1999) 169–191

Cruz Villalón, J, 'El trabajo autónomo: nuevas realidades, nuevos retos' in *Revista Temas Laborales* (2005) 81 11–22

Cruz Villalón, J, 'Propuestas para una regulación del trabajo autónomo' in *Documentación Laboral* (2005) 73 9–54

Cruz Villalón, J, 'Il lavoro autonomo economicamente dipendente in Spagna' in *Diritto lavoro mercati* (2013) 287–315

Curzi, Y and Fabbri, T (eds), *Lavoro e salute. Approcci e strumenti per la prevenzione dello stress e la promozione del benessere al lavoro* (Torino, Giappichelli, 2012)

Davies, A, 'Regulating Atypical Work: beyond Quality' in N. Countouris, M Freedland (eds) *Resocialising Europe in a Time of Crisis* (Cambridge, Cambridge University Press, 2013) 230–249

Davies, P, and Freedland, M, *Kahn-Freund's Labour and the Law* (Stevens, 3rd edn, 1983)

Däubler, W, *Tarifvertragsgesetz mit Arbeitnehmer-Entsendegesetz*, 3rd edn (Baden-Baden, Nomos, 2012)

Däubler, W, 'Der Arbeitgeber—ein Fixpunkt des Arbeitsrechts?' in *Kritische Justiz* (2013) 133–144

Däubler, W et al (eds), *Betriebsverfassungsgesetz*, 14th edn (Frankfurt am Main, Bund-Verlag, 2014)

Däubler, W, 'Crowdworker—Schutz auch außerhalb des Arbeitsrechts?' in C Benner (ed), *Crowdwork, zurück in die Zukunft* (Frankfurt am Main, Bund-Verlag, 2014) 248–276

Däubler, W, 'Der gesetzliche Mindestlohn—doch eine unendliche Geschichte?' in *Neue Juristische Wochenschrift* (2014) 1924–1929

Däubler, W and Klebe, T, 'Crowdwork: Die neue Form der Arbeit—Arbeitgeber auf der Flucht?' in *Neue Zeitschrift für Arbeitsrecht* (2015) 1032–1042

Davidov, G, 'Setting Labour Law's Coverage: Between Universalism and Selectivity' in *Oxford Journal of legal Studies* (2014) 34 543–566

Davidsson, J and Naczyk, M, *The Ins and Outs of Dualization: a Literature Review* (Oxford, Department of Social Policy and Social Work, 2009)

Davies, A, *Employment Law* (Pearson 2015)

Deakin, S, 'A New Paradigm for Labour Law?' in *Melbourne University Law Review* (2007) 31 1161–1167

Deakin, S, and Morris, G, *Labour Law* (Hart, 6th edn, 2012)

Deckers, H and Mortier, A, 'Durée du contrat de travail et durée du travail' in S Plasschaert and O Ryckaert (ed), *Le droit social en chantier(s)* (Bruxelles, Larcier, 2012) 261–266

Deinert, O, 'Zahlung der Sozialversicherungsbeiträge' in *Arbeitsrecht im Betrieb* (2012) 255–259

Deinert, O, *Internationales Arbeitsrecht* (Tübingen, Mohr Siebeck Verlag, 2013)

Deinert, O, 'Kernbelegschaften—Randbelegschaften—Fremdbelegschaften: Herausforderungen für das Arbeitsrecht durch Reduzierung von Stammbelegschaften' in *Recht der Arbeit* (2014) 65–77

Deinert, O, *Soloselbstständige zwischen Arbeitsrecht und Wirtschaftsrecht* (Baden-Baden, Nomos Verlagsgesellschaft, 2015)

Deinert, O and Kittner, M, 'Die arbeitsrechtliche Bilanz der Großen Koalition 2005-2009' in *Recht der Arbeit* (2009) 265–279

Del Rey Guanter, S (ed), *Comentarios al estatuto del trabajo autónomo* (Madrid, Lex Nova, 2007)

Deter, G, 'Zahl der Leiharbeiter steigt wieder' in *Arbeit und Recht* (2015) 268

Di Martino, V and Wirth, L, 'Telework: A New Way of Working and Living' in *International Labour Review* (1990) 529–554

Dittberner, N, 'Fünf Fragen an Nicolas Dittberner' in C Benner (ed), *Crowdwork, zurück in die Zukunft* (Frankfurt am Main, Bund-Verlag, 2014) 93–98

Dewhurst, E, 'Intergenerational Balance, Mandatory Retirement and Age Discrimination in Europe: how Can the ECJ Better Support National Courts in Finding a Balance between the Generations' in *Common Market Law Review* (2013) 1333–1362

Dorssemont, F, 'Trade Union Representation in Belgium' in C La Macchia (ed), *Representing Employee Interests: Trade Union Systems within the EU* (Albecete, Editorial Bomarzo, 2012) 53–74

Dorssemont, F, Naert, K and Van Regenmortel, A, 'Well-Being at Work in Belgium: A Matter of Co-operation' in E Ales (ed), *Health and Safety at Work. European and Comparative Perspective* (Alphen aan den Rijn, Kluwer Law International, 2013) 67–98

Drahopoupil, J (ed), *The Outsourcing Challenge. Organizing Workers across Fragmented Production Networks* (Bruxelles, European Trade Union Institute, 2015)

Düwell, FJ, *Deutscher Bundestag, Ausschussdrucksache* 17 (11) 431, 56

Felstiner, A, 'Working the Crowd: Employment and Labor Law in the Crowdsourcing Industry' in *Berkeley Journal of Employment and Labor Law* (2011) 143–204

Fernández Costales Muñiz, J, 'Los trabajadores autónomos en la Ley de Prevención de Riesgos Laborales' in Aa Vv, *La Seguridad Social de los Trabajadores Autónomos* (Granada, Editorial Laborum, 2007) 181–186

Fiorillo, L and Perulli, A (eds), *Il contratto a tutele crescenti e la Naspi, Decreti legislativi 4 marzo 2015, n. 22 e n. 23* (Torino, Giappichelli, 2015)

Forst, G 'Null-Stunden-Verträge' in *Neue Zeitschrift für Arbeitsrecht* (2014) 998–1002

Forster, KM, 'Strategic Reforms of Contingent Work' in *Southern California law Review* (2001) 74 541–576

Franken, JP, 'Erforderliche Nachbesserungen im Arbeitnehmerüberlassungsgesetz' in *Neue Zeitschrift für Arbeitsrecht* (2013) 1192–1194

Franzen, M, 'Neuausrichtung des Drittpersonaleinsatzes—Überlegungen zu den Vorhaben des Koalitionsvertrags' in *Recht der Arbeit* (2015) 141–152

Fredman, S and Spencer, S (eds), *Age as an Equality Issue* (Oxford, Hart Publishing, 2003)

Freedland, M, *The Contract of Employment* (Clarendon Press 1976)

Freedland, M, *The Personal Employment Contract* (OUP 2003)

Freedland, M, 'From the Contract of Employment to the Personal Work Nexus' in *Industrial Law Journal* (2006) 1–29

Freedland, M and Countouris, N, *The Legal Construction of Personal Work Relations* (Oxford, Oxford University Press, 2011)

Freudhofmeier, M and Höfle, W, 'Geringfügige Beschäftigungsverhältnisse' in *ASoK-Spezial: Sozialversicherung kompakt* (Wien, Linde Verlag, 2015)

Frey, CB, Osborne, MA, *The Future of Employment: How susceptible are Jobs to Computerisation?* (Oxford, Oxford Martin School, 2013)

Frick, K and others (eds), *Systematic Occupational Health and Safety Management. Perspective on an International Development* (Amsterdam, Pergamon, 2000)

Friedrich, M, 'Rahmendienstvertrag und Arbeitszeit—Zugleich eine Entscheidungsbesprechung zu OGH 8 Ob A 116/04' in *Arbeits- und SozialrechtsKartei* (2006) 12–16

Friedrich, M, 'Flexibilisierung durch Befristungen und Bedingungen in Vertragsklauseln und Betriebsvereinbarungen' in *Zeitschrift für Arbeits- und Sozialrecht* (2011) 109–117

Fuchs, M, 'Das Gleichbehandlungsgebot in der Leiharbeit nach der neuen Leiharbeitsrichtlinie' in *Neue Zeitschrift für Arbeitsrecht* (2009) 57–63

Fuchs, M and Marhold, F, *Europäisches Arbeitsrecht* (Wien, Verlag Österreich, 2014)

Fudge, J, 'Blurring Legal Boundaries: Regulating for Decent Work' in J Fudge, S McCrystal and K Sankaran (eds), *Challenging the Legal Boundaries of Work Regulation* (Oxford, Hart Publishing, 2012) 1–26

Fudge, J, 'Labour as a 'Fictive Commodity': Radically Reconceptualizing Labour Law' in Davidov, G, and Langille, B, (eds), *The Idea of Labour Law* (OUP 2011) 120–136

Galantino, L (ed), *La sicurezza del lavoro* (Milano, Giuffrè, 1996)

Gallagher, C and Underhill, E, 'Managing work health and safety: recent developments and future directions' in *Asia Pacific Journal of Human Resources* (2012) 50 227–244

Gamonal, SCF and Rosado Marzán, C, 'Age Discrimination and Labour Law in Latin America: The Challenges of Equality Law in Light of Underdevelopment', in A Numhauser-Henning and M Rönnmar (eds), *Age Discrimination and Labour Law. Comparative and Conceptual Perspectives in the EU and Beyond* (Alphen aan den Rijn, Kluwer Law International, 2015) 357–378

García Murcia, J, 'El sistema de fuentes de la relación laboral' in J García Murcia (ed), *Estudios ofrecidos al profesor Martín Valverde* (Oviedo, Universidad de Oviedo, 2007) 19–75

García Murcia, J, 'Trabajo autónomo' in J García Murcia (ed), *El trabajo autónomo y otras formas de trabajo no asalariado* (Pamplona, Thomson-Aranzadi, 2007) 21–24

Gerhartl, A, 'Geringfügig entlohnte Beschäftigungen—Arbeits- und sozialversicherungsrechtliche Besonderheiten' in *Arbeits- und SozialrechtsKartei* (2010) 394–399

Gerhartl, A, 'Geringfügige Beschäftigung im Arbeitslosenversicherungsrecht' in *Zeitschrift für Arbeits- und Sozialrecht* (2012) 161–168

Gibbons, R, 'Firms (and Other Relationships)' in P Di Maggio (ed), *The Twenty-First-Century Firm: Changing Economic Organization in International Perspective* (Princeton, Princeton University Press, 2003) 186–199

Gleitsmann, M and Kircher, M, 'Soziale Errungenschaften für Selbständige aus rechtspolitischer Sicht' in P Aschauer and E Kohlbacher (eds) *Sozialversicherungsrecht: Jahrbuch 2014* (Wien, NWV Verlag, 2014) 87–98

González Díaz, FA, 'Régimen profesional del trabajador autónomo' in J Luján Alcaraz (ed), *El Estatuto del Trabajador Autónomo* (Murcia, Editorial Laborum, 2007) 69–96

González Ortega, S, *La presunción de existencia del contrato de trabajo* (Madrid, Ministerio de Trabajo y Seguridad Social, 1990)

González Ortega, S, 'El tratamiento de los riesgos de los trabajadores autónomos' in *Temas Laborales* (2005) 81 152–172

Greiner, S, '"Personalhoheit" als Schlüsselbegriff der Abgrenzung von echtem Fremdpersonaleinsatz und verdeckter Arbeitnehmerüberlassung' in *Recht der Arbeit* (2014) 262–271

Gunningham, N, 'Integrating Management Systems and Occupational Health and Safety Regulation' in *JL & Soc* (1999) 26 192–214

Gutiérrez-Solar Calvo, B and Lahera Forteza, J, 'Ámbito y fuentes de regulación del trabajo autónomo' in J Cruz Villalón and F Valdés Dal-Ré, *El Estatuto del Trabajo Autónomo*, (Madrid, La Ley, 2008) 63–114

Gyulavári, T, 'A bridge too far? The Hungarian regulation of economically dependent work' in *Hungarian Labour Law E-journal* 82 (2014) 95–98

Hamann, W, 'Fremdpersonal in Unternehmen—Industriedienstleistung statt Leiharbeit?' in *Neue Zeitschrift für Arbeitsrecht* (2014) 1st Suppl. 3–9

Hárs, Á, 'Atipikus foglalkoztatási formák Magyarországon a kilencvenes és a kétezres években' in *Közgazdasági Szemle* (2013) 224–250

Hárs, Á, *Az atipikus foglalkoztatás: mítoszok, lehetőségek és korlátok az atipikus foglakoztatási formák lehetőségeinek kihasználásában*' (Budapest, Kopint Konjunktúra Kutatási Alapítvány, 2013)

Helfen, M, 'Netzwerkförmige Tertialisierung und triangularistische Beschäftigung: Braucht es eine interorganisationale Personalpolitik?' in *Managementforschung* (2014) 24 171–206

Helfen, M and Nicklich, M, 'Gewerkschaften zwischen Konkurrenz und Kooperation? Inter-organisationale Beziehungen in der Facility Services-Branche' in *Industrielle Beziehungen* (2013) 21 (2) 181–204

Hendrickx, F, (ed), *Active Ageing and Labour Law. Contributions in Honour of Professor Roger Blanpain* (Cambridge, Intersentia Publishing Ltd, 2012)

Heuschmid, J, 'Leiharbeit kann durch TV eingeschränkt werden' in *Arbeit und Recht* (2015) 279–281

Heuschmid, J and Klauk, M, 'Zur Primärrechtswidrigkeit der Leiharbeits-Richtlinie" in *Soziales Recht* (2012) 84–94

Heuschmid, J and Hlava, D, 'Keine Anwendung des europäischen Kartellrechts auf TV, die Regelungen für Selbstständige enthalten' in *Arbeit und Recht* (2015) 193–195

Hohendanner, C and Walwei, U, 'Arbeitsmarkteffekte atypischer Beschäftigung' in *WSI-Mitteilungen* (2013) 239–246

Hohmeister, F and Küper, A, 'Individualvertragliche Arbeitszeitgestaltung bei der alternierenden Telearbeit' in *Neue Zeitschrift für Arbeitsrecht* (1998) 1206–1208

Horváth, I and Szabó, T, *Munkajogi Navigátor—Az új Munka Törvénykönyve a gyakorlatban*, (Kaposvár, Adónet Zrt., 2012)

Hötte, DA, 'Crowdsourcing—Rechtliche Risiken eines neuen Phänomens' in *MMR—MultiMedia und Recht* (2014) 795–798

Houwerzijl, M, 'Regulating temporary work in the Netherlands after the Temporary Agency Work Directive' in R Blanpain, F Hendrickx, and M Houwerzijl (eds) *Temporary Agency Work in the European Union and the United States*—BCLR (Bulletin Comparative Labour Relations) (2013) 82 125–143

Howes, V, 'Who Is Responsible for Health and Safety of Temporary Workers? EU and UK Perspectives' in *European Labour Law Journal* (2011) 2 379–400

Huertas Bartolomé, T, *Mediación mercantil en el ordenamiento laboral* (Madrid, Tecnos, 1991)

Ichino, P, 'La riforma dei licenziamenti e i diritti fondamentali dei lavoratori' in L Nogler and L Corazza (eds), *Risistemare il diritto del lavoro. Liber amicorum Marcello Pedrazzoli* (Milano, F Angeli, 2012) 792–823

Irani, LC and Silberman, MS,' Turkopticon' in C Benner (ed), *Crowdwork, zurück in die Zukunft* (Frankfurt am Main, Bund-Verlag, 2014) 131–166

Jahn, E and Weber, E, 'Zusätzliche Jobs, aber auch Verdrängung' in *IAB-Kurzbericht* (2013) 2 1–6

James, P and others, 'Regulating Supply Chains to Improve Health and Safety' in *Industrial Law Journal* (2007) 163–187

Jeandidier, W, 'Note on Cour de cassation. Chambre criminelle, 4 February 1985, no 84-91581' in *Semaine juridique édition générale* (1986) II n. 20585

Jenkins, R, Pearson, R and Seyfang, G (eds), *Corporate Responsibility and Labour Rights: Codes of Conduct in the Global Economy* (London, Routledge, 2013)

Julén Votinius, J, 'Young Employees—Securities, Risk Distribution and Fundamental Social Rights' in *European Labour Law Journal* (2014) 387–410

Julén Votinius, J, 'Age Discrimination and Labour Law in Sweden', in A Numhauser-Henning and M Rönnmar (eds), *Age Discrimination and Labour Law. Comparative and Conceptual Perspectives in the EU and Beyond* (Alphen aan den Rijn, Kluwer Law International, 2015) 279–295

Kajtár, E, 'A munkáltatói utasítás helye a 21. Század munkajogában' in *II JURA* (2014) 214–224

Kalleberg, AL, 'Organizing Flexibility: The Flexible Firm in a New Century' in *British Journal of Industrial Relations* (2001) 479–504

Karl, B, 'Die Einbeziehung geringfügig Beschäftigter in die Sozialversicherung' in *Arbeits- und SozialrechtsKartei* (1997) 383–391

Karl, B, 'Die Sozialversicherungspflicht geringfügig Beschäftigter nach der 55. ASVG-Novelle' in *Arbeits- und SozialrechtsKartei* (1998) 357–370

Karthaus, B and Klebe, T, 'Betriebsratsrechte bei Werkverträgen' in *Neue Zeitschrift für Arbeitsrecht* (2012) 419–426

Kempen, O and Zachert, U (eds), *Tarifvertragsgesetz*, 5th edn (Frankfurt am Main, Bund-Verlag, 2014)

Kenner, J, 'Statement or Contract?—Some Reflections on the EC Employee Information (Contract or Employment Relationship) Directive after *Kampelmann*' (1999) 28 ILJ 205

Kenner, J, 'New Frontiers in EU Labour Law: From Flexicurity to Flex-Security' in Dougan, M, and Currie S, (eds), *50 Years of the European Treaties: Looking Back and Thinking Forward* (Hart 2009) 279–310

Kietaibl, C, *Arbeitsrecht I—Gestalter und Gestaltungsmittel* (Wien, New Academic Press, 2013)

Kilpatrick, C, 'The Court of Justice and Labour Law in 2010: A New EU Discrimination Law Architecture' in *Industrial Law Journal* (2011) 280–301

Kim, I-H, 'Welfare States, Flexible Employment, and Health: A Critical Review' in *Health Policy* (2012) 99–127

Kittner, M, Zwanziger, B and Deinert, O (eds), *Arbeitsrecht: Handbuch für die Praxis*, 7th edn (Frankfurt am Main, Bund-Verlag, 2013)

Kittner, M, Zwanziger, B and Deinert, O (eds), *Arbeitsrecht Handbuch für die Praxis*, 8th edn (Frankfurt am Main, Bund-Verlag, 2015)

Kiss, G, *Munkajog* (Budapest, Osiris Kiadó, 2005)

Kiss, G, 'The Problem of Persons Having a Similar Legal Status as Employees (Workers), and the Absence of Regulating this Legal Status in the Hungarian Labour Code: The "Third Estate" of the Labour Market', in G. Kiss, *Recent Developments in Labour Law* (Budapest, Akadémiai Kiadó, 2013) 259–279

Kiss, G, 'A munkavállalóhoz hasonló jogállású személy problematikája az Európai Unióban és e jogállás szabályozásának hiánya a Munka Törvénykönyvében', in *Jogtudományi Közlöny* (2013) 1–14

Klebe, T, 'Workers of the crowd unite?' in C Benner (ed), *Crowdwork, zurück in die Zukunft* (Frankfurt am Main, Bund-Verlag, 2014) 277–284

Klebe, T and Jacquemin, T, 'Die Zukunft der Betriebsratsarbeit 2.0' in *Arbeitsrecht im Betrieb* (2014) 11 33–36

Klebe, T and Neugebauer, J, 'Crowdsourcing: Für eine Handvoll Dollar oder Workers of the Crowd Unite?' in *Arbeit und Recht* (2014) 4–7

Kohlbacher, E, 'Fortbestehen der SV-Beitragspflicht bei einvernehmlicher Auflösung im Krankenstand mit gleichzeitiger Wiedereinstellungszusage' in *Arbeits- und SozialrechtsKartei* (2011) 15–18

Kokemoor, A, 'Neuregelung der Arbeitnehmerüberlassung durch die Hartz-Umsetzungsgesetze' in *Neue Zeitschrift für Arbeitsrecht* (2003) 238–244

Koukoulaki, Th, 'New trends in work environment—New effects on safety' in *Safety Sci* (2010) 936–942

Kovács, E, 'Hungarian Unions: How Representative? How Effective?' in *Comparative Labor Law and Policy Journal* (2011) 891–914

Krause, R, 'International Framework Agreements as Instrument for the Legal Enforcement of Freedom of Association and Collective Bargaining? The German Case' in *Comparative Labor Law & Policy Journal* (2012) 749–774

Krause, R, 'Neue tarifvertragliche Regeln für die Leiharbeit in der Metallindustrie' in *Neue Zeitschrift für Arbeitsrecht* (2012) 830–836

Krause, R, 'Tarifverträge zur Wiederherstellung von Equal Pay' in *Arbeit und Recht* (2012) 55–61

Krause, R, 'Arbeit in der Holzklasse—Gesetzliche und kollektivvertragliche Rahmung der Leiharbeit' in *Kritische Justiz* (2013) 119–132

Krause, R, 'Arbeitnehmerüberlassung als Instrument zur Flexibilisierung von Arbeitsmärkten' in *Zeitschrift für internationales und ausländisches Arbeits- und Sozialrecht* (2014) 113–152

Krause, R, 'Flexibler Personaleinsatz—Arbeitnehmerüberlassung und Werkverträge zwischen Markt und Regulierung' in *Zeitschrift für Arbeitsrecht* (2014) 349–394

Krause, R, *Tarifverträge zur Begrenzung der Leiharbeit und zur Druchsetzung von Equal Pay* (Frankfurt am Main, Bund-Verlag, 2014)

Krebber, S, *Unternehmensübergreifende Arbeitsabläufe im Arbeitsrecht* (München, C.H. Beck-Verlag, 2005)

Krejci, H, 'Das Werkvertragserkenntnis' in *Verwaltungsrundschau* (1997) 81–85

Lai, M, 'Tutela della maternità nella legislazione europea' in *Diritto e pratica del lavoro* (1993) 2 77–83

Lazzari, C, 'L'obbligo di sicurezza nel lavoro temporaneo, tra ordinamento interno e diritto comunitario' in *Giornale di Diritto del Lavoro e di Relazioni Industriali* (2009) 633–672

Leimeister, JM et al, 'Crowdwork—digitale Wertschöpfung in der Wolke' in C Benner (ed), *Crowdwork, zurück in die Zukunft* (Frankfurt am Main, Bund-Verlag, 2014) 9–43

Lester, G, 'Careers and Contingency' in *Stanford Law Review* (1998) 73–145

Liebman, S, 'Prestazione di attività produttiva e protezione del contraente debole fra sistema giuridico e suggestioni dell'economia' in *Giornale di diritto del lavoro e delle relazioni industriali* (2010) 571–593

Link, M, 'Labour Law and the New Inequality' (2009) 59 UNBLJ 14–47

Linsenmaier, W and Kiel, H, 'Der Leiharbeitnehmer in der Betriebsverfassung—"Zwei-Komponenten-Lehre" und normzweckorientierte Gesetzesauslegung' in *Recht der Arbeit* (2014) 135–157

Lokiec, P, *Il faut sauver le droit du travail* (Paris, Odile Jacob, 2015)

López Gandía, J, *Contrato de trabajo y figuras afines* (Valencia, Tirant lo Blanch, 1999)

Lluis y Navas, J, 'Los acuerdos de interés profesional de los trabajadores autónomos' in *Actualidad Laboral* (2010) 4 405–418

Luján Alcaraz, J, *El Estatuto del Trabajo Autónomo. Análisis de la Ley 20/2007, de 11 de julio* (Murcia, Ediciones Laborum, 2007)

Macaulay, S, 'An Empirical View of Contract' *Wisconsin Law Review* (1985) 465–482

Macneil, I, 'The Many Futures of Contract' in *Southern California Law Review* (1974) 691–816

Magnani, M, 'La riforma dei contratti e del mercato del lavoro nel c.d. Jobs Act. Il Codice dei contratti' in *Dir. Rel. Ind.* (2015) 961–977

Mancini, GF, *La responsabilità contrattuale del prestatore di lavoro* (Milano, Giuffrè, 1957)

Marhold, F, 'Atypische Arbeitskräfteüberlassung?' in *Arbeits- und SozialrechtsKartei* (2008) 162–168

Marhold, F and Friedrich, M, *Österreichisches Arbeitsrecht* (Wien, Springer Verlag, 2012)

Marhold, F, Burgstaller, G and Preyer, H, *AngG, Angestelltengesetz—Kommentar* (Wien, Manz Verlag, 2013)

Martín Valverde, A, 'Fronteras y zonas grises del Derecho del Trabajo en la jurisprudencia actual (1980-2001)' in *Revista del Ministerio de Trabajo y Asuntos Sociales* (2002) 38 21–50

Martínez Barroso, MR, *Régimen profesional, prevención de riesgos y derechos colectivos de los trabajadores autónomos* (Madrid, Centro de Estudios Financieros, 2006)

McCrystal, S, 'Designing Collective Bargaining Frameworks for Self-Employed Workers: Lessons from Australia and Canada' in *International Journal of Comparative Labour Law and Industrial Relations* (2014) 30 217–242

McGaughey, E, 'Are Zero Hours Contracts Lawful?' (20 Nov 2014) SSRN

Melzer-Azodanloo, N, 'Erster Kollektivvertrag für Tele-Arbeit' in *Arbeits- und SozialrechtsKartei* (1997) 349–351

Melzer-Azodanloo, N, *Tele-Arbeitsrecht—der virtuelle Arbeitsplatz: Formen, Bedingungen, Gefahren* (Wien, Linde Verlag, 2001)

Mengoni, L, 'Il contratto di lavoro nel diritto italiano' in Aa.Vv., *Il contratto di lavoro nel diritto dei paesi membri della C.E.C.A.* (Milano, Giuffrè, 1965) 407–504

Molero Manglano, C, *El contrato de alta dirección* (Pamplona, Thomson/Civita, 2011)

Monda, M, 'La valutazione dei rischi per la sicurezza e la salute dei lavoratori' in L Zoppoli, P Pascucci and G Natullo (eds), *Le nuove regole per la salute e la sicurezza dei lavoratori* (Milano, Kluwer—Ipsoa, 2008) 327–344

Montuschi, L, *Ambiente, salute e sicurezza* (Torino, Giappichelli, 1998)

Montuschi, L (ed), *La nuova sicurezza sul lavoro. D.lgs. 9 aprile 2008, n. 81 e successive modifiche* (Bologna, Zanichelli, 2011)

Morin, ML, 'Sous-traitance et relations salariales' in *Travail et Emploi* (1994) 60 23–43

Morin, ML, 'Les frontières de l'entreprise et la responsabilité de l'emploi' in *Droit social* (2001) 478–483

Napoli, M, *La stabilità reale del rapporto di lavoro* (Milano, F Angeli, 1980)
Napoli, M, 'Elogio della stabilità' in *Quaderni di diritto del lavoro e delle relazioni industriali* (2002) 26 9–18
Natullo, G, *La tutela dell'ambiente di lavoro* (Torino, UTET, 1995)
Natullo, G, *Salute e sicurezza sul lavoro* (Torino, UTET, 2015)
Nebe, K, 'Spaltung des Arbeitsmarktes durch Krisengesetzgebung—eine kritische Analyse des deutschen Arbeits- und Sozialrechts vor und nach der Krise' in *Soziales Recht* (2013) 1–16
Neumayr, M and Reissner, G P, *Zeller Kommentar zum Arbeitsrecht* (Manz, Wien, 2011)
Nesi, G, Nogler, L and Pertile, M (eds), *Child Labour in a Globalised World. A legal Analysis of ILO Action* (Farnham, Ashgate, 2008)
Nielebock, H, 'Regelung europarechtskonformer Ausnahmen vom Gleichbehandlungsgrundsatz durch die Änderung des AÜG 2011?' in *Festschrift für Klaus Bepler* (München, C.H. Beck-Verlag, 2012) 463–474
Nießen, T and Fabritius, B, 'Gleichbehandlungsgebot in der Arbeitnehmerüberlassung durch Bezugnahmeklauseln und bei Befristungen' in *Fachanwalt Arbeitsrecht* (2013) 294–296
Nogler, L, 'La subordinazione nel d.lgs. n. 81 del 2015: alla ricerca dell' «autorità del punto di vista giuridico»' in WP CSDLE 'Massimo D'Antona'
Ortiz Chaparro, F, *El Teletrabajo* (Madrid, McGraw-Hill, 1996)
Oscarsson, E, *Ungdomsarbetslöshet—Mått, orsaker och politik* (Stockholm, SACO, 2013)
Owens, R, 'Decent Work for the Contingent Workforce in the New Economy' in *Australian Journal of labour Law* (2002) 15 209–234
O'Cinneide, C, *Age Discrimination and European Law* (Brussels, European Commission, 2005)
O'Cinneide, C, 'Constitutional and Fundamental Rights Aspects of Age Discrimination' in A Numhauser-Henning and M Rönnmar (eds), *Age Discrimination and Labour Law. Comparative and Conceptual Perspectives in the EU and Beyond* (Alphen aan den Rijn, Kluwer Law International, 2015) 51–70
O'Dempsey, D and Beale, A, *Age and Employment, Report from the Network of Legal Experts in the non-discrimination field to the European Commission*, 1 July 2011
Pacic, J, 'Arbeitslosenversicherung für Selbständige' in *Zeitschrift für Arbeits- und Sozialrecht* (2008) 156–161
Pallini, M, *Il lavoro economicamente dipendente* (Padova, CEDAM, 2013)
Papadopoulos, G and others, 'Occupational and public health and safety in a changing work environment: An integrated approach for risk assessment and prevention' in *Safety Sci* (2010) 943–949
Pascucci, P, 'Il campo di applicazione soggettivo delle nuove regole sulla salute e sicurezza nei luoghi di lavoro' in *Diritti lavori mercati* (2008) 2 297–338
Pascucci, P, 'Dopo la legge n. 123 del 2007. Titolo I del d.lgs. 9 aprile 2008, n. 81 in materia di tutela della salute e della sicurezza nei luoghi di lavoro' in *WP CSDLE "M. D'Antona".IT*,—73/2008

Pasquarella, V, 'La tutela della salute e della sicurezza negli appalti' in M Aimo and D Izzi (eds), *Esternalizzazioni e tutela dei lavoratori* (Torino, UTET, 2014) 138–193

Pedrazzoli, M, *Democrazia industriale e subordinazione* (Milano, Giuffrè, 1985)

Peers, S et al (eds), *The EU Charter of Fundamental Rights: A Commentary* (Oxford, Hart Publishing, 2014)

Pellecchia, R, 'Il Mobbing: fattispecie e tutele' in G Natullo (ed), *Salute e sicurezza sul lavoro* (Torino, UTET, 2015) 958–991

Pennycock M, Cory, G and Alakeson, V, *A Matter of Time: The rise of zero-hours contracts* (Resolution Foundation 2013)

Périn, PL, 'Devoir de vigilance et responsabilité illimitée des entreprises: qui trop embrasse mal étreint' in *Rev. Trimestrielle de droit commercial* (2015) 215–224

Perraudin, C, Thèvenot, N and Valentina, J, 'Avoiding the employment relationship: Outsourcing and labour substitution among French manufacturing firms, 1984–2003' in *International Labour Review* (2013) 152 525–548

Persiani, M, *Contratto di lavoro e organizzazione* (Padova, CEDAM, 1966)

Persiani, M (ed), *Il nuovo diritto della sicurezza sul lavoro* (Torino, UTET, 2012)

Perulli, A, 'Prestazioni organizzate dal committente e collaborazioni coordinate e continuative. Il nuovo quadro normativo' in L Fiorillo and A Perulli (eds), *Tipologie contrattuali e disciplina delle mansioni, Decreto legislativo 15 giugno 2015, n. 81* (Torino, Giappichelli, 2015)

Pessi, R, Pisani, C, Proia, G and Vallebona, A (eds), *Jobs Act e licenziamento* (Torino, Giappichelli, 2015)

Pfeil, WJ, *Österreichisches Sozialrecht* (Wien, Verlag Österreich, 2014)

Pipeschi, G, 'La responsabilità nei cantieri' in G Natullo (ed), *Salute e sicurezza sul lavoro* (Torino, Utet, 2015) 896–936

Powell, W, 'The Capitalist Firm in the Twenty-First Century: Emerging Patterns in Western Europe', in P Di Maggio (ed), *The Twenty-First-Century Firm: Changing Economic Organization in International Perspective* (Princeton, Princeton University Press, 2001) 33–68

Prassl, J, *The Concept of the Employer* (Oxford, Oxford University Press, 2015)

Preis, U 'Flexicurity und Abrufarbeit' *Recht der Arbeit* (2015) 244–248

Preis, U and Sagan, A (eds), *Europäisches Arbeitsrecht* 1st edn. (Köln, Otto-Schmidt-Verlag, 2015)

Prosser, Th, 'The implementation of the Telework and Work-related Stress Agreements: European Social Dialogue through 'Soft' Law?' in *European Journal of Industrial Relations* (2011) 245–260

Prugberger, T and Kenderes, G, 'Az atipikus munkaviszonyok a munkaerő-kölcsönzés és a távmunkavégzés tükrében' in *Miskolci Jogi Szemle* (2009) 2 30–55

Pyper, D, and Dar, A, *Zero-hours contracts* (House of Commons Briefing Paper Number 06553, 10 November 2015)

Quesada Segura, R, *El contrato de servicio doméstico* (Madrid, La Ley, 1991)

Quinlan, M, Mayhew, C and Bohle, Ph, 'The global expansion of precarious employment, work disorganization, and consequences for occupational health: a review of recent research' in *International Journal of Health Services* (2001) 335–414

Rauch, T, 'Angemessenes Entgelt bei Arbeitskräfteüberlassung' in *ecolex* (2013) 676–678

Razzolini, O, 'Contitolarità del rapporto di lavoro nel gruppo caratterizzato da unicità di impresa' in *Giornale di diritto del lavoro e di relazioni industriali* (2009) 263–304

Razzolini, O, 'La nuova disciplina delle collaborazioni organizzate dal committente', in *WP CSDLE 'Massimo D'Antona'.*

Rebhahn, R,' Arbeitnehmerähnliche Personen—Rechtsvergleich und Regelungsperspektive' in *Recht der Arbeit* (2009) 236–253

Reim, U, 'Neue Flexibilität bei der Leiharbeit' in *Zeitschrift für Tarifrecht* (2003) 106–113

Rieble, V and Klebeck, U, 'Lohngleichheit für Leiharbeit' in *Neue Zeitschrift für Arbeitsrecht* (2003) 23–29

Riesenhuber, K, *Europäisches Arbeitsrecht* (Heidelberg, C.F. Müller Verlag, 2009)

Riesenhuber, K, *European Employment Law* (Antwerp, Intersentia, 2012)

Risak, M, 'Crowdwork—Erste rechtliche Annäherungen an eine "neue" Arbeitsform' in *Zeitschrift für Arbeits- und Sozialrecht* (2015) 11–19

Robson, LS and others, 'The Effectiveness of Occupational Health and Safety Management System Interventions: A Systematic Review' in *Safety Sci* (2007) 329–353

Rodríguez Ramos, P, *La relación laboral especial de los estibadores portuarios* (Madrid, Trotta, 1997)

Rodríguez-Piñero y Bravo Ferrer, M, 'Contrato de trabajo y relación de trabajo' in *Anales de la Universidad Hispalense* (1967) vol. XXVII 1–92

Rödl, F and Ulber, D, 'Unvereinbarkeit von § 9 Nr. 2 Halbs. 4 AÜG mit der Leiharbeitsrichtlinie' in *Neue Zeitschrift für Arbeitsrecht* (2012) 841–845

Rönnmar, M, 'The Managerial Prerogative and the Employee's Obligation to Work: Comparative Perspectives on Functional Flexibility' in *Industrial Law Journal* (2006) 56–74

Rönnmar, M, Numhauser-Henning, A, 'Swedish Employment Protection in Times of Flexicurity Policies and Economic Crisis' in *International Journal of Comparative Labour Law and Industrial Relations* (2012) 443–467

Rönnmar, M, 'Age Discrimination and Labour Law: A Comparative Analysis' in A Numhauser-Henning and M Rönnmar (eds), *Age Discrimination and Labour Law. Comparative and Conceptual Perspectives in the EU and Beyond* (Alphen aan den Rijn, Kluwer Law International, 2015) 415–447

Rojo Torrecilla, E, 'Cambios en el mundo del trabajo: nuevos empleos y nuevos trabajadores' in *Revista de fomento social* (2002) 241–276

Runggaldier, U, 'Probleme der Einführung einer alle Erwerbseinkommen umfassenden Sozialversicherungspflicht' in *Österreichische Juristen-Zeitung* (1998) 494–501

Rusciano, M and Natullo, G (eds), *Ambiente e sicurezza del lavoro* (Torino, UTET, 2007)

Sachs-Durand, C, 'Occupational Health and Safety in France: A Good Formal Protection, but a Problematic Efficiency' in E Ales (ed), *Health and Safety at Work. European and Comparative Perspective* (Alphen aan den Rijn, Kluwer Law International, 2013) 99–126

Sala Franco, T and López Mora, F, 'Contrato de trabajo' in E Borrajo Dacruz (ed), *Comentarios a las leyes laborales. El Estatuto de los Trabajadores*, 1st edn (Madrid, Edersa, 1990) 3–34

Salminen, S, 'Have Young Workers more Injuries than Older Ones? An International Literature Review' in *Journal of Safety Research* (2004) 513–521

Sansone, P, *Gleichstellung von Leiharbeitnehmern nach deutschem und Unionsrecht* (München, C.H. Beck-Verlag, 2011)

Sansone, P, 'Leiharbeit' in U Preis and A Sagan (eds), *Europäisches Arbeitsrecht* (Köln, Otto Schmidt, 2015) 439–473

Santoro Passarelli, F, *Nozioni di diritto del lavoro* (Napoli, Jovene, 1944)

Santoro Passareli, G, 'I rapporti di collaborazione organizzati dal committente e le collaborazioni continuative e coordinate ex art. 409, n. 3, c.p.c.', in WP CSDLE *'Massimo D'Antona'*—278/2015

Schaub, G (ed), *Arbeitsrechts-Handbuch*, 16th edn, (München, Beck, 2015)

Schiek, S, 'Age Discrimination before the ECJ—Conceptual and Theoretical Issues' in *Common Market Law Review* (2011) 777–799

Schiller, S and Hannoun, C, 'Quel devoir de vigilance des sociétés-mères et des sociétés donneuses d'ordre?' in *Revue de Droit du Travail* (2014) 441–448

Schlachter, M, 'Mandatory Retirement and Age Discrimination under EU Law' in *International Journal of Comparative Labour Law and Industrial Relations* (2011) 287–299

Schlachter, M, 'Transnational Temporary Agency Work: How Much Equality Does the Equal Treatment Principle Provide?' in *International Journal of Comparative Labour Law and Industrial Relations* (2012) 177–197

Schlachter, M (ed), *EU Labour Law. A Commentary* (Alphen aan den Rijn, Kluwer Law International, 2015)

Schmechel, T, 'Die Rolle des Betriebsrats bei der Einführung und Durchführung von Telearbeit' in *Neue Zeitschrift für Arbeitsrecht* (2004) 237–241

Schömann I and Clauwaert S, 'Temps de travail et travail atypique au cœur des réformes du droit du travail en Europe' in *Revue de Droit de Travail* (2014) 582–591

Schörghofer, F, 'Zur Umsetzung der Leiharbeits-RL im AÜG' in *Zeitschrift für Arbeits- und Sozialrecht* (2012) 336–344

Schrammel, W, 'Vom "Werkvertragserkenntnis" zur umfassenden Sozialversicherungspflicht' in *Arbeits- und SozialrechtsKartei* (1997) 333–342

Schrank, F, 'Die wichtigsten Neuerungen zur Arbeitskräfteüberlassung (Teil 1 und 2)' in *Recht der Wirtschaft* (2013) 31–36; 84–87

Schüren, P, 'Tarifunfähigkeit der CGZP wegen Missbrauchs der tariflichen Normsetzungsbefugnis in der Leiharbeit' in *Arbeit und Recht* (2008) 239–244

Schüren, P and Brors, C, 'Neue gesetzliche Rahmenbedingungen für den Fremdpersonaleinsatz' in *Neue Zeitschrift für Arbeitsrecht* (2014) 569–573

Schüren, P and Hamann, W (eds), *Arbeitnehmerüberlassungsgesetz*, 4th edn (München, C.H.Beck-Verlag, 2010)

Schüren, P and Wank, R, 'Die neue Leiharbeitsrichtlinie und ihre Umsetzung in deutsches Recht' in *Recht der Arbeit* (2011) 1–11

Schumann, D, 'Tarifverträge zur Leiharbeit in der Metall- und Elektroindustrie—Verbesserte Arbeitsbedingungen für Leiharbeitnehmer' in *Arbeitsrecht im Betrieb* (2012) 423–426

Sebardt, G, *Redundancy and the Swedish Model. Swedish Collective Agreements on Employment Security in a National and International Context* (Uppsala, Iustusförlag, 2005)

Segonds, M, 'Les limites imposées à l'optimisation sociale par la loi n. 2014-790 du 10 juillet 2014 visant à lutter contre la concurrence sociale déloyale' in *Revue sciences criminelles* (2014) 828–835

Selma Penalva, A, *Los límites del contrato de trabajo en la jurisprudencia española* (Valencia, Tirant lo Blanch, 2007)

Selma Penalva, A, 'El Trabajador autónomo económicamente dependiente' in J Luján Alcaraz (ed), *El Estatuto del Trabajador Autónomo* (Murcia, Editorial Laborum, 2007) 125–205

Siebenhüter, S, 'Der Betrieb als Projekthaus—Wie Werkverträge die Arbeitswelt verändern' in *WSI-Mitteilungen* (2014) 306–310

Sonntag, M (ed), *ASVG—Allgemeines Sozialversicherungsgesetz, Jahreskommentar* (Wien, Linde Verlag, 2015)

Standing G, *The precariat—the new dangerous class* (Policy Network 2011)

Steinberg, M, 'Occupational Health and Safety in a Diverse, Post-Industrial Society: A Swedish Dilemma' in E Ales (ed), *Health and Safety at Work. European and Comparative Perspective* (Alphen aan den Rijn, Kluwer Law International, 2013) 281–328

Stone, KVW and Arthurs, H (eds), *Rethinking Workplace Regulation: Beyond the Standard Contract of Employment* (New York, Russell Sage Foundation Press, 2013)

Summers, C, 'Contingent employment in the United States' in *Comparative Labor Law Journal* (1996–97) 503–522

Supiot, A, 'Les nouveaux visages de la subordination' in *Droit Social* (2000) 131–145

Tárraga Poveda, J, 'Cuestiones procesales' in J Luján Alcaraz (ed), *El Estatuto del Trabajador Autónomo* (Murcia, Ediciones Laborum, 2007) 291–321

Tárraga Poveda, J, 'La protección social del trabajador autónomo' in J Luján Alcaraz (ed), *El Estatuto del Trabajador Autónomo* (Murcia, Ediciones Laborum, 2007) 253–273

Tárraga Poveda, J, 'Los derechos colectivos del trabajador autónomo' in J Luján Alcaraz (ed), *El Estatuto del Trabajador Autónomo* (Murcia, Ediciones Laborum, 2007) 207–251

ter Haar, B and Rönnmar, M, *Intergenerational Bargaining, EU Age Discrimination Law and EU Policies—an Integrated Analysis* (Amsterdam, AIAS—iNGenBar, 2014)

Tiraboschi, M, (ed.), *Il testo unico della salute e sicurezza nei luoghi di lavoro. Commentario al decreto legislativo 9 aprile 2008, n. 81* (Milano, Giuffrè, 2008)

Tiraboschi, M, 'Il lavoro etero-organizzato' in M Tiraboschi (ed), *Le nuove regole del lavoro dopo il Jobs Act* (Milano, Giuffré, 2016) 261–268

Thüsing, G (ed), *Arbeitnehmerüberlassungsgesetz*, 3rd edn (München, C.H. Beck-Verlag, 2012)

Thüsing, G, 'Equal Pay bei Leiharbeit—Zur Reichweite der Gleichbehandlungspflicht nach dem AÜG' in *Der Betrieb* (2003) 446–451

Thüsing, G, 'Dauerhafte Arbeitnehmerüberlassung: Neues vom BAG, vom EuGH und auch vom Gesetzgeber' in *Neue Zeitschrift für Arbeitsrecht* (2014) 10–12

Tolosa Triviño, C, 'Comentarios a la Ley 20/2007', del Estatuto del Trabajador Autonomo' in *Informaction Laboral-Jurisprudencia* (2007) 8 2–17

Tomandl, T and Aigner, W, 'Verfassungsprobleme bei der Sozialversicherung dienstnehmerähnlicher Beschäftigungsverhältnisse' in *Zeitschrift für Arbeits- und Sozialrecht* (1997) 1–12

Tomandl, T, 'Rechtsprobleme einer umfassenden Sozialversicherung' in *Zeitschrift für Arbeits- und Sozialrecht* (1998) 9–17

Tomandl, T, *Wesensmerkmale des Arbeitsvertrages in rechtsvergleichender und rechtspolitischer Sicht* (Wien, Springer Verlag, 1971)

Tosi, P, 'L'art. 1, comma 1, d.lgs. n. 81/2015: una norma apparente?' in *Argomenti di Diritto del Lavoro* (2015) 6 1117–1133

Treu, T, 'In tema di Jobs Act. Il riordino dei tipi contrattuali' in *Giornale di Diritto del Lavoro e delle Relazioni Industriali* (2015) 155–181

Ulber, J, 'Personal-Service-Agenturen und Neuregelung der Arbeitnehmerüberlassung' in *Arbeit und Recht* (2003) 7–15

Ulber, J, 'Die Richtlinie der Leiharbeit' in *Arbeit und Recht* (2010) 10–15

Ulber, J (ed), *Arbeitnehmerüberlassungsgesetz*, 4th edn (Frankfurt am Main, Bund-Verlag, 2011)

Ulber, J and Stang, D,' Die geplante Neuregelung der Leiharbeit' in *Arbeit und Recht* (2015) 250–255

Vacarie, I, 'Le travail dans un marché sans frontières' in *Revue de droit du travail* (2015) 634–641

Val de Tena, A, *Los trabajadores directivos de las empresas* (Pamplona, Thomson/Aranzadi, 2010)

Valdés de la Vega, B, 'Occupational Health and Safety: A EU Law Perspective' in E Ales (ed), *Health and Safety at Work. European and Comparative Perspective* (Alphen aan den Rijn, Kluwer Law International 2013) 1–28

Veneziani, B, 'The Employment Relationship' in B Hepple and B Veneziani (eds), *The Transformation of Labour Law in Europe—A Comparative Study of 15 Countries 1945–2004* (Oxford, Hart Publishing, 2009) 99–128

Virtanen, M and others, 'Temporary employment and health: a review' in *International Journal of Epidemiology* (2005) 610–622

Vosko, LF, *Managing the Margins. Gender, Citizenship, and the International Regulation of Precarious Employment* (Oxford, Oxford University Press, 2010)

Waas, B, 'Der Gleichbehandlungsgrundsatz im neuen Arbeitnehmerüberlassungsgesetz' in *Zeitschrift für Europäisches Sozial- und Arbeitsrecht* (2012) 7–13

Wachter, G, *Wesensmerkmale der arbeitnehmerähnlichen Person* (Berlin, Duncker & Humblot, 1980)

Walker-Said, Ch and Kelly, JD (eds), *Corporate social responsibilty? Human rights in the new global economy* (Chicago, University of Chicago Press, 2015)

Waltermann, R, 'Fehlentwicklung in der Leiharbeit' in *Neue Zeitschrift für Arbeitsrecht* (2010) 482–487

Walters, D and James, PH, 'What Motivates Employers to Establish Preventive Management Arrangements within Supply Chains?' in *Safety Sci* (2011) 988–994

Wiebauer, B, 'Arbeitsschutz im Fremdbetrieb' in *Zeitschrift für Arbeitsrecht* (2014) 29–83

Williamson, O, *The Economic Institutions of Capitalism: Firms, Markets, Relational Contracting* (London, Free Press, 1985)

Wynn, M and Leighton, P, 'Will the Real Employer Please Stand Up? Agencies, Clients Companies and the Employment Status of the Temporary Agency Worker' in *Industrial Law Journal* (2006) 301–320

Zanko, M and Dawson, P, 'Occupational Health and Safety Management in Organizations: A Review' in *International Journal of Management Reviews* (2012) 14 328–344

Zekic, N, *Werkzekerheid in het arbeidsrecht* (Deventer, Kluwer, 2014)

Zimmer, R, *Soziale Mindeststandards und ihre Durchsetzungsmechanismen: Sicherung internationaler Mindeststandards durch Verhaltenskodizes?* (Baden-Baden, Nomos, 2008)

Zimmer, R, 'Der Grundsatz der Gleichbehandlung in der Leiharbeitsrichtlinie 2008/104/EG und seine Umsetzung ins deutsche Recht' in *Neue Zeitschrift für Arbeitsrecht* (2013) 289–294

Zoppoli, L, Pascucci, P and Natullo, G (eds), *Le nuove regole per lasalute e lasicurezza dei lavoratori, Commentario al D.lgs. 9 Aprile 2008, n. 81* (Milano, Ipsoa-Wolter Kluwer, 2008)

INDEX

www.ingramcontent.com/pod-product-compliance
Ingram Content Group UK Ltd.
Pitfield, Milton Keynes, MK11 3LW, UK
UKHW020134290926
15471UKWH00003B/480

9 781509 930180